Office Planning and Design Desk Reference

Edited by

James E. Rappoport, AIA
Daroff Design Inc.
Philadelphia, Pennsylvania

Robert F. Cushman, Esquire
Pepper, Hamilton & Scheetz
Philadelphia, Pennsylvania

Karen Daroff, IBD
Daroff Design Inc.
Philadelphia, Pennsylvania

A Wiley-Interscience Publication
JOHN WILEY & SONS, INC.
New York • Chichester • Brisbane • Toronto • Singapore

This publication is designed to provide accurate and
authoritative information in regard to the subject
matter covered. It is sold with the understanding that
the publisher is not engaged in rendering legal, accounting,
or other professional services. If legal advice or other
expert assistance is required, the services of a competent
professional person should be sought. *From a Declaration
of Principles jointly adopted by a Committee of the
American Bar Association and a Committee of Publishers.*

Library of Congress Cataloging-in-Publication Data:
Office planning and design desk reference / edited by James E.
    Rappoport, Robert F. Cushman, Karen Daroff.
        p.   cm.
        "A Wiley-Interscience publication."
        Includes bibliographical references and index.

    1. Office layout.   2. Office buildings—United States.
    3. Offices—United States—Location.   4. Office buildings
    -Environmental aspects—United States.   5. Office decoration.
    I. Rappoport, James E.   II. Cushman, Robert F.   III. Daroff, Karen.
    HF5547.2.O34   1991
    658.2—dc20   91-33863
    ISBN 0-471-50820-9   CIP

Printed in the United States of America

10 9 8 7 6 5 4 3 2 1

This book is dedicated to
Jason and *Joshua*
and to *Robert* who was born
as we completed our first draft.

A special thank-you to
Lisa O'Kane
whose diligence and hard work
helped transform our draft into the final text.

Contributors

Larry C. Baucom, Esquire
Jones Lang Wootton
Washington, DC

C. Jaye Berger, Esquire
Law Offices of C. Jaye Berger
New York, NY

Robert F. Cushman, Esquire, *Editor*
Pepper, Hamilton & Scheetz
Philadelphia, PA

Karen Daroff, IBD, *Editor*
Daroff Design Inc.
Philadelphia, PA

Joel J. Goldberg, Esquire
Venable, Baetjer, Howard & Civiletti
Washington, DC

Gary Goldman, Esquire
CDI Corporation
Philadelphia, PA

Jay R. Hendler, AIA
Hendler & Hendler
San Francisco, CA

Barry M. Nealon, Esquire
Jones Lang Wootton
Washington, DC

Piero Patri, FAIA
Whisler-Patri
San Francisco, CA

James Rappoport, AIA, *Editor*
Daroff Design Inc.
Philadelphia, PA

Richard Carl Reisman, AIA
Interland
San Mateo, CA

Daniel W. Winey, AIA
Gensler & Associates
San Francisco, CA

Contents

Preface

Decisions affecting the location of corporate office facilities and decisions pertaining to their design, development, renovation, financing, construction, furnishing, leasing, occupancy, management, and operation are seldom an individual or personal effort.

Most of the professionals associated with these decisions and activities—most notably, architects, interior designers, developers, corporate facility managers, lawyers, real estate brokers, engineers, contractors, bankers, and others—require years of professional education and apprenticeship and are licensed or otherwise supervised by local, state, or federal authorities. The required spectrum of professional and technical talent is rarely found within the organization that is planning the office facility relocation or within a single consulting firm.

Long before Theory Z and the resulting trend toward project team management, the office facility industry in the United States and elsewhere had practiced the art and science of a unified team approach to project management. This approach relies on the check-and-balance interaction of many individuals. Team members not only must be knowledgeable in their particular area of expertise, but also they must have enough experience with and understanding about the expertise of other team members to be able to participate comfortably in the formation and organization of the team,

- to be an advocate for their own specialty if necessary, and
- to offer the counterbalancing comments and criticisms required during review of other members' recommendations, without undermining the unified team effort.

Most seasoned office facility team members practicing today learned their skills in the years since World War II's Manhattan project, which fostered the basic guidelines for major project team management, frequently referred to as CPM (critical path method). This underlying theory remained the basis for most of the project team organizations in the office facility industry until the early 1970s. During the mid-1970s, the energy crisis years, with their double-digit interest rates for construction loans and building mortgages, new methods of project team organizational theory had to be learned. Clients could no longer afford the time-consuming, step-by-step sequential project management process.

Management by objectives (MBO) theory taught that the end product was realizable in a shorter period of time by means of a more interactive and overlapping project team management approach, frequently called "fast track" project management. IBM has coined the phrase "helical project management," a quite graphic explanation of how the various team members come together to determine goals and objectives and then return to their individual professional pursuits for interdisciplinary best-case recommendations (see Figure A). Independently, they are able to refine their goals and objectives and return again and again to the team's meeting table until the best-case scenario from each member's point of view is established, documented, approved, and implemented as being the best-case scenario from the entire team's point of view.

In this text, the editors have brought together contributors from many of the professional consultancies typically represented on a major office facility project management team. These professionals were asked to write chapters that would help the other team members to interact better with their counterparts. The compendium presented here not only fosters improved office facility project team management, but guides those who employ a project team.

A typical office facility project team can include all or some of the professional and corporate participants represented in Figure B. The chart has been prepared as a matrix, rather than a time-sequential ordering or a pyramidal form of project management organization. Earlier forms of project management clearly placed a "boss" at the head. The matrix form of team management given here is the most effective team approach, because each participant has an

FIGURE A

The Helical Design Process

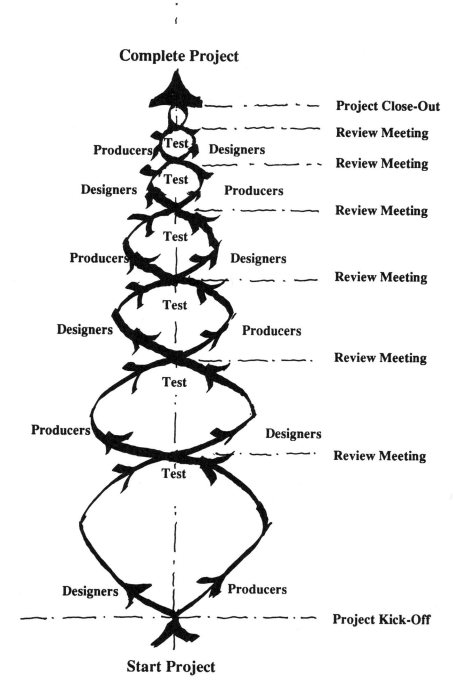

FIGURE B

Landlord/Tenant Project Team Organization Chart

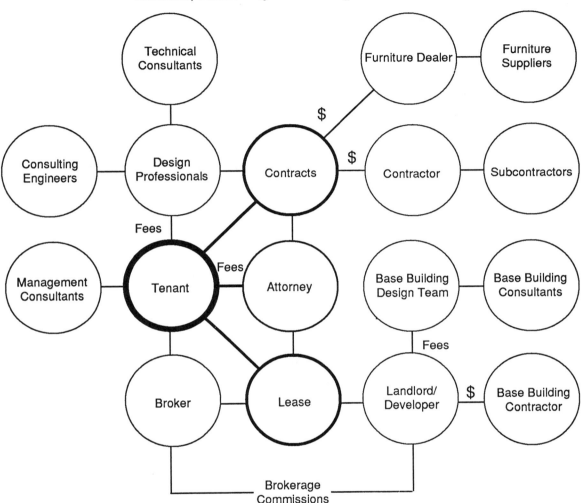

equal but separate and distinct professional responsibility to the enterprise.

The premise of this book is that, by the integration of individual and collective professional and corporate know-how, and by the sharing of diverse backgrounds and experiences, office facility professionals and their projects gain substantial benefits. We define these benefits in terms of the following goals and objectives:

1. More effective application of individual and collective management problem solving and of creative talents to the client's projects, the community as a whole, those who will use and occupy the developed facilities, and the practicing professionals themselves;

2. More efficient and productive use of individual and collective professional efforts, to achieve project completion in less time while more fully responding to the client's specific intended use, both now and in the future;

3. Fewer errors and omissions, to ensure less peril to the life and safety of those using and occupying the facilities and fewer individual and collective professional liabilities and related claims;

4. An overall lowering of costs, as calculated by the use of the costs per employee housed (the method

described in Chapter 4), and evaluations of both the initial cost and the life cycle cost, incurred over the useful life of the project.

These four goals and objectives have become more important to the office facility industry as the "velocity" of professional practices has increased over the past decade. We use the term "velocity" to express the fourth dimension, which is time and the effects of time on our professional practice(s), the office facility industry as a whole, and each office facility project.

The velocity has increased in the office facility industry for several reasons:

- The growing population of the office work force, caused in part by the trend toward a more service-oriented economy, requires more private industry office space.

- Growth in the governmental sector of the economy is causing a need for additional office space—in part, to house more governmental employees who oversee growth in the private sector.

- Increased awareness of international trade and foreign competition has caused an expansion in research and development (R&D) aimed toward new products and processes as well as more productive methods and procedures in the office environment. Complex R&D project teams include all levels of organization and have increased the need for more team meeting facilities, conference and training facilities, and a closer association of office and plant employees.

- Regional relocations of corporate office facilities, based on individual marketing and supply-side regional opportunities and constraints, have shifted the location requirements of certain types of office facilities.

- The urban/suburban relocation cycle constantly causes adjustments in the demand for specific office space locations in a given region.

- Frequent variations in real estate tax rates or the imposition of wage or other taxes at the municipal level of government become the impetus for regional relocations.

- Corporate mergers, takeovers, and other aspects of corporate finance and management have recently led to more frequent revision, downsizing, or relocation of offices.

- Redundancy in staff and equipment subsequent to a merger; macroeconomic business cycles; or internal management productivity improvement programs often trigger a relocation to more efficient new offices.

- The growth of electronic banking and computer-linked communications has supported a shift in location preferences and may in the near future allow many office workers to join the growing work force in cottage industry, working at home or in mobile units.

- During the 1980s, the substantial new influx of both urban and suburban speculative office facility construction was spurred by many factors: the economic recovery provisions of the 1981 tax act, IRA (Individual Retirement Account) investment programs, and the relatively stable and peaceful U.S. and European economies. The incredible growth in the Japanese economy and Japanese investment in real estate throughout the world led to increased speculative building and to higher costs for new facilities. Insurance, IRA, and retirement fund investment managers began promoting the "selling of America" to foreign investors as they sought liquidity for their investment portfolios. This substantial influx of new office facilities reached a peak at the end of the 1980s, when changes in the tax laws, problems in the banking industry, and other macroeconomic conditions resulted in an oversupply of office space in many regional markets. This oversupply has created a highly competitive tenant (buyer's) market, which has encouraged trading-up for many tenants who seek to improve productivity, downsize their operations, and implement enhanced computer networks. The oversupply offers many office tenants economic opportunities for improving the productivity of their operations while lowering their office use and occupancy costs.

- A growing understanding of the economic effect of present value project cost accounting (an accounting method that takes into account the impact of inflation on current and future financial obligations) has produced more effective and accurate methods of accounting for preoccupancy development costs. These include mortgage and construction loan interest, insurance costs, code and environmental impact costs, and all of the other "soft costs" of the office facility industry, tempered by the ever changing tax codes related to these investments.

- Vastly increased costs of land, compliance with environmental impact codes, on-site building construction labor, and Occupational Safety and Health Administration (OSHA) rules and related costs and expenses have spurred use of faster, pre-fabricated building materials systems, techniques, and methods of construction.

- Increased emphasis on access for the handicapped, energy conservation, and occupational safety in the office environment has resulted in the need to reno-vate many older buildings that lacked aspects of

these safety requirements that are now retroactive under many local, state, and federal regulations.

- Increased emphasis on preventive medicine and on the application of human factors engineering and ergonomic design principles to the office en-vironment, has given added impetus to renovation of antiquated buildings and to incorporation of human factors engineering principles into the planning of new buildings.

- The technical and legal debate surrounding the "sick building syndrome," which challenges the

FIGURE C

Comparison of Construction Put in Place and Vacancy Rate, U.S. Office Market (Copyright © 1991 by Real Estate Research Corporation (RERC). Used with permission of RERC, *Construction Review*, and Coldwell Banker Commercial.)

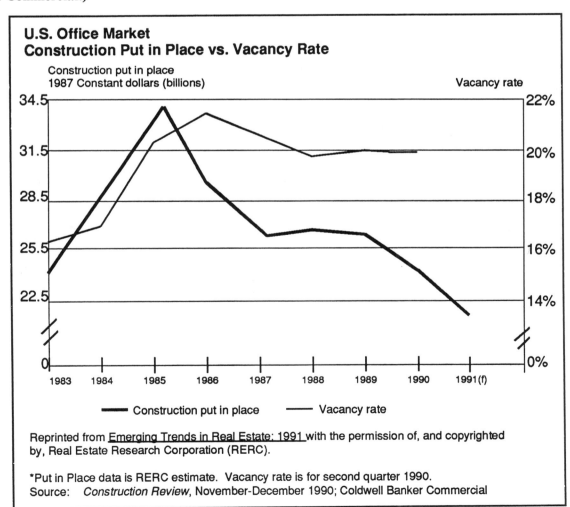

Reprinted from Emerging Trends in Real Estate: 1991 with the permission of, and copyrighted by, Real Estate Research Corporation (RERC).

*Put in Place data is RERC estimate. Vacancy rate is for second quarter 1990.
Source: *Construction Review*, November-December 1990; Coldwell Banker Commercial

techniques used to achieve energy-efficient buildings, requires a rethinking of the basic design and legal principles that the office facility industry has followed since the mid-1970s.

- A more active, articulate, and concerned office work force is seeking a higher quality of life (even in the office work environment), demanding improvements, and even going to litigation when their quality of life has become abused. Courts increasingly are willing to entertain both individual and class actions to resolve life safety and perils to quality of life.

For these and other related reasons, office facility projects are being planned to provide more office facilities in less time and with a higher degree of overall quality and suitability for the owner/occupant's intended use (See Figure C). Based on the value of office building permits authorized annually, expenditures for new office construction in the United States experienced a dramatic surge during the 1980s, with an all-time high in 1985 of $16.2 billion, an increase of 260 percent from a decade earlier. In comparison, the 1970s, with their double-digit inflation and energy crisis, saw a significant drop in construction spending, with a decade low in 1975 of $4.5 billion.

The value of building permits is only a fraction of the total cost of office building construction, which includes the base building enhancement features and

FIGURE D

Chart of Nonresidential Reconstruction Expenditures (Copyright © 1991 by Cahners Economics. Used with permission.)

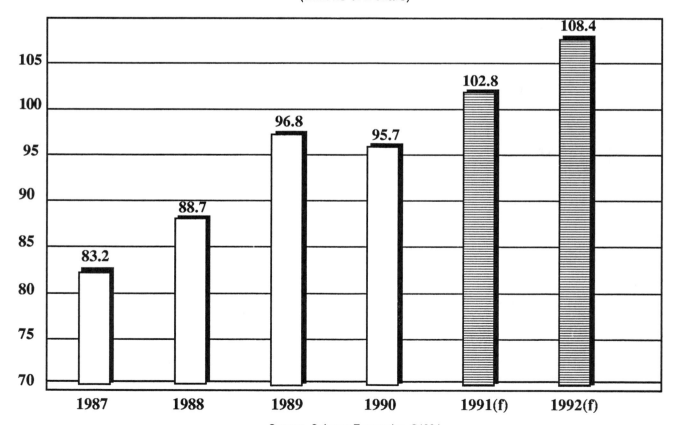

Nonresidential Reconstruction Expenditures
(Billions of Dollars)

Source: Cahners Economics, ©1991

tenant improvement costs not associated with the permit value formula.

It is difficult to determine data on base building enhancements, tenant improvements, and renovations, but the Tax Act of 1981 supposedly fostered at least as much renovation as it did new construction. Supporting this claim was the first-ever comprehensive study of remodeling of commercial buildings, released by the U.S. Department of Commerce; in 1986, the only year covered by the survey, total expenditures on commercial improvements and upkeep totaled $78 billion. For comparison, the study included the value of new construction for commercial buildings without expenditures for improvements. This exclusion lowered total new construction to $70 billion in 1986, or 10 percent less than the amount spent on remodeling. Dollar for dollar, therefore, remodeling is now known to be a larger market than new construction. Cahners Economics expected nonresidential remodeling during 1990 to exceed $91 billion—a 17 percent increase over 1986 levels (see Figure D).

Interior Design Magazine, in its yearly survey of office facility industry project budgets, calculated that no less than $23.05 billion would be spent in 1990 for the specifications and purchasing of design products for office facilities. This annual average was based on the "Universe Study," the first total design market study that surveyed the entire interior design universe, including independent interior design firms (employing at least one designer), architectural firms, major corporations with planning or facilities departments, chain hospitality firms, and office furniture dealers. The clear evidence from these statistics is that the 1990 market basket of services represents a substantial dollar volume and a large portion of the entire country's gross national product.

This text offers those engaged in the office facility industry, and students who seek to work in this industry, a comprehensive study of professional practice designed to improve interdisciplinary communications and thereby foster the matrix form of project team management. Because so many of us employ personal computers in our daily professional practice, many of the forms and legal documents presented assume an availability of electronic media.

The authors, editors, and publisher encourage readers' comments and suggestions for improvement of this text in a future edition. Please address all inquiries to Daroff Design Inc., 2300 Ionic Street, Philadelphia, PA 19103.

JAMES E. RAPPOPORT
ROBERT F. CUSHMAN
KAREN DAROFF

Philadelphia, Pennsylvania
September 1991

Overview

The process of office facility planning and design requires a concerted effort, over a substantial period of time, from the executives and staff of the organization being relocated. This book outlines the methods and procedures to plan and manage the office facility relocation process cost effectively and expeditiously.

Two types of planning processes are usually involved in a relocation. The first is the typical corporate or professional office relocation into a new facility of less than 10,000 rentable square feet of space. Eighty percent of all office facilities occupied in any given year are of this type. These relocations may be into owner/user facilities: the organization being relocated decides to buy and renovate, to build a new structure, or otherwise to develop their own new office facilities. However, the vast majority of relocations into new office space of under 10,000 square feet represent a leasing of space as a tenant in an office building owned by a landlord or developer who is unrelated to the relocating organization. Because these relocations require leases, they involve lawyers, real estate brokers, and related professional consultants.

The second type of office facility relocation seeks a much larger space, frequently 100,000 or more square feet. For these larger relocators, there is a likelihood of equity participation in the office building and a more influential role than that of the smaller tenants. Their participation has two major implications:

1. The larger tenant or owner/user, by nature of its specific office facility requirements, can and should have a major impact on the design, the construction, and perhaps the financing and operations of the office building. This impact is described in Chapter 4 as "inside-out design."

2. The larger tenant is likely to have on staff or on retainer many of the professional consultants required to plan and manage the office relocation process.

This book will guide the facility management team of the larger tenant in communicating effectively with its professional consultants during the office facility relocation process.

Smaller tenants may be tempted to embark on relocation using in-house managers and staff who have limited experience in the office facility relocation process. For these smaller tenants, the book's glossaries, forms, and exhibited documents may seem useful initially as a do-it-yourself guide, but they are offered to allow informed interviewing of professional consultants and knowledgeable interaction with them during the relocation process. (In that regard, Chapter 6, on recruiting, selecting, and contracting with the project's design professionals, underlines the need to document the project's scope, goals, objectives, and overall requirements in a lucid format prior to proceeding.)

Chapter 1, on determining the needed type, size, cost, and configuration of office space (known in the industry as "programming") will help small tenants to establish their project requirements firmly so that the relocation process can avoid the costs of restating the organization's use and occupancy needs.

A number of aspects of the office relocation process simply cannot be accomplished on a do-it-yourself basis. Leases frequently involve real estate brokers who must be state-licensed. Construction drawings are subject to review by local building departments and environmental agencies, and architects and engineers are required to prepare and sign the plans. Lawyers experienced in real estate issues are frequently retained to document lease agreements and to assist with the preparation of construction contracts, following approval of architects' and engineers' specifications.

Professional consultants are therefore frequently required for even the smallest office facility relocation, and their fees are cost-justified by the ongoing nature of the office facility relocation costs and expenses. For example, a 10,000-square-foot lease in a midsize city's urban center may cost the relocating organization more than $5 million over a 10-year period or from $10,000 to more than $15,000 per employee housed per year. Frequently, this market

FIGURE E

Office Market Ratings for 40 Cities, Stated as Years to Exhaust Existing Available Supply
(Used with permission of *Contract Design,* January 1990.)

	Years to Exhaust Supply*	Vacancy Rate 1989	Available Space 1989**
Up to One Year's Supply			
Charleston, SC	0.3	10.0	185
West Palm Beach, FL	0.4	22.0	1,640
Cleveland	0.5	11.0	3,288
Tucson	0.7	23.0	1,346
Phoenix	0.9	22.0	7,044
San Diego	0.9	22.3	8,000
Orlando	1.0	21.0	4,312
One- to Two-Year Supply			
Seattle	1.1	14.4	5,500
Tampa	1.1	24.1	6,000
Baltimore	1.2	14.6	5,000
Hartford	1.2	16.5	4,900
Ft. Lauderdale	1.3	26.6	5,000
Wilmington, DE	1.5	12.8	2,000
Detroit	1.5	16.0	8,779
Charlotte	1.5	16.2	3,000
Milwaukee	1.5	22.7	3,700
Miami	1.5	22.5	7,000
Minneapolis/St. Paul	1.6	17.7	8,778
Kansas City	1.6	17.1	6,000
Memphis	1.7	18.9	6,000
Atlanta	1.8	19.1	18,000
San Francisco	2.0	16.1	8,100
Two- to Three-Year Supply			
Dayton	2.1	20.1	2,500
Indianapolis	2.2	19.4	5,300
Philadelphia	2.2	15.3	13,500
Boston	2.3	14.0	19,000
San Antonio	2.3	31.5	6,000
Cincinnati	2.4	15.0	5,000
Jacksonville	2.4	N/A	3,000
Los Angeles	2.5	19.4	47,800
Washington, DC	2.9	14.2	34,000
Three- to Five-Year Supply			
New York	3.8	14.6	41,200
Pittsburgh	3.8	16.1	6,500
St. Louis	4.0	21.9	7,000
Chicago	4.4	16.2	36,300
Five or More Years' Supply			
Houston	5.2	28.3	41,300
New Orleans	5.5	25.9	6,000
Stamford	5.7	27.6	12,000
Denver	6.8	27.7	19,000
Dallas/Ft. Worth	8.7	26.5	39,500

* Years of supply are calculated by the current amount of rentable space divided by the projected amount of office demand for each metro area.
** Space listed in thousands of feet.

Source: *Contract Design,* January 1990

basket of use and occupancy costs, which includes rent, real estate taxes, water and sewer usage, light, heat, and power, and interior furnishings, finishes, and equipment, will consume more than 30 percent of an organization's annual total gross receipts and be second only to employee wages and related benefit expenses in the overall yearly company budget. Moreover, unlike wages, the lease is fixed for a long period of time and is not subject to easy revision, reduction, or adjustment.

Because of the substantial amount of money involved, the office facility relocation decision must be made with the greatest of care and with the best consultation affordable. Frequently, building developers and landlords seeking smaller tenants will offer to provide, on a rent-inclusive basis, some, if not all, of the professional services required by the tenant for the relocation. This may appear to be a cost-effective method to achieve the desired results, but unwary prospective tenants may overpay their rent and occupancy costs for an undersupply of the necessary professional services.

To judge whether lease inclusion is a practical and cost-effective solution, the first thing a prospective tenant needs to know is how competitive the market for tenants has become. Office facility construction reached a peak late in the 1980s and resulted in an oversupply of office facilities. Figure E rates 40 cities for their availability or saturation of office rental space.

Vacancy rates in many cities exceed 20 percent and will require more than two years of rental business to exhaust the supply. In each subsequent year, more vacancies will be added through renovation and new construction, so the oversupply is likely to continue for the foreseeable future. This high vacancy rate results in a substantial amount of competition among developers and landlords who are seeking tenants to relocate into their available space. (Chapter 4 outlines how a prospective smaller tenant can take advantage of a highly competitive real estate market. Chapters 8, 9, and 10 provide cost-effective insights into the lease negotiation process.)

Those who seek to purchase or net-lease older buildings for renovation and upgrading will find Chapter 5 of interest; the authors describe the methods and procedures related to retrofitting older buildings for modern office needs. Because modern office occupancy is a "moving target," any building constructed prior to 1980 is likely to require some upgrading for office operations of the 1990s.

Throughout, this book provides to architects, interior designers, facility managers, and staff of large and small organizations practical know-how on leasing, designing, or relocating their office facilities.

J.E.R.
R.F.C.
K.D.

CHAPTER 1

Determining the Type, Size, Cost, and Configuration of the Office Space an Organization Will Require

James E. Rappoport and Karen Daroff

After an initial discussion but before a decision is made to initiate the office planning and design process, an organization should document the type, size, and configuration of the office space it will require. This preliminary needs analysis will serve as the basis for all subsequent and ongoing discussions associated with the office facility relocation process. The analysis must precede the decision of whether to recruit, select, and retain a professional-contract interior designer or interior architect or to rely on the selected developer or landlord to provide space planning service.

The preliminary needs analysis is frequently called a *space utilization program,* or "the program" for short; if properly generated and documented, the program can serve as the basis for the project from the planning and negotiating stages to far beyond the move-in date, as the company expands, adjusts, and forecasts its space requirements.

The term of most office leases is likely to exceed the fiscal planning period of even the best managed corporations. A long-range (5 to 10 years) space utilization program is therefore, by definition, a forecast of the future. Because office automation and professional practice are bound to be different in the future than they are today, the most accurate forecast will include known facts, calculated projections, documented assumptions, and allowances for future innovations. The flexibility that allows change frequently requires redundancy. Moreover, for a program to provide an accurate forecast of future requirements, it must rely on as many points of view as possible within a given organization.

The Programming Process

We call the recommended programming process "top-down–bottom-up" programming (see Figure 1.1). The process begins with strategic planning sessions at the senior executive level. The time frame for completion of the program is determined, and benchmark points that will measure progress and affirm forecasts for future periods of the program are established. The strategic planning sessions should produce statements as to overall corporate goals and objectives for the relocation. As much guidance as possible should be given to all levels in the organization, regarding the macroeconomic and marketing direction foreseen by the senior executives of the company as the impetus and basis for the space utilization program. Figure 1.2 shows how these projections can be plotted graphically.

If the impetus for the relocation is a merger or consolidation, a strategy that eliminates redundancy and realizes economics of scale will be as critical to the success of the planning process as the increased sales that are forecast for the merged or consolidated organization.

After these meetings have generated and documented strategic plans, a questionnaire should be developed and made mandatory for each area of the organization's operations. Appendix 1A, at the end of this chapter shows an example, prepared by the authors' professional interior design office facility programming consultants.

The senior executives of the organization should invite every department manager of the company to a programming kick-off meeting at which the goals and objectives of the proposed office facility relocation are clearly outlined and discussed, and the questionnaire is handed out. A deadline for the return of the completed questionnaires is critical. One to two weeks is generally adequate.

In very small organizations, the questionnaire may be completed during the kick-off session, but frequently, even in smaller organizations, managers

FIGURE 1.1

"Top-Down/Bottom-Up" Programming Process

Senior Executive Projections

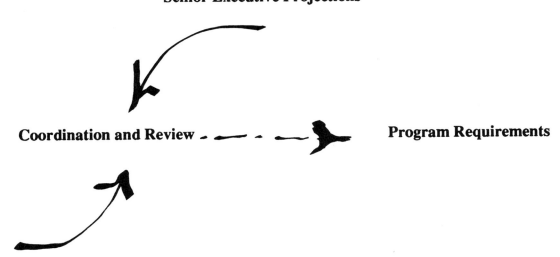

Coordination and Review   **Program Requirements**

Management and Staff Projections

may want to review personnel projections, discuss equipment and supplier issues, and test various departmental ideas and forecasts before responding to the questionnaire.

In larger organizations, many department managers will want to consult with their staff prior to responding; in most organizations, the interaction of staff from the bottom up becomes an exciting opportunity for everyone to participate in and help plan for the future of the organization while testing each other's ideas.

The questionnaires should be collected on the deadline date. When they are tabulated, the unified document that results from the replies becomes the space utilization program. An example of a tabulated program is provided in Appendix 1B.

If the process were this simple, professional interior design office facility programming consultants would be put out of business by do-it-yourselfers. There are at least three pitfalls to the do-it-yourself programming process:

1. It may be difficult for certain organizations to generate bottom-up responses without creating internal political trauma. For these organizations and for others with 50 or more persons, an outside professional interior design office facility programming consultant is recommended. By applying expertise garnered from many parallel assignments, the professional consultant will quickly and accurately gather and compute the needed data while reducing tensions by "merchandising" the office facility relocation process.

2. Department managers may determine unilaterally that day-to-day sales, marketing, and administrative activities come before strategic planning activities. An outside professional programming consultant, given appropriate authority by the senior executives of the company, may elicit a more timely and more accurate response.

3. Departmental responses frequently do not correlate or coincide. For example, when asked what size office the department manager should occupy, some managers may select the smallest office offered, to appear to be cost-conscious or otherwise "political"; others may select the largest office available, to show peers the force and merit of their position within the company. A professional consultant can frequently assist in reaching the most appropriate compromise within a given organization by drawing upon examples and experiences from parallel or peer-group organizations.

Whether the space utilization program is prepared in-house or with the aid of a professional interior design office facility consultant, the resulting document

FIGURE 1.2

Square Footage Projections

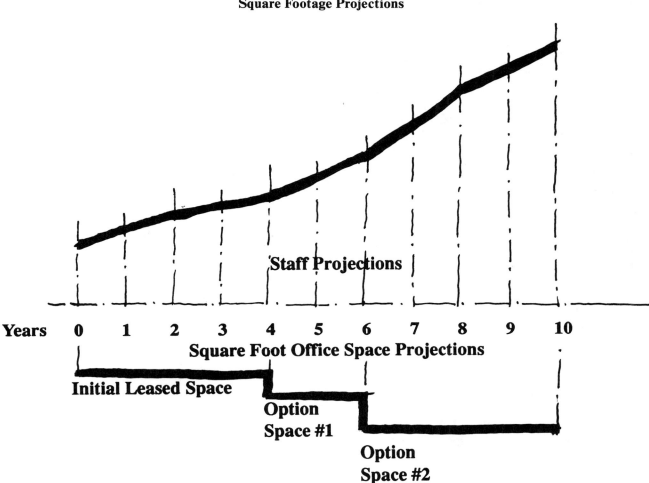

or office facility program thereafter becomes the basis for discussions with competing developers, landlords, real estate agents representing various office facilities, and all of the other professional consultants that are likely to be retained to assist in the office relocation process. The office facility program is perhaps most critical for initiating the relocation process, because it serves as the basis for all subsequent decisions throughout the office relocation process.

An interesting aspect of the program is its forecast of space requirements, defined in *usable* square feet, at the key points in time identified in the strategic plan. Usable square feet are the measured and estimated amounts of floor space required to house all of the offices, workstations, support spaces, and circulation or access spaces outlined in the office facility program. However, the calculation of usable square feet

will not determine the amount of rentable square feet required, because rentable square feet are determined unilaterally by those developing and marketing the various office facilities. The real estate industry markets office space on a rentable-square-feet basis. The next step in the relocation process is therefore to determine the amount of space, in *rentable* square feet, that is required to accommodate the program's usable square feet, in the various office buildings under consideration.

For at least two reasons, the program cannot accurately forecast rentable square feet of space. These reasons are outlined in detail in Chapter 3 and will be stated only briefly here. The main reason is that, in each office building, the architectural elements that create the usable office space are likely to vary in dimensions and configuration, so that they provide

FIGURE 1.3

Components of Total Rentable Square Footage Required

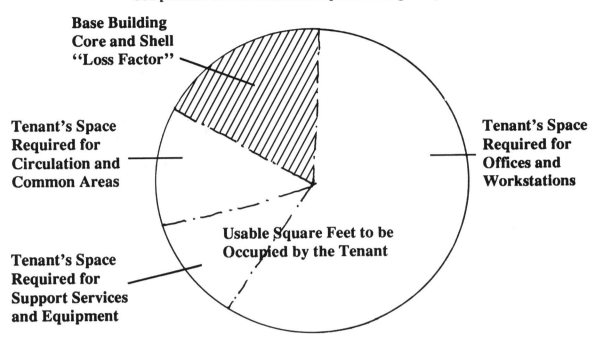

**TOTAL RENTABLE SQUARE FEET REQUIRED
YEAR XXXX**

more or less pure usable office space for a given tenant's program requirements (see Figure 1.3).

The second reason is that there are no hard and fast rules for defining rentable square feet of space. "Rentable" is a marketing term loosely defined by various local and national real estate and building managers' trade associations; it is not a set of dimensions that can be measured or computed using a standard formula. Because many terms used in office facility leases have various definitions, those entering the office facility real estate marketplace are well advised to understand clearly *every term* used by the industry and to question those who use the terms, to determine their precise meaning for any particular project application.

A glossary of office facility and design terms appears on pages 6–9 of this chapter.

The Office Facilities Relocation Team

Competition for office tenants is presently high. Professional consultants assisting and guiding tenants that seek to relocate therefore work closely together, to provide their tenant clients with a clear, concise, and comparative analysis of the available office facilities. Because no two pieces of real estate are equal, the consultants' analysis of the objective and subjective issues related to the differences between available relocation options and a tenant's present office facilities requires a multidisciplinary approach to the tenant's relocation decision.

A relocation team is likely to include the following members. *The tenant* is the principal in the decision-making process. The ultimate real estate decision will be made by the tenant, who will pay the rent and operate the business in the resulting office facility after the project team consultants' assignment is completed.

Typically, the tenant company will appoint various managers and employees from within the company to serve as the tenant's relocation committee, entrusted with recommending to the company's senior officers the most appropriate course of action. The project team consultants will report to the head of this tenant committee. To function effectively, the tenant committee must be granted clear authority and responsibility from the senior officers of the tenant company.

The developer has purchased the site, hired the base building architects and engineers, financed the project, won governmental approvals, awarded construction contracts, and constructed (or is in the process of constructing) the building. In older buildings, the developer may have sold its interests to another landlord, or hired a management agent to keep the building filled with tenants, or begun a process of modernizing and upgrading the building. In any case, the lease will be negotiated on behalf of the developer or its agent.

Developers typically hire space planners and leasing specialists to help tenants understand the features and benefits offered by their building, and, specifically, how best to fit the prospective tenant into a mutually convenient space available within the building. A developer's team usually will offer space planning assistance at no cost to the prospective tenant, but these "tenant plans" alone will not offer the comparative analysis of various available buildings most tenants desire. It then becomes advisable for a prospective tenant to employ the services of a project relocation team—a real estate broker, a space planning firm, and a real estate attorney.

The broker is a licensed real estate professional who seeks out prospective tenants for various office buildings in a particular geographic region and assists in closing leases with these tenants. The broker will assist a tenant in gathering data about available office facilities, arrange for tours and inspections, help negotiate leases, and analyze the comparative lease offerings.

The broker typically will receive a commission from the developer after a tenant's lease is signed and may offer real estate consulting services, for fees paid by the tenant.

Most developers appoint one broker in a community to serve as the broker for a building. This broker prepares the marketing materials for the leasing of the building and receives brokerage commissions from the developer after tenants sign their leases. If a tenant selects another independent broker to represent the tenant in the transaction, the brokerage commissions may be shared between the tenant's broker and the developer's building broker. A wise tenant selects one (tenant) broker to assist in the comparative real estate selection and to represent the tenant in the competitive lease negotiation process.

The interior design/space planning firm will provide the tenant with the programming, design, and construction documentation, including plans and other drawings and the preliminary comparative cost analysis of the real estate proposals negotiated by the broker. The firm will assist the tenant in making financial, functional, and esthetic design decisions related to the office relocation, and will prepare the space plans, interior designs, furniture location plans and documents with which the tenant or developer will contract for construction, furniture, equipment purchases, telephone and data wiring, and relocation services required by the tenant. (These services are outlined in detail in Chapter 3.)

The architect for the tenant fit-out project may be the interior design/space planning firm, if the firm is registered to practice in the locale of the project site. If the firm is not registered and local codes require an architect's seal on the building code filing documents, then the interior design firm may retain an architect as a project team consultant, or the client may seek to retain the project architect directly. If a developer or landlord has built a speculative office building into which the tenant is to relocate, two architects may be working on the project: a base building architect, responsible for the building itself, and a tenant architect, responsible for the tenant fit-out.

The attorney working for the tenant, will assist in the lease drafting and negotiations and in the actual contract drafting for the various construction and relocation services specified by the interior design/space planning firm. The developer, other parties to the lease, and various contractors will have their own attorneys.

The contractor retained to construct the tenant space may be the contractor hired by the developer to build the base building or an independent contractor selected with the help of the interior design/space planning firm to build the tenant's office facility. A new building's construction contract will separate the construction materials of the base building (core and shell) from a tenant's fit-out: interior (nonstructural) walls, ceilings, lighting, and interior finishes. Some contractors provide tenants with construction management services for a fee; others contract with their clients in the traditional manner at a fixed contract price that includes their profit over and above the costs of their various subcontractors, who provide labor and materials within particular areas of technical expertise (i.e., plumbers or electricians).

The construction management services are defined by industry standard forms of owner/construction manager contracts. They include preconstruction budget and scheduling services and a full range of consulting services, which many tenants require during the design process.

The furniture dealer will be a specialized contractor with expertise in the delivery and installation of office furniture and equipment. Frequently, since passage of the 1981 tax act, these personal property items are bid separately from the fixed assets provided by the contractor, because personal property items are more quickly depreciated and need to be segregated from depreciated fixed assets that have a longer useful life.

Other project consultants required by the specific project may include:

- Engineers who specialize in heating, ventilating, and air conditioning (HVAC), electrical, plumbing, mechanical, structural, and other related building trades;

- Telecommunications and data consultants who assist in the specifications of these specialized systems' equipment and associated wiring;

- Security consultants who recommend the processes, procedures, and equipment needed to protect the new office facility;

- Audiovisual and display consultants who provide designs and equipment specifications for these specialized functions;

- Lighting consultants who assist the design team in selecting and specifying appropriate energy-efficient lighting equipment and controls;

- Acoustic consultants who review the acoustic requirements of the project and recommend architectural and electronic equipment that will reduce unwanted noise while amplifying sound for conference and training requirements;

- Art consultants who assist in the selection and placement of new art and recommend the husbanding and reuse of existing art objects.

Typically, the tenant becomes the direct client of the broker, interior design/space planning firm, attorney, and contractor. The other relocation team members work as consultants, as illustrated in Figure 1.4.

Glossary

The tenant's real estate broker, attorney, and space planner will all assist in the lease negotiations with the developer. The following glossary of terms discussed in this book or typically found in an office facility lease is offered to acquaint prospective tenants with the basic language used in the lease negotiations and documents.[1]

Aggregate total rent: the sum of the base rental and all escalations over the full term of the lease.

Base building: the portion of the office building constructed by the building owner or developer prior to the tenant fit-out (workletter) construction.

Base rent: the rent stated exclusive of escalation.

Base year: that year beyond which escalation increases. Although it should be the year immediately prior to the lease commencement, the base year is whatever it is stated to be.

Building code: the ordinance used by the governmental agency that regulates the construction and life-safety issues in the region where the building is being built. Building codes frequently require that all tenant occupancy plans be filed for approval prior to construction commencement. These filing drawings must be signed and stamped by licensed architects and engineers who have supervised the preparation of the documents and who certify that they meet the technical requirements of the building code. The tenant's occupancy plans must conform to the provisions of the building code.

Column centerline dimensions: the dimensions from the center of each column to the center of the next adjacent column(s) in the building. These dimensions are critical to the efficient planning of an office facility because furniture and other equipment come in factory-made standard sizes and must fit efficiently within the space between the columns.

Core-to-glass dimension: the dimension from the window glazing to the building's core; a critical dimension because it affects the ability to lay out offices and plan open workstations in an efficient manner.

Core space: the part of a floor taken up by bathrooms, public corridors, lobbies, janitors' closets, and other spaces not assigned to tenants. It does not include spaces that cut through the floors, such as elevator shafts.

CPI escalation: an increase in base rent matched to the percentage increase in the consumer price index (CPI) or a portion of that increase from a fixed point in time, usually referred to as the base

[1] Definitions of terms used in commercial office leases have been prepared with the assistance of Donald Schnabel of Julien J. Studley Inc., New York.

FIGURE 1.4

Tenant Bubble Chart

XXX Company World Headquarters
Project Team Organization Chart

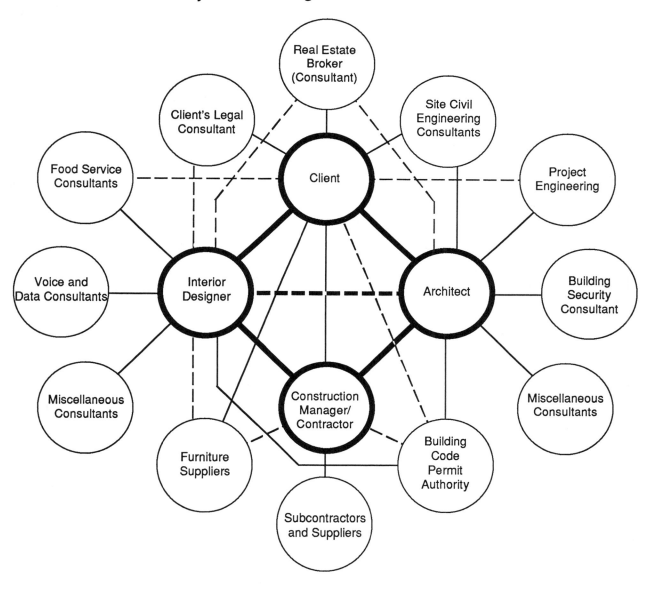

year. An alternate term is *cost of living adjustment (COLA)*. Typically, a tenant's rent is increased by 25 percent of the increase in the CPI over the base year. If the CPI increases at an annual rate of 8 percent, then the tenant pays a 2 percent increase in rent; if the base rent is $20 per square foot, the rent goes up $0.40 per square foot in the first year. Warning: It compounds thereafter.

Demised premises: the floor space defined in the lease as being the tenant's space for the term of the lease.

Demising wall: the wall that separates a tenant's office from neighboring space. City codes require that demising walls achieve a certain level of fire resistance.

Electricity: the power required for lighting, computers, and other equipment. Various methods for connection and payment include direct metering, included, rent inclusion, and submetering.

Electricity/direct metering: purchase of electricity directly from the utility by the tenant. There is a direct relationship between the amount of electricity the tenant consumes and what the tenant pays.

Electricity/included: inclusion of the costs of all electricity serving the tenant's space within the tenant's rental payments under the terms of the lease.

Electricity/rent inclusion: inclusion of electricity costs in rent as $/square foot × number of square feet; dollar amount may increase because of a utility rate increase or by lease agreement in the event that the landlord determines that a tenant's potential demand for electricity has increased because the tenant is adding new equipment.

Electricity/submetering: purchase of the electricity from the utility by the building owner, who then submeters it to the tenants. The submeter becomes the empirical calculator in determining the amount of electricity the tenant has consumed.

Lease commencement date: the date when the tenant moves in, usually the first or the fifteenth day of the month. This may not be the first day on which the tenant pays rent.

Loss factor: the difference between rentable and usable area, expressed as a percentage of rentable area.

Net present value: the discounted present value (at the opportunity rate) of future payments. (See Chapter 3 for a more detailed explanation of this real estate economics concept.)

Operating expenses: the total cost of operating a building. A portion of a tenant's rent reflects the tenant's pro-rata portion of the operating expenses.

Operating pass through: agreement by the tenant to pay a proportionate share of the increase of operating expenses and/or real estate taxes over some stated base year.

Options: rights to renew or expand a lease, which may be part of the lease negotiation and should be described in the lease.

Pass through escalation: a means of adjusting rent whereby the owner and tenant agree on a base year or an amount per square foot, and the tenant pays a proportionate share of any increase over the base year.

Porter's wage escalation: an increase in rent stated as a penny (or some multiple thereof) per square foot for each penny per hour that the wages of a building's porter go up. Tenants should distinguish between those porter's wages that include fringe benefits and those that do not. The increase in rent escalation and the increase in hourly compensation of a porter are not directly related. If the escalation were gauged penny for penny, a tenant occupying 10,000 square feet in a building where porter's wages increased by $0.65/hour would see a rent escalation of $6,500 annually.

Proportionate share: that percentage of the building which the tenant occupies, usually defined as a fraction: the numerator is the tenant's rentable square feet, the denominator is the total rentable square feet of the building.

Quiet enjoyment: a tenant's right to use and occupy the leased and demised premises for the purposes stated in the lease during the entire term of the lease, regardless of changes in ownership, mortgages, ground leases, and so on.

Real estate taxes: a combination of the tax rate and the assessed valuation on a building. For example, a building assessed at $3.5 million with a tax rate of $6 per $100 would pay real estate taxes of $210,000; a tenant occupying 100,000 square feet in this building would pay $2.10/square foot.

Recapture: the part of a sublease clause that specifies the landlord's right to take back that portion of the tenant's premises that is offered for sublease.

Rentable space: the total floor area on which a tenant's rent will be determined, including the space actually occupied by the tenant plus allocations of the tenant's floor and other floors that service the tenant's floor, such as elevators, toilets, electrical closets, janitors' closets, fire stairs, mechanical equipment, and air conditioning equipment, plus or minus a "marketing" factor determined by the landlord.

Step-up: the specific time when and the fixed dollar amount by which base rent is to be increased, as stated in the lease.

Substantial completion: a date, spelled out in the lease, when the majority of the construction work to fit out the tenant's space has been completed.

Tenant allowance: dollars provided by the building landlord to the tenant to pay for all or a portion of the tenant's fit-out expenses.

Tenant fit-out: the interior partitions, ceilings, wiring, lighting, finishes, and all of the related tenant-required features constructed within the tenant's demised premises, including the fees billed to the tenant by the tenant's consulting team.

Usable space: the space that a tenant actually occupies, which is generally less than the rentable space.

Utility pass through: an increase to cover costs of electricity or steam for a building, to be passed directly through to the tenants from the utility on a proportional basis.

Workletter: a document attached as an exhibit to the lease, where a building standard installation, rather than a tenant allowance form of lease agreement, is used. The owner defines in the workletter the quantity and quality of walls, doors, ceilings, lights, electrical outlets, painting, wall covering and floor covering to be constructed in the tenant's space.

Zoning code: the ordinance used by the governmental agency regulating the use of land in the region where a building is being built. Zoning codes frequently require that all building plans, site plans, and subsequent renovations and additions be filed for approval prior to the commencement of construction. These filing drawings must be signed and stamped by a licensed architect and a surveyor who have supervised the preparation and calculations of the plans and documents being submitted. Zoning codes regulate land use and the use of buildings within the region. The tenant's use of the rented space must conform to the allowed uses within the region and zoning district.

Rentable Square Feet Calculations

Because an understanding of rentable square feet of space is so critical to the office facility relocation process, all tenants are well advised to understand the basis for this term and how it varies from building to building. This section offers a brief explanation of how rentable square feet are calculated.

In the course of lease negotiations with various tenants during the years of a building's occupancy, office buildings are typically assigned a variety of rentable square feet calculations by their various owners or developers. Recently, owners and developers have taken a stronger and more consistent approach to the assignment of rentable square feet within their buildings. Interior design firms specializing in space measurement have been retained to measure new buildings or remeasure existing buildings and prepare documentation, in a computer-aided drafting format, of the computed rentable square feet of space for an entire building, for typical full floors of a multifloor building, and for partial-floor suites in buildings marketing multitenanted floors. These documents are used for day-to-day management of the demised premises within the building as well as for lease attachments defining the demised premises.

The information in these documents becomes the audit trail for negotiating various rent escalation clauses. These clauses are based on a proration of certain landlord taxes and operating costs assigned to a specific tenant on the basis of the tenant's percentage of occupancy of the total rentable square feet calculated and verified for the building as a whole.

Typically, the building owner will want to measure the entire building at one time, to prepare a verifiable spreadsheet analysis similar to the one shown in Figure 1.5.

For existing buildings, this analysis may result in a substantial increase in the leased rentable square feet of the building as stated in the architect's original construction documents. When a consistent measuring concept is applied to a building, square footage calculations typically increase for the following reasons:

- The building's architect prepared calculations based on zoning definitions of tenant square footage measurements; these may not always correspond to the real estate marketing goals of the owner.

- Earlier leases often allowed for "negotiation" of the rentable square feet.

- Leases signed earlier may not have used a consistent formula for determining rentable square feet lease-to-lease within the building.

- Leases signed earlier used various definitions of rentable square feet.

- Leases may have been signed using drawings that were not accurate renditions of actual floor layouts, planned areas, common areas, or public areas within the building.

- Building common corridors, tenant common spaces, tenant mechanical spaces, and other non-habitable spaces may not have been counted in the rentable square feet calculations.

- Building additions may have occurred.

FIGURE 1.5

Lease Management Chart

DDI Lease Management
Comparison of Existing to New Rentable Sq.Ft. Calculations
Building Analysis: 1234 W. Main Street Property, XXX Property Owners

6 October 19XX

Tenant Space and Floor Number Designation	1 Existing Lease Date	2 Lease Expiration Date	3 Existing Usable Sq.Ft. (Net)	3A % of Total Building Usable Sq.Ft.	4 Existing Rentable Sq.Ft. (Gross)	4A % of Total Building Rentable Sq.Ft.	5 Net to Gross Ratio	6 New Usable Sq.Ft. (Net)	6A % of Total Building Usable Sq.Ft.	7 New Rentable Sq.Ft. (Gross)	7A % of Total Building Rentable Sq.Ft.	8 Net to Gross Ratio	9 Variation Between Columns 4 & 7	10 Variation % of Increase Between Columns 4 & 7
1st Floor														
#102 ABC Company	1/1/80	12/31/84	8500	12.50%	10,000	12.82%	85.%	8,500	12.50%	10,241	12.50%	83.%	+241	+1.82%
#103 XYZ Company	1/1/75	12/31/84	8500	12.50	10,000	12.82	85	8,500	12.50	10,241	12.50	83	+241	+1.82
1st Floor Subtotal			17,000	25.88	20,000	25.64	85	17,000	25.00	20,482	25.00	83.	+482	+1.82
2nd Floor														
#201 XX Company	2/1/82	1/31/90	6,000	8.82	7,000	8.97	86	6,000	8.82	7,229	8.82	83	+229	+1.832
#202 YY Company	2/1/82	1/31/90	6,000	8.82	7,000	8.97	86	5,800	8.53	6,988	8.53	83	-12	(99.%)
#203 ZZ Company	2/1/82	1/31/90	5,000	7.36	6,000	7.70	83	5,200	7.65	6,265	7.65	83	+265	+1.84
2nd Floor Subtotal			17,000	25.00	20,000	25.64	85	17,000	25.00	20,482	25.00	83	+482	+1.82
3rd Floor														
#301	5/1/88	4/30/90	17,000	25.00	16,000	20.51	106	17,000	25.00	20,482	25.00	83	+4,482	+1.28
3rd Floor Subtotal			17,000	25.00	16,000	20.51	106	17,000	25.00	20,482	25.00	83	+4,482	+1.28
4th Floor														
#401	6/1/81	5/31/88	17,000	25.00	22,000	28.21	77	17,000	25.00	10,482	25.00	83	-1,518	(93.%)
4th Floor Subtotal			17,000	25.00	22,000	28.21	77	17,000	25.00	10,482	25.00	83	-1,518	(93.%)
TOTAL ALL FLOORS			68,000	100.00	78,000	100.00	87	68,000	100.00	81,928	100.00	83	+3,928	+1.05

- Errors may have been made in the original architect's plans, the real estate agent's documentation, the lawyer's lease documents, or the as-built condition of the existing building and its various tenant demising walls. These errors may have caused the square feet measurements to vary from the actual.

For a new building, the square feet measurements become the basis for all tenant presentations, negotiations, and lease documents. For an existing building, the new measurements, with their new assignment of rentable square feet, may not impact the existing leases with existing tenants, but they will be used for all subsequent lease negotiations within the building, including renegotiations with existing tenants when their original leases come up for renewal. Over a period of time, the new rentable square feet calculations can replace the earlier rentable square feet numbers. The building is thereafter marketed with a unified definition of rentable square feet and a uniform (lease-to-lease) ratio of usable square feet to rentable square feet (the "building factor").

Tenants will want their interior designer/space planner to review the developer's stated rentable square feet calculations and to measure the actual space being rented, to establish the usable square feet available for tenant planning purposes. A simplified definition of usable square feet is: the amount of actual measured floor area within the demised premises of specific office space being rented.

The tenant's program of required usable square feet of space and the rentable square feet calculations must be verified, and the usable square feet must be measured. The tenant and the interior designer/space planner can then proceed to establish tenant space plans and comparative analyses of the various competing office facilities under study. To document these various measurements, the tenant's interior designer/space planner should receive from the developer original Mylar™ or computer-aided drafted (CAD) base drawings, or, if they are not available from the developer, will prepare the base building drawings on which the tenant's plans are to be drafted.

As a first step in the evaluation of the base building's opportunities and constraints, the plans are cross-hatched in six patterns, representing the types of building floor space illustrated in Figure 1.6.

Building common spaces: Base building spaces, such as lobbies, are shared by all tenants of the building and are included as an allocation in the rentable square feet of all of the tenants' leases.

Floor common spaces: Corridors, toilet rooms, and similar common spaces shared by tenants on a specific floor are included as an allocation in the rentable square feet of all of the tenants on that floor.

Shaftways and stairs: These base building spaces are not typically counted in the rentable square feet calculations.

Mechanical, air conditioning, and telephone and electrical equipment spaces: These base building spaces are typically allocated in the rentable square feet of all of the tenants' leases.

Tenant occupied space: All space within an individual tenant's demising walls is in this category.

Tenant mechanical and shaft spaces: Within the tenant occupied space, there is space that has been planned and used by the tenant in a manner that causes it to vary from the original building code floor area ratio (FAR) calculation (e.g., tenant stairs, shafts, mechanical rooms with low ceiling heights, and so on).

Figure 1.6 illustrates the various building floor spaces, which are elements of a set of floor plans for a typical office building.

As noted earlier, variations in the configuration of the office buildings will be a major factor in determining the rentable square feet of space needed to accommodate a given tenant's program of space requirements in a given office building. There is no shortcut method of determining precisely the amount of rentable space required in a given building. A preliminary tenant plan must be prepared, based upon the given program, and then the landlord's representatives must be asked to advise how many rentable square feet of space have been demised by the plans.

The process is further complicated because, in any given marketplace, so many different types of office buildings are offered at different rental rates and under various lease terms and conditions.

Frequently, a less efficient building (one with less usable space for the stated rentable square feet) will offer a lower cost per rentable square foot of space, to compensate for the building's inefficiency. The would-be tenant will know the relative efficiency or inefficiency of a particular building only by proceeding as indicated below:

- Documenting the tenant's space requirements into a program of present space needs and a forecast of future space requirements. (See Appendixes 1A and 1B.)

FIGURE 1.6

Types of Building Floor Spaces

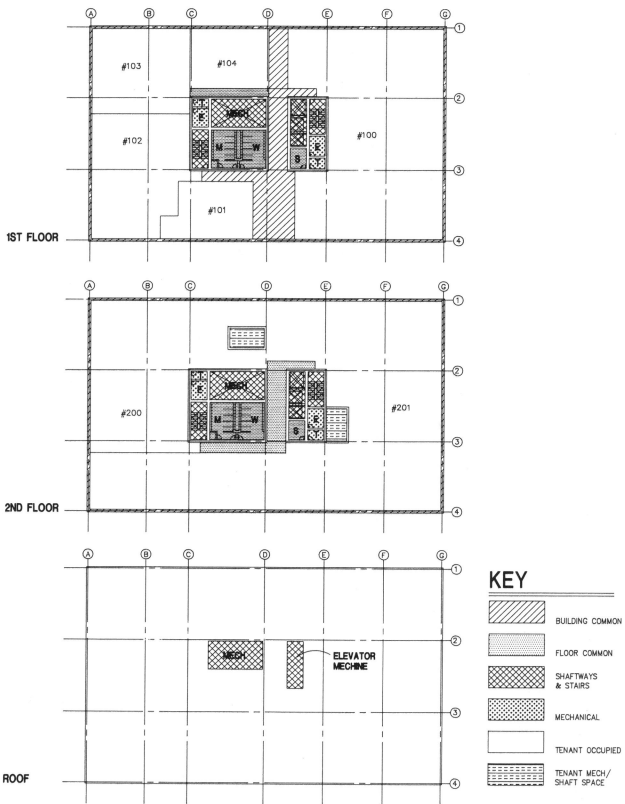

- Sketching the stated program of space needs within the various base building floor plates under consideration. (See Appendix 1C.)
- Determining the relative efficiency of these alternate floor plates for housing the tenant's requirements and then the subjective enhancement features offered by the various sketched plans, which will vary from building to building. (See Chapter 4 for this comparative analysis.)
- Calculating all of the use and occupancy costs, from year to year and over the term of the proposed lease, on a present value basis.
- Dividing the rental and operating costs, for each facility being compared, by the number of employees that can be housed, to compute the costs per employee housed.

Costs per Employee Housed

The costs per employee housed are the true measure of the features, benefits and associated costs of one real estate opportunity as compared to others (see Figure 1.7; these costs are discussed in detail in Chapter 4). From evaluation of these costs, a best-case opportunity frequently can be deduced. Location, proximity, and many other subjective features and amenities of the building (e.g., its neighborhood, the availability of parking) should also be evaluated. To make a reasonable comparison, the prospective tenant will require, from various landlords and developers in the region, information on available space that is of interest to the tenant.

Available Space

In the current marketplace, a number of options are available in three basic types of office buildings:

- Modern office towers built or being built to respond to current tenant requirements and current building codes;
- Older buildings that have recently been enhanced and upgraded to provide for current tenant requirements and to comply with most current codes.
- Older buildings that are being cosmetically renovated but, for a variety of reasons, cannot respond to certain current tenant requirements or current building codes.

A would-be tenant can use a number of methods to secure landlord proposals. One method is for the tenant to draft a request for proposal based on its program of space requirements. Covering letters might be sent with the request for proposal directly to any and all building owners and real estate brokers in the community.

A relatively more efficient method would be to employ a tenant real estate consultant to represent the tenant throughout the selection process.

Real Estate Consultant

A tenant real estate consultant/broker can be employed to assist in the relocation process under a fee agreement or a commission agreement. Frequently, a

FIGURE 1.7

Costs per Employee Housed

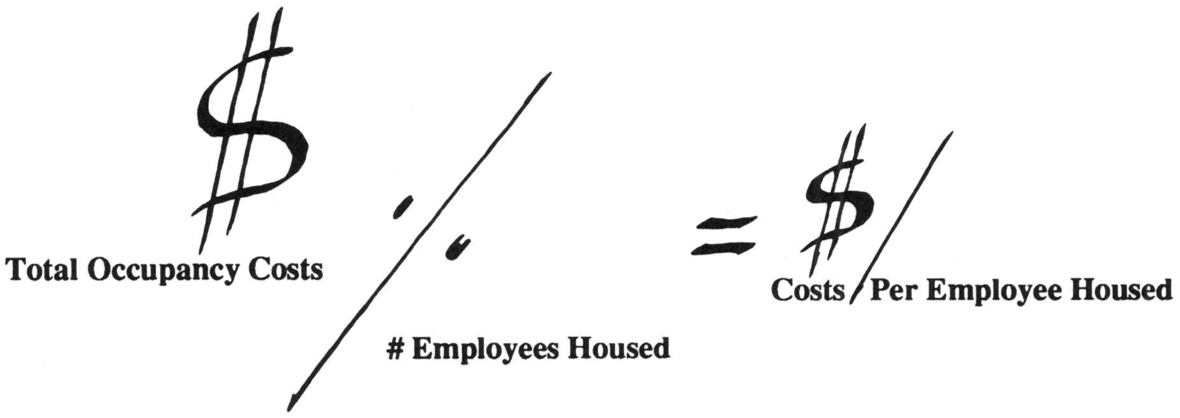

fee agreement is more cost-effective if the prospective tenant has a good idea of what is available and is interested in reaching closure in a timely manner. In this scenario, the request for proposal is drafted by the consultant, using the program's information with respect to the physical requirements of the project and the associated costs.

The real estate consultant will also prepare the lease terms and conditions, which will include the term and options of the proposed agreement and the various legal and operational issues that affect the tenancy over the term of the lease.

The request for proposal will then be issued to the owners of buildings that appear on a short list of buildings recommended by the tenant real estate consultant.

The Building Owners

The initial response by the building owner's representative to the request for proposal will be to provide price, availability data, and a base building plan of the space the owner proposes to offer. From this base plan, the tenant's space planner, applying the tenant's program of space requirements, will prepare what is known as a tenant plan. From combined tenant plans, the various building owners will compile their own estimates of fit-out costs and, from these estimates, will prepare more detailed responses to the tenants' requests for proposal.

The Negotiations

The entire process described in the preceding sections generally occurs within three to four weeks. A number of proposals will result, each representing the tenant's requirements and each documenting legal, real estate, architectural, and budgetary terms and conditions, thus forming a complete preliminary proposal.

From this response to the request for proposal, the tenant, the tenant real estate consultant, and the interior designer/space planner can begin the negotiation process, which results in active bidding by the competing building owners until an apparent best-case deal is negotiated.

This latter phase can occur in a few weeks' time or may extend for many months, depending on the willingness of the parties to meet, to review each other's points of view, and to arrive at a mutually acceptable agreement.

Project Initiation

The design and documentation of a complete set of tenant fit-out construction and furnishing plans—one that responds to the tenant's requirements and includes the engineering, telephone, and data features package—requires 4 to 12 weeks to complete, depending on the project's complexity.

Frequently, during the documentation phase of the project, the lease documents are being refined with the provision that, if the deal is not confirmed, the building owner pays the tenant's interior designer's fees earned to the date of termination of the deal. With this arrangement, the project proceeds with all due speed while placing some pressure on the building owner to close the deal with the tenant.

It is critical to the financial success of all tenant fit-out projects that the tenant fit-out budget be confirmed by the building owner and/or the owner's contractors prior to the lease confirmation. Budget confirmation is accomplished by issuing a preliminary set of documents from which a very accurate budget can be prepared. The tenant then knows for certain what the final cost will be, and both parties know whether the available building allowance provided by the building owner is sufficient to complete the project to the satisfaction of the tenant.

In many urban centers (using 1990 as a base year), landlords frequently offer tenants dollar allowances of $30 to $45 per rentable square foot for tenant fit-out and related project expenses. Some tenants agree to trade off more rental dollars in the future for more cash up front, by taking the tenant allowance from the building owner. For example, a number of the executive office facility, professional, and legal firm relocations (in the base year) negotiated allowances of $60 to $70 per square foot, while many operational office facilities opted for $40 to $45 allowances that resulted in much lower per-square-foot rents.

Adding $10 per square foot to the landlord's up-front costs, assuming 10 to 12 percent mortgage loan rates, may add $1.50 to $2.00 per square foot per year to a 10-year lease's rental cost.

From the first day of project initiation until the documents are ready for bidding, including final lease negotiations after the pre-bid budget has been used to confirm the lease agreements, the project will require a minimum of 6 to 8 weeks.

Construction

Construction cannot begin until there is a lease. Many leases require lender approvals and all construction projects require a building permit. This process requires 3 to 4 weeks and usually overlaps the time the contractor needs to mobilize the subcontractors, order equipment and materials, and deliver them to the project site.

From the date of receipt of the permit until the date of substantial completion, most 10,000- to 20,000-square-foot tenant projects require 10 to 14 weeks of on-site construction effort. More time is required for a multifloor tenant or for multiple enhancement features.

The installation of the tenant's carpeting, furniture, and final finishing generally adds another 2 to 3 weeks to the project's duration.

Conclusion

A full-floor tenant fit-out project requires approximately 27 weeks from initial fact-finding and programming until installation of the final furniture and finishing package. The main phases of this process and their duration are graphically described in Figure 1.8.

Cash Costs

As noted earlier, the presently competitive market makes it possible to negotiate with a building owner to front the fit-out costs—the professional fees and all of the hard costs associated with the project. Some tenants build their secretarial desks into the architecture, to make the landlord pay for these workstations within the fixed asset budget, but frequently they find that these fixed items become outdated or otherwise require relocation. Substantial dollars must be spent at a later date, to rebuild and reconfigure what was thought to be a bargain initially.

Usually, the tenant pays out-of-pocket for furniture and for telephone and data equipment. The telephone and data wiring, carpeting, and window treatment may be allocated to the landlord's allowance or the tenant's cash budget, depending on the deal negotiated between the parties. In general, allocations follow Internal Revenue Service (IRS) guidelines as to the definition of fixed assets and useful life versus items of personal property. For shorter leases, fewer items are considered fixed assets and more are personal property. Leases with options seem to qualify for longer useful life treatment, but IRS rulings continue to fluctuate on this treatment.

Partnerships, more than corporations, are interested in the tax effect because it may pass directly to the individual partners. A quick write-off may be better for the partners than more rent, especially if the building owner is going to mortgage the incremental cost above the landlord allowance of $30 to $45 per rentable square foot and thereby charge the tenant costs plus financing costs for the additional tenant allowance.

The Large Office Facility Relocation Project Process

The preceding discussion of the office facility programming and planning process that leads to a leasing decision and a related tenant fit-out construction documentation package is appropriate for small and medium size office facility relocation projects. For large corporate relocations, the tenant's facility relocation committee and the entire project consulting team are advised to prepare, during their initial strategic planning sessions, a project-specific schedule of key benchmark dates, milestones, and to-do lists, in a workbook format. This dynamic document can be used as a framework for planning, a depository for data, and a record of decisions by the senior executives of the tenant company and their consultants.

An outline of the workbook's projected contents may be useful during the preliminary stages of the process. The workbook should help to uncover issues that relate to various points and that can be expanded appropriately when the project's key documents are drafted. As additional topics arise during the planning process, the outline can be revised and modified to include these new topics. The outline can provide a framework for subsequent report writing and serve as a guide during the lease negotiation process.

To gain full advantage from the workbook, it is important to record all relevant issues and information that may be related to the office facility relocation

FIGURE 1.8

Tenant Relocation Project Time Line

Typical 10,000- to 20,000-square-foot Tenant Relocation Project Time Line

Weeks

1 2 3 4 5 6 7 8 9 10 11 12 13 14 15 16 17 18 19 20 21 22 23 24 25 26 27

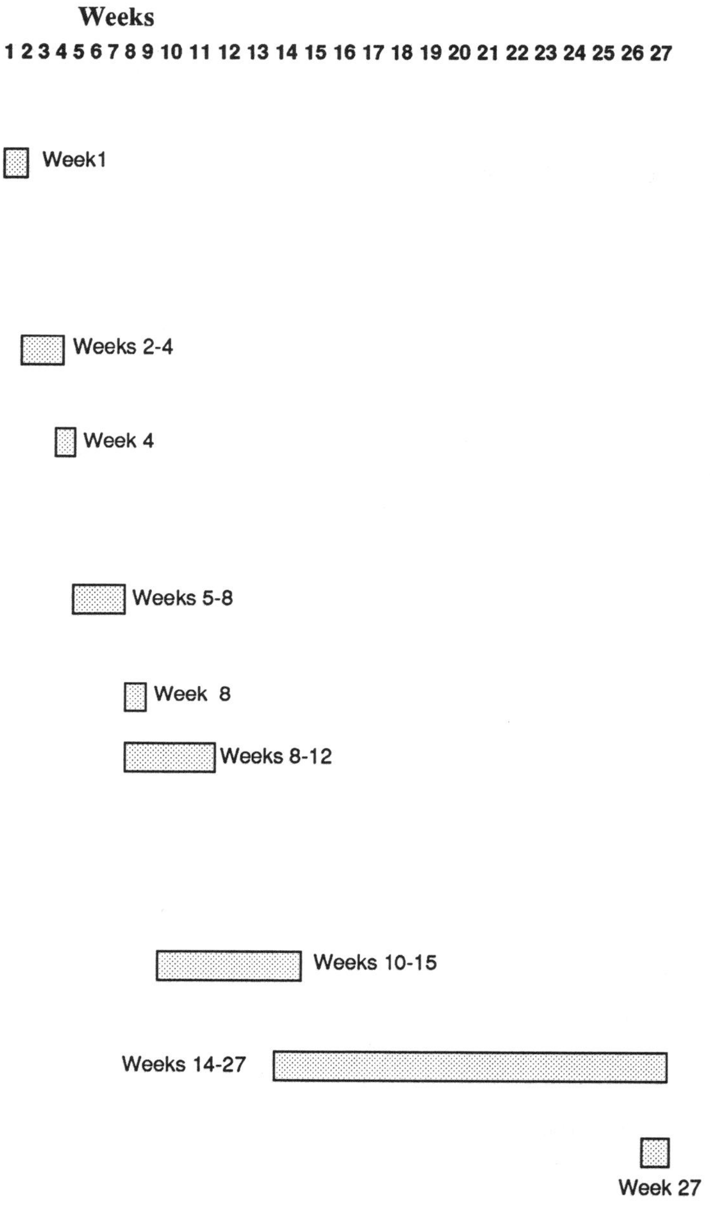

Project Phases

1. Retain a tenant interior designer/space planner, seek out short list of available office buildings, prepare program of space requirements, project budget, send request for proposal to building owners, retain real estate consultant.

   Week 1

2. Prepare tenant plans for each facility on the short list.

   Weeks 2-4

3. Receive back from building owners their proposals and compare features and benefits using the plans and proposals as the basis of comparison.

   Week 4

4. Negotiate with those building owners offering the best deals.

   Weeks 5-8

5. Select the best deal and proceed.

   Week 8

6. Release interior designer/space planner (and consulting engineers) to prepare designs, contract documents, final budgets, and work with the real estate consultants and lawyers to confirm and document the lease agreement.

   Weeks 8-12

7. Initiate construction process, permits, buy-out, and mobilize on site.

   Weeks 10-15

8. Proceed with construction process, substantial completion, furnish and finish.

   Weeks 14-27

9. Accomplish substantial completion, relocation, and final punch list of construction, furniture and finishing packages.

   Week 27

plans. Two major reasons for preparing the workbook are to codify various assumptions and directions provided to the project planning team during the programming phases of the project by senior executives and other tenant representatives, and to orient new members of the planning and development team to the process in a time-efficient manner.

The workbook will encompass the full range of the project team's analysis and will ensure that the work is done in the context of the client's objectives.

Ultimately, each of the project-related consultants' professional contracts will reference the workbook as the basis for the client's design intent and the source of specific direction in the design process.

Figure 1.9 shows an indexed outline for a complete office facility relocation project workbook. Entries for each category would carry the index number for that category (e.g., 006, 007). As new issues arise, subcategories can be created and designated (e.g., 006.1, 006.2).

FIGURE 1.9

Index Outline of Office Facility Relocation Project

I. INTRODUCTORY

    001   Cover sheet
    002   Title sheet with date of the report presentation
    003   Names of senior executives for whom the report was prepared
    004   Names of project team members who prepared the report
    005   Table of contents
    006   Executive summary of the process used to prepare the workbook
    007   Description of the project team's role in the process

II. CORPORATE PHILOSOPHY AND GROWTH GOALS

    008   Client corporate image statement
    009   Client facility image statement
    010   Statement concerning flexibility for future expansion
    011   Philosophy of corporate growth and acquisition
    012   Operational basis for office and workstation standards
    013   Discussion regarding key dates of planning periods and relationship between client's economic forecast(s) and facilities planning process
    014   Description of appropriate window wall and natural light relationships within company hierarchy (who is to get a window and how many?)
    015   Organizational theory (i.e., centralization versus decentralization; variations at different points of maturity of company)

III. EMPLOYEE/COMMUNITY/PUBLIC RELATIONS ISSUES

    016   Management of internal and external communications and related issues prior to project development
    017   Criteria related to health and occupational safety
    018   Criteria related to community relations and local political considerations
    019   Criteria related to recreation, both on-site and off-site

IV. FACILITIES PLANNING AND DEVELOPMENT PROCESS

    020   Recommendation for expanding the project team into a development team
    021   Flow diagram of the interrelation of the proposed project development team
    022   Task list for the proposed development process
    023   Key dates for the proposed development process
    024   Recommendations for the time line required to meet key dates
    025   Outline of key contract types required to facilitate time-line dates
    026   Client location goals
    027   Client facility component goals and sublocation implications
    028   Size(s) foreseen for the location(s)

(continued)

FIGURE 1.9 *(Continued)*

029	Phased occupancy assumptions
030	Quality expectations
031	Productivity improvement expectations
032	Occupancy cost reduction expectations
033	Criteria for managing the existing client facilities in the future
034	Criteria for managing the existing client facilities during the development process
035	Criteria for managing energy conservation in existing and new structures
036	Criteria for risk avoidance in the location and operation of client facilities
037	Development master planning concepts
038	Development parking concepts
039	Development food service concepts
040	Development computer center concepts
041	Development telecommunications concepts
042	Office and workstation sizes and related occupancy concepts
043	Conference facilities and related management concepts
044	Library and filing concepts and management concepts requirements
045	Training center requirements and related management concepts
046	Outline program of specific space allocations for proposed project development site(s)
047	Outline budgets for proposed project development site(s)
048	Statement as to assumptions leading to project budget(s)
049	Project development design concepts
050	Criteria for managing natural and artificial light in new facilities
051	Criteria for determining cost-effective structural and planning grids or modules
052	Criteria for relocation and inter- and intradepartmental moves during the development process
053	Criteria for relocation and inter- and intradepartmental moves during the initial facility move-in process
054	Criteria for relocation and inter- and intradepartmental moves subsequent to the initial facility move-in process
055	Management of data base
056	Management of computer-aided design (CAD) documentation
057	Management of project consulting team
058	Facility management of resulting as-built new and renovated facilities
059	Stated goals to be achieved by facilities computerization
060	Budget calculations for various levels of office and workstation furniture (allowances)
061	Discussion of the formation, content, and use of the computer-aided data base of current and future program information
062	Discussion of the future prospects of the client company as they relate to current and future space planning and facilities needs
063	Discussion of electronic data processing and its future, in relation to current and future space planning needs
064	Discussion related to current locations of client's facilities, historic reasons for these locations, likely future location criteria, and political consequences, productivity, and marketing of these location concepts
065	Issues related to "smart" buildings and their inter- and intrafacility wiring and wire distribution systems
066	Criteria for selection of project engineers and other consultants
067	Criteria for selection of project land planners and master planning project team
068	Criteria for dissemination of the information contained in this workbook
069	Issues of client internal security
070	Criteria for individual relocation costs of client employees
071	Criteria for determining an appropriate set of life-cycle points in time against which various comparisons are to be made
072	Discussion of the interview process and the results of the interviews
073	Various subjective issues raised in the interview process and during the walk-through
074	Issues of redundancy and the use of redundancy for risk avoidance
075	Issues of redundancy and the ability to shed certain redundant facilities and equipment in a consolidated master plan

FIGURE 1.9 *(Continued)*

076 Issues of insurance in effect currently, during the development process, and after facilities are up and operating

077 Criteria for analysis of various service activities (food service, transportation, security, maintenance, and the like) that are employee-based and/or contractor-based

078 Use of computer-aided design and drafting (CADD) techniques for management of current facilities as well as facilities to be developed

V. REGIONAL PLANNING ISSUES

079 Sources of employees' transportation linkage and concepts
080 Criteria for project site analysis
081 Criteria for project site land use regulations
082 Criteria for project site access and traffic modes
083 Market and target market patterns
084 Communication linkages and capabilities

VI. REAL ESTATE ECONOMIC ANALYSIS

085 Identification of potential land and existing real estate sites within defined locations
086 Determination of acquisition costs
087 Determination of development costs—hard and soft costs
088 Development pro formas and cash flow projections
089 List of site alternatives and extent to which objectives are met
090 Life expectancy of proposed developed properties
091 Financing requirements and concepts for proposed development process
092 Analysis and cost comparisons of lease/rent and owner/user opportunities
093 Agreement as to assumption of rate of inflation during various life-cycle periods against which present value analysis and related calculations can be made
094 Cash flow analysis of various development concepts
095 Analysis of facility costs, currently and in the future, based on various development concepts

VII. REAL ESTATE IMPLEMENTATION

096 Negotiation of acquisition agreements
097 Supervision of site plans/building designs
098 All necessary zoning and public approvals
099 Selection of in-house and out-of-house professional team
100 Preparation of construction cost analysis
101 Financial structuring and financing of project
102 Negotiation of construction contract and supervision of construction work
103 Preparation of financial statements and progress reports
104 Assignment of accounting responsibilities
105 Securing of financing

VIII. EXTERNAL COMPARISON

106 Human resources and survey ratios from studies of peer/competing companies
107 Relationship of expected costs to current costs and to costs at peer companies
108 Proposed field trips to similar project sites for inspiration and confirmation of project goals and objectives
109 Proposed interrelationship with facility managers in similar client companies, to share project data

IX. CONCLUSIONS

110 Statement of project conclusions
111 Next steps
112 Related appendices
113 Rear-cover graphics

Facility Management Process

Large office facility relocation projects will require what has been called a facility management systems approach to the relocation process. The backbone of this approach is facilities management software, which is available from a variety of software vendors.

We recommend that a major relocation project should be begun with an end result in mind—a facilities management data base tool—and that each of the project development and design decisions, from project initiation through move-in and beyond, should be managed in a systematized manner within the overall data base management concepts described here.

Facilities management software systems encompass, in a single data base, the client's program of space requirements; the individual and departmental space requirements, detailed at key points in time; the individual, departmental, and company-wide budgets for all interior fit-out and furnishings items designed, specified, and installed in the new facility; perpetual inventories of these items, with warranty and subsequent fill-in purchase order information; the computer-drafted tenant plans and all related engineering and construction plans; commercial terms and conditions for each of the construction contracts; and agreements with all of the vendors and suppliers to the project.

The general goals and objectives of establishing a computer-aided facilities management system are:

- To consolidate all project-related drawings and data into one relational data base,
- To facilitate change by allowing for cost-effective and timely revision(s) to the plans over the useful life of the project,
- To manage the inventory of furniture and equipment,
- To facilitate subsequent relocations while honoring the master plan and design concepts of the facility,
- To develop departmental charge-back facilities management techniques,
- To ensure ongoing warranty services,
- To facilitate reorders and ensure accurate reorder specifications and pricing,
- To manage a changing facility with a minimum of time delay from receipt of directives to revise the facility until completion of the desired revision.

Detailed goals and objectives are shown in Figure 1.10.

Facilities Management Case Study: Comparison of Manual and Computer Approaches to Office Facility Relocation

For a large office facility relocation process to prove its cost effectiveness to the senior executives of the company, the resulting facility must provide ongoing flexibility for a changing program of space requirements during the entire useful life of the facility. Constant change must be accommodated through a systematic approach to the planning and facility management process because, in many large organizations, in-house relocations may affect more than 30 percent of the employees of the company each year. The act of planning for the initial relocation is only the first step in an ongoing process of facility management.

The following analysis compares a computer-aided facilities management process (Process C) to two alternate manual processes (Process A and Process B).

In Process A, a facility is managed on an ad hoc basis without a programming, space planning, or furniture standard. Inventory of furniture and equipment is outdated, and there is no master plan of departmental locations or of office and workstation positioning within various nonstandard architectural columns, walls, and cores of a building.

Process B, a semisystematized process of a well-established master plan, could occur with a well-planned modern office facility. A programming, space planning, and furniture standard has been implemented; inventory of new furniture and equipment is up-to-date; suppliers have committed to given prices, discounts, and delivery terms for certain quick-ship items; a master plan of departmental locations and of office and workstation positioning has been fulfilled; and the planning guidelines regarding the architectural columns, window walls, partitions, and cores of the building have been clearly understood.

In this case study, an operating division has identified the need to increase its present requirement of 10,000 usable square feet by adding 2,000 usable square feet to accommodate 10 new employees, who have been hired to report for work within four weeks' time (see Figure 1.11). There is no contiguous room into which this division may expand. The facilities

FIGURE 1.10

Comprehensive Facilities Management Approach

COMPREHENSIVE FACILITIES MANAGEMENT APPROACH

1. Define Strategic Project Management Issues with Client

- Goals and objectives of the proposed relocation
- Corporate philosophy related to the office environment
- Client marketing goals and objectives
- Analysis of the present deficiencies of the existing facility
- Growth criteria and expectations
- Economic issues governing the relocation
- Client corporate principals' personal desires related to the relocation
- Regional planning and location-related issues
- Real estate economic issues
- General management issues
- Employee and community and client relationship issues
- Establish project time line and key benchmark dates for the relocation

2. Create a Facility Management Database of Project Needs

- Prepare strategic criteria for database development (cost, timing, objectives, etc.)
- Customize the programming form(s) to correspond to client requirements
- Prepare motivational presentation of planning process
- Present planning process to client executives
- Present planning process to client managers and employees
- Walk-through existing facilities
- Document existing facilities (account for existing people, places and things)
- Establish key benchmark dates for client analysis of future facility requirements
- Interview client executives and managers using the programming form to take notes
- Establish a consensus of facilities criteria (who, what, when, where, what type, how many, at what cost, etc.)
- Input data into facilities management computer system
- Edit with senior client project management
- Publish a working report illustrating the project needs as thus defined

3. Develop the Facilities Management Database During the Course of the Project

A. Project Needs Analysis	B. System Requirements Data	C. Site Requirements Data	D. Interior Criteria Data	E. Peer Comparison	F. Publish Project Workbook	G. Assemble Project Team Data
• Existing conditions	• Window wall	• Parking	• Existing FF&E	• Trade journals	• Document criteria	• Issue RFPs to consultants
• Forecasts at key dates	• Mechanical	• Safety	• Quality goals	• Visit peers	• Establish budget	• Analyze bids
• Best case affinities	• Electrical	• Security	• Style goals	• Visit suppliers	• Determine location	• Select consultants
• Bubble diagrams	• Structural	• Traffic	• Image goals	• Meet consultants	• Determine timing	• Project team kick-off
• Block diagrams	• Telephone	• Signage	• Work patterns	• Analyze peer data	• Grant approvals	• Enter fees in database
• Stack diagrams	• Data	• Proximity	• Visitors' needs	• Test data		
• Circulation analysis	• Computers	• Utilities	• Marketing needs	• Adjust criteria		
• Tenant plan/floor	• Fire protection	• Fiber optics	• Efficiency factors	(if appropriate)		
• Lease data	• HVAC	• Microwave	• Filing requirements			
• Work letter data	• Plumbing	• Expansion	• Storage needs			
• Budget data	• Security	• Recreation	• Conferencing needs			
• Staffing data	• Wire distribution	• Cultural	• Food services			
• Departmental data	• Elevatoring	• Food service				
• Existing furniture data	• Mail distribution	• Budget criteria				
• Existing equipment data	• Truck loading	• Office work needs				
• Planning factors	• Vaults and safes	• Workstation needs				
• Loss factors	• Acoustics	• Special requirements				
• Option space analysis						

FIGURE 1.10 (*Continued*)

H. Project Management Data

- Glossary of project terms
- Consultant's contract data
- Consultant's fee data
- % complete project analysis
- Project cash flow analysis
- Project budget analysis

I. Design and Documentation Data

- Tenant plans
- Coded furniture plans
- Ceiling plans
- Carpet plans
- Finish plans
- Telephone & data wiring plans
- Departmental plans
- Lease charge back plans
- Sublease allocation plans
- Option year(s) plans
- Security system plans
- Furniture plans
- Furniture component plans
- Art feature location plans
- Lighting plans
- Tel. and data address plans

J. Bid and Buy Data

- Project specifications
- Specification addenda
- Specification bulletins
- Pre-bid conference issues
- Bid timing requirements
- Bid receipts
- Bid review and analysis
- Bid comparisons with peers
- Bid negotiations
- Contract confirmation terms
- Order confirmation terms
- Expediting activities
- Bills of lading
- Product receipt and review
- Warranty data
- Reorder data
- Payment accounting
- Quality assurance analysis
- Lease management data

K. Construction Management Data

- Project specifications
- Specifications addenda
- Specifications bulletins
- Pre-bid conference issues
- Bid timing requirements
- Bid receipt
- Bid review and analysis
- Bid comparisons
- Award bids
- Track % complete
- Observe work in progress
- Sample submission review
- Process payments
- Change orders
- Quality control

L. Project Close-out Data

- Final payments to consultants
- Final payments to suppliers
- Final payments to contractors
- Subsequent additional services
- First rent payments
- First equipment lease payments

M. Facilities Management Training

- DDI trains client managers in use of system
- Client purchases software and hardware package
- Database turn over to client

Install Database at Client Facility
Location and Conduct On-Site Training and Follow-up as Required

A Project Needs Analysis
B System Requirements Data
C Site Requirements Data
D Interior Criteria Data
E Peer Comparison
F Publish Project Workbook
G Assemble Project Team Data
H Project Management Data
I Design and Documentation Data
J Bid and Buy Data
K Construction Management Data
L Project Close-out Data
M Facilities Management Training

Use of the Facilities Database by the Client Facilities Manager to:

- Maintain the design inventory of the as-built facility
- Honor terms and conditions of all facilities contracts, leases, etc.
- Develop internal charge-back systems per department
- Manage any subleased facilities
- Manage any optioned facilities
- Facilitate subsequent relocations and replanning
- Maintain perpetual inventory of people, places and things
- Warranty management
- Maintenance management
- Spare parts and inventory management
- Telephone and data address management
- General ledger accountability
- Risk avoidance and security accountability
- Equipment maintenance
- Refurbishment specifications
- Subsequent external relocations
- Maintain and update drawings file
- Maintain and update specifications file
- Maintain and update suppliers file
- Maintain and update lease file(s)

FIGURE 1.11

Case Study: How Ten New Hires Will Add Square Footage to Departmental Space Requirements

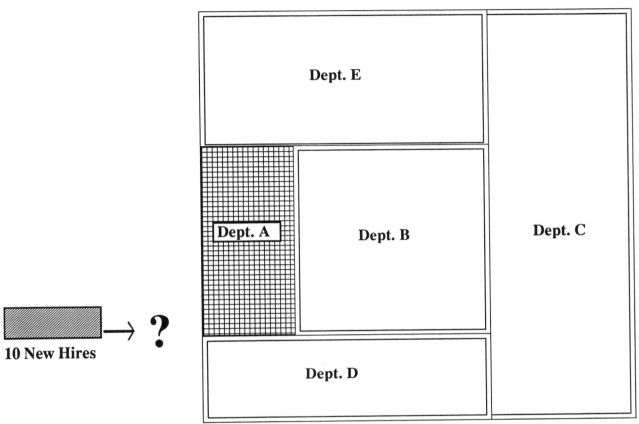

management team must find a suitable space for the division's relocation in 12,000 square feet of space, plus reasonable space for future expansion. This new space should conform to the interdivisional adjacencies of the company as a whole, and the relocation of the division should be accomplished with a minimum of disruption and relocation of other divisions of the company, to avoid a "domino effect."

As will be seen in the following analysis, the proposed computer-aided facility management process produces the lowest overall project cost, with the most reliability and the quickest time frame.

Estimates in a relative quantitative analysis (in 1990 dollars) are as follows:

	Square Feet Required	Facilities Staff Total Costs	Project Time (Days)
Computer-aided project process (C)	11,000	$ 1,287.50	40
Semisystematized manual process (B)	11,200	5,081.25	100
Prior ad hoc process (A)	11,500	12,425.00	201

Process A (Ad Hoc Process)

The following in-house space planning project process is what might occur under the circumstances of an existing pre-renovated or non-standardized office facility:

Item #	Hours	Elapsed Time in Days	Item
1.	1.00	Day 1	Facilities manager receives a visit from the division manager to request verbally the need for additional space that is thought to be approximately an additional 2,000+ square feet. A meeting date is set to substantively review these requirements with the division manager, and, in preparation,
2.	0.50	Day 1	The space planners and architects are asked to print and publish the relevant as-built plans of division offices.
3.	2.00	Day 5	Review these as-built plans.
4.	2.00	Day 6	Walk through division space.
5.	1.00	Day 7	Meet with the division manager to show the as-built plans and to discuss the forecasted additional need for space, take notes on the types of new employees that have been hired, and the other additional space requirements, and promise to report back in a few days.
6.	4.00	Day 7-8	Determine, once back at the facilities department, that in fact contiguous space is not sufficient to accommodate the additional 2,000 square feet of space.
7.	8.00	Day 9-10	Review the present use of space in that division, and compare this use with other similar divisions, to build a case for the actual need of 1,000 usable square feet of space, by instilling an unpublished, but implicit, space standard on the space allocation(s).
8.	0.50	Day 10	Call a meeting to present the "bad news" to the division manager.
9.	2.00	Day 12	Tell the division manager (a) that too much additional space is required, and (b) a full relocation is required, since not enough contiguous space is available into which to expand.
10.	1.50	Day 12	Receive a call from the group senior VP calling for a meeting between facilities and the Division A management to review the division's complaints that they are not receiving effective service from facilities;
		Day 12-17	Explain the rationale for the problem(s) and promise to come back within a week with an effective answer.
11.	16.00		Ask the space planners and architects for a full printout of the plans of the building, put the drawings on the wall in a large conference room, and begin to game likely relocations to allow for the needed expansion.
12.	8.00		Prepare, at the same time, an analysis of the use of space company-wide and attempt to build a stronger case for the space standards allowing for lower than the 2,000 square foot allocation the division management requested.

Item #	Hours	Elapsed Time in Days	Item
13.	8.00		Select the least worse relocation alternate and sketch in block format that relocation concept.
14.	2.00	Day 17	Meet with the division manager and the SVP to present the least worst solution and the space standards argument. Convince them of the space standards but receive many questions about the relationship of the new location of the division to others in the company, and the effect of the least worst relocation strategy on other divisions and the company as a whole.
		Day 18-23	Promise to come back in five days with alternate least worst relocation(s) strategy(s).
15.	32.00		Seek out alternate strategies and document each in sketch form. In cases where vertical adjacencies are also required, prepare building sections or study models to illustrate the three dimensionality of the relocation and the resulting effects on each division. Color code these documents for ease of presentation.
16.	3.00	Day 23	This time, meet with the division's managers, the SVP, and the managers of each division affected;
17.	24.00 2.00	Day 23-25	Go through another round of revisions, and Call a final meeting where you present three options for them to select from.
18.	1.00	Day 25	Finally, receive an approval to proceed into the planning stages.
19.	2.00	Day 26	Call an orientation meeting with the division manager(s) to determine the expected time line--now way past due--and the budget and other project constraints.
20.	1.50	Day 27	Orient facilities management staff to the project and the proposed time line, constraints, goals, and objectives.
21.	2.00	Day 27	Establish the internal procedures and budgets for the remainder of the facilities management service required by the compromise reached in the division manager's meeting.
22.	2.00	Day 28	Meet with the division manager to begin from scratch to learn the program of space requirements; meet with other division managers affected by the relocation.
23.	10.00	Day 29-30	Create a sketch plan of the division, illustrating the best case layout from a required space point of view and present this hypothetical plan for review.
24.	20.00	Day 30-35	Receive comments and criticisms of the plan, prepare revised plan(s) until the division manager is satisfied (note that without a space standard and verifiable data as to space requirements, it is ''open season'' for custom design features and non-standard uses of space, thus fostering many subjective design and layout decisions).
25.	2.00	Day 36	Finally reach agreement as to the plan.

Case Study
Page 2

Item #	Hours	Elapsed Time in Days	Item
26.	2.00	Day 37	Measure the plan to determine that the plan required 11,500 square feet of space--500 more than had been anticipated (due to the lack of specificity and standards).
27.	3.00	Day 37	(We assume for this study that the other divisions can be modified slightly to effect this relocation, thus avoiding the full relocation of the other divisions). Advise the SVP that the agreement reached earlier is no longer valid, owing to the additional requirement of space and call another meeting to present the minor domino effect to each of the affected divisional managers.
28.	2.00	Day 38	After some discussion, receive approval to move the additional 500 square feet around, and proceed with the design development process.
29.	16.00	Day 38-40	Using the sketch plan as a basis, survey the existing location of the division to prepare an inventory of existing furniture and equipment, including the wiring requirements of each piece of equipment and the condition, color, and finish of each piece of furniture.
30.	16.00	Days 40-42	Determine, in this empirical method, what components may be required to effectuate the new plan, learning that the new plan cannot be built with many of the existing components.
31.	24.00	Day 43-50	Prepare a list of the required new components; call in the sales reps for the items required, and ask them to submit quotations.
32.	4.00	Day 51	Present these quotations together with the other facilities costs to the division manager, who will no doubt find the total costs beyond the budget, advise that you can redesign to change the plan again, and, in the process, reuse more of the existing furniture and equipment and seek a compromise to that end.
33.	16.00	Day 52-54	Replan
34.	16.00	Day 54-60	Request new quotations from the suppliers' reps, who this time don't grant as long a discount, and also note that many of the needed items are still specials and not on the list for special corporate discounts.
35.	2.00	Day 61	Resubmit this revised budget for management approval and receive same.
36.	4.00	Day 62	Issue purchase order requisitions to word processing, using the quotations as the basis.
37.	40.00	Days 62-66	Prepare final drafted plans for implementing the relocation, including: · Furniture plans · Relocation and move plans · Use of existing furniture plans · Telephone and electric plans · Other furniture, plants, planters, etc. Create these plans one at a time, including the base building elements, which need to be drafted on each plan package.

Case Study
Page 3

Item #	Hours	Elapsed Time in Days	Item
38.	16.00	Day 67-68	Revise the plans as required, each time revising each package of plans to coordinate the complete set of documents.
39.	4.00	Day 69	Issue purchase orders to various suppliers.
40.	4.00	Day 76	Review the order confirmations and work orders and discover errors.
41.	8.00	Day 77	Issue bulletins to correct the errors.
42.	4.00	Day 80	Receive new order confirmations and still discover errors.
43.	2.00	Day 84	Issue final bulletins and receive back final order confirmations that appear to be correct.
44.	16.00	Day 84-124	Expedite as required, but from memory, since there is a lack of CADD expediting to recall what has been ordered and what the promised delivery date(s) are--note, since there are no standards, many items are custom orders.
45.	16.00	Day 124-144	Review the bills of lading, signing for the goods at the dock, without full knowledge of what has been ordered or received, or how it will be installed to meet the plan.
46.	16.00	Day 124-144	Discover during supervision of installation that some items have been shipped improperly, others ordered improperly, and in general discover missing components preventing completion of the project.
47.	4.00	Day 145	Partially punch list the job.
48.	2.00	Day 146	Order the replacements.
49.	4.00	Day 142-167	Expedite the replacements.
50.	4.00	Day 168	Supervise the installation of the replacements.
51.	2.00	Day 170	Punch list the replacements and discover still some compromise solutions which are thought to be acceptable and let them go.
52.	16.00	Day 171	Prepare an as-built plan for the record.
53.	4.00	Day 172	Prepare a take-off of the as-built plan for the allocation of the space square feet with accounting.
54.	16.00	Day 172-175	Prepare a manual inventory document from an actual as-built inspection and count for accounting.
55.	8.00	Day 176	Authorize payment of invoices.
56.	16.00	Day 176-200	Resolve warranty claims from initially defective items by searching through the manual records for who supplied the goods and what the warranty terms are.
57.	2.00	Day 201	Authorize payments for the replacement of items contracted for to be under warranty.

Case Study
Page 4

Item #	Hours	Elapsed Time in Days	Item
58.	8.00	Day 176-200	Resolve errors in telephone and address, issue new listing to corporate telephone directory for republishing
59.	2.00	Day 201	Meet with facility staff to wrap up project and rethink process so that fewer ''glitches'' might occur the next time.

	497.00 hours	Total estimated project time
$12,425.00		x $25/hour estimate of value of project service
	$1.08/sqft	on 11,500 square feet
	201.00 days	elapsed time

In this case study analysis, the project requires 497 facilities staff hours to complete, an imputed cost of $12,425 in staff time. The project ultimately requires 11,500 square feet of space, 500 square feet more than had been foreseen, and with associated increased operating costs over the years of the facility. Moreover, the project requires additional furniture and equipment, and redundancies, owing to the overall lack of a clear inventory or furniture and equipment standards program. The project requires approximately 201 days to complete.

Process B (Semisystematized Process)

The following project process is what might occur under the circumstances of the strong space standard and the furniture and equipment standards program, but without the fully integrated computer-aided facilities:

Item #	Hours	Elapsed Time in Days	Item
1.	0.25	Start	Facilities manager receives from the division manager a written request for additional space that is thought to be approximately 11,500 square feet in total, based upon the approved space standards program already established.
			A meeting date is set to review these requirements with the division manager and, in preparation,
2.	1.00	Day 1	The as-built drawings of the division are taken from the plan files and reproduced.
3.	4.00	Day 1	These plans are reviewed.
4.	2.00	Day 2	A walk-through is required, since changes might have occurred subsequent to the drafting of the plans.
5.	4.00	Day 3	The plans are updated based upon the walk-through.
6.	1.50	Day 5	During the meeting with the division manager, the standard programming form is used to record the needed information, but, at that meeting, certain requests for nonstandard items surface.
7.	2.00	Day 6	The program is reviewed by the facilities manager, who calls a meeting with the facilities staff to orient staff to the project.
8.	8.00	Day 7	A planner plans the required additional space and determines that no contiguous space exists to grow the division, and that a relocation is required.
9.	1.00	Day 8	A meeting is called to explain these findings to the division manager and further discussion occurs as to any changes in operations that might affect the relocation decision.
10.	8.00	Day 9	Tack up the full set of drawings for the entire facility on a conference room wall, and manually game where the division might move to allow for the needed expansion.
11.	4.00	Day 10	Select the least worst relocation alternate and sketch in block format that relocation concept.
12.	1.50	Day 11	Meet with the division manager, the Senior Vice President, and any division managers that may also be relocated to allow for this expansion, and explain the least worst relocation strategy. Receive comments and promise to return within a few days with alternate strategies.

Item #	Hours	Elapsed Time in Days	Item
13.	8.00	Day 12-15	Seek out the alternate relocation strategies, color code the plans to ease the presentation, and meet with the managers again to illustrate these options.
14.	1.00	Day 16	Receive an approval to proceed into the planning stages.
15.	1.00	Day 17	Meet again with the division managers affected by the relocation to determine the expected time line, budget, and other project constraints.
16.	1.00	Day 17	Reorient the facilities team to the project and the proposed time line, constraints, goals, and objectives.
17.	1.00	Day 17	Establish internal procedures and budgets for the remainder of the facilities management service required to complete the project under the agreements reached with management.
18.	16.00	Day 18-20	Using the planning standards and the manual or nonintegrated computer based furniture inventory, prepare a detailed plan for the relocation and additional offices and workstations.
19.	8.00	Day 21	Using manual methods, color code those existing elements on the plan, leaving the uncolored items for manual counting into a shopping list of needed items.
20.	8.00	Day 22	Refer to the specifications and manually assemble the specifications, suppliers, and prices for the needed items.
21.	8.00	Day 23	Word process this list in a purchase order requisition format and present this list to the manager for budget approval. (We will assume that all standard items have finally been the basis of design).
22.	1.00	Day 24	Receive comments and criticism of the plan and the budget, and revise the plans, budgets, and take-offs until the manager is satisfied. Reach agreement.
23.	4.00	Day 25	Measure the plan to determine that 11,200 square feet have been required.
24.	40.00	Day 24-29	Prepare final drafted plans for implementing the relocation including: · Furniture plan · Relocation and move plans · Use of existing furniture plans · Telephone and electric plans · Other required furniture, plants, planters, etc., plans Create these plans one at a time, including the base building elements, which need to be drafted on each plan package.
25.	4.00	Day 30	Issue purchase orders using the specifications as the basis.
26.	8.00	Day 30	Revise the plans as required, each time revising each package of plans to coordinate the complete set of documents.
27.	2.00	Day 31	Issue revised purchase orders, if required.

Item #	Hours	Elapsed Time in Days	Item
28.	4.00	Day 34-40	Review order confirmations and work orders, and discover errors.
29.	2.00	Day 41	Issue bulletins to correct the errors.
30.	1.00	Day 45	Receive new order confirmations and still discover errors.
31.	1.00	Day 46	Issue final bulletins and receive back final order confirmations that appear to be correct.
32.	4.00	Day 50-70	Expedite, as required, from a check-off process (assuming quick ship items).
33.	4.00	Day 70-75	Review bills of lading, sign for goods at the dock without full knowledge of what has been ordered or received, since the integrated computer aided system has not been used.
34.	4.00	Day 70-75	Discover during supervision of the installation that some items have been shipped improperly, others ordered improperly, and, in general, discover missing components, preventing timely completion of the project.
35.	2.00	Day 76	Partially punch list the job.
36.	2.00	Day 77	Order replacements.
37.	2.00	Day 77-90	Expedite replacements.
38.	2.00	Day 91	Supervise the installation of the replacements.
39.	1.00	Day 91	Punch list the replacements.
40.	4.00	Day 92	Prepare an as-built plan for the record.
41.	4.00	Day 93	Prepare a take-off of the as-built plan for the allocation of square feet with accounting.
42.	8.00	Day 94	Prepare a manual inventory document from an actual as-built inspection and count for accounting.
43.	2.00	Day 95	Authorize payments of the invoices.
44.	4.00	Day 96-100	Resolve warranty claims from initially defective items by searching through the specifications for the appropriate terms and conditions.
45.	2.00	Day 96-100	Resolve errors in the manually prepared telephone and data address plans, issue new listings to the corporate telephone and data directory for republishing.
46.	1.00	Day 100	Meet with division manager to receive his comments of appreciation.

Item #	Hours	Elapsed Time in Days	Item
47.	1.00	Day 100	Meet with facilities staff to wrap up the project and rethink the process so that fewer problems might occur the next time.

203.25 hours	Total estimated project staff hours
$5,081.25	x $25/hour = imputed staff cost
$0.45/sqft	on 11,200 square feet planned = cost of the service per square foot
100.00 days	elapsed time

In this case study analysis, the project requires 203.25 facilities staff hours to complete, an imputed cost of $5,081.35 in staff time. The project ultimately requires 11,200 square feet of space, slightly more than the 11,000 forecast. Standard furniture and equipment has been used, but with some errors, owing to the manual drafting and ordering process. The project requires approximately 100 days to complete.

Process C (Computer-Aided Facility Management Process)

The following project space planning process is what is likely to occur under the circumstances of a strong space standard, with the fully integrated computer-aided facilities management systems approach to the office facility relocation process.

Item #	Hours	Elapsed Time in Days	Item
1.	0.25	Start	Review formal written request from the division manager that a relocation or expansion is required, received on a preprinted form.
2.	1.00	1-3	Call an orientation meeting with the division's manager to acquaint the manager with the process and to establish a time line, budget, and other project constraints.
3.	1.00	1	Orient facilities management staff to the project and the proposed time line, constraints, goals and objectives of the division management.
4.	0.50	1	Establish internal procedures and budgets for the facilities management service required by the division manager.
5.	1.00	1	Search the database for stack plans and adjacencies of the division's as-built plan and program of space requirements, and forecast for future requirements, and issue these reports to the division's management.
6.	0.25	1	Issue the self-paced computer-aided space planning program form, together with the approved space standards and space utilization guidelines to the division's management, together with written instructions as to the steps they need to take to set in motion the relocation.
7.	1.00	5-6	Review the completed planning program form, together with the division's management, and verify the requirements.
8.	1.50	6	Input the new data into the system and run the forecast requirements report.
9.	2.50	6	Review the divisional adjacency requirements for all divisions to learn where best to fit the relocated division to maintain the most optimal divisional adjacencies.
10.	1.50	6	Review the existing stack and block plans to verify the most likely relocation within an unassigned space (or) if the total space required by the division is not available in an unassigned space suitable for their use.
11.	3.00	6	Using the stack and adjacency reports, shuffle divisions within a particular area of the facility by "gaming" the reassignment of various divisional locations on the computer tube, until a reasonable solution is found.
12.	2.50	6	Prepare a new block and stack plan for the relocation(s) and publish this new plan for review by any divisions involved in the proposed relocation.
13.	1.5	8-9	Call a meeting of the affected divisional managers to review the proposed relocation, and, if required, bring the managers into the computer area to regame the solutions until a compromise has been reached.

Item #	Hours	Elapsed Time in Days	Item
14.	1.50	9	Publish the revised block and stack, and issue a memorandum of the agreement reached at the planning meeting.
15.	1.00	9	Activate forecast program and run main divisional reports for those divisions to be relocated.
16.	1.00	9	Activate inventory program to run reports on equipment assignments, listings of furniture, equipment, and people, and furniture specification information, voice and data addresses, etc.
17.	8.00	9-10	Using the approved space standards of offices and workstations, replan the affected areas, using the appropriate office and workstation sizes, and available modules of furniture and equipment (which should fit together in the reconfigured arrangement as they now do in the original layout).
18.	4.00		Plot the new space plans and issue for review and sign-off.
19.	1.00	11-12	Receive back sign-off and/or comments and further direction--assume that sign-off can be achieved with a first pass, since the planning has previously been approved as to program and standards.
20.	2.00	12	Activate the CAP to verify if new equipment or component parts are required to effectuate the plan.
21.	1.00	12	Issue a computer generated purchase order from the data base for these new parts (or) if required, first issue a shopping list and budget from the data base for prior management approval.
22.	4.00	12	Issue final plans for the implementation, including: · Furniture plans · Relocation and move plans · Telephone and electrical plans · Other furniture, plants, planters, etc., plans. These are produced by overlaying various layers of the database of plan data so that various trades can be provided just the information they require for their individual work orders or contracts.
23.	2.00	12	Issue the related purchase orders, work orders, and other documents.
24.	0.50	12	Issue a new tenant report to indicate to accounting that the division will henceforth occupy the stated and CADD measured amount of space; copy the division manager.
25.	1.00	19-22	Review order confirmations and bills of lading in conformance with purchase order.
26.	1.00	22-37	Expedite as required (quick ship program).
27.	2.00	38	Supervise the relocation and new furniture installation.
28.	1.00	38	Punch list the relocation and new furniture installation.

Case Study
Page 11

Item #	Hours	Elapsed Time in Days	Item
29.	1.00	38	Issue new computer data and telephone addresses for inclusion in corporate address book.
30.	N/R	0	Order additional parts found missing in the relocation process.
31.	N/R	0	Repeat the order, order confirmation, expediting, installation, and punch listings process for the missing parts.
32.	N/R	0	Meet with division managers to discuss delayed project completion.
33.	1.00	38	Enter the warranty information into the system for subsequent review and "wear dating."
			Authorize payments for all invoices in the system.
34.	1.00	39-40	Pass on congratulatory memo of thanks from division management to facilities management staff for a job well done.

51.5 hours	Total estimated project time
$1,287.50	x $25/hour estimate of value of project service
$0.12/sqft	
40.00 days	Elapsed time

In this case study, the project requires 51.5 facilities staff hours to complete, at an imputed cost of $1,287.50 in staff time. The project ultimately requires the forecasted 11,000 square feet of space. Moreover, the project has been completed within the office and workstation standards from quickly available components with a minimum of error in installation, and overall resulting in lower costs for the fit-out components and the installation, and an elapsed time of approximately 40 days.

The case study just presented shows that the computer-aided facility management approach to office facility relocation projects establishes the basis for subsequent and ongoing in-house relocations of departments within the completed facility over its useful life.

For this reason, managers of large office facility relocations will want to initiate their projects using the recommended computer-aided systems approach and will want each of their consultants to participate in the development of the data base during the course of the planning and implementation process.

Appendix 1A

As noted earlier in this chapter, the office facility relocation process begins with a program of space requirements. This appendix presents a program questionnaire prepared for a medium size consulting company that has 21 operating divisions. As noted in the memo to senior executives and department heads, this growing company seeks a short-term solution to space requirements while it studies various relocation opportunities.

(Appendix 1B begins on page 71.)

Departmental Facility Requirements Questionnaire

XXX Corporation
XYZ Building
City, State 00000

Department

_____

Department manager

_____

Present location of department

_____

Interview Date   Time

_____

Place of interview

_____

MEMORANDUM

Date   **1 November XXXX**

To   **Senior Executives and Department Heads**

From   **XXX, President**

Re   **Staffing and Office Facility Space Requirements**

We realize that our present office facilities at the XXX location are becoming over-crowded and that, eventually, we will need to resolve our office facility requirements with a medium range strategy of renovations and/or relocations.

In the meantime, our business plans require that we increase our present staffing here at XXX by approximately 24 employees. These requirements will necessitate a modest renovation project we hope to complete in a few months.

In order to accomplish this short-term goal with minimal disruption to each of you, we have retained the assistance of the XYZ design firm of Anytown, USA, who have substantial experience in the analysis of corporate space planning program requirements and the design of cost-effective and award-winning office facilities.

They have recommended that we initiate a fact-finding process to determine our space requirements here at XXX location in the short run, as well our medium range requirements for the future. The short run data will be used as the basis for our immediate renovation program, while the medium range data will be used as the basis for our ultimate renovation and/or relocation.

The programming process the XYZ design professionals recommend is as follows:

1. Each of you is invited to attend a programming kick-off meeting to be held in the classroom at 8:45 a.m. on Thursday, the 9th of November. Please arrive promptly. At this meeting, we will discuss the programming process and explain the self-paced programming questionnaire the XYZ design professionals will distribute.

2. The questionnaire will necessitate your preparation of a zero-based analysis of your department's staffing and office facility requirements at three points in time:

- Current requirements, assuming you could, in fact, change your present departmental office space to suit your present requirements;
- Your forecast of requirements one year from today;
- Your forecast of requirements three years from today.

We will discuss at our kick-off meeting on the 9th our mutual projections for company-wide growth, and this discussion will guide us in determining:

3. Our company-wide projections for central services, conference and meeting rooms, word processing, copy, mail and related services and other required support spaces at the above-noted three benchmark points in time.

4. Once you have prepared your analysis, using the questionnaire the XYZ design professionals will provide, the XYZ design firm's team will meet with each of you privately in your department's offices to walk through your existing facilities, assist you in completing your departmental questionnaire and respond to any issues of facility design and management you wish to discuss.

5. After all of the departmental meetings have been completed, the XYZ design professionals will prepare a computer-aided database indicating the space requirements for the company as a whole and for each department within the company. This database will compute the space requirements at each of the above-noted three benchmark points in time.

The database for current requirements will guide our immediate space planning renovations and, shortly thereafter, the XYZ design professionals will prepare a plan and schedule to accomplish these goals and objectives. Once the plans have reached a preliminary stage, we will reconvene a meeting of all department heads and senior executives to review these plans and to prepare for the short term renovations.

We hope to complete steps 1 thru 5 above in the next 3-4 weeks.

I urge each of you to clear your calendar to attend this important meeting. If client business prevents you from attending, please send someone else to represent your department. Also, please bring your calendars with you to the meeting so that you can make a date with the XYZ design firm's programming team for your departmental interview.

Contents

XXX***XXX Corporation***   ***Page 3***

INTRODUCTION

XYZ Design Firm is a professional interior architectural and space planning firm headquartered in Anytown, USA. We have been retained by the management team at the XXX Corporation's XXX facility to review the use and occupancy of this facility, and to plan for the short term occupancy of 24 additional personnel into this facility.

Our initial assignment is to make recommendations to renovate and plan for modest additions to the existing office and support spaces of the XXX facility. To accomplish this assignment, we have recommended a zero-based approach of data gathering to learn how each department that will be using this facility currently functions and plans to function in the future.

The basis of our data gathering process will be this self-paced questionnaire and a subsequent interview that we will schedule with each department manager who will use the renovated and expanded facility. The purposes of this departmental facility questionnaire is to systematically identify the present and projected uses of the facility.

The format of this questionnaire will allow you to provide us with your comments on the present facilities, and your individual departmental requirements for a more efficient and enhanced workplace, both currently and at key benchmark dates in the future. Referring to the attached memo from XXX, we will be gathering data from each department manager responding to requirements at three key benchmark dates, being:

- The current period of data gathering (Period I - month, year)
- Approximately one year from this period (Period II)
- Approximately 3 years from this period (Period III)

We will report back the data we gather, using our relational database software which, when edited and reviewed by your management team, will become the basis for our subsequent design recommendations. This three year projection will be used to establish the basis for an ultimate renovation and/or relocation from the XXX facility.

We ask that you review the contents of this questionnaire, fill in the spaces with the requested information, and have this questionnaire completed by the time of our interview date.

During the personal departmental interview, we will review your responses to the questionnaire, discuss the operations of your department and any ideas you may have to improve the use and occupancy of the XXX facilities. You are, of course, at liberty to bring as many of your department's staff with you as you would like, to this interview.

Ideas related to company-wide facility design and operational improvements, productivity, marketing and general perceptions of the office facilities at XXX will be topics of an open discussion. You may also wish to discuss operational issues which affect your work or the progress or productivity of your work, such as concerns for light, heat, air conditioning, power, security, glare, acoustics, etc. We will also discuss issues of the physical proximity of your department to others in the XXX facility, to help determine how future expansions and revised space planning might improve overall interrelationships between departments and service functional areas in the building.

We will walk through your department's current operational areas to verify and record existing office furniture and equipment in use by your department.

Once the data has been gathered from all of the departments in this survey, we will prepare our database reports, review them with your management team and publish a final version for your use and as a guide to our subsequent design efforts.

We look forward to our personal interview with you and to your active participation in this data gathering process. If you have any questions regarding this questionnaire, please contact James XXX, who will be leading our firm's programming effort. He can be reached at 800.555.9900.

Thank you for your timely participation.

XXX Corporation   *Page 4*

In this section of the questionnaire, we are requesting information about your department's office and support space requirements in the facility.

XXX Corporation   *Page 5*

ITEM 1. BASIC DESCRIPTION OF YOUR ORGANIZATION

Please describe here the basic operations of your department and your goals for the improvement of these operations in the planning years of Periods I, II and III.

Be as specific as you can as to the functions your department performs and how it serves the company and its customers.

_____

_____

_____

_____

_____

_____

_____

_____

_____

_____

_____

_____

_____

_____

_____

_____

_____

_____

_____

_____

_____

_____

_____

_____

_____

_____

_____

_____

_____

ITEM 2. DEPARTMENTAL ORGANIZATIONAL CHART

To help us study your department within and among the various units or subunits within your department, please draw an organizational chart like the sample shown below. Please include all units currently in your department, in addition to any new units proposed for the future. Within the organizational blocks, list the name and title of the individual managing that particular unit.

Sample Organization Chart:

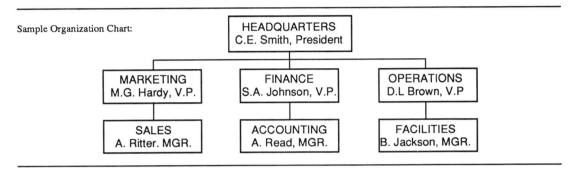

XXX Corporation   ***Page 7***

ITEM 3. ADJACENCY CHART

Often within an organization, certain departments need to be located near one another to allow for the sharing of personnel, equipment or support spaces (conference rooms, duplication rooms, file rooms). By filling in the adjacency chart, you can help us to track any adjacency requirement critical to the smooth operation of your department and the company as a whole.

We have learned from the company's organizational chart that it currently operates with 21 departments, 17 of which are currently operating out of the XXX facility. Some of these departments may only consist of an executive and his or her assistants, but it is important to list each department here to develop the data that will assist in a best-case physical relationship of each department within the facility.

Most likely, there are some departments within your organization that you feel must be located nearby, while there are probably others to which proximity would be undesirable. In still other cases, the location of another department may not be important. Please fill out the chart by specifying the required relationship between your department and each of the others listed. A legend has been provided to describe each code letter. Circle one letter (A, I, U, X) in the column to the right of each department's listing.

A = Closeness Absolutely Necessary   U = Closeness Unimportant
I = Closeness Important   X = Closeness Undesirable

Department Name	Manager's Name and Present Office Location (W) = Located at XXX (E) = Located Elsewhere		Your Preference for Adjacency

List of Departments Currently Located at the XXX Headquarters Facility:

1.	Senior Executive's suite	Mr. A	(W)	A I U X
2.	Management Information Systems	Mr. B	(W)	A I U X
3.	Project Development	Mr. C	(W)	A I U X
4.	Business Development	Mr. D	(W)	A I U X
5.	Finance	Mr. E	(W)	A I U X
6.	Law & Administration	Mr. F	(W)	A I U X
7.	Graphic Arts Department	Mr. G	(W)	A I U X
8.	Strategic Planning & Development	Mr. H	(W)	A I U X
9.	XXX Management Services Inc.	Mr. I	(W)	A I U X
10.	XXX Corporation	Mr. J	(W)	A I U X
11.	XXX Corporation Business Development	Mr. K	(W)	A I U X
12.	XXX Corporation Law	Ms. L	(W)	A I U X
13.	XXX Corporation Human Resources & Administration	Ms. M	(W)	A I U X
14.	XXX Corporation Management Development	Mr. N	(W)	A I U X
15.	XXX Corporation Finance	Mr. O	(W)	A I U X
16.	XXX Corporation Claims Management (Eastern)	Mr. P	(W)	A I U X
17.	XXX Corporation Project Management (Eastern)	Mr. Q	(W)	A I U X

List of Departments Currently in Other Locations:

18.	XXX Corporation Chairman's Office	Mr. R	(E)	A I U X
19.	XXX Inc.	Mr. S	(E)	A I U X
20.	XXX Inc.	Mr. T	(E)	A I U X
21.	XXX Lab Services Inc.	Ms. U	(E)	A I U X

XXX Corporation   **Page 8**

ITEM 3. ADJACENCY CHART

If any of the adjacencies listed in the matrix are based upon sharing of equipment, conference rooms, duplication rooms, reception areas, or similar support spaces, please let us know by filling in the blanks below.

My department needs to be near _____ because _____

My department needs to be near _____ because _____

My department needs to be near _____ because _____

My department needs to be near _____ because _____

My department needs to be near _____ because _____

My department needs to be near _____ because _____

Please feel free to add any additional comments about adjacency requirements which you feel may be helpful to us in our planning process. We are particularly interested in any information regarding required proximity to loading docks, computer rooms, or any public areas which have not been discussed previously. Also, you may have entered the (X) code within the adjacency chart designating an undesired adjacency between two units. Please enter any additional information concerning the nature of those undesired adjacencies so we may be sure to add that information to the adjacency planning, too.

_____

_____

_____

_____

_____

_____

_____

_____

_____

_____

_____

_____

_____

_____

_____

_____

_____

_____

XXX Corporation   **Page 9**

ITEM 4. RECEPTION AREA REQUIREMENTS

We understand that it is the current policy to receive all visitors in the main lobby of the facility, and to usher them to the adjacent offices and work areas in the other areas of the building. As such, there seem to be few, if any, departmental waiting areas within departmental suites of the facility.

We are considering the pros and cons of locating vendor and other visitor's conference and meeting rooms near the central reception area of the facility. One benefit of a central reception area is to limit the access of visitors to your department's confidential work in progress. Nevertheless, there may be other business reasons why your department might require a departmental reception space within your department's office area. If your department would function more productively with a departmental waiting area within your department, please advise us here as follows:

A.   The number of visitors your department receives in your department's office area in a typical day

     _____ visitors per day

B.   The average period of time your visitors must wait prior to being ushered into an employee's work area or into a conference or meeting room on the second floor of the building

     _____ minutes of waiting

C.   The average number of visitors that you might expect to be waiting for this period of time

     _____ visitors waiting at any one period of time

Does your department have a designated departmental receptionist?

     ☐ yes   ☐ no

Does your department have a designated usher to bring visitors up from the lobby?

     ☐ yes   ☐ no

If you were to share an inter-departmental reception/waiting area with other departments, please indicate here those departments that you might find it convenient to share a reception area with:

ITEM 5. CONFERENCE AND TRAINING AREAS

In this section, we would like you to advise us as to your department's requirements for conference spaces. Our goal is to provide conference rooms for the various types and configurations of conferences, meetings and presentations that all of the departments require simultaneously during a typical business day. As noted earlier, one way to accomplish this goal is to group many of the conference and meeting rooms around a central reception area of the company.

Referring to the sketches of various types of conference rooms on the next page, please indicate the use and occupancy of any of the conference room sizes and configurations that your department may require.

ITEM 5. CONFERENCE AND TRAINING AREAS

For your convenience in determining the type of conference/training room(s) required, we illustrate some typical conference and training rooms with their codes for insertion in the space provided on pages 12 and 13.

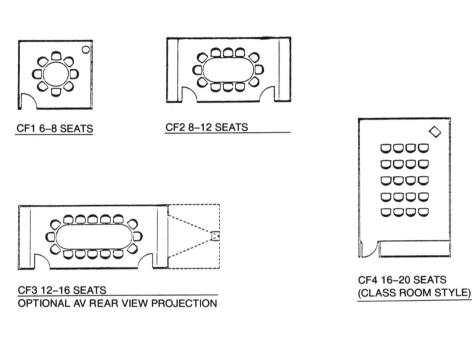

CF1 6–8 SEATS   CF2 8–12 SEATS

CF3 12–16 SEATS
OPTIONAL AV REAR VIEW PROJECTION

CF4 16–20 SEATS
(CLASS ROOM STYLE)

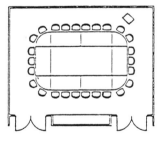

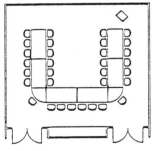

CF5 20–30 SEATS   CF6 30+ SEATS

Conference room CF Designation		The number of individual meetings per week in each period		
		Period I	Period II	Period III
CF-1	6-8 seats	_____	_____	_____
CF-2	8-12 seats	_____	_____	_____
CF-3	12-16 seats	_____	_____	_____
CF-4	16-20 seats	_____	_____	_____
CF-5	20-30 seats	_____	_____	_____
CF-6	30+ seats	_____	_____	_____
Other (describe on next page)		_____	_____	_____

Conference room CF Designation		The approximate period in hours of a typical meeting*		
		Period I	Period II	Period III
CF-1	6-8 seats	_____	_____	_____
CF-2	8-12 seats	_____	_____	_____
CF-3	12-16 seats	_____	_____	_____
CF-4	16-20 seats	_____	_____	_____
CF-5	20-30 seats	_____	_____	_____
CF-6	30+ seats	_____	_____	_____
Other (describe on next page)		_____	_____	_____

---

* Note here your comments if a particular meeting program requires substantial set-up time or if your department requires a semipermanent set-up of equipment or other marketing materials or props which would render the particular conference or marketing room ''reserved'' for a period of time by your department.

_____

_____

_____

_____

_____

_____

_____

_____

Please refer to the list of typical meeting room equipment packages and indicate in the spaces provided below the equipment your department might require in each of the conference room types designated. If your department requires materials and equipment specific to XXX's operations, including exhibits and related hardware products, please indicate those requirements as well:

Conference room CF designation		Equipment packages required from the list below. Please ◯ requirements	Additional XXX specific materials and equipment
CF-1	6-8 seats	1 2 3 4 5 6 7 8 9 10 11 12 13 14 15 16 17 18 19 20 21 22 23 24 25 26 27 28 29 30 31 32 33	_____ _____ _____ _____
CF-2	8-12 seats	1 2 3 4 5 6 7 8 9 10 11 12 13 14 15 16 17 18 19 20 21 22 23 24 25 26 27 28 29 30 31 32 33	_____ _____ _____ _____
CF-3	12-16 seats	1 2 3 4 5 6 7 8 9 10 11 12 13 14 15 16 17 18 19 20 21 22 23 24 25 26 27 28 29 30 31 32 33	_____ _____ _____ _____
CF-4	16-20 seats	1 2 3 4 5 6 7 8 9 10 11 12 13 14 15 16 17 18 19 20 21 22 23 24 25 26 27 28 29 30 31 32 33	_____ _____ _____ _____
CF-5	20-30 seats	1 2 3 4 5 6 7 8 9 10 11 12 13 14 15 16 17 18 19 20 21 22 23 24 25 26 27 28 29 30 31 32 33	_____ _____ _____ _____
CF-6	30+ seats	1 2 3 4 5 6 7 8 9 10 11 12 13 14 15 16 17 18 19 20 21 22 23 24 25 26 27 28 29 30 31 32 33	_____ _____ _____ _____

Other (describe on next page)

List of typical conference room/marketing equipment packages and features:

1. Lecture training table
2. Lectern
3. Commercial TV
4. VCR
5. Teleconferencing
6. Flip chart
7. Slides
8. Monitors (for TV)
9. Monitors (for computers)
10. PC or terminal
11. Plotters or printers
12. Telephone
13. Speaker phone
14. Rear view projection
15. Light dimmers
16. Closed circuit TV
17. Tack surfaces
18. Chart rail
19. Motion picture projector
20. Video projector
21. Front projection screen
22. Audio tapes or disks
23. Video disks & players
24. Electronic blackboard
25. Black-out shades
26. Remote control equipment
27. Coffee service
28. Food service
29. Long term prop storage
30. Copier
31. Tablet arm chairs
32. Marker board
33. TV satellite

XXX Corporation

Please sketch and describe here any special conference or marketing presentation facilities your department may require now or in the future.

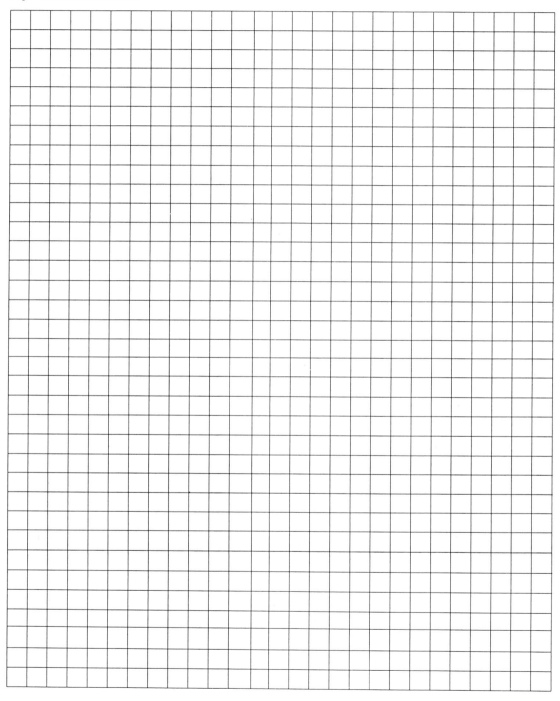

XXX Corporation   *Page 15*

ITEM 6. CRITICAL OPERATIONAL FACTORS

In our review of your department's space requirements, we would like to learn of any operational relationships of sub-units, or support areas, which may effect the productive operations of your department. For instance, if your department supports a particular computer room or central filing area, we ask that this information be described below (as an example). Please cross reference to adjacency sheets if applicable.

Unit Name	Size	Description of Critical Operational Factor
Audit Unit Vault (example)	400 sq ft.	Fire Safe records retention must be near the building core, not at window wall.

ITEM 7. PERSONNEL REQUIREMENTS

In order to obtain a comprehensive overview of a particular organization's space requirements for the present and the future, we ask you to help us by projecting you personnel requirements for the future using current requirements and projected future requirements.

The following page will provide you with a format to follow to collect the information. If your department is comprised of various sub-units, you may wish to rely on your unit managers to collect the data as it pertains to each unit. If this is the procedure you wish to follow, you will need to provide each unit manager with a copy of the attached personnel listing sheet along with a copy of this instruction page.

Prior to the start of this data collection process, projection periods were established to study the growth of XXX Corporation from the present through Year XXXX. Therefore, we ask you to use the following projection periods for your personnel forecast:

Period I (Month, Year)   Period II (Month, Year)   Period III (Month, Year)

While we understand that it is difficult to forecast the future, especially for your dynamic company, please do not be afraid to state your assumptions and forecast accordingly. We need this data to study the rate of organizational growth, which will help us to track facilities requirements in relation to the company's overall goals.

In the past, we have found many situations where the personnel headcounts varied in number from the so-called "full-time equivalent" employee count. For the purpose of this phase of data collection, we would like you to consider personnel headcount numbers, not "full-time equivalent" numbers. Full-time equivalent employee counts are applicable in an organization that has part-time, shift, or temporary personnel among their departments. We are concerned basically with the total number of offices, workstations and support spaces required by your department, whether they are occupied by employees, consultants or shared support equipment.

Accordingly, we would like you to provide us with information describing the existence of any part-time, multishift, or temporary personnel assigned to your department. Also, include the nature of the work assigned to these specific employees. This information will help us to track any situations where a particular workstation or space is shared by more than one individual, so we can avoid duplication in the workstation requirement projection figures. A personnel headcount comments page has been provided for your use to describe these situations.

To summarize, please provide us with:

Headcount numbers = total number of employees in your department's employee roster

and -- please note the existence of any part-time or shared offices or workstation occupants.

Section 2 / Second Floor   **Page 17**

ITEM 7. PERSONNEL REQUIREMENTS

INSTRUCTIONS

First, you will need to use a separate page or pages for each unit within your department. List all applicable job titles in the designated space to the left of the form. Then enter the personnel requirement projections in the spaces provided. Finally, in the "special requirements" column, please note the existence of part-time, shift, or temporary personnel. Any notation here will require further explanation on the personnel headcount comment page.

Sample entries have been provided on a partial form below for your review. Please use as many lines as required, adding additional pages if necessary.

Department __Computers__   Unit_____

Code	Job Title	Personnel Required			Special Requirements
		Period I	Period II	Period III	
	Project Manager	2	3	4*	*This person is a consultant, not employee
	Clerk	60	66*	75	*4 of these share 2 desks; they are part-timers
	Word Processing	20*	24*	28*	*In each year we need 2 WP stations more than this count for clerks to use part-time
	Secretaries	10*	12*	14*	This is our headcount but only in December. For 11 months, we need 2 fewer people

Codes will be completed by the XYZ design professionals.
Remember, please prepare a separate sheet for each unit within your department.

Please check if this department or unit is continued on additional worksheets ☐

XXX Corporation   *Page 18*

ITEM 7. PERSONNEL REQUIREMENTS

Department_____   Unit_____

| Code | Job Title | Personnel Required | | | Special Requirements |
		Period I	Period II	Period III	

Codes will be completed by the XYZ design professionals.
Remember, please prepare a separate sheet for each unit within your department.

Please check if this department or unit is continued on additional worksheets ☐

XXX Corporation   **Page 19**

ITEM 7. PERSONNEL REQUIREMENTS

In your present office facilities, various sizes are currently being occupied by various levels and types of employees, and most of the administrative and clerical employees are currently working at traditional desks, while a few employees are working at more up-to-date workstations.

While it is clearly not appropriate to employ new office and workstation sizes, configurations and furnishings in the short run renovation program, it may be appropriate to establish a company-wide standards program on the occasion of the ultimate renovation or relocation process. For this reason, we ask that you consider on the following pages the sizes, configurations and furnishings which you feel are most appropriate for each of the employees in your department.

Using a zero base approach, please refer to the sketches of various types and configurations of offices and workstations on the following page, and write in the job title of those employees in your department that you believe would best be functionally supported by the designated office or workstation.

Please use the same job titles used in the preceding departmental staffing projection pages of this questionnaire. For example:

    word processor
customer clerk
telephone respondent

This is an example of just one of many office furniture systems which offer computer support wiring and convenient storage capabilities.

ITEM 7. PERSONNEL REQUIREMENTS

Please write below each of these typical office and workstation configurations the job title of the individuals in your department that you believe would best be functionally supported by the designated office or workstation.

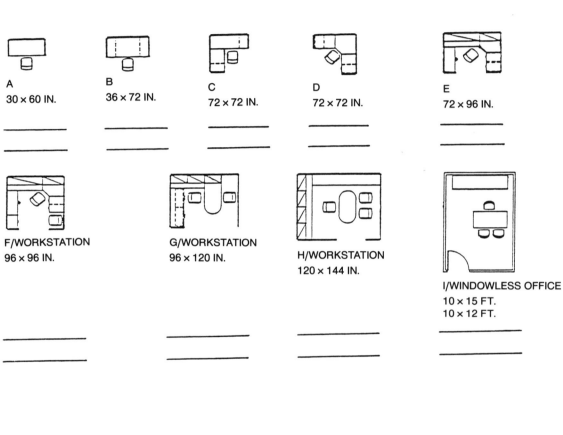

A
30 × 60 IN.

B
36 × 72 IN.

C
72 × 72 IN.

D
72 × 72 IN.

E
72 × 96 IN.

_____

_____

F/WORKSTATION
96 × 96 IN.

G/WORKSTATION
96 × 120 IN.

H/WORKSTATION
120 × 144 IN.

I/WINDOWLESS OFFICE
10 × 15 FT.
10 × 12 FT.

_____

_____

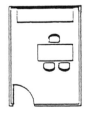

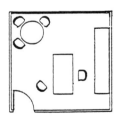

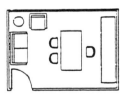

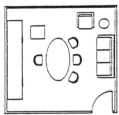

J/OFFICE
10 × 15 FT.
10 × 12 FT.

K/OFFICE
15 × 15 FT.
12 × 12 FT.

L/OFFICE
15 × 20 FT.
12 × 16 FT.

M/OFFICE
20 × 20 FT.
16 × 16 FT.

_____

_____

XXX Corporation   **Page 21**

ITEM 8. TELEPHONE AND DATA WIRING REQUIREMENTS

On the preceding page, you have listed by title or job description those in your department that will assist us in our planning effort, and have outlined their special requirements.

On this page, we would like you to advise us of your goals related to telephone and data requirements for each of these types of employees.

Please list again the job titles and then place an (X) in the space provided below the electronic equipment codes these employees require.

Code	Description
(t)	is a typical telephone set
(e)	is an executive telephone set with multiple features and lines
(tt)	is a second telephone instrument in the lounge or conference area of the particular office or workstation
(cd)	is a call director telephone set, typical of receptionists/secretaries who handle calls for various managers
(pc)	is a personal computer with printer
(w)	is access to the various off-premises wire service data bases for that computer
(fx)	is facsimile equipment
(o)	is other (please describe)
(tx)	is telex service, either as a part of the computer terminal or a separate terminal devoted to telex

Job Title	Telephone and Data Code Requirements								
	(t)	(e)	(cd)	(tt)	(pc)	(w)	(fx)	(o)	(tx)
SECRETARIES	x					x	x		

ITEM 9. FILING AND STORAGE REQUIREMENTS

In order to complete an understanding of your department's functional requirements, we need to analyze your filing and storage requirements. Not only do we need to know about your current filing and storage system but we need to know if you plan to make any changes to your existing system in the future. We are particularly interested in any plans you may have to change from standard filing methods to space-saving microfilm, microfiche, or computer-related equipment. As you can imagine, any change to these data storage systems can greatly impact the amount of building space your department will require.

The following questions will help us to track your existing requirements and your future requirements in a way that will allow us to look at your overall requirements without getting too specific. Later in our planning process, we will return for more specific information about your needs. Again, we understand that it is often difficult to forecast future needs, but we would appreciate your "best guess."

Please briefly describe any special filing or storage equipment that your unit will require.

_____

_____

_____

Do you foresee any changes in your present system? If so, please explain.

_____

_____

_____

Of your department's total current storage requirements,

(A) _____ % could be disposed of or sent to a long-term warehouse
(B) _____ % could be in a warehouse available on 4 hours notice
(C) _____ % could be in a central file location immediately available for your use.
(D) _____ % must be within your department's office suite

Total = 100%

XXX Corporation **Page 23**

ITEM 9. FILING AND STORAGE REQUIREMENTS

Please provide us with a current inventory of the number of each type of filing equipment now in use in your department, and then estimate the number you will require at the various planning dates in the future.

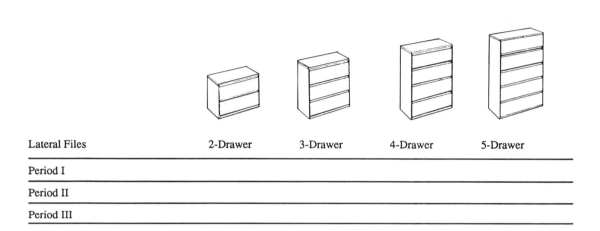

Lateral Files	2-Drawer	3-Drawer	4-Drawer	5-Drawer
Period I				
Period II				
Period III				

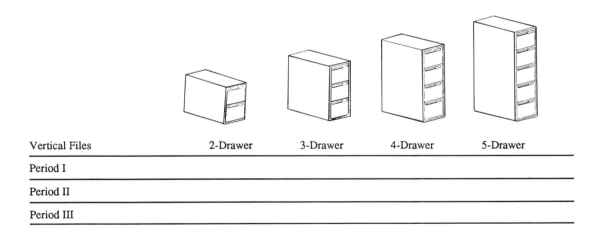

Vertical Files	2-Drawer	3-Drawer	4-Drawer	5-Drawer
Period I				
Period II				
Period III				

XXX Corporation   **Page 24**

ITEM 9. FILING AND STORAGE REQUIREMENTS

Please provide us with a current inventory of the number of each type of filing equipment now in use in your department, and then estimate the number you will require at the various planning dates in the future.

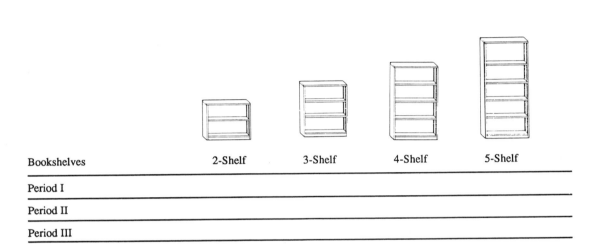

Bookshelves	2-Shelf	3-Shelf	4-Shelf	5-Shelf
Period I				
Period II				
Period III				

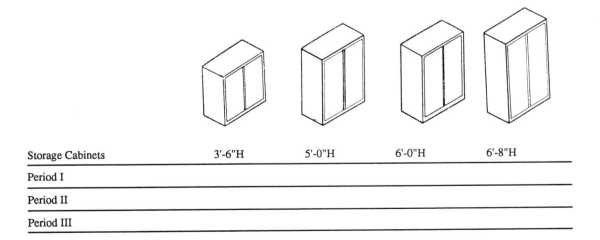

Storage Cabinets	3'-6"H	5'-0"H	6'-0"H	6'-8"H
Period I				
Period II				
Period III				

XXX Corporation   *Page 25*

ITEM 9. FILING AND STORAGE REQUIREMENTS

Please provide us with a current inventory of the number of each type of filing equipment now in use in your department, and then estimate the number you will require at the various planning dates in the future.

EDP Card Files	6-10 Drawer	12-20 Drawer	22-30 Drawer
Period I			
Period II			
Period III			

Tab Card Files	3x5 Cards	6x9 Cards	5x8 Cards	4x6 Cards
Period I				
Period II				
Period III				

ITEM 9. FILING AND STORAGE REQUIREMENTS

Please provide us with a current inventory of the number of each type of filing equipment now in use in your department, and then estimate the number you will require at the various planning dates in the future.

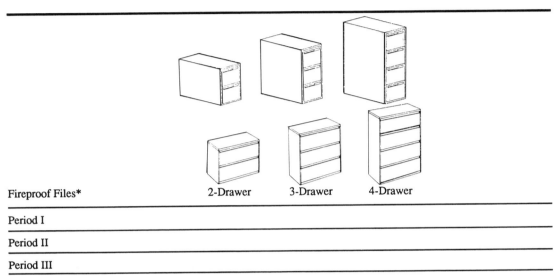

Fireproof Files*	2-Drawer	3-Drawer	4-Drawer
Period I			
Period II			
Period III			

* Please indicate either vertical or lateral

Plan Files	5-Drawer
Period I	
Period II	
Period III	

XXX Corporation   ***Page 27***

ITEM 10. EQUIPMENT REQUIREMENTS

EQUIPMENT NEEDS

In order to develop a better understanding of your use and occupancy of office space to serve the needs of your department now and in the future, we would like to learn of any office equipment that is in use throughout your department.

Because office equipment is in a constant state of "flux" as to type and configuration, we recommend that you provide information for just those items now in use or on order.

By providing the name of the user, we will understand which office or workstation requires that particular piece of equipment. If the equipment is free-standing and shared by various people in your department, rather than indicating a name of a user, please use the word "shared."

EQUIPMENT INVENTORY SHEETS

Please follow the example on the next page and list all of the equipment currently being used by your unit. List the manufacturer, model number and the size. Specify whether the piece is a table-top or free-standing model by circling the appropriate code letter. Next, look for either the Underwriters Laboratory (UL) plate or the manufacturer's plate that holds the information on the equipment's electrical requirements. Transfer the information, specifying the volts, amps and BTU requirements for each piece of equipment onto the Equipment Inventory Sheet. Finally, please list the name(s) of the people who use each piece of equipment. If the equipment is shared by two or more units, list the names of the units.

FUTURE EQUIPMENT REQUIREMENTS

Once you have listed all of your existing equipment and the related information, please use the Future Equipment Requirement page to list any pieces of equipment that are currently on order or that will be ordered within the next three months. Next to the items you list, please provide the information as indicated.

Please make a copy of the equipment pages and this instruction page for each of the units in your department.

XXX Corporation   *Page 28*

ITEM 10: EXISTING EQUIPMENT REQUIREMENTS

DEPARTMENT_____EXAMPLE_____   UNIT_____

EQUIPMENT INVENTORY SHEET

Equipment Type	Manufacturer & Model No.	Size	Table-top or Free-standing	Volts/Amps/BTUs	Equipment Users
Xerox (Example)		30 " W x 40 " D x 30" H	T (F)	120/30/5000	Art Dept.
		____" W x ____" D x ____" H	T F		
		____" W x ____" D x ____" H	T F		
		____" W x ____" D x ____" H	T F		
		____" W x ____" D x ____" H	T F		
		____" W x ____" D x ____" H	T F		
		____" W x ____" D x ____" H	T F		
		____" W x ____" D x ____" H	T F		
		____" W x ____" D x ____" H	T F		
		____" W x ____" D x ____" H	T F		
		____" W x ____" D x ____" H	T F		
		____" W x ____" D x ____" H	T F		
		____" W x ____" D x ____" H	T F		
		____" W x ____" D x ____" H	T F		
		____" W x ____" D x ____" H	T F		
		____" W x ____" D x ____" H	T F		
		____" W x ____" D x ____" H	T F		
		____" W x ____" D x ____" H	T F		
		____" W x ____" D x ____" H	T F		
		____" W x ____" D x ____" H	T F		
		____" W x ____" D x ____" H	T F		
		____" W x ____" D x ____" H	T F		
		____" W x ____" D x ____" H	T F		
		____" W x ____" D x ____" H	T F		
		____" W x ____" D x ____" H	T F		
		____" W x ____" D x ____" H	T F		

Additional comments _____

_____

_____

ITEM 11. OTHER FACILITIES REQUIREMENTS

Does your department require immediate, sole and exclusive access to any of these special spaces:

	Circle One	Size Required in Square Feet
Lobby and main reception	Yes No	_____
Coat rooms or locker areas	Yes No	_____
Mailrooms or distribution areas	Yes No	_____
Supply or storage areas	Yes No	_____
Central file areas	Yes No	_____
Computer rooms	Yes No	_____
Photocopy areas	Yes No	_____
Cafeterias or dining areas	Yes No	_____
Vending areas	Yes No	_____
Libraries	Yes No	_____
Marketing displays	Yes No	_____
Quiet rooms	Yes No	_____
Sound masking	Yes No	_____
Reception desk in lobby	Yes No	_____
Training rooms	Yes No	_____
Multi-purpose room	Yes No	_____
Emergency showers	Yes No	_____

Special structural or architectural consideration must be given to areas housing any of the following items or conditions. Does your department require any of the following?

STRUCTURAL	Circle One	Size Required in Square Feet
Motorized files	Yes No	_____
Safes	Yes No	_____
Mainframe computers	Yes No	_____
Heavy machinery	Yes No	_____
Mail distribution	Yes No	_____
Multi-purpose elevator	Yes No	_____

ACOUSTICAL		
Noisy machinery	Yes No	_____
Testing areas	Yes No	_____
Multi-purpose	Yes No	_____
Training areas	Yes No	_____
Conference rooms	Yes No	_____

MECHANICAL/PLUMBING		
Kitchens	Yes No	_____
Vending areas	Yes No	_____
24-hour operations	Yes No	_____
Telephone switch areas	Yes No	_____

XXX Corporation   **Page 30**

ITEM 11. OTHER FACILITIES REQUIREMENTS

FIRE CODE ISSUES	Circle One	Size Required in Square Feet
High density areas	Yes No	_____
Computer rooms	Yes No	_____
Computer tape storage	Yes No	_____

ELECTRICAL		
PC network wiring	Yes No	_____
Cellular deck wire distribution system	Yes No	_____
Low glare lighting system	Yes No	_____

SPECIAL LIGHTING		
Art	Yes No	_____
Artifacts	Yes No	_____
Displays	Yes No	_____
Client presentations	Yes No	_____
Computer areas	Yes No	_____
Product storage	Yes No	_____

SPECIAL AUDIOVISUAL		
Presentation rooms	Yes No	_____
Teleconferencing	Yes No	_____
Multi-purpose	Yes No	_____
Video deposition	Yes No	_____
Video teleconferencing	Yes No	_____
Equipment or closet storage	Yes No	_____

SPECIAL SECURITY REQUIREMENTS		
For demo rooms	Yes No	_____
For art, artifacts	Yes No	_____
For records/files	Yes No	_____
For computers/computer files	Yes No	_____
For storage rooms	Yes No	_____
For equipment rooms	Yes No	_____
Video monitoring	Yes No	_____
Computer tapes	Yes No	_____

ITEM 12. CRITIQUE OF YOUR PRESENT ENVIRONMENT

We are very interested in your comments, critique and feelings about your department's present working environment, and any suggestions you have for (a) improving your working environment at XXX location, and (b) so as to avoid repeating a similar environmental error in the design and development of your new location.

Please be as direct and forthright as you would like in describing your present facility and in outlining your suggestions for improvements to be built into the new departmental locations. Please write or sketch your suggestions in the space provided below. Provide additional pages, if necessary.

_____
_____
_____
_____
_____
_____
_____
_____
_____
_____
_____
_____
_____
_____
_____
_____
_____
_____
_____
_____
_____
_____
_____
_____
_____
_____

CONCLUSION

The information you have provided will be reviewed with you in the face-to-face interview in your office. We will call you to schedule an appointment, once we have reviewed your response to this questionnaire.

During that interview, our professional programmers will assist you in completing any portion of this questionnaire that may have been difficult for you to complete on your own, and they will assist in amplifying any issues which you may wish to describe or discuss.

After the scheduled interview, our programmers will tour your department's office suite to review the existing working conditions and layout.

Once the data gathering process has been completed, you will be provided with the printout of the data for your department, and the management of your company will be provided with the overall database for the company. Once this data has been verified and adjusted for company-wide goals and objectives, we will publish a facilities needs analysis workbook, which will be distributed to each department manager for review and comment prior to the development of the designs for the proposed departmental renovation.

We thank you for your assistance in this very important data gathering process, and assure you of our professional and personal interest in meeting your individual department's requirements for the proposed short-term renovation, and for your ultimate renovation or relocation project.

XYZ Design Professionals/Project Team

Appendix 1B

The computer-aided forecast of space requirements shown in this appendix was prepared by calculating and evaluating each of the departmental question-naires received from XXX Corporation's depart-ment managers. The appendix also shows a summary report for the company as a whole.

Because this assignment included the as-is condi-tion of an existing office facility with a known "loss factor" (18 percent) of usable to rentable square feet, the study calculated both usable and rentable square feet per department and for the whole company. The company's department managers predicted the num-ber of employees would grow from 133 to 244 by the end of the third period of the study; the program of space requirements was calculated at 62,497 square feet, to house the third-period requirements. The current requirement was computed at 33,831 square feet on a zero basis—approximately 6,000 square feet more than the actual space plan of the company today. The present space plan lacks many of the features re-quired by the zero-based program.

(Appendix 1C begins on page 76.)

Daroff Design Inc.

Strategic Facility Planner

FORECAST

M A I N   R E P O R T   W I T H   A L L   D E T A I L S

for units matching: *

Client: XXX Corporation
Project: ABCD

Corporate Headquarters Building

01-JAN-1999

Date: 01 JAN-1999 Page 2

Project: ABCD   Client: XXX Corporation   Corporate Headquarters Building

Main Forecast Report with All Details for Organizational Units matching: *
Organizational Unit Code: PRES-   Color Code: 1
Organizational Unit Name: President

Code	Name	Space Std	Area	Resouce Counts P1 JAN-1999	P2 Jan-2000	P1 JAN-1999	P2 JAN-2000	Space Requirements (sq.ft.)
Resource Type: Personnel								
PRES	President P	450.00	1.00	1.00	450.00	450.00		
SECY	Secretary	125.00	1.00	1.00	125.00	125.00		
Personnel Totals			2.00	2.00	575.00	575.00		
Resource Type: Support Space								
BRDRM	Boardroom (30 x 20)	675.00	1.00	1.00	675.00	675.00		
CLOSET	Storage Closet	15.00	1.00	1.00	15.00	15.00		
LNGE	Lounge area	150.00	1.00	1.00	150.00	150.00		
Support Space Totals					840.00	840.00		
Resource Type: Filing & Fitments								
3S3624	Linear shelves - 24 ft	12.00	3.00	4.00	36.00	48.00		
5D36LG	5 Dwr 36"w Lat File	12.00	5.00	7.00	60.00	84.00		
Filing & Fitment Totals					96.00	132.00		
Resource Totals for Organization Unit					1511.00	1547.00		
Internal Circulation Factor					0.0%	0.0%		
Totals for PRES -			2.00	2.00	1511.00	1547.00		

Typical Departmental Database

| Project: ABCD | Client: XXX Corporation | Corporate Headquarters Building | | | | Date: 01 JAN-1999 Page 3 |

Main Forecast Report with All Details for Organizational Units matching: *
Organizational Unit Code: PRES-ACTR-   Color Code: 2
Organizational Unit Name: Actuarial Services

Code	Name	Space Std	Area	Resouce Counts P1 JAN-1999	P2 Jan-2000	Space Requirements (sq.ft.) P1 JAN-1999	P2 JAN-2000
Resource Type: Personnel							
AVP-A	Asst. VP-Actuarial	AVP	450.00	1.00	1.00	450.00	450.00
DIR-A	Off-dir-Actuarial	DIR	125.00	1.00	1.00	125.00	125.00
SVP-A	Sr. VP-Actuarial	SVP	350.00	1.00	1.00	350.00	350.00
WS-E	Workstation size E	E	137.00	2.00	2.00	274.00	274.00
WS-F	Workstation size F	F	100.00	8.00	9.00	800.00	900.00
WS-F+	Workstation size F+	F+	67.00	4.00	4.00	268.00	268.00
WS-H	Workstation size H	H	67.00	2.00	3.00	134.00	201.00
Personnel Totals				22.00	24.00	2641.00	2808.00
Resource Type: Support Space							
CLOSET	Storage Closet		15.00	1.00	1.00	15.00	15.00
FLRM-A	File room		500.00	1.00	1.00	500.00	500.00
STDY	Study room (10 x 15)		175.00	1.00	1.00	175.00	175.00
Support Space Totals					690.00	690.00	
Resource Type: Filing & Fitments							
5D36LG	5 Dwr 36"w Lat File		12.00	3.00	4.00	36.00	48.00
5D36RM	5 Dwr 36"w Lat File	RM		31.00	35.00		
Filing & Fitment Totals						36.00	48.00

Typical Departmental Database

Project: ABCD   Client: XXX Corporation   Corporate Headquarters Building

Main Forecast Report with All Details for Organizational Units matching: *

SUMMARY PAGE	Personnel Counts		Space Requirements (sq.ft.)		
	P1 JAN-1999	P2 Jan-2000	P1 JAN-1999	P2 JAN-2000	
Resource totals for selected units	185.00	190.00	30440.00	30929.00	
Totals including Internal Circulation			30440.00	30929.00	
Inter-departmental Circulation, 0%					
Grand totals for selected Units			30440.00	30929.00	

-- END OF REPORT --

Departmental Summary Page

Project: ABCD   Client: XXX Corporation   Corporate Headquarters
Main Forecast Report - Resource Summary for Organizational Units matching: *

Code	Name	Space Std	Resouce Counts Area	P1 JAN-1999	Space Requirements (sq.ft.) P1 JAN-1999
Resource Type: Personnel					
AVP-A	Asst VP-Actuarial	AVP	175.00	3.00	525.00
AVP-BD	Asst VP-Budget	AVP	175.00	1.00	175.00
AVP-IN	Asst V-Insurance	AVP	175.00	1.00	175.00
AVP-IS	Asst VP-Info Survey	AVP	175.00	1.00	175.00
AVP-L	Asst VP-Legal	AVP	175.00	1.00	175.00
AVP-RP	Asst VP-Finan Report	AVP	175.00	1.00	175.00
CASH	Cashier	RM	0.00	2.00	
DIR-A	Off dir-Actuarial	DIR	145.00	2.00	290.00
DIR-BD	Off dir-Budget	DIR	145.00	1.00	145.00
DIR-BR	Off dir-Broker/Dealr	DIR	145.00	7.00	1015.00
DIR-CM	Off dir-Communicatns	DIR	145.00	1.00	145.00
DIR-E	Off dir-Info Serv	E	137.00	1.00	137.00
DIR-FC	Off dir-Facilities	DIR	145.00	1.00	145.00
DIR-HR	Off dir-Human Resrce	DIR	145.00	1.00	145.00
DIR-IS	Off dir-Info Serv	DIR	145.00	1.00	145.00
DIR-L	Off dir-Legal	DIR	145.00	1.00	145.00
DIR-M	Off dir-Marketing	DIR	145.00	2.00	290.00
DIR-S	Off dir-Struct Settl	DIR	145.00	1.00	145.00
MAIL	Mailroom Clerk	RM	0.00	2.00	
PRES	President	P	450.00	1.00	450.00
RECEP	Receptionist	RM	0.00	1.00	
SECY	Secretary		125.00	1.00	125.00
SVP-A	Sr. VP-Actuarial	CVP	350.00	1.00	350.00
SVP-F	Chief Financial Offr	SVP	350.00	1.00	350.00
SVP-HR	Sr. VP-Human Resourc	SVP	350.00	1.00	350.00
SVP-L	Sr. VP-Legal	SVP	350.00	1.00	350.00
SVP-M	Sr. VP-Marketing	SVP	350.00	1.00	350.00
VP-IN	vp-Insurance Agency	VP	263.00	1.00	263.00
VP-IS	vp-Information Serv	VP	263.00	1.00	263.00
VP-M	vp-Marketing	VP	263.00	2.00	526.00
VP-S	vp-Struct Settl	VP	263.00	1.00	263.00
WS-E	Workstation size E	E	137.00	11.00	1507.00
WS-F	Workstation size F	F	100.00	41.00	4100.00
WS-F+	Workstation size F+	F+	67.00	65.00	4335.00
WS-H	Workstation size H	H	67.00	24.00	1608.00
Personnel Totals				185.00	19357.00

Resource Summary

Project: ABCD   Client: XXX Corporation   Corporate Headquarters

Date: 01 JAN-1999 Page 3

Main Forecast Report - Resource Summary for Organizational Units matching: *

| | | | Resouce Counts | | Space Requirements (sq.ft.) |
| | | Space | | P1 | P1 |
Code	Name	Std	Area	JAN-1999	JAN-1999
Resource Type: Support Space					
BRDRM	Boardroom (30 x 20)		675.00	1.00	675.00
CASHRM	Cashier's rm (18 x 12)		260.00	1.00	260.00
CLOSET	Storage Closet		15.00	8.00	120.00
COMP	Computer room		565.00	1.00	565.00
CONF I	Conference (34 x 48)		1360.00	1.00	1360.00
CONF 2	Conference (12 x 15)		180.00	2.00	360.00
COPY	Copy area		100.00	3.00	300.00
FLRM-A	File room		500.00	1.00	500.00
FLRM-P	File room		250.00	1.00	250.00
FLRM-R	File room		500.00	1.00	500.00
KITCN	Kitchen/Vending		100.00	3.00	300.00
LIBRY	Library (10 x 15)		175.00	2.00	350.00
LNGE	Lounge area		150.00	3.00	450.00
LUNCH	Lunchroom (12 seats)		350.00	1.00	350.00
MAILRM	Mailroom		400.00	1.00	400.00
RECEPT	Reception area		400.00	1.00	400.00
STDY	Study room (10 x 15)		175.00	1.00	175.00
STRGBR	Storage room (10 x 12)		145.00	1.00	145.00
STRGCM	Storage room (10 x 15)		175.00	1.00	175.00
STRGFC	Storage room (26 x 20)		585.00	1.00	585.00
STRGIN	Storage room (10 x 12)		145.00	1.00	145.00
STRGIS	Storage room (10 x 15)		175.00	1.00	175.00
TELE	Telephone room		150.00	1.00	150.00
Support Space Totals				185.00	19357.00
Resouce Type: Equipment					
RACK	Literature rack		10.00	2.00	20.00
Equipment Totals					20.00

Resource Summary (Cont'd)

Project: ABCD   Client: XXX Corporation   Corporate Headquarters

Date: 01 JAN-1999 Page 4

Main Forecast Report - Resource Summary for Organizational Units matching: *

| | | | Resouce Counts | | Space Requirements (sq.ft.) |
| | | Space | | P1 | P1 |
Code	Name	Std	Area	JAN-1999	JAN-1999
Resource Type: Filing & Fitments					
2D42GL	2 Dwr 42" Lat file		12.00	2.00	24.00
3S3621	Linear Shelves-21 ft		12.00	3.00	36.00
3S3624	Linear Shelves-24 ft		12.00	3.00	36.00
5D30LG	5 Dwr 36"w Lat file		12.00	1.00	12.00
5D36C	5 Dwr 36"w File/Cabs		12.00	33.00	396.00
5D36LG	5 Dwr 36"w Lat File		12.00	140.00	1680.00
5D36RM	5 Dwr 36"w Lat File	RM	0.00	70.00	
5D4112	41"w Bookcases		12.00	2.00	24.00
5S3612	5 Shelf 36"w Bookcase		12.00	4.00	48.00
5S3615	5 Shelf 36 x 15 Bookcase		12.00	2.00	24.00
5S4218	5 Shelf 42"w Bookcase		12.00	2.00	24.00
7H3612	36" x 12" x 84" Bookcase		11.00	3.00	33.00
BOOK	Bookcases (lirbary)	RM	0.00	8.00	
BOOK1	36"w Bookcases	RM	0.00	3.00	
BOOK2	8-4" Bookcase	RM	0.00	1.00	
CHECK	31" x 18" Check File	RM	0.00	4.00	
DATA	36"w Data File	RM	0.00	3.00	
FF4030	Flat File 40w x 30d		18.00	2.00	36.00
SHELF	Shelves in mailroom	RM	0.00	7.00	
Filing & Fitments Totals					2373.00

SUMMARY PAGE (not including circulation)

| Personnel Counts | | Space Requirements (sq ft) | |
| P1 | | P1 | |
JAN-1999		JAN-1999	
Resource totals for selected units	185.00		30440.00

-- END OF REPORT --

Resource Summary (Cont'd)

Appendix 1C: Tenant Planning Case Study

The tenant planning documents in this appendix were prepared for a prospective tenant seeking approximately 65,000 usable square feet of space in a high-rise office tower in a major urban center. Most of the available floors in the office towers in the community offered 20,000 to 25,000 square feet; this tenant therefore required all or most of three sequential floors of office space. Because of the tenant's multifloor requirement, a first step in this tenant planning process was to prepare affinity bubble diagrams to illustrate various options for distributing the departments of the company among the three floors of space. These computer-generated diagrams illustrate, by the relative proximity of the departmental bubbles, the affinity of one department to another; the relative size of the bubbles shows the square footage requirements of each department. From this diagram, the space planners were easily able to determine which departments could be located on each of the company's three floors.

(Text continues on page 80.)

Project:ABCD

Study:FL8 Period:01-JAN-1999:P1 Building:LOGAN Floor:8

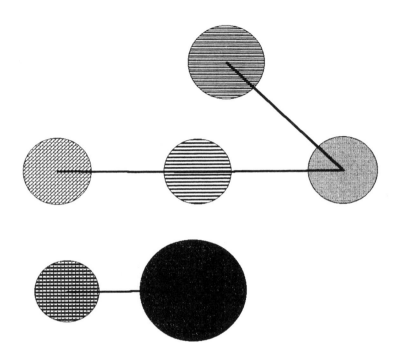

Color	Num	Tot-Area	UnBlocked	Code				Name
	67	1537.50	1537.50	Circulation				
	49	1511.00	1511.00	PRES-	-	-	-	President
	56	3770.00	3770.00	PRES-FINA-INFO-		-		Information Services
	53	1396.00	1396.00	PRES-FINA-BROK-		-		Broker/Dealer
	63	1568.00	1568.00	PRES-LEGL-	-	-		Legal
	64	1616.00	1616.00	PRES-MKTG-	-	-		Marketing
	65	1952.00	1952.00	PRES-MKTG-INSR-		-		Marketing-Insurance

BUBBLE DIAGRAM - DEPTS ON FLOOR 8

Project:ABCD

Study:FL9 Period:01-JAN-1999:P1 Building:LOGAN Floor:9

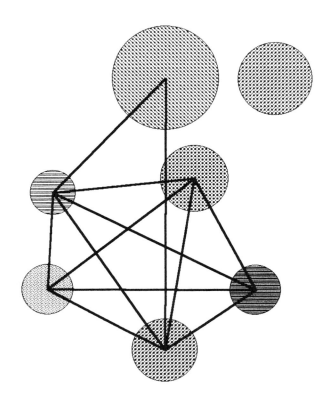

Color	Num	Tot-Area	UnBlocked	Code			Name
	67	1537.50	1537.50	Circulation			
	50	3367.00	3367.00	PRES-ACTR-	-	-	Actuarial Services
	51	1634.00	1634.00	PRES-ACTR-STRU-		-	Structured Settlements
	52	623.00	623.00	PRES-FINA-	-	-	Financial
	54	775.00	775.00	PRES-FINA-BUDG-		-	Financial-Budget
	55	795.00	795.00	PRES-FINA-CASH-		-	Financial-Cashier
	57	1380.00	1380.00	PRES-FINA-PENS-		-	Financial-Pension
	58	1280.00	1280.00	PRES-FINA-REPT-		-	Financial-Reporting

BUBBLE DIAGRAM - DEPTS ON FLOOR 9

Project:ABCD

Study:FL10 Period:01-JAN-1999:P1 Building:LOGAN Floor:10

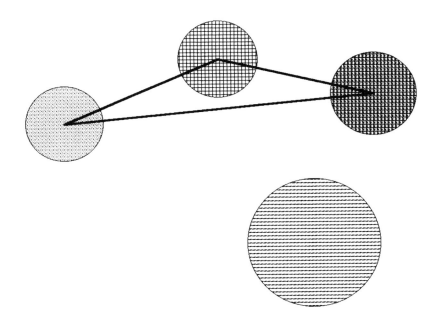

Color	Num	Tot-Area	UnBlocked	Code			Name
	67	1537.50	1537.50	Circulation			
	66	3785.00	3785.00	PRES-SPAC-	-	-	Common Spaces
	60	1362.00	1362.00	PRES-HRES-	-	-	Human Resources
	61	1299.00	1299.00	PRES-HRES-COMM-	-		Corporate Communication
	62	1585.00	1585.00	PRES-HRES-FACL-	-		Facilities

BUBBLE DIAGRAM - DEPTS ON FLOOR 10

Stack Plan

The next step in the planning process was to prepare a stack plan, to illustrate the departmental relationships on each of the three floors (page 81). A stack plan also assists the building management and leasing agents in meeting present and future tenants' requirements for relocation on sequential floors within the building.

Once the available spaces within the building have been identified, and documented in a stack plan, the tenant planning process determines which space(s) are indeed most appropriate for the intended use of the tenant, and at which point(s) in time the tenant may want to acquire additional space, preferably immediately above or below the space(s) occupied initially. This additional space is typically established as a tenant's "option" within the lease and is known as "option space."

Comparative Building Analysis

The spreadsheet on pages 91–92 is a short-form comparative building analysis of the "fit" and "features" offered by a variety of office buildings to accommodate the tenant's requirements.

(Chapter 2 begins on page 93.)

Project:ABCD

Study:2LOG Period:01-JAN-1999:P1 Building:LOGAN

Color	Num	Tot-Area	UnPlaced	Code				Name
	49	1511.00	0.00	PRES-	-	-	-	President
	50	3367.00	0.00	PRES-ACTR-	-	-		Actuarial Services
	51	1634.00	0.00	PRES-ACTR-STRU-		-		Structured Settlements
	52	623.00	0.00	PRES-FINA-	-	-		Financial
	53	1396.00	0.00	PRES-FINA-BROK-		-		Broker/Dealer
	54	775.00	0.00	PRES-FINA-BUDG-		-		Financial-Budget
	55	795.00	0.00	PRES-FINA-CASH-		-		Financial-Cashier
	56	3770.00	0.00	PRES-FINA-INFO-		-		Information Services
	57	1380.00	0.00	PRES-FINA-PENS-		-		Financial-Pension
	58	1280.00	0.00	PRES-FINA-REPT-		-		Financial-Reporting
	59	742.00	742.00	PRES-FINA-TAXX-		-		Financial-Tax
	60	1362.00	0.00	PRES-HRES-	-	-		Human Resources
	61	1299.00	0.00	PRES-HRES-COMM-		-		Corporate Communication
	62	1585.00	0.00	PRES-HRES-FACL-		-		Facilities
	63	1568.00	0.00	PRES-LEGL-	-	-		Legal
	64	1616.00	0.00	PRES-MKTG-	-	-		Marketing
	65	1952.00	0.00	PRES-MKTG-INSR-		-		Marketing-Insurance
	66	3785.00	0.00	PRES-SPAC-	-	-		Common Spaces

STACK STUDY - XXX CORPORATE HEADQUARTERS

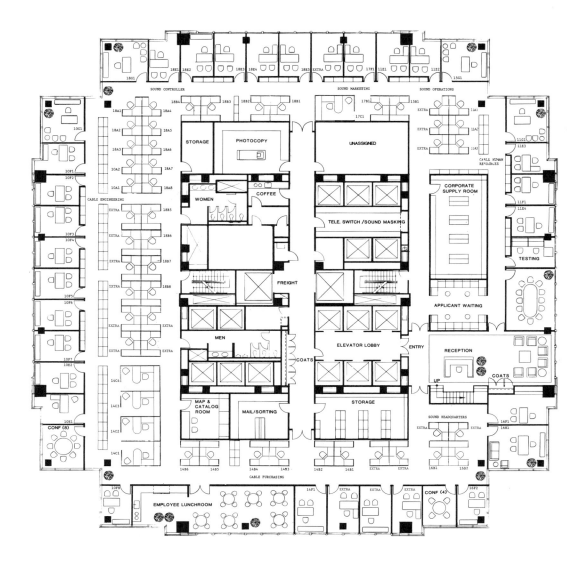

Building A, Floor 1

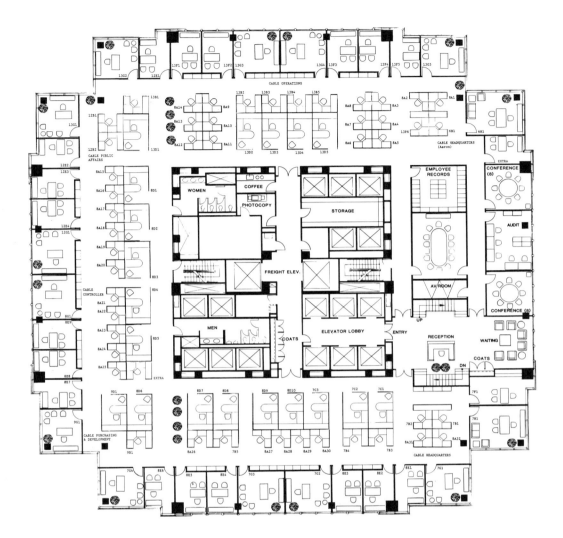

Building A, Floor 2

Building A, Floor 3

Building B, Floor 1

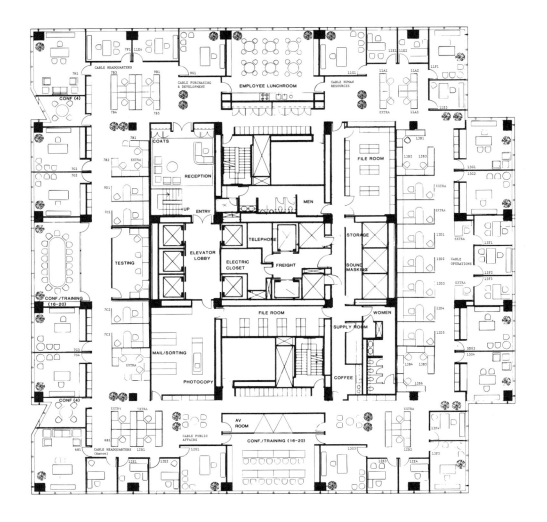

Building B, Floor 2

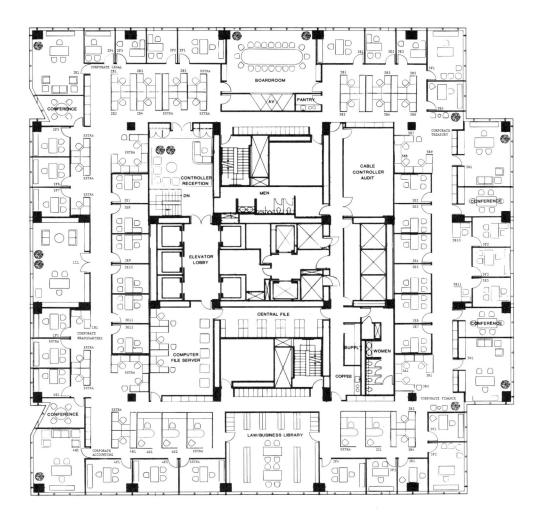

Building B, Floor 3

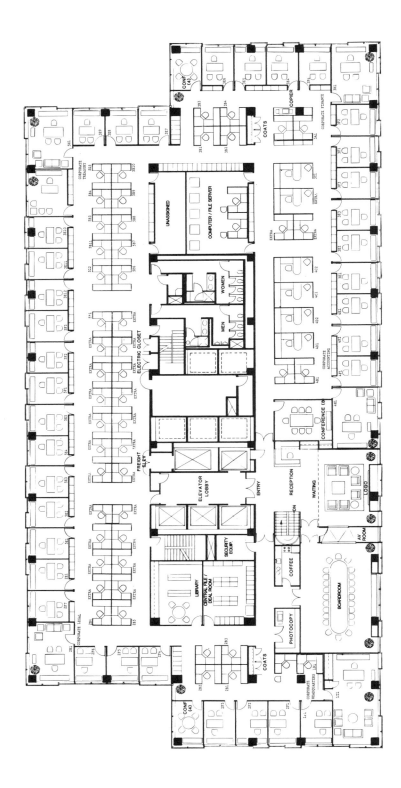

Building C, Floor 1

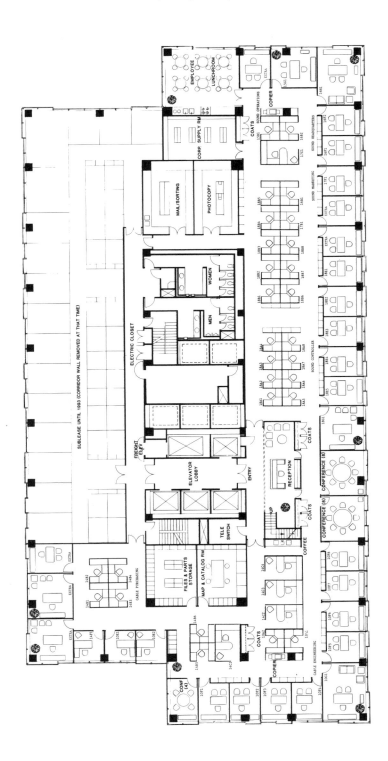

Building C, Floor 2

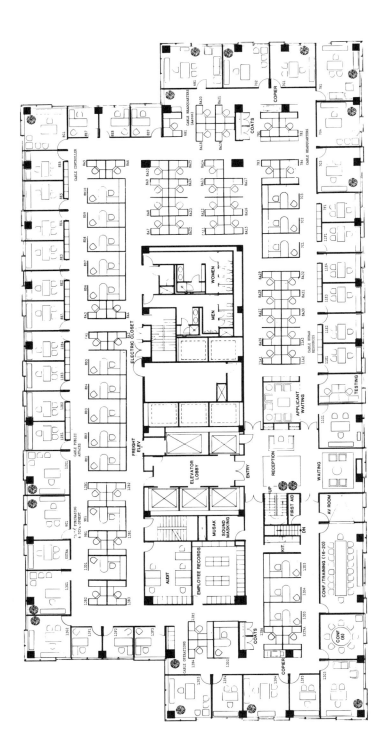

Building C, Floor 3

COMPARATIVE BUILDING ANALYSIS
DAROFF DESIGN INC.

Items Being Evaluated	1993 Requirements CM3 of 6/6/86 Computer Forecast	A Building	B Building	C Building	D Building	E Building	Revised September Forecast	F Building	C Building With Revised Program (September)
Floors studied/usable sq.ft. (Usable = carpeted areas only)	1/ 19360	19/ 19045	22/ 17409	33/ 19608	7/ 15463	20/ 11000	1/ 17150	34/ 17249	33/ 18038
	2/ 19360	20/ 19045	24/ 17409	34/ 19608	8/ 15463	19/ 16761	2/ 17150	35/ 17249	34/ 19608
	3/ 19360	21/ 19045	25/ 17409	35/ 19608	9/ 15463	5/ 41634	3/ 17150	36/ 14520	35/ 19608
Total usable sq.ft.	T/ 58080	T/ 57135	T/ 52227	T/ 58824	T/ 46389	T/ 69395	T/ 51450	T/ 49018	T/ 57254
Less Sublet Potential	2370	5280	0	0	0	9650	0	0	8540
Total Net Usable sq.ft. To Be Planned	T= 55710	T= 51855	T= 52227	T= 58824	T= 46389	T= 59745	T= 51450	T= 49018	T= 48714
Floors studied/rentable sq.ft. (To be confirmed by real estate negotiation)	1/ 22000	19/ 21312	23/ 23037	33/ 23500	7/ 19620	20/ 12170	1/ 19500	34/ 23600	33/ 21733
	2/ 22000	20/ 21312	24/ 23037	34/ 23500	8/ 19620	19/ 18667	2/ 19500	35/ 23600	34/ 23500
	3/ 22000	21/ 21312	25/ 23037	35/ 23500	9/ 19620	5/ 46425	3/ 19500	36/ 19400	35/ 23500
Total rentable sq.ft.	T/ 66000	T/ 63936	T/ 69111	T/ 70500	T/ 58860	T/ 77262	T/ 58500	T/ 66600	T/ 68733
Less Sublet Potential	2692	6140	N/A	N/A	N/A	10722	N/A	N/A	10289
Total Net Rentable sq. ft. To Be Planned	T= 63308	T= 57796	T= 69111	T= 70500	T= 58860	T= 66540	T= 58500	T= 66600	T= 58444
Ratio of RENTABLE to USABLE=	88%	90%	76%	83%	79%	90%	88%	74%	83%
Loss Factor Percentage (%)	12%	10%	24%	17%	21%	10%	12%	26%	17%
Lin. ft. window wall *req'd if E's with windows ** req'd if E's inboard w/o windows	1195 ft req'd.* 715 ft. req'd.**	1693 ft.	1872 ft.	1926 ft.	1240 ft.	1660 ft.	1060 ft. 640 ft.	1440 ft.	1706 ft.
Offices & Workstations / usable sq.ft. (Qty. / Extension)									
Type 6x6 A=51 sq.ft.	46 / 2346	47 / 2397	62 / 3162	46 / 2346	49 / 2499	42 / 2142	19 / 969	24 / 1224	15 / 765
6x8 B=68 sq.ft.	54 / 3672	81 / 5508	72 / 4896	61 / 4148	56 / 3808	77 / 5236	73 / 4964	91 / 6188	91 / 6188
8x8 C=84 sq.ft.	11 / 924	12 / 1008	14 / 1176	11 / 924	11 / 924	6 / 504	1 / 84	0 / 0	1 / 84
8x12 D=116 sq.ft.	18 / 2088	18 / 2088	17 / 1972	18 / 2088	18 / 2088	25 / 2900	43 / 4988	46 / 5336	53 / 6148
10x12 E=126 sq.ft.	48 / 6048	42 / 5292	50 / 6300	48 / 6048	38 / 4788	51 / 6426	42 / 5292	20 / 2520	49 / 6174
10x15 F=188 sq.ft.	31 / 5820	43 / 8084	30 / 5640	32 / 6016	42 / 7896	33 / 6204	21 / 3948	58 / 10904	21 / 3948
15x15 G=262 sq.ft.	16 / 4192	18 / 4716	19 / 4978	16 / 4192	15 / 3930	16 / 4192	12 / 3144	9 / 2358	10 / 2620
15x20 H=350 sq.ft.	7 / 2450	7 / 2450	7 / 2450	7 / 2450	8 / 2800	7 / 2450	6 / 2100	6 / 2100	6 / 2100
15x25 I=438 sq.ft.	1 / 438	1 / 438	1 / 438	1 / 438	1 / 438	1 / 438	1 / 438	1 / 438	1 / 438
Total SF for Offices & Workstations	27986	31981	31012	28650	29171	30492	25927	31068	28465
Files, Special Spaces and Intradepartmental Circulation (sq.ft.)	27724	19874	21215	30174	17218	29253	25522	17958	27635
Total number of office and workstation occupants	232	269	272	240	238	250	218	255	247
TOTAL USABLE SQ.FT. PLANNED	55,710	51,855	52,227	58,824	46,389	59,745	51,449	49,026	56,100
TOTAL RENTABLE SQ.FT. PLANNED	63,308	57,796	69,111	70,500	58,860	66,540	58,500	66,600	58,444
USABLE SQ.FT. PER PERSON	240	193	192	245	195	232	236	192	227
RENTABLE SQ.FT. PER PERSON	273	215	254	294	247	258	268	261	237

91

Items Being Evaluated	1993 Requirements CM3 of 6/6/XX Computer Forecast	A Building	B Building	C Building	D Building	E Building	Revised September Forecast	F Building	C Building With Revised Program (September)
NOTES AND COMMENTS									
Planning fit to program		Good fit	Good fit	Good fit	Doesn't fit	Good fit		Tight fit	
Quality of resulting plan		High quality	HQ. quality	HQ. quality	Business-like	HQ. quality		HQ. quality	
Efficiency of plan		Efficient	Generous	Generous	Tight	Generous		Efficient	
Building quality		Superior	Superior	Superior	Dated	Updated		High	
Core of building efficiency		Efficient	Efficient	Efficient	Inefficient	Inefficient		Efficient	
Quality of view(s)		50% Good/50% OK	Superior	Superior	50% Good/50% N.G.	80% Superior/20% OK		Superior	
Ease of configuring sublet space		Easy to configure	Difficult	Difficult	Need 5,000 sf more	Easy to configure		May need more space	
Location of floors within building		Good	Superior	Superior	Poor (low rise)	Superior?		Superior	
Treatment of "E" Offices		All w/windows	38 w/windows	All w/windows	No windows	Mostly no windows		Mostly windows	
Core-to-glass dimension	37'-0 to 39'-0	37'-6	36'-6	45'-0	49'-0 w/column	Varies w/columns		37'-6 & 46'-0	
Special spaces configuration		Meets program	Exceeds program	Exceeds program	Less than program	Exceeds program		Varies	

TOTAL ESTIMATED COSTS
less workletter allowance

NET 10 YEAR ESTIMATED COSTS

AVERAGE NET COST PER YEAR
(Total net estimated cost/10 years)

TOTAL $ EMPLOYEES INDICATED IN PLANS

AVERAGE YEARLY COST PER EMPLOYEE
(average net cost per year)

CHAPTER 2

Evaluating Building and Space Suitability

Piero Patri and Daniel W. Winey

When choosing a facility for relocation or expansion, it is no longer enough for an organization to be knowledgeable about such traditional factors as base rent, lease terms, and building efficiency. The constantly changing business environment has complicated the manner in which organizations function. Unlike the past, when most firms were concerned with competition on the home front, today many businesses operate on a global scale. Office automation and advanced telecommunications systems are permeating the workplace. As technological systems change and one system is substituted for another, many organizational, building, and technological relationships are disturbed, and more complex issues are left in their wake. The need to keep up with these changes and succeed in the face of increased competition is forcing firms continually to evaluate methods of maximizing return on investment and employee productivity.

To choose intelligently a building that will best suit a user's needs, the tenant must also consider the building's ability to support present and future technological demands. This means addressing such issues as wiring and cable distribution systems, power and air conditioning requirements, structural load capacity, equipment space provisions, and satellite/microwave access. Often, commercial brokers are not prepared to address these issues, leaving firms without the information they need to make intelligent building choices.

As the situation grows in complexity, tenants find that they must increasingly rely on qualified staff or outside architectural, engineering, and design consultants to provide them with the necessary data for making critical building choices—choices that will ultimately affect the firm's overall profitability. Thus, it is important that a program be developed

Reprinted with minor modifications from *The Commercial Real Estate Tenant's handbook,* edited by Alan D. Sugarman, Robert F. Cushman, and Andrew D. Lipman (New York: John Wiley & Sons, 1987). Used with permission.

early, to analyze a tenant's immediate and future needs. This program should be developed from the organization's mission statement. It is the first step in the building selection process, and it will serve as the basis for all ensuing activities, including interior space design, pre-move, move-in, facility acceptance or "commissioning," postoccupancy evaluation, and continuing facility management. In addition to staff or consultants, organizations that serve as a resource include: National Research Council's Building Research Board, Urban Land Institute, Industrial Development Research Council, Building Owners and Managers Association, Building Owners and Managers Institute International, and the International Facilities Management Association.

Building Selection Criteria

When reviewing buildings to house tenant operations, organizations should heed certain precautions. Fierce competition in today's real estate market has led to a growing number of building owners who lure tenants with free rent, upgraded materials, and high-style facilities. Though these factors may be important to corporate image and should not be overlooked when choosing a building, neither should they become the only concerns. To compete effectively in today's business world, an organization must first address the critical organizational, building, and technological issues.

Early in the building selection process, organizations are faced with choices that will affect their ability to function effectively and efficiently within a facility. An analytic approach to this process has been developed by our London-based colleagues, Duffy Eley Giffone Worthington (DEGW), architects. It goes well beyond traditional concerns of location, square footage, and design to encompass specific usability issues of capacity, flexibility, adaptability, and manageability. With this approach, development of a usable building or interior space through intelligent planning is assured.

When used within the DEGW approach, the term "capacity" refers not only to available square footage, but also to a building's ability to accept additional installation of wiring, cabling, and other equipment. As a user's staff and technological demands change, does the building have the dimensional ability to accommodate a raised floor for cabling if and where needed? Can the roof accept the added weight of a satellite dish or other equipment, should the need arise?

As organizations grow and change, layout, working style, and staff expectations are altered. The building's degree of "flexibility" in accommodating these changes is its ability to accept repositioning of walls, ceilings, floors, furniture, and equipment in an economical and time-efficient manner.

Organizations are continually evolving in response to market demands and other pressures. Thus, a building's "adaptability" is the measure by which an organization can rework interior space to accommodate an altered mix of functions or uses.

"Manageability" is the building's ability to minimize disruption when modifying location and configuration of equipment. In other words, how easily can the building provide for facility management over time?

Organizational Issues

Some organizational concerns that significantly impact productivity are: image, structure and hierarchy, staff requirements, adjacencies, and economic constraints. A firm may choose a building with a pleasing facade because it can enhance the corporate image—this is especially true if the building is afforded a high degree of visibility. Image, however, is not limited to building exterior; it must also be directly related to the interior architecture. Quality of interior materials in public spaces and on tenant floors is another important image factor. A high-profile advertising agency, for example, might require upgraded materials while a lower-profile insurance firm would be satisfied with standard materials.

Organizational structure and hierarchy have a direct relationship with an organization's function and its need for a specific type of space. In general, the larger the floor plate and leasing depth in a building, the more easily an open plan can be accommodated. Insurance firms tend to be open-office intensive, and for this type of organization a large floor plate would normally be required. A law firm, on the other hand, is more private-office intensive and would make more efficient use of a building with a smaller floor plate and leasing depth. Corporate hierarchy, space standards, size, and growth patterns dictate the size and configurations of optimal floor plates.

Another organizational issue is staff requirements. In determining whether a building offers enough space to house an organization in the present and future, consultants analyze the nature and scope of the potential tenant's operations. In such cases, the facility must be reviewed in terms of accommodating increased (or decreased) space requirements over time. If the firm's staff is relatively stable with a minimal amount of turnover or expansion, then space needs for the future may not be a priority.

The relationship between an organization and its client base may greatly influence building selection, but the organization's internal operations dictate specific interior adjacencies. Within the facility, interdepartmental and intradepartmental adjacencies are of prime importance. When adjacencies are optimized, travel distances and paper flow are minimized, leading to enhanced personal communication and, ultimately, increased staff productivity. If so desired, employees can become involved in the planning process at this time. This has the additional benefit that the staff may be more comfortable and effective in the new space. To ensure that the building will be responsive to an organization's needs, consultants must study the manner in which specific departments function and the working relationships among those departments. Such studies reveal specific interdepartmental and intradepartmental requirements which the organization can use to optimize adjacencies.

The future impact of advanced telecommunications and office automation on adjacencies must also be considered, both within the building and elsewhere. For example, many corporations have found that computer and telecommunications technologies have given organizations the flexibility to maintain executive functions in higher cost, downtown space while relocating back office operations to less expensive, suburban locations.

Along with office automation comes a potential for space savings. Analysis of these savings, however, should be made on a case-by-case basis. For example, while automation may help thin the ranks of clerical and middle-management personnel, it may conversely lead to an increase in the number of technical staff who can operate the automated equipment.

These highly skilled, highly paid technicians also demand greater spaces within which to work. More space may also be needed in the future to accommodate mainframes, minis, video display terminals, printers, other technological support equipment, and storage. It is generally predicted that a one-to-one ratio of worker to desktop terminal will exist in the future.

Economic constraints are always a major organizational concern, and one variable that should not be omitted from the economic equation is cost of tenant improvements. Because this cost reflects the corporate image to be portrayed, it can vary significantly from organization to organization. It is up to the organization to determine an appropriate quality level of tenant improvements, and it is the consultant's function to establish the cost of these improvements.

Building Issues

At an early stage in the building selection process, it is important to view the facility from an employee's perspective. To attract and maintain a work force, corporations must first examine such issues as local housing conditions, quality of educational systems, shopping, and recreation. Once these and other similar issues are addressed, the organization can continue to more specific concerns, including accessibility, traffic patterns, parking, landscaping, views, amenities, tenant standards, building efficiencies, code requirements, and the ability of the building to accommodate advanced technology.

Accessibility, traffic patterns, and parking constraints are important elements of building review. The degree of ease or difficulty in reaching the building—whether by public transportation or private methods—is important. What is the building's proximity to bus or railroad stops? How close to the building can employees park? Is the quantity of parking spaces sufficient to accommodate employees and visitors? Other issues associated with parking are lighting and access as they relate to safety and security. In addition, cities may impose particular parking requirements which simply may not be adequate in meeting tenant needs. It is especially important to consider the impact of future growth within the building and in surrounding areas upon parking.

In terms of landscaping and views, what an employee sees when looking through a window can have tremendous impact on his or her morale. Thus, important considerations are whether the facility takes advantage of well-landscaped grounds and whether the building maximizes views and natural light.

The proximity of the building to restaurants, retail shops, and other amenities is also a consideration. Does the building provide a cafeteria or dining room? How close are banks, post offices, and other services? The time associated with employees traveling to and from these types of amenities may greatly affect productivity.

The quality of tenant improvement standards is a building issue but is also an internal image consideration in that it may relate to the attraction and retention of employees. Can the design and type of wall system used accommodate the tenant's needs? Whereas a demountable system may be appropriate to an organization with a high "churn" (change rate), expensively finished drywall may be more appropriate for a law firm. Doors, frames, and hardware—all important aspects of an organization's image—vary significantly from facility to facility. Overall finishes and materials, such as floor coverings, wall coverings, and glass allowances, all impact the construction budget. This is especially true if upgrades from the building standard are anticipated. It should be noted that in a soft leasing market, such as today, many if not all lease conditions are negotiable.

When analyzing building efficiencies, building geometry should be studied for its ability to meet user needs. For example, building core layout, leasing depths, column spacing, and window modules can greatly impact space planning, requiring tenants in some buildings to modify customary workstation and office area standards to avoid inefficient use of space. Particular column spacing and leasing depths can also greatly affect the building's ability to accommodate private offices or open planning. Ultimately, all of these issues affect overall square footage requirements and the building's ability to adapt to organizational change.

All aspects of building usability—capacity, flexibility, adaptability, and manageability—should be addressed in terms of expansion (as dictated by departmental moves) on a specific floor and expansion to adjacent floors. As organizational units expand, the divisions created by those expansions can also contribute to inefficiencies. One of the most important functions of a design professional is to help the tenant ascertain potential growth patterns over the life of the lease and to analyze the building's ability to accept that growth.

The difference between a building floor's rentable and usable areas can economically impact tenant operations. A floor's rentable area refers to the entire floor, as measured to the inside finished surface of the permanent, outer building walls or window line. It includes all columns and other elements necessary to the building's structure, but excludes such major vertical elements as elevator shafts, stairwells, vents, and vertical ducts. On a multitenant floor, rentable space includes proportional shares of such common areas as elevator lobbies, restrooms, and telephone, electrical, and maintenance closets.

Usable space on a multitenant floor does not include these types of areas because they are not available to house the firm's personnel, equipment, and furniture. Therefore, usable area is the prime consideration to a tenant when evaluating a space because it is a representation of the actual space available.

Design professionals are skilled in computing rentable and usable area from architectural floor plans. Computations can also be accurately and automatically generated from computer-aided design and drafting (CADD) plans. If computations are furnished by the landlord, the method and figure should be verified by the tenant because of the differing methods of computation used. Building Owners and Managers Association standards are widely accepted and generally used as a basis.

To relate rentable and usable areas when a portion of a floor is under review, the landlord should provide the tenant with the load factor. Once the load factor is ascertained, a more accurate picture of building efficiency and value can be achieved. The greater the load factor, the less space-efficient the building. When comparing efficiencies of different buildings, the cost per usable square foot should therefore be compared, rather than the cost per rentable square foot or total dollar figures. The following formulas can be used to determine both rentable and usable areas:

$$\frac{\text{Rentable area}}{\text{Usable area}} = \text{load factor or rentable usable ratio}$$

$$\text{Usable area} \times \text{load factor} = \text{rentable area}$$

Codes and regulations can also greatly impact floor plate efficiency. This is especially true in older structures that were built prior to the adoption of more stringent codes. Provisions for fire-rated corridors, potential dead-end corridors, and maintenance of minimum separation of exits all directly affect and constrain space planning.

The existence or nonexistence of life-safety provisions is a code-related consideration that also has economic implications. Does the floor have a sprinkler system? Do restrooms accommodate handicapped persons? Is an annunciator system available? Do smoke detectors exist? If not, then the tenant faces potential costs for upgrading and safety.

While the existence of indoor pollution, from formaldehyde, asbestos, and polychlorinated biphenyls (PCBs), may not necessarily be code issues at this time, they remain significant problems which many landlords are finding must be addressed. Users should be aware of such conditions and of what landlords are doing to mitigate these and any other potential hazards.

Technological Issues

Rapidly changing and expanding workplace technology dictates that firms guard against moving into buildings that do not offer the usability of "future-proofing" factors of capacity, flexibility, adaptability, and manageability. Tenants should not assume that a newer building is any more accommodating than an older building. Such a mistake could land a tenant in a structure that may soon be rendered functionally obsolete, thus defeating the purpose of using technology: increased productivity and economic gains. (A detailed analysis of this entire subject is provided in Chapters 10 and 11, *High Tech Real Estate,* Dow Jones-Irwin, Homewood, IL, 1985.)

As sophisticated office automation and telecommunications technology continues to permeate the workplace—with varying degrees of impact on the building and its interior spaces—organizations are learning to use it as a recruiting tool to attract and retain skilled employees.

Many tenants, developers, and building owners were introduced to advanced technology through the idea of shared tenant services. A lack of immediate success of shared tenant services left tenants with the impression that preparing a building to accommodate advanced technology either now or in the future was not a concern. However, nothing could be further from the truth. What we are currently seeing is just the beginning of an evolving office technology market. Thus, the more important consideration to users is not necessarily that a facility provides enhanced telecommunications and office automation services, but that the building can accommodate the changing technology (which is the basis for these services) over time.

Unfortunately, this more important consideration has been obscured by the highly visible failures and lesser known successes that shared tenant services have had. What users must realize is that there is nothing wrong with shared tenant services if marketed and managed properly. Shared tenant services is merely a method—and not the only method—of providing organizations with advanced telecommunications and automation technology. As technology grows more functional and cost-effective to have, many larger corporations are buying their own equipment. As it grows more efficient and affordable, it also moves within closer reach of smaller companies. In addition, local telephone operating companies have started marketing similar services to tenants from their central facilities.

Typically, intelligently planned buildings are designed to accommodate or include enhanced telecommunications, expanded office automation services, and the building management system (BMS). Listed among enhanced telecommunications services are basic telephone service, least-cost routing, voice mail, and teleconferencing. Expanded office automation services include word and data processing, personal computing, document scanning, printing, and more.

The most common component of advanced building technology is the BMS, a system that many buildings had, in some form, prior to the hype over "smart" buildings. Perceived as a service to the building rather than to the tenant, the BMS has as its objective cost control and efficiency through effective management of energy, life-safety, elevators, security, lighting, and other building systems. The BMS is important to the tenant, in that pass through energy costs, for example, can be affected by the energy management and control system.

As discussed previously, it is important not to underestimate the impact of technology. It is just as important not to overreact. Technology is changing rapidly. With each generation, each individual piece of equipment occupies less space than the equipment being replaced, and also weighs less, requires less power, and emits less heat. On the other hand, as costs of the equipment decrease, more pieces of equipment are being located in offices. It is incumbent upon consultants to apply good judgment by combining past experience with research into the future direction of technology, to ensure both farsighted as well as cost-effective responses to technology in the selection and design of the workplace.

There is no doubt that advanced technology has brought a new dimension to what architects, interior designers, space planners, facility managers, and engineers must consider when fully evaluating a building or space for a potential user. As noted in the discussion

of BETA, later in this chapter, Whisler-Patri has a well-developed procedure for evaluating buildings and spaces. As part of this procedure, technology and its impact on the full range of architectural, electrical, mechanical, structural, equipment space, and site components are reviewed.

One element examined is the building's capacity to meet a user's needs for present and future distribution of signal (i.e., voice, data, and video systems); power; and heating, ventilation, and air conditioning (HVAC). In the course of past reviews, it was found that many new as well as older buildings contain major deficiencies in their existing vertical and horizontal distribution systems. These deficiencies make it very difficult or cost-prohibitive for users to install and manage additional wiring or cable.

The recent Federal Communications Commission ruling that holds building owners—rather than telephone companies—responsible for signal cabling within the building, underscores the importance of reviewing the capacity of the building's vertical signal distribution system. This review should start with the system's point of entry—whether it be from landlines underground, satellite earth stations, or microwave antennas on the roof. It is a necessary review, because it is often found that the capacity of the existing vertical distribution system must be at least doubled to accept evolving technology.

The proliferation of desktop equipment necessitates review of horizontal signal distribution capacity as well. Whether horizontal distribution is accomplished by through-, under-, or over-the-floor methods, it is a key factor in total building evaluation.

Electrical power is another important consideration that must be addressed early. Increased use of office technology has boosted power demands, and many new as well as older buildings are falling short of supply. Though each new generation of equipment requires less power and generates less heat, offices continue to experience an increase in the amount of equipment used. But, supply is only one issue. Is interference-free or "clean" power available to ensure smooth computer operations? Is there a reliable, uninterrupted power supply (UPS) available to protect valuable data bases? And, with many firms running portions of their operations on a 24-hour, 7-day-week basis, the issue to users in a multitenant building is whether the power metering system ensures equitable utilities charges.

Lighting is also important when determining overall power requirements. Currently, many organizations can spend approximately one-half of their energy budgets on lighting and on increased cooling due to lighting. Design professionals try to minimize rising lighting power demands by using more natural illumination, reflected ambient light, and task lighting in their plans. Reflected ambient and task lighting is helpful in reducing glare on terminal screens as well.

Along with an increase in heat-generating office equipment has come a need for increased cooling and ventilation. Just as important as overall HVAC requirements is the need to cool hot spots caused by heat from concentrations of equipment. Twenty-four-hour operations can cause additional problems in that the entire air conditioning system may have to run during off hours. A multizoned air conditioning system can accommodate hot spots and give individual users more control over their own environments.

Usually not as critical but still a consideration is the question of whether the building has the structural capacity to support the extra weight of mainframe computers, heavy batteries for UPS, extra cooling towers, and other heavy equipment. Is the roof structure sufficiently stable to accommodate microwave and satellite dishes? If not, additional bracing may be required.

Equipment space requirements and location must also be addressed when evaluating a building's ability to support changing technology. Can additional equipment be installed without substantial alteration to existing construction? Are telephone closets distributed in a manner that minimizes wiring congestion and length? Along with the common practice of installing wiring for data transmission and various building systems in the same telephone closets, there has come a need for compartmentalization and control of access to these closets.

When evaluating a building site, the building's connection with regional, national, and international telecommunications networks is an important criterion. Thus, it is becoming increasingly necessary to perform a signal propagation study to ensure interference- and obstruction-free transmission of microwave and satellite signals. Ready availability of landline (underground) connection is also studied, particularly with regard to high-speed, high-quality data transmission.

Interior Architecture Issues

In the building selection process, growing numbers of tenants are retaining consultants to determine whether a structure helps maximize economic efficiency and employee productivity. Frequently, this is because a potential tenant's own staff either lacks the expertise or is too busy to do so. Architectural and related consultants possess the skills to prepare a detailed architectural program, evaluate and recommend buildings, prepare the design and necessary construction documents, oversee construction, and accept the completed facility. In the past, this has been a function of the consulting architect and team. However, the traditional team, which consists primarily of the real estate consultant, the architect, and the mechanical, electrical, and structural engineers, is no longer sufficient. Advanced technology has made it necessary to expand this team to include a telecommunications and office automation consultant, at a minimum.

Typically, a real estate consultant has the critical function of preparing an in-depth marketing analysis of existing market supply and demand. This analysis would take into consideration historical, current, and projected absorption and development.

A real estate consultant also usually has a computerized inventory system which contains specific market data and relocation possibilities. The system provides a thorough lease analysis and the financial implications of various alternatives, and it illustrates the impact of individual lease variables. Thus, a true comparison of different locations is revealed. Another provision of the system allows specific users to evaluate various leasehold and equity opportunities as well as the potential advantages and disadvantages of each. Most important, all of these programs are usually used to evaluate operating efficiency as projected over the entire lease term in relation to various relocation alternatives.

Once the choice of facilities has been narrowed to two or three potential candidates, the architect and consultants begin evaluating the building in detail. Key individuals from various departments are surveyed to verify the organization's forecasting data. This procedure should include a review of corporate space standards, based on individual, functional, and task requirements. The architect typically makes recommendations as to whether corporate space standards should be modified to work effectively within a specific building module. Requirements for support functions will also be verified. Consultants assist users in determining departmental adjacencies and relationships between departments and support functions.

From the preceding information, specific criteria are developed and applied to the various buildings under consideration. The architect's functions are to provide a preliminary space plan and block diagrams for each facility and to evaluate the effects of the building configuration and core on planning and functional adjacencies. Computer-aided design and automated programming can be employed to forecast user needs for stacking, blocking, and space planning functions.

To determine a building's ability to support or accommodate a tenant's changing technological needs in both the present and future, there are existing procedures which can be used for analysis. The seminal study, Office Research: Buildings and Information Technology (ORBIT), was completed in 1983 in the United Kingdom. The group that conducted the study was led by London-based DEGW. The basis for ORBIT was a concern that existing buildings in the United Kingdom were not properly accommodating changing electronic technology and were thus in danger of becoming prematurely obsolete.

This original ORBIT study led to a related, multiple-client research and development project called ORBIT 2. Conceived by Xerox's Harbinger Group, the study defined interactions between organizations, technology, facilities, facility management, and related economics for both the present and future.

The method we use to make similar types of decisions is called Building Evaluation and Technology Assessment (BETA) and Site Selection Matrix. Developed in conjunction with Peter Valentine and William Luyties from COMSUL Ltd., telecommunications and office automation consultants, this process involves reviewing buildings and interior spaces to determine their ability to meet a tenant's current and future space requirements plus office automation and tele-communications needs. The process provides tenants and corporate users with "hidden" information relating to the financial implications of a space over life of occupancy. With this information in hand, tenants will be able to avoid the disruption and expense of later renovations or moves caused by a building's inability to meet changing demands.

Not only is the BETA and Site Selection Matrix used to evaluate the organizational, building, and technological issues associated with a move, but it also provides the financial data associated with site selection. This includes capital budgeting, cost benefit analyses, cash flow projections for strategic facilities, and asset planning. Clients can then use this information to determine where organizations should

or should not spend money to make changes, based on the benefits expected to be derived from those changes.

A real estate consultant and architect may also assist in analyzing lease proposals in terms of cost, schedules, rent commencement clauses, tenant improvements, and other important financial considerations. A thorough analysis will consider tenants' first cost as well as costs over time. Additionally, the architect can provide the tenant with a generic workletter. This will outline the needs of the tenant and become the basis for negotiations.

Once a building has been selected, consultants assist users in developing detailed space plans for future organizational and technological change. During creation of final space plans, consultants do not apply the same set of criteria for all tenants, for the obvious reason that each tenant and building combination is unique. By the same token, space planners who ignore a firm's potential for future change are doing the tenant a disservice. For example, an organization that experiences frequent change or is in the midst of rapid growth will benefit from a highly flexible space plan that incorporates such materials as carpet tiles and demountable partitions.

When creating interior spaces, interior architects have the expertise to select finishes, furniture, and equipment that result in an esthetically pleasing and comfortable environment. They remain up-to-date on product innovations and are adept in utilizing available resources. Well-designed offices that are secure, clean, and efficient contribute to increased productivity and go a long way in attracting and retaining workers. Workplace esthetics and ergonomics are especially significant in the automated office, where they can be used to help minimize an otherwise dehumanizing environment. For example, sound-absorbing fabric on walls, padded carpet, and acoustical ceiling tile can be used to lessen the noise impact from high-speed printers and other equipment.

Many corporations are also retaining outside consultants to assist with other aspects of relocation, postoccupancy evaluation, and ongoing facilities management. In today's complex world, many tenants prefer that one point of contact be responsible and accountable for the relocation process, thus paving the way for a smoother transition. Observant architectural and interior design firms recognize this fact and are now providing clients with a full cycle of design services. Such services range from coordinating the move to developing programs that will orient employees to their new facility. These services can also have long-term implications; studies have shown that employee acceptance is critical to maximizing productivity.

After an organization has completed its move, the consultant can play an important role in managing the facility and minimizing occupancy costs. With the use of computer-aided design, space plan changes, asset tracking and control records, space allocation plans, and wire management plans can be accomplished quickly and economically.

It is evident that as buildings become more technologically advanced and therefore more complex, additional steps must be taken to ensure quality control over the completed facility. The evolving discipline of diagnostics is beginning to perform this function. This quality control is accomplished by developing performance criteria during the programming and early design stages, and by testing and assessing these criteria at appropriate times during and after construction and, ideally, throughout the life of the project. This will help ensure cost-effective and productive utilization of the facility.

CHAPTER 3

Elements of a Typical Office Facility

Karen Daroff and James E. Rappoport

This chapter presents, in alphabetic order, each of the elements of a typical office facility. The components of a base building construction project and of the interior space planning and fit-out package are described in detail. Where appropriate, sketches are introduced to illustrate the elements being described.

At the end of the chapter, a series of layered drawings is presented to illustrate the interrelationship of some of the elements discussed. The reader may use these drawings to prepare transparencies which, when registered one over the other, will allow visualization of the interrelationship of the diagrammed elements.

The process of generating a program of tenant requirements and reviewing their three-dimensional layering is the basis for the inside-out office facility design process and the means for producing a cost-effective facility design. This programming process is described in Chapter 1.

Descriptions of Elements

Access to building. Ease of entry and lobby circulation to the building's core are critical issues, when analyzing traffic flow at peak periods during each business day. (See Figure 3.1.)

Approximately 15 percent of the total building population should be factored when estimating access to the building during each of the following six peak periods:

7:55 to 8:00 A.M.	5:00 to 5:05 P.M.
8:25 to 8:30 A.M.	5:30 to 5:35 P.M.
8:55 to 9:00 A.M.	6:00 to 6:05 P.M.

Most individuals require five to six seconds to approach and pass through a lobby's entrance doorway. Slightly less time is required for entry through

FIGURE 3.1

Circulation Vectors Entering Office Building

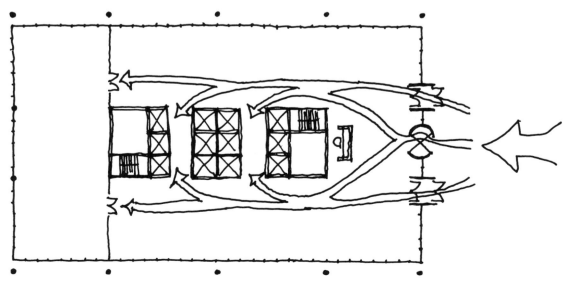

revolving doors on clear days, and slightly more time for entry through a pair of swinging doors into a vestibule on a windy day, or through revolving doors under wet conditions. (Extra time allowances should be made for handicapped individuals.)

Rarely will individuals go two abreast through a pair of doors; more often, individuals select the right-hand door only and file through one at a time.

A building with 200,000 usable square feet of space would require, by the above criteria, no fewer than three to four doorways for approximately 750 to 900 employees working in the facility each day. A building of 1 million square feet should have no fewer than 15 to 20 doors, using the same formula.

Having fewer doorways causes frustration and ultimately anger among employees when they are late to work, or inconvenienced, or must wait to gain access to the lobby or building elevator core during inclement weather.

Escalators rising up from a street-level lobby to a second-floor elevator lobby, typical of some 1960s office towers, also delay building access. The cost in employee morale and in lost hours worked per employee per year is significant.

Access floors. Access floor systems are recommended for many office facilities where office automation and occupancy plans require many points of access or constant change and relocation of the wiring infrastructure. These access floor systems are typically employed in computer rooms, telephone switchboard rooms, and word processing areas.

Rarely, however, can a full access floor installation be cost-justified for a client's typical office facility.

Access floors are manufactured with the same 2 ft.-0 in. module as ceiling systems. (See Figure 3.2.) Various heights are possible above the finished floor, from as little as 6 inches to more than 24 inches. The height is determined by the engineering space specification for pipes, ducts and wireways, and fire suppression systems, required for protection of the space between the finished floor and the access floor panels, and the wires and elements within this space.

Acoustic Issues

Core Design. It is not unusual to find a core design where noise generated by base building elements (such as the elevator machinery, flushing toilets, fans and mechanical equipment, and the rush of high-velocity air distribution systems) is not properly isolated acoustically at the core walls.

Acoustic engineers state that a cumulative opening the size of a dime in a core wall allows enough sound to transfer into the tenant's space to give the effect of having no core wall. This equivalent illustrates the point that core walls contiguous to occupied tenant space must be acoustically opaque, with both mass and acoustic insulation, to provide the required isolation of core noise and prevent it from intruding into tenant space.

A noise coefficient index (NCI) of at least 35 to 40 should be considered the minimum standard of acoustic isolation from core-to-tenant spaces.

Office Planning. When searching for a new apartment, experienced tenants have learned to inspect shared or "party" walls for acoustic problems. All tenants have experienced at some time the annoying sounds of neighbors' slamming doors, flushing toilets, and playing loud music, and know that one should reject units not offering acoustic privacy.

Unfortunately, most prospective office tenants forget the lessons learned in their residential house hunting, when they are planning an office relocation. Because office leases tend to be much longer than residential leases, selection of a new office facility with acoustic problems may later seem like a "noisy life sentence."

Although the theory of sound transference is a subject taught in all architectural schools, acoustic problems still persist in new office construction. The reason lies in the sheer physical difficulty of acoustically isolating one space from another. As noted earlier, if all of the minute gaps typical of a wall separation exceed the size of a dime, then sound will "leak" into adjoining rooms as if the wall did not exist.

Because every architectural space is separated from its adjoining space by a combination of floor, ceilings, window walls, doors, pipe and duct chases, wireways, and other penetrations, there will always be some element of sound transference between adjoining rooms. Uninsulated or "flimsy" partitions may act as a drum, allowing sound to pass through the wall by means of vibration transference.

Today's architect and interior designer is equipped with a variety of tools and techniques to help reduce acoustic gaps, stiffen and insulate walls, and otherwise minimize acoustic problems. The following measures are especially recommended:

- To reduce gaps where walls and floors meet, a combination of techniques can be used: insulate the wall cavities and fill the small gaps left between wallboard and joists; place a neoprene gasket between the wall's bottom plate and the concrete

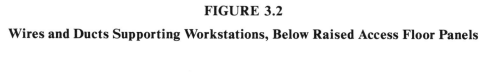

FIGURE 3.2

Wires and Ducts Supporting Workstations, Below Raised Access Floor Panels

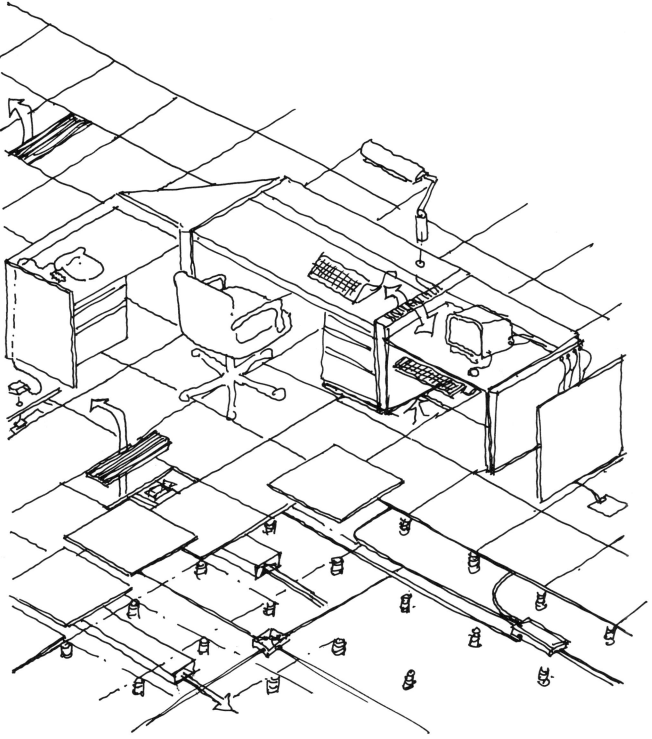

floor; carpet up to the wallboard; and use a vinyl wall base.

- Address similar details between walls and window mullions, walls and ceilings, and door frames and surrounding walls.
- Never place outlets back-to-back in party walls; undercut doors to a minimum; provide reducer strips between office doorways and corridors; gasket pipe chases; and fill continuous window-wall fan coil units with acoustic blankets.
- Never locate acoustically quiet spaces below or next to rooms with hard-surface floor finishes, adjacent to fan rooms or high-velocity duct chase spaces, or alongside elevator hoistways and machine rooms.

In practical terms, a well-detailed and planned interior fit-out will reduce acoustic problems and help ensure a higher degree of speech privacy. To be sure that acoustic techniques and sound absorptive materials are employed, a prospective tenant should always review the fit-out specifications of the future office space prior to signing the lease.

The cost of acoustic details will add significantly to overall construction costs—perhaps as much as $5 per square foot. This explains why all of these techniques are rarely employed on any one project and why sound transference is a frequent problem.

If a prospective tenant must accept the realities of some sound leakage, it is still possible to create a quiet office environment. The answer is not found solely in eliminating noise but rather in generating background noise to "mask out" objectionable sounds. This "sound masking" theory led to the creation of a quantifiable acoustic criterion known as the "Speech Privacy Index." (See Figure 3.3.)

In practice, the most objectionable noises in the office environment are within the human voice frequency range. It has been determined that the sound of air moving at approximately 800 feet per minute through a properly engineered air duct system produces a sound frequency level within this human frequency range. "Masking" the sound of human voices creates the perception of speech privacy. Because air conditioning systems are not always operational and acoustic frequency generation is not totally reliable, acoustical engineers developed a synthetic acoustic generator that simulates the sound of rushing air and can be adjusted to match the level of speech privacy desired within an office environment. Known as a sound masking system, this equipment is available as a base building feature or as a tenant-installed

fit-out item at a cost of less than $1.00 per square foot of office space.

By intention or default, all office environments are instilled with unique acoustic characteristics. As with many subliminal forces, when acoustic levels are appropriate, they tend to go unnoticed. When room acoustics are unsatisfactory, however, tenants and their employees suffer and office productivity may be reduced. In response, full-service engineering firms and interior architectural specialists routinely specify sound masking in conjunction with acoustic detailing for both owner/user and tenant fit-out assignments.

Additional Structural Support

Certain tenants frequently require additional support for their central file rooms, will and money safes, libraries, and other office facility spaces that carry greater than typical floor loadings.

Building codes typically specify that office floors must accept 60 pounds per square foot of space for the tenant's furniture, equipment, and employees. However, file rooms, for example, can easily concentrate loads in excess of 120 pounds per square foot. Such additional loading may require additional structural steel, either by increasing the size of the beams and joists below the heavy-load area, or as a plinth above the structural floor, providing a spreading out of the otherwise concentrated load.

Areas requiring structural reinforcing must be determined initially during the programming data collection process.

Appliance Cords

In keeping with regulations developed by the Underwriters Laboratories (UL), appliance cords are typically 6 feet long. For this reason, outlets need to be located within close proximity to the work surfaces where the appliances are to be positioned. The use of extension cords, in addition to being against the building code, may cause tripping conditions when used throughout an office facility, and therefore should be avoided.

Office and workstation furniture manufacturers provide convenient wireways and outlets within the furniture itself, so that a pod or grouping of workstations can be "plugged in" at one location, with the wires running within the workstation panels to the various outlet locations positioned according to the occupancy plan.

FIGURE 3.3

How Sound Masking Yields "Speech Privacy"

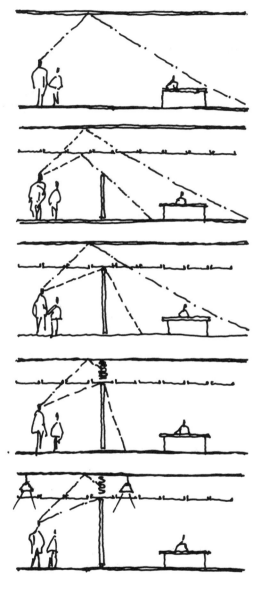

Open office without acoustic treatment results in 100% sound transference

Open office with acoustic ceiling and low panels results in 80% sound transference

Office with acoustic ceiling and full height walls results in 50% sound transference

Office with acoustic ceiling and full height insulated walls with ceiling blanket results in 25% sound transference

Office with acoustic ceiling and full height insulated walls with ceiling blanket and sound masking system results in "speech privacy"

Atria

An atrium and an interior courtyard are frequently employed to increase the available window wall for companies needing many windowed offices or to provide employees with the desirable features of a planted area. Because an atrium stops and starts the planning rhythm or module of an office workstation layout, its size and configuration should be studied as it relates to that rhythm or module.

Auxiliary Ventilation

Tenants that employ artists and others using glue and paints, or require blueprinting and photostat equipment, or maintain certain food service operations, may need special ventilation shafts. Their exhaust requirements frequently cannot be accommodated within available exhaust ductwork serving the base building toilet rooms and other core requirements. If these tenants occupy lower floors in large office towers, they may require ducts passing through spaces on floors above them and incur substantially increased rents. The availability of tenant ventilation duct shafts is therefore a critical aspect to the planning of certain types of tenant use and occupancy.

A lack of auxiliary ventilation may result in the so-called "sick building" syndrome because the various noxious fumes and odors are not filtered and ventilated to the outside.

Base Building Core and Shell Cost Considerations

Specific costs and expenses are difficult to determine. There are many ways to construct an office building, and many more features that can be combined in finishing it. Cost ranges for base buildings vary substantially from building to building and from location to location.

In most instances where a tenant is impacting the construction of a base building, the tenant will be guided by competent design professionals throughout the entire development process. Improved methods of construction will frequently cost more to provide and install, but alternate solutions may cost more to operate over the life of the facility. For example, if a 32-foot column spacing is desired because it offers 15 percent more density of employees housed in a given amount of usable floor area, this factor usually overcomes the structural engineer's advice that the heavier steel cross section may add 3 to 4 percent to the overall costs of the building.

Because there may be no fewer than 100 such items in an overall tenant/base building construction package, no shortcut is available in this evolution process other than to proceed to document and discuss each feature as to its pros and cons, its effect on first costs and life-cycle costs, and the cumulative effects of available features versus alternate features.

As is discussed in later chapters, a variety of leasing terms and conditions help to protect tenants engaged in either the fit-out of their demised premises or the development of a customized office building for their use and occupancy.

A wise tenant will try to predict potential problems and negotiate lease terms and conditions to protect its interests. The key to this process is to proceed, prior to lease confirmation, through the schematic design and preliminary budgeting steps recommended in Chapter 1. Most of the vagaries of the tenant fit-out costs package will then become clarified, and the resulting lease and financial agreements can proceed with known costs and expenses, to the benefit of both the tenant and the tenant's prospective landlord or developer.

Bites. The building corners may be designed with indentations, cut backs, or bites—opportunities for more corner offices—but if the bites are not of the correct size or shape, a substantial waste of space may result. (See Figure 3.4.) The building's resulting corner conditions may also fuel a demand to provide such large offices that a particular corporate hierarchy will become upset by the assignment of these larger offices to otherwise equal individuals.

Building Configurations. Many architects seek to develop esthetically pleasing or unusual architectural features for their buildings by designing buildings with curved, sawtooth, or diagonal, rather than rectangular, shells. Others seek to provide multiple corner conditions (to satisfy senior executives, who typically request corner offices). Interior atria, courtyards, and other features may be employed to offer more varied window wall configurations than can be offered by the typical office tower "box" or "block." A site location or zoning reason may dictate why a particular architect will position and shape a building in other than a rectangular shape.

Nevertheless, it is an axiom of modern office design that 99 percent of the most efficient and best designs will be rectangular.

When architects propose nonrectangular buildings, a number of considerations need to be reviewed in relation to the building's overall efficiency and the cost per employee housed.

Building Core. "Core" is the term used to define the services and vertical circulation areas of a building. The core usually includes:

- Elevators (passenger and service)
- Stairs and fire stairs
- Mail chutes and mail conveyance systems
- Toilet rooms
- Janitor's closets
- Building maintenance rooms
- Fan rooms and air conditioning equipment rooms
- Areas set aside for ducts
- Areas set aside for wire risers
- Telephone closets
- Electric closets
- Data wiring closets

FIGURE 3.4

How a Building Configuration with Many Bites (Cut-Out Shapes) Can Result in Inefficient Tenant Space

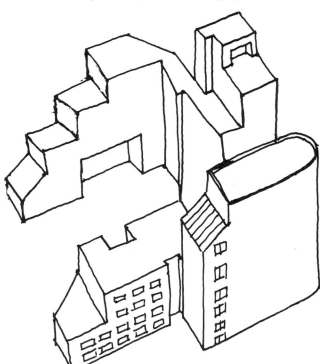

- Service or freight vestibules
- Fire protection equipment areas
- Structural elements employed for wind bracing and other major structural functions.

An example of placement of core elements is shown in Figure 3.5. Typically, the larger the building, the larger the core. However, in a ratio of the square feet devoted to core compared to the square feet available for tenant occupancy, a larger building's larger core may offer more efficiency.

With careful attention to the details of the core's design, efficiencies that impact the overall efficiency of the tenant's space can be achieved. The two major elements of the core that substantially affect the efficiency of tenant space are (1) the core's width, and (2) the location of the fire/exit stairs and other access points within the core.

The major determinant of the core width is the sum of the width(s) of the passenger elevators plus the structural walls to either end of the core. Generally, three 3,500-pound-capacity elevators require a minimum 25 ft.-10 in. width; four elevators require a 34 ft.-6 in. width. The structural walls can range from

steel construction of 1 ft.-6 in. thickness to a concrete structural wall of 2 ft.-6 in. thickness (or more).

These structural elements can be either load-bearing or a combination of load-bearing and lateral wind-bracing elements.

In very tall office towers, the structural elements become the major components of a core and determine its overall efficiency.

Because the core typically contains two or more sets of fire stairs (as required by the building code), fire exit corridors, and fire stair doorways, access to these stairs becomes a major space utilization element.

The most recent national building code requires a direct circulation pattern throughout the occupied spaces and ending at each set of fire stairs, and at least two such fire stairways are required in all buildings. Access for the handicapped is also a code requirement.

The recent building code(s) requires a loop of circulation and does not allow a dead-end corridor (common within earlier office tower installations).

For a full-floor tenant, access to the fire stairs can and usually does occur directly from the tenant's occupied space. However, the building code requires that passengers on the building's elevators must be

FIGURE 3.5

Typical Base Building Core Features

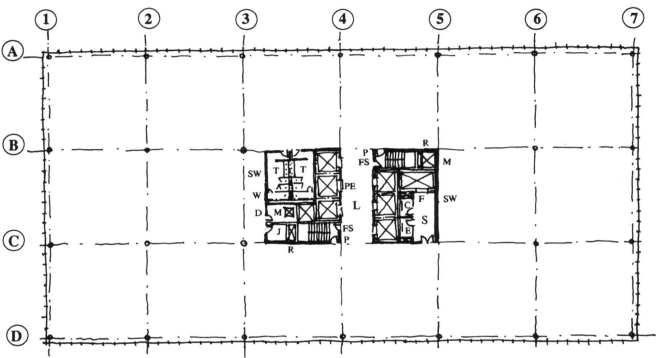

C - Telephone (communications) riser closet
D - Drinking fountain
E - Electrical riser closet
F - Freight elevator
FS - Fire exit stairs (2 required)
J - Janitor's closet
L - Passenger elevator lobby
M - Mechanical ventilator riser and fan equipment
P - Fire safety pull boxes / emergency phone
PE - Passenger elevators
R - Fire suppression system / water risers and hose cabinets
S - Service vestibule
SW - Structural shear walls
T - Men's and women's toilet rooms
W - Wet (water and waste) riser for core and tenant (pantry) use

able to access the fire stairs from the full-floor tenant's space, in case a fire alarm stops the elevator and passengers are discharged into the elevator foyer of the full-floor tenant.

In such a fire emergency, the discharged passengers would break the security of the full-floor tenant's space to gain access to the fire stairs, unless the access is provided directly within the elevator foyer itself.

An alternate solution for both full-floor and partial-floor tenants is to place the fire stairs near the elevator foyers, thus reducing the amount of office planning space that must be devoted to access to the fire stairs.

In very tall or multiheight office towers that have multiple banks of elevators, it may not be possible to position the stairs within the core and reduce the access or circulation space. The stairs may be located in one area of the core in the low-rise towers and in another area in the high-rise towers. A crossover circulation pattern would be needed within the core, on some intermediate floor of the tower.

Building Shell. "Shell" is the term used to define the skin areas of a building. The shell typically includes:

- The actual glass, aluminum, steel, concrete, and masonry skin of the building
- The decorative or architectural details of the building's exterior facade
- The decorative, architectural, or mechanical details of the building's interior facade
- The window sill condition, including the heating and ventilation radiation and/or the air distri-

FIGURE 3.6

Building Shell Thickness

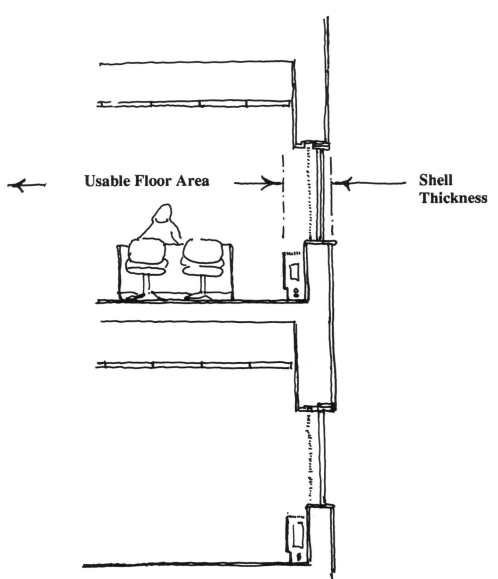

bution system, typically located at the window wall (shell)

- The structural columns, typically located within or outside of the glass line at the window wall (shell)
- Any wet columns carrying water, or waste, or roof drainage, typically located within, in, or outside of the glass line at the window wall (shell).

The design of building shells is always the purview of the base building architect and engineers and impacts substantially on the overall efficiency of the office and workstation planning of the tenant spaces.

The shell of the building has a thickness that is, in effect, part of the gross floor area but is not usable by the tenant. (See Figure 3.6.) By this measure, the thinnest shell offers the most efficient use of available gross floor area.

In recent years, mechanical engineers have begun to provide high-velocity air distribution at the head of the window wall; formerly, hot water radiation was distributed below the glass line at the window wall. The high-velocity air distribution has substantially reduced the thickness of the window wall, making for a more efficient building.

In some cases, when below-the-glass radiation has been eliminated, the window sill has been lowered below the traditional 30-inch table (or credenza) height from the finished floor. A greater expanse of glass may be beneficial, but the inability to furnish up to the window wall may cause inefficiencies that should be studied.

Moreover, if the architect lowers the glass line to the finished floor, there may be no room for wire distribution at the window wall. Frequently, line voltage, telephone, and data communications wiring will be distributed to the offices most efficiently at the window wall.

The advantages of a greater expanse of glass should be compared to the disadvantages of more costly wire distribution and the inability to furnish up to the window wall, to determine the most appropriate decision.

The shell of the building has the main function of protecting or sealing the interior space from outside elements.

Since the energy crisis of the mid-1970s, architects have taken very aggressive steps to meet what President Carter called then a "corporate responsibility" to reduce energy consumption in all private and public buildings. Smaller windows and more use of insulated granite on the facades of the recent office towers are some results of this edict.

Techniques for using fixed double-glazing and metallic semimirrored glass elements have further improved a shell's ability to reduce solar and climatic intrusion into a building's interior. These glazing techniques offer lower energy costs and less daylight intrusion into the interior, which results in less glare at the window wall and less need for interior illumination to overcome the window wall glare.

A disadvantage of these glazing techniques is a tinted, colored, or "dulled" vision through the window wall glass shell to the outside view. In some buildings, the opacity becomes so great that plants cannot be grown in the interior office areas. This new breed of mirrored glass office environments requires careful interior design detailing, to liven up the space and make up for the lack of incoming sunlight.

The recommended window wall will allow approximately 60 footcandles of sunlight illumination to pass through on the north facade. Window treatments on the east, west, and south facades must allow for modification during periods of the day when the sunlight passing through those facades exceeds the 60-footcandle level.

Carpet Tiles. As indicated below in the description of *wiring,* especially flat wire installations, carpet tiles are a highly desirable feature for most office facilities. Each of the major carpet manufacturers has developed technology to produce individual carpet tiles, each typically 18 inches square (some manufacturers also produce 24-inch square tiles), using broadloom materials that are compatible with their standard tile product line. (See Figure 3.7.)

Carpet tiles are used in places where access to the floor-mounted wiring is a critical design factor. Carpet tiles are also recommended because the floor's appearance over time can be ensured. Carpet tiles that are damaged or soiled beyond their ability to be cleaned can be easily replaced and are thus cost-justified on a life-cycle cost basis.

There is a premium cost of approximately $4.00 per yard for carpet tile installations versus broadloom installations of the same general quality. A large proportion of this additional cost can be avoided if the areas to be carpeted are sized to correspond to the carpet tile standard sizes, thus avoiding cutting and the resulting waste of carpet tile materials during installation.

It appears that carpet tiles are increasingly the floor covering of preference for operational facilities.

FIGURE 3.7

Typical 18″ x 18″ Carpet Tiles (Direct Lay-Down Installation Method Illustrated)

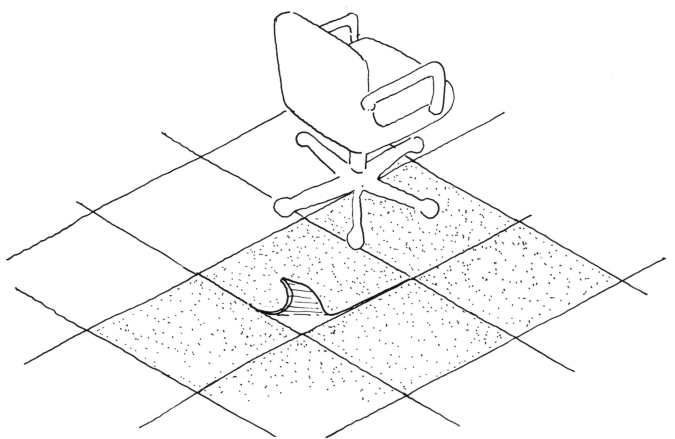

Ceiling Grids. Typically constructed on a 1 × 1 ft., 2 × 2 ft., or 2 × 4 ft. module, these tile carriers or supports are manufactured in many cross sections of steel or aluminum and are shaped to support various types and configurations of ceiling tiles and acoustic ceiling boards. (See Figure 3.8.)

Ceiling Systems. Most modern office facilities must offer direct access to the layers of infrastructure installed above the ceiling line. There are many types and configurations of ceiling systems, but, in general, these systems consist of hangers, ceiling tile supports, and the ceiling panels themselves. The hangers and ceiling tile supports are also used to support fluorescent luminaires and various other elements of the infrastructure that penetrate the ceiling system.

The ceiling system is a major structural element that modulates the location and contains many infrastructure items. It is best, therefore, to allow the ceiling plane to freely pass over all of the partitioning, furniture, and other interior elements located below the ceiling plane. To interrupt the ceiling plane with protrusions from partitions and other elements interrupts the modulation of the ceiling and requires a cut-and-fit operation at each vertical-to-horizontal juncture. (See Figure 3.9.)

Major features of modern ceiling systems are acoustic isolation and fire isolation. Acoustically, the ceiling panels are designed to absorb airborne sound from the office space below and to prevent sound of an airborne and vibration nature from passing through the ceiling plane and bouncing back down into a contiguous office space below. In regard to fire

FIGURE 3.8

Typical 2'-0" x 2'-0" Suspended Ceiling Grid Framing Acoustic Ceiling Panel (Tiles)

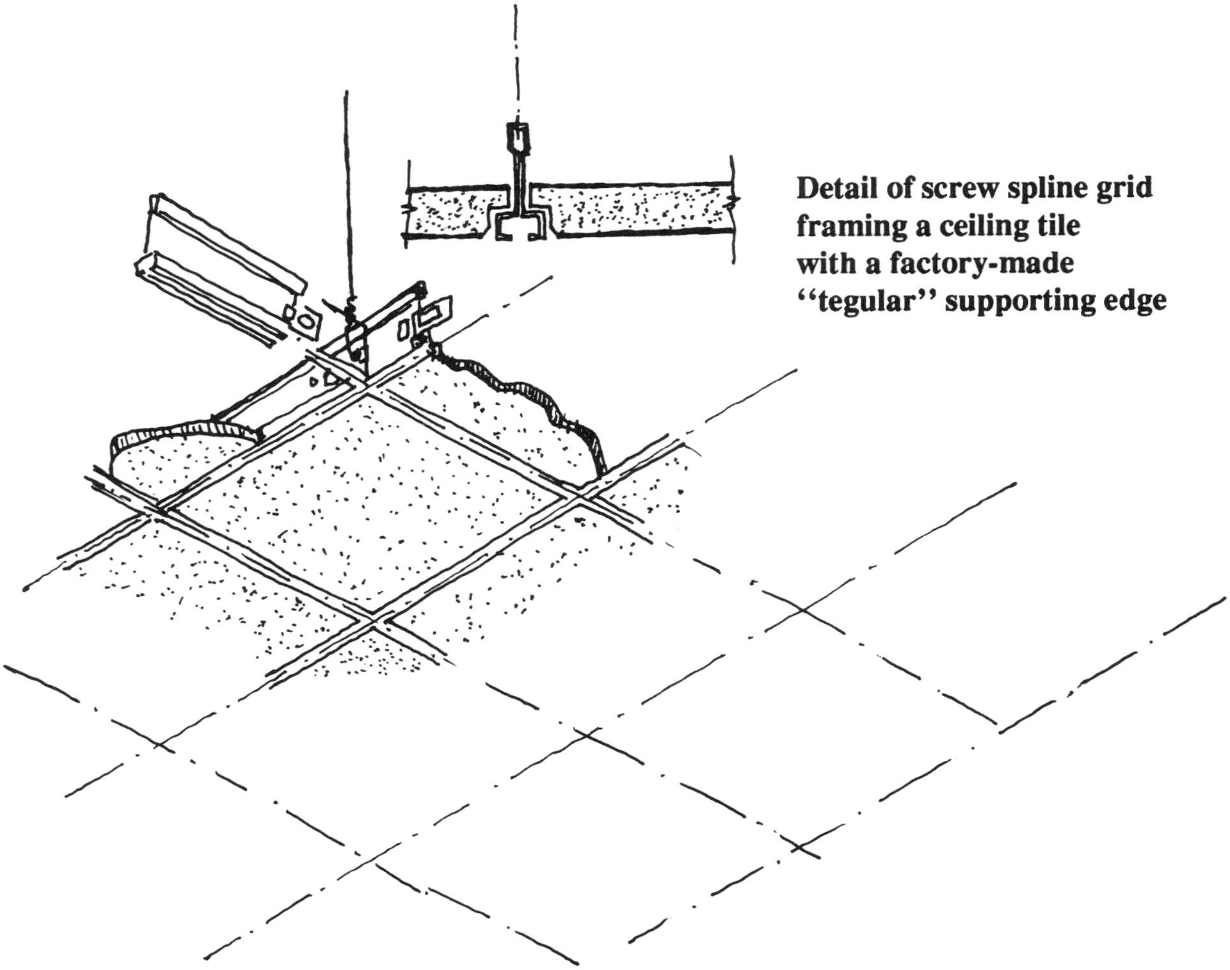

Detail of screw spline grid framing a ceiling tile with a factory-made "tegular" supporting edge

protection, some ceiling systems offer one hour of containment by preventing a fire burning in one office area from passing through the ceiling plane and into a contiguous occupied office space.

Traditionally, the office partitions of senior-level executives and of most conference rooms pass through the ceiling plane to the underside of the structural slab above the hung ceiling. These full-height partitions are required by the building code for demising walls between tenants, or between tenants and common public corridors or building cores. These structural partition elements give a better acoustic separation of one space from another and offer more fire protection, assuming that the joints are properly cut and fitted.

In practice, reliance on full-height partitions for acoustic and fire isolation often results in leaks.

Additionally, the partitions require interruption of the structural and infrastructural elements located between the ceiling and the structural slab above.

To assure future flexibility and lower operating costs, partitions should be constructed from the floor to the underside of the ceiling. The wiring, ductwork, piping, and other elements of the infrastructure can thus be installed continuously, providing flexibility for future partition relocations. However, additional technical considerations may be required to resolve acoustic and fire isolation issues.

Center of Tile. This term refers to the design directive that all ceiling-mounted elements, such as downlights, sprinkler heads, exit signs, fire prevention sensors, and other ceiling mounted elements,

FIGURE 3.9

Full-Height Partition Types

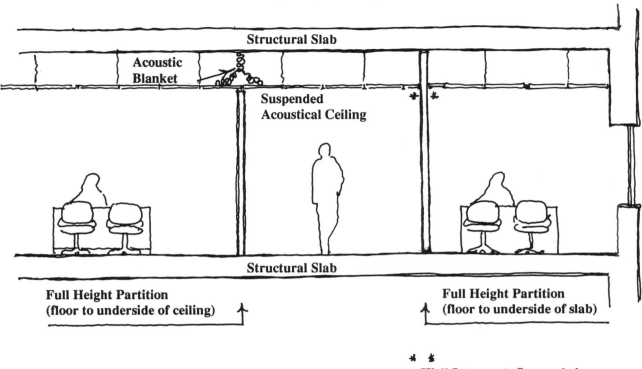

Structural Slab

Acoustic Blanket

Suspended Acoustical Ceiling

Structural Slab

Full Height Partition
(floor to underside of ceiling)

Full Height Partition
(floor to underside of slab)

* *
**Wall Interrupts Suspended
Acoustic Ceiling**

FIGURE 3.10

Grills, Sprinkler Heads, and Recessed Downlights Located on "Center of Tile"

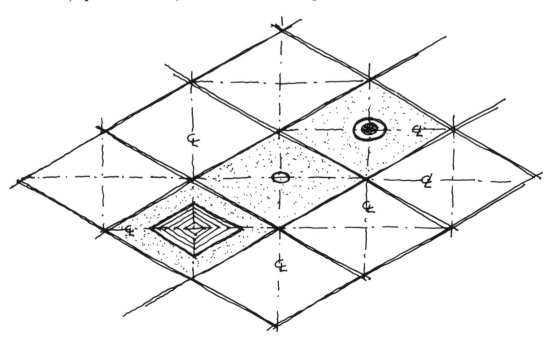

should be located on the center line of the ceiling tiles. (See Figure 3.10.)

If the tiles are 2 × 2 ft., as is typical of many office facility installations, the center of tile is on axes in both directions.

If the tiles are the less costly 2 × 4 ft. tiles, the center of tile may mean any one of three locations, and must be specified in the contract documents.

Ceiling-mounted elements that are otherwise located appear haphazard; they indicate an "ad hoc" design effort and should be avoided wherever possible.

Circulation. Spaces for circulation (see Figure 3.11) are a major element in any interior space planning effort, and account for more than 20 percent of the overall space requirements. (See also

FIGURE 3.11

Circulation Factors

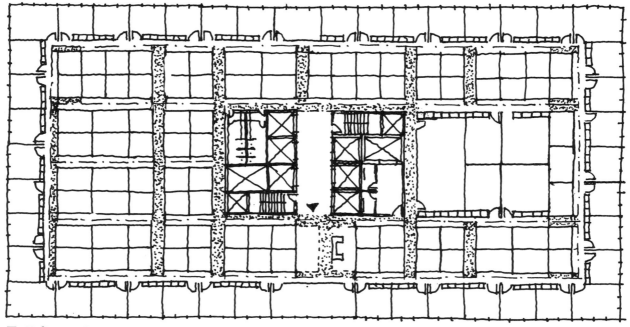

Full floor plan

By planning with double-loaded corridors, the total circulation factor in this illustration is less than 22% of the rentable square feet.

By accounting for 50% of the typical double-loaded corridor accessing each office and workstation within each office and workstation sq. ft. program allocation, less than 8% of the rentable area (the cross aisles) need be accounted for as a "departmental circulation factor".

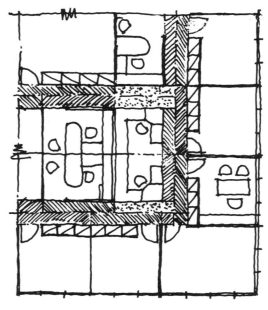

Detail @ corner

Interdepartmental circulation and *Intradepartmental circulation*.)

Clerestory Glass. This design device is frequently employed to provide an illusion of openness and some view of daylight passing through a private perimeter office into the open workstation area of a typical office facility. The clerestory glass can be located on top of a partition, if the partition is coincidental with the screw spline ceiling. The glass or plastic glazing can actually be fitted up and into the screw spline grid above.

Common Corridor Widths and Access Doors. In tenant suites, these elements should be established as part of the core design and as the determinants for the core-to-glass dimension. Doors to tenant spaces must swing toward the means of egress (see Figure 3.12). On multitenant floors, all tenant doors are required to swing outward. Because these doors may

FIGURE 3.12

Multitenant-Floor Common Tenant (Fire Exiting) Corridor

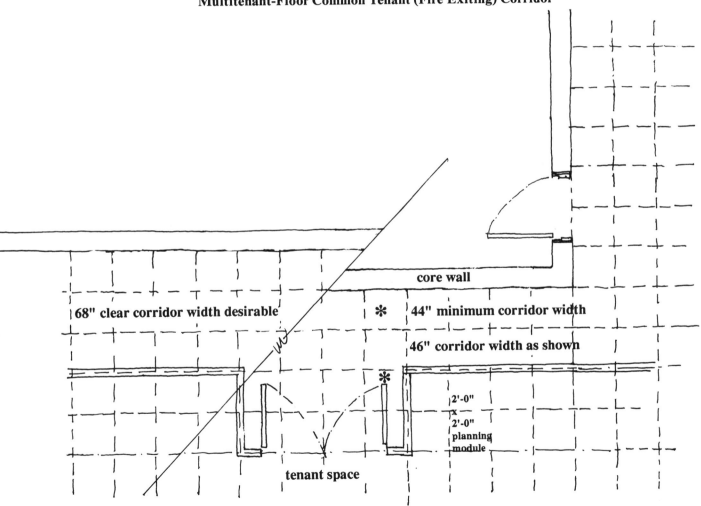

Minimum corridor width sized for fire and handicapped code (with recessed tenant doorway).

Note: In this illustration the core walls follow the 2'-0" planning module line, while tenant partitions are located on center lines of the planning module.

*Handicapped code requires 48" minimum from edge of door to wall; in this example, 58" is provided.

not obstruct the minimum corridor width of 44 inches, the corridors must either be increased in size to 44 inches plus the door width (usually 36 inches)—a sum of 80 inches—or the tenant doors must swing outward within a niche in the corridor wall provided for this purpose. This niche can also be used to meet the 60-inch turning radius required for the handicapped (see Figure 3.13).

A typical multitenant corridor of minimum dimensions is illustrated in Figure 3.14.

Core Design Recommendations. In general, a core design should address the following features:

- A width that starts and ends on the building's window bay module

FIGURE 3.13

Wheelchair 180° Turning Space Requirement

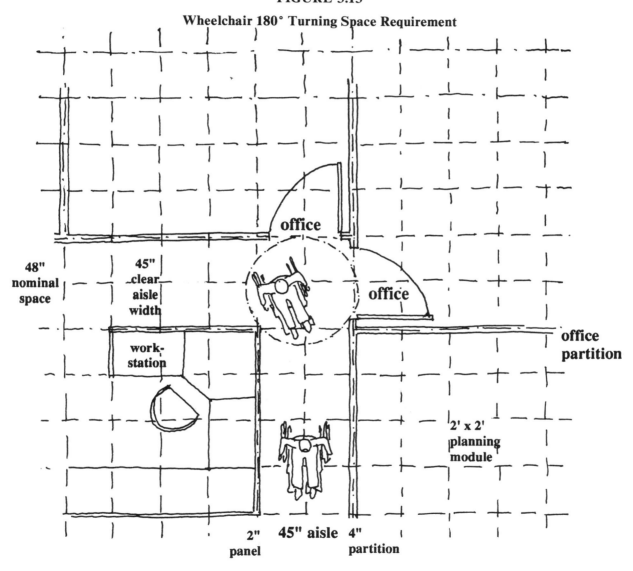

Code-required 60" diameter turning space is provided in this example with a 2'-0" x 2'-0" planning grid, nominal 4'-0" aisle with 2" thick furniture panels, and 4" thick office partitions encroaching 50% to either side of the planning module line (the actual space provided is 63.6" with the office doors closed within a 45" clear aisle width).

FIGURE 3.14

Minimum Wheelchair Turning Spaces

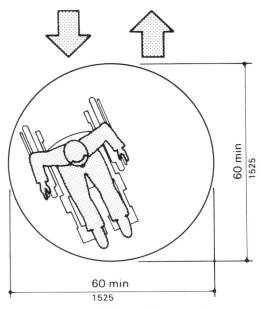

(a) 60-in (1525-mm)-Diameter Space

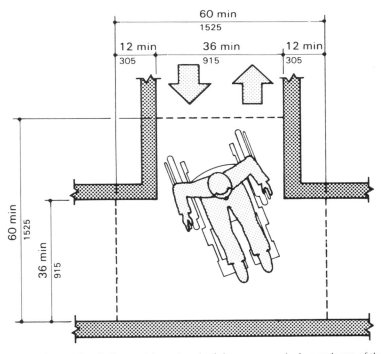

NOTE: Dashed lines indicate minimum length of clear space required on each arm of the T-shaped space in order to complete the turn.

(b) T-Shaped Space for 180° Turns

- Stair locations with access directly from the elevator foyer
- A minimal number of openings from tenant space into the core
- Minimum square feet devoted to the core
- A location of core and core elements that avoids crossover circulation patterns on intermediate floors of a tower building
- Elevator foyer face-to-face dimensions of 9 ft.-0 in., with 8 ft.-0 in. being too narrow for most facilities, and more than 9 ft.-0 in. being generous
- Elevator intervals of 18 seconds or less
- Cross-core circulation paths
- Mail distribution systems for multifloor tenants.

Corridor Dimensions. Corridors vary according to their purpose, their length, and the esthetic criteria of the particular project. In general, the minimum corridor width is set by the building code at 44 inches, the criterion for a fire exit. Fire marshals and code enforcement agents will sometimes allow a structural column to protrude into the exit way, even when it reduces the corridor to 36 inches in width at a few points along the way.

File cabinets with drawers or cupboard-type doors that open into the exit way are also permitted to constrict the width to 36 inches in some municipalities, but, in general, 44 inches should be maintained as a minimum dimension throughout the interior planning.

The nominal width for most office planning should approach 60 inches, so that two employees can pass side by side, a wheelchair employee can turn around easily, and a door or drawer can open up into the corridor and still allow for the 44-inch minimum dimension.

Major circulation paths—where many employees walk to and from departments and/or where the mail delivery carts travel—should exceed the 60-inch nominal width, becoming, wherever possible, at least 72 to 84 inches in width.

Crossing the Core. Where the core is longer than 50 feet, crossing the core becomes an important design feature for full-floor tenants and for owner/user office facilities. Frequently, the base building architect will seek to use the space between the high-rise elevators for the toilet rooms on the low-rise floors. This will prevent crossing the core unless a secondary path is designed into the core. (See Figure 3.15.)

It has been calculated that office occupants walk at a rate of approximately 200 feet per minute. Having numerous employees walk around a large core several times a day becomes a major waste of valuable staff time and should be given consideration when reviewing base building core designs. For example, on a typical floor of a 25,000-square-foot office tower with a core 100 feet long, *five to six hours of cumulative wasted staff time could be saved daily* if the core had a central crossing point.

Curves and Angles. These design features may offer esthetic advantages, but every curved or angled building is built at a major premium price, because each element of the structure, infrastructure, shell, and interior must be customized and cut to fit.

Deflection. The bounce or sag of a particular structural element or combination of structural components is described as its deflection. There are two types of deflection. Initial deflection occurs as soon as the structure is put into place and loaded with its own weight, including the weight of the poured-in-place floor slab(s). Live load deflection is the bounce one feels when walking over the structural elements of the floor slab. Figure 3.16 shows the effect. (See *Initial deflection* and *Live load deflection,* below.)

Double-Loaded Corridor. The most efficient method to develop circulation patterns is with double-loading, the planning method in which either side of the circulation path provides access to offices, workstations, files, special spaces, and other features of the facility. (See Figure 3.17.)

If the overall dimensions of a particular building do not allow for double-loading, then the overall efficiency and cost effectiveness of that building will be dramatically reduced. In many cases, a loss of efficiency of 10 to 20 percent has been attributed to the inability to plan with double-loaded corridors.

Each of the building's interior dimensions must be carefully studied, to create the opportunity to plan space using the double-loading technique. This technique is desirable because it substantially increases space planning efficiency, thus lowering costs per employee housed.

Electric Outlets. The positioning of electric outlets within offices, workstations, and other areas is derived from the occupancy plan. Additional building code requirements for the location of outlets

FIGURE 3.15

Crossing the Core

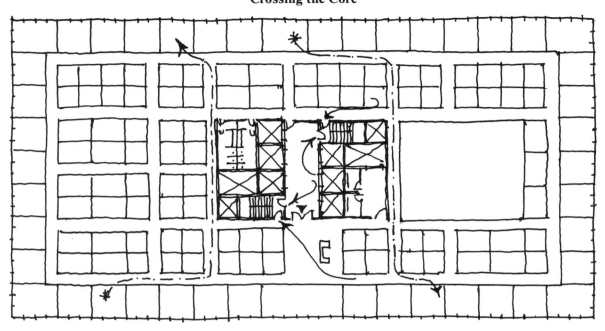

Illustration of a full floor tenant floor plan with a core configuration designed so that fire exiting can occur without encroachment on the tenant's internal security, and providing "short-cuts" so that tenant employees can easily cross the core for access to employees on the other side of the building.

FIGURE 3.16

Effect (Exaggerated) of Floor Slab Deflection

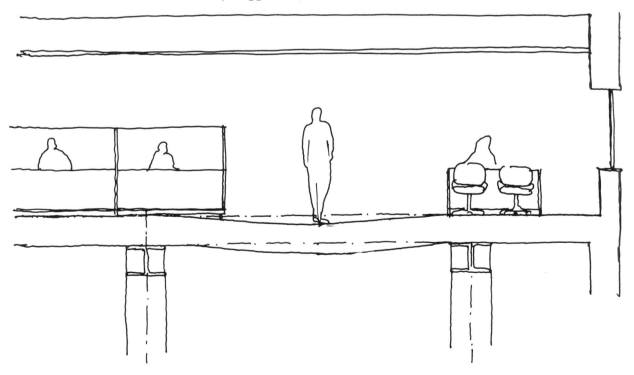

FIGURE 3.17

Efficient "Double Loaded" Circulation Patterns

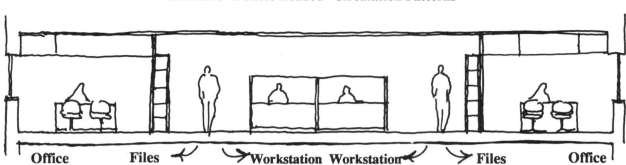

Office   Files   Workstation   Workstation   Files   Office

along office and corridor partitions vary with each municipality.

Electric Utilization and Metering. For any office facility built under President Carter's "corporate responsibility" edict, utilization and metering of electricity is a key requirement.

Many pre-1975 office buildings required tenants to share one electric meter, thus providing the landlord with an opportunity for additional income as electric utility rates increased over the years. If the electric charges are included within the rent, there may be no responsibility or impetus for discussion between the landlord and the tenant.

At current utility rates, a tenant in a pre-1975 office facility that has pre-1975 lighting concepts and no energy conservation will use as much as $4.25 of electricity per square foot per year. A modern, fully insulated, office building with double "thermopane" glazing, low-brightness lighting and a well-planned energy conservation program will require less than $1.50 of electricity per square foot per year.

Most older buildings now undergoing renovation and seeking new tenants are installing submeters for each tenant. Most new leases are net of electricity and require the tenant to pay the landlord, a third party, or the utility directly for the energy consumed and metered.

Metered electricity is recommended for all tenants. If a building has yet to be submetered, a tenant-installed submeter should be placed on the tenant's floor and appropriate lease language should be developed to provide the tenant with a pay-as-you-go electric utilization policy.

Elevator Buttons. There was a period of time between 1960 and 1970 when "soft-touch" elevator buttons were considered desirable design features. "Soft-touch" elevator buttons are designed to respond to the slightest heat of an approaching finger, which seemed at the time to be a great convenience over the spring-loaded mechanical buttons that preceded this invention.

However, it was quickly discovered that, in a fire emergency situation, all elevators are attracted to the floor with the fire, and many lives have been lost because elevator passengers found themselves stranded on the floor where the fire emergency had occurred.

All tenants are encouraged to request that their landlords remove these soft-touch elevator buttons as a condition of the lease.

Elevator Capacity and Elevator Service. These design determinations are critical both during the peak periods of the morning and evening and during the business day, when multifloor tenants are likely to use the elevators to travel between their various floors.

The building's elevator consultant can provide a calculation of the interval of waiting time during peak periods. This calculation requires an analysis of cab size and capacity, speed of travel (in feet per minute), the number of floors of travel, the floor-to-floor dimensions (in feet), and the number of expected passengers, based on an assumed occupancy of the building.

For a quality office facility, the goal should be an interval of approximately 18 to 24 seconds waiting time during peak periods.

Once the programming has been completed, it will be possible for the tenant to advise the building's elevator consultant of actual occupancy loading per floor, which will help to verify the elevator interval and to establish the effect of a multifloor tenant's employees' use of the elevators for floor-to-floor travel in off-peak hours.

Elevator systems can be adjusted prior to occupancy, if a lead tenant provides design criteria to the landlord or developer in time. Owner/users can clearly have a system engineered to meet their precise requirements.

Elevator Fire Safety. All elevators must return to the ground floor in the event of a fire emergency. This is accomplished by a preprogrammed feature in the elevator control system and a backup generator that allows the elevator motors to function in the event of a blackout. In addition to these automatic controls, a modern elevator fire safety system must include annunciators between the elevator cabs and the central alarm station. In the best design solution, a video camera should observe each elevator cab interior and a rotating monitor control station should be built into a central alarm station staffed 24 hours per day by building security personnel.

Ergonomics. The science of biotechnology, as it is applied to office facility planning and design, forms the basis for the various dimensions and configurations that are recommended. Ergonomics has been defined in a variety of ways, depending on its usage. Physiologists, human factors engineers, product designers, health insurance agencies, and life safety standards codes and ordinances all have varying definitions of the term. Simply stated, ergonomics is the fit and measure of the human body to its environment—how well the human body fits and functions with furniture, equipment, machines, and the overall physical environment. (See Figure 3.18.)

Most modern office configurations do not fit within pre-1960s office buildings because the 72-inch dimension for computer support workstations has replaced the earlier 60-inch desk width common for typewriter usage. For example, a unit of five desks, each 60 inches wide, would easily fit in a 1960s office facility built with columns 28 feet on center; only four workstations will fit at the new 72-inch width. To achieve a layout of five workstations in a row, the columns must be set at no less than 32 feet, which is the minimum column bay recommended for a modern office building.

Ergonomics is critical to productivity enhancements, often the major impetus for an office relocation.

The emergence of ergonomics in the office environment can be dated back to January 1, 1976, when West German employers became legally obligated to replace all office chairs with chairs that met new federal life-safety regulations. Failure to comply would result in the cancellation of all health insurance coverage for employees by the German equivalent of Blue Cross/Blue Shield.

Since 1976, German office furniture and equipment manufacturers have embraced ergonomics as the mainstay of all new product engineering and production and have taken the lead in new product design. Northern European competitors for the Euromarket were quick to follow suit, and U.S. contract office furniture and equipment manufacturers also responded to these new ideas.

The thrust of this discussion is the cost-effective design of the office environment, but it is relevant to compare the pre-1976 American automobile industry with its Italian, German, and Japanese competitors. Clearly, ergonomic factors induced many consumers to change their buying habits, to the detriment of the American designed and manufactured products.

It is not uncommon to experience a strong "sticker shock" reaction from clients, when recommending a more costly ergonomic-feature package over the reuse of antiquated existing furniture and equipment or the purchase of new equipment with fewer ergonomic features. This reaction does not seem to be a stylistic or design resistance but simply one of economics. In the United States, the propensity to consider ergonomics as a prime criterion for purchasing one product over another has increased manyfold in recent years, but there is still resistance in some corporate quarters to paying more for ergonomic furniture, equipment, and overall office environments.

Orgatechnik, the German office furniture trade fair, traditionally introduces new products that have been designed to further enhance ergonomics and life safety in the modern office facility. Some of these products are refinements of ergonomic and human factors engineering; others represent completely new ideas and concepts. Based on these new offerings, designs for today's ergonomic office might include any or all of the following features and products:

1. Entry security systems designed to guard against intrusion by allowing only one individual at a time to pass through a portal and then only after a voice, touch, video, dip card, proximity card, or coded number pad access device has been activated.

2. Clear signage and graphics programs providing a variety of locational information, including

FIGURE 3.18

Office Ergonomics and Life Safety Features

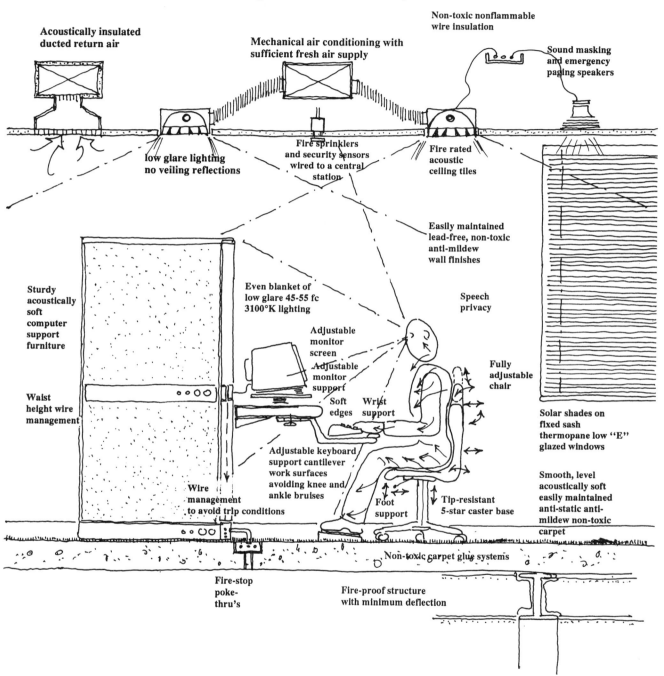

directions to maneuver within the facility, messages pertaining to the location of and paths to fire exits, and various other life-safety, informational, and motivational message systems. These signage systems may appear in the form of print, rolling light emitting diode (LED) panels, or video and video projection techniques, and frequently employ international symbology to communicate across language barriers and to assist blind and handicapped individuals.

3. Advanced fire, smoke, panic, and security monitors, including sprinkler systems, next-generation Halon® fire suppressor systems for electronic environments, central station controls, annunciator panels with automatic police and fire department dialers, sequencing multistation video monitors, motion sensors, "bug" sensors, and other electronic eavesdropping sensors and controls.

4. Office and workstation locking devices that can be operated by the handicapped and by arthritic individuals who are unable to turn knobs; various keying and electronic locking systems that can be easily reprogrammed when an employee resigns or relocates from the office or workstation.

5. Exterior facade glazing materials that are bulletproof, bomb-proof, and shatter-proof, and are treated or tinted with antiglare and thermal protection coatings to reduce eye strain and energy consumption.

6. A revolutionary new glazing product that can be used both on the exterior facade and on office and workstation partitions. Using liquid crystal technology, the glazing can be charged or uncharged to black out glass panels for visual privacy or permit views indoors or out.

7. Various wire distribution systems for electric current, voice, data, television, computer, and other wiring requirements. These new wiring systems can be installed within the floor slab, within raised (or depressed) access floor units, and within factory-made cavity walls and ceilings. Other available systems allow instant disconnect/reconnect and constant monitoring of faults in the wiring path(s).

8. Carpet products with permanent antistatic features well below the levels that damage a computer tape or diskette or induce a static shock. These carpet tiles enhance wearability by introducing antifungus, antimildew, and instant clean-up fibers. Their backings and glue systems are non-PVC-based, which is highly desirable because PVC has been shown to produce toxic chemicals during a smoldering fire and because initially PVC leaches out noxious gases into the office environment, which has been described as a cause of the "sick building" phenomenon.

9. Ceiling products that absorb acoustic vibration and sounds, providing speech privacy from room to room or workstation to workstation; sound-masking products that introduce white noise into the office environment to drown out voices and further enhance speech privacy.

10. HVAC equipment that is silent, effective, and easy to control, and provides the moisture, the antifungus and antibacteria agents, and the increased fresh air changes needed to respond to the "sick buildings" issue; electronic controls that monitor performance at critical points in the overall office environment and automatically adjust supply to changing demand while reducing overall energy consumption.

11. Ambient lighting with new light sources, engineered to provide higher overall quantities of light with more accurate qualities and color temperatures. Luminaires are currently available that allow one fluorescent tube to replace two or three tubes in one fixture, thus reducing overall energy consumption and providing the glare-proof overall blanket of illumination required for the modern video display tube and PC environment.

12. Lighting controls that sense the presence of occupants and turn the lights on and off as required, and that modulate the staging of lights within the entire facility to avoid spikes or peaks that increase demand meter readings and overall utility costs. Other controls turn off lights at night while providing just enough light for housekeeping functions, and offer battery back-up lighting for emergencies and constant monitoring of the electronic controls.

13. Office and workstation furniture with soft, rounded surfaces and convenient waist-high troughs that manage workstation and peripheral equipment-to-equipment wiring. Recently introduced C-shaped legs for tables and desks help reduce trip conditions and bruised ankles, typically experienced at the lower portions of more traditional double-pedestal desks; glide feet and other features allow for easy movement. Table tops that tilt and can be raised and lowered to adjust to

users' needs; drawer units that stop and do not pull out all the way; furniture edges that are soft and warm to the touch; surfaces that are non-glare and cannot be scratched; details designed to avoid catching one's fingers or clothes; and similar features that create fully adjustable office and workstation furniture are also available.

14. Office seating providing for new articulations below the seat's center of gravity, thus offering a full range of motion while seated and the ability to constantly adjust that range of motion throughout the day; seating designs that support the small of the back and the upper shoulders and offer adjustable arm rests, adjustable heel rests, tip-resistant five- and six-star caster bases with constant height adjustments and with electronic sensors that store the various settings and return to an adjusted setting on command; seating that offers upholstery selections that avoid the "hot seat" phenomenon; flame-resistant upholstery techniques; plastic materials that prevent the off-gassing problems of earlier plastic materials; finishes that are soft and do not damage the surrounding office furniture or its occupant(s); and a myriad of other "patent-pending" features.

15. Office filing systems for hard copy, which use graphic indicators, such as color and form, to avoid visual difficulty in reading tabs; filing that automatically retrieves file folders or larger case files; systems that present files to the viewer at a 45° angle, thus allowing easier file recognition and less eyestrain; file cabinets that are safer and quieter to operate and can be automatically locked up at night.

16. Computer terminals that have, along with ergonomic functions noted earlier, articulated keyboards, finger-reach keyboard systems, smaller front-to-back VDT tubes incorporating flat screen technology, faster access time, less dwell time, simplified software, and peripheral equipment that offers the user more productivity, less stress of failure, less typing, quieter laser printers, easier automatic tape backups, and central LAN control.

17. Safer tape and diskette storage equipment and retrieval systems with less cumbersome fire-proof storage facilities, including the new 3-inch diskette, higher density tape backups, and much larger core memories and hard disks, all of which ease the risk avoidance and security procedures of relocating tapes and other electronic records in the modern office.

18. No-smoking policies; smoke eater ashtrays for those who must smoke, and point-of-use smoke control and personal HVAC units.

19. On-site food service, either cafeteria-style or in full-service vending equipment, with automatic dip card debiting for no-cash-required payment.

20. True 100 percent handicapped accessibility everywhere.

21. Telephone systems with comprehensive features and instant learning curve capabilities; video phones and video teleconferencing as an affordable off-the-shelf product line; data systems, from the now imperative FAX transmission systems to related communications improvements such as the vastly improved LANs and PBXs; double-redundant equipment packages to avoid down time and monitor glitches.

22. Improved fire retardant interior finishes; factory-made interior partitioning and storage wall elements that divide space and serve the storage and filing needs of the occupants; office partitions offering quick assembly and disassembly; door systems and other instant office systems with snap-together integrals, wiring troughs, and harnesses.

23. Senior executive and conference room furniture and equipment that offer conservative styling while supporting computer, communications, and audiovisual equipment in an ergonomic manner; related lounge and soft seating manufactured from fire-resistant materials.

As is evidenced by this vast array of product offerings, the process of improving office furniture and equipment products is evolutionary. Although some of these items are not yet currently in the mainstream of the American office facility market, most are readily available. With the availability of these ergonomic office products, the true challenge for today's office planners and designers is to promote these products' benefits and encourage their use within today's office environment. Undoubtedly, the continuing education of corporate America as to the benefits of working within an ergonomically "sound" office environment is required; of equal importance is consultation as to lost productivity and the potential employee hazards if ergonomics is ignored.

Floor-to-Ceiling Height. The floor-to-ceiling height is developed by the layering effect of the various elements located in the space between the hung ceiling and the floor above. (See Figure 3.19.)

FIGURE 3.19

Typical Office Furniture Systems Panel with Power, Communications, and Data "Power-in" Feed (Served by Three-Septum Cellular Floor Dock System)

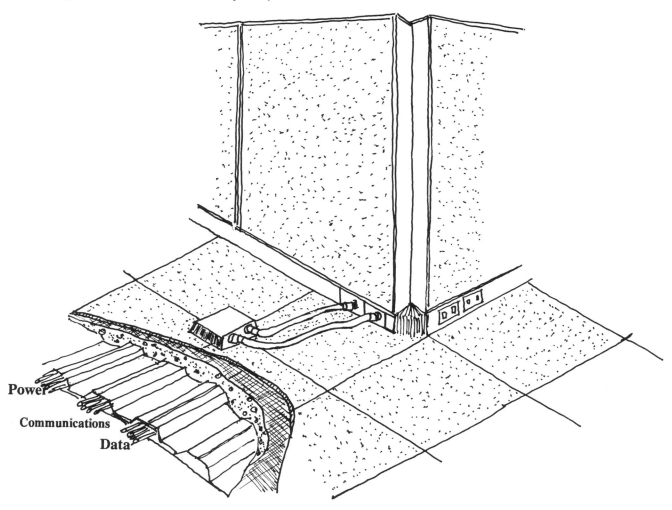

As described in Chapter 4, these elements typically include:

- The finished slab of the floor above
- Structural members supporting the floor
- Wireways and poke-throughs for the tenant of the floor above
- Wireways for the subject tenant
- The duct system and various ceiling-plenum-mounted HVAC equipment
- Sprinkler piping and sprinkler heads
- Telephone wireways
- Data wireways

- Sound-masking wireways and speakers
- Fire and emergency wireways and related sensors and other devices
- Ceiling support elements
- Ceiling tile elements
- Ceiling-mounted lighting fixtures

These elements can be layered within the plenum or overlapped and compressed within a limited amount of space. Precisely how these elements are laid out vertically within the plenum affects the amount of space that will be required from the finished floor above to the ceiling.

In general, it is desirable that larger expanses of floor area and special-use rooms within a given office facility be provided with higher ceiling heights than the traditional 8 ft.-0 in. minimum ceiling height.

A review of the base building ceiling-plenum design and engineering features will reveal to the tenant the typical ceiling height available within the base building standard, and areas where ceiling height options might be created by relocating ductwork and other plenum-mounted elements to the side(s) of areas where the higher ceiling heights are desirable.

Floor-to-Floor Height. Architects use this term to measure the dimension from one structural finished floor to the finished floor of the floor above (see Figure 3.20). This dimension helps to determine the cost of the base building structure and shell, but does not necessarily determine the floor-to-ceiling height, which will be of greater interest to tenants.

Floor Sizes. In office towers, floor sizes vary within the same building, in usable square feet and, frequently, in core-to-glass dimensions. In the lower portions of a typical office tower, the full complement of elevators is present in the core; on the upper floors, only the high-rise and service elevators are present. An office tower that maintains the same shell configuration from the first floor to the penthouse floor will have more usable space in the top floors than in the lower floors.

In towers where the architect has varied the shell configuration from floor to floor, floor plates on lower floors may be larger than on higher floors, or other floor plates may vary from floor to floor.

On "crossover" floors, the usable square feet available may be substantially less than on other floors in the same building. Both high-rise and mid-rise elevators may be present; the stair towers may cross over within the core; or air intake equipment, fan rooms, or other mechanical features may be present. These added base building impediments may substantially affect the ability to cost effectively plan certain floors in an otherwise efficient office tower.

The tenant's program of space requirements will determine the best floor plate to house those requirements. As an aside to their program criteria, many smaller tenants will seek out a building with a smaller floor plate so that they can enjoy the prestige of occupying an entire floor in a smaller office tower rather than being perceived as a small user by renting a partial floor of a larger office tower.

A large office facility tenant's program of space requirements may best be served by a combination of large and small floor plates. For instance, a bank or insurance company may require a large floor plate for the operational aspects of the program while desiring smaller floor plates for the senior executive suite. Frequently, large banking and insurance company office towers are designed with larger floors at the base of the building and smaller floors above. In addition, there may be a requirement for a very large floor plate of central filing and back-of-the-house functions placed at a below-grade or concourse level.

Planning efficiency may not be the only determinant of floor plate size and configuration. Many owner/users in urban centers seek to enjoy the marketing and image benefits of occupying the tallest tower in the community. Within a given zoning envelope of available gross floor area for a particular site, one of the options is to go higher while reducing each of the tower's floor plates. This option is frequently not cost-effective in regard to the inside-out design concepts, but the perceived marketing and image benefits to the owner/user may outweigh all other design and planning considerations.

Prior to selecting a specific office tower or a particular floor or suite of floors in the tower, tenants are well advised to test the vagaries of the particular floors being offered against other floors in the same building and other buildings seeking their tenancy.

Fluorescent Ambient Lighting. Since the energy crisis of the mid-1970s, fluorescent ambient lighting has become a major design determinant. In general, as more computer terminals have come into use at office desks and workstations, the need to avoid glare on these terminals has gained special concern. President Carter's edict on "corporate responsibility" resulted in lighting levels being lowered to less than 2.5 watts per square foot of energy usage for most office facilities.

The General Services Administration and many independent testing organizations have been studying the effects of lower levels of lighting on productivity since 1975. Their early findings were that buildings constructed between 1945 and 1970 were illuminated at levels exceeding 100 footcandles and were using more than 5 watts of electricity per square foot; only 5 footcandles of light were required to recognize individual faces and to read a newspaper without eyestrain.

Twenty-five to 30 footcandles is the range recommended for most casual and business conferences and meetings, with a reduction to 10 to 15 footcandles for taking notes during a slide presentation meeting. Thirty-five to 50 footcandles is the range

FIGURE 3.20

Typical Floor-to-Floor "Sandwich" of Structural, Mechanical, Electrical, and Fire Safety Features

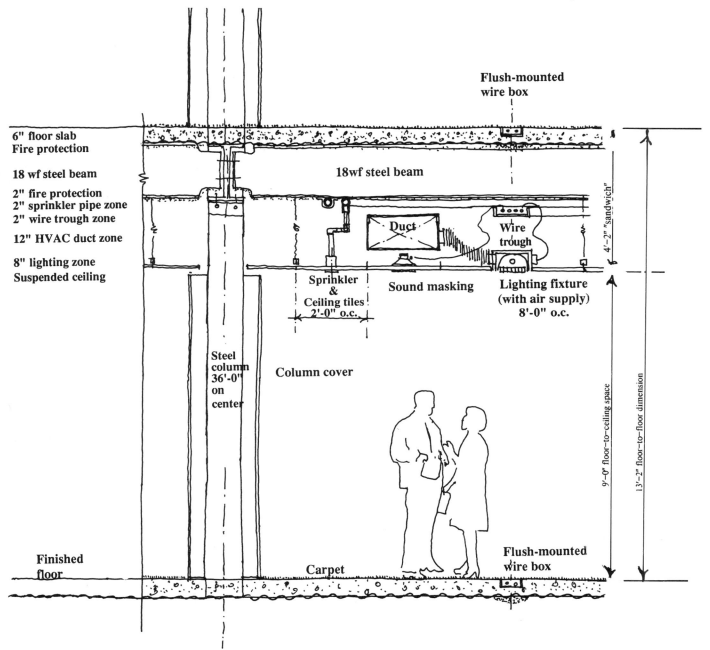

6" floor slab
Fire protection

18 wf steel beam

2" fire protection
2" sprinkler pipe zone
2" wire trough zone

12" HVAC duct zone

8" lighting zone
Suspended ceiling

Flush-mounted
wire box

18wf steel beam

Duct

Wire
trough

Sprinkler
&
Ceiling tiles
2'-0" o.c.

Sound masking

Lighting fixture
(with air supply)
8'-0" o.c.

Steel
column
36'-0"
on
center

Column cover

4'-2" "sandwich"

9'-0" floor-to-ceiling space

13'-2" floor-to-floor dimension

Finished
floor

Carpet

Flush-mounted
wire box

required for most office functions, including reference to text and spreadsheets while inputting data into a computer terminal. Individuals who perform accounting or drafting tasks and older employees who have myopia may require a level of illumination of 65 to 85 footcandles.

Technically, footcandles are expressed both as to the quantity of light and the quality of light. The qualitative aspects provide the basis for evaluating glare conditions. By reducing glare, a given quantity of light will appear to be easier on the eyes, allowing one to see more clearly, with less eyestrain.

Because one design goal is to lower overall electric consumption (and operating cost), glare should be reduced in order to provide the appropriate quantity of light for various office tasks while using the least amount of electrical energy.

To provide ample amounts of the illumination required for most office use and to maintain a glare-free working environment, illumination levels should be within the range of 50 to 60 footcandles, with energy consumption of less than 2 watts per square foot.

Ambient lighting elements should typically be located in the ceiling. Additional lighting, known as task lighting, may be located near the work surface(s) when and as required. Ambient lighting is a fixed infrastructural element; task lighting is placed according to the occupancy plan.

One appropriate location or modulation of ambient ceiling-mounted lighting is in a continuous line of single-tube fluorescent luminaires, either 6 ft.-0 in. on center for paper-intensive operations, or 8 ft.-0 in. on center for computer terminal-intensive operations.

With ceiling heights of 8 ft.-0 in. to 9 ft.-0 in., the 6-foot module will produce approximately 60 footcandles of evenly distributed lighting throughout the work area, while the 8-foot module will produce approximately 50 footcandles of evenly distributed light. (See Figure 3.21.)

The type and quality of the fluorescent fixtures (luminaires) and the color temperature and wiring systems of the fixtures are also critical design factors when using the above-recommended spacing.

Technically, low-brightness parabolic luminaires are recommended, with 11 to 15 2-inch to 3-inch baffles per 4-foot section, and single-tube Octron® or generic T8 fluorescent tubes burning at 3100° Kelvin on 277-volt circuits wired with plug-together modular wiring harnesses.

Tenants who require synthetic north light, and who work with advertising and print color reproductions or have other color-sensitive specialized working conditions, should employ a twin-lamp ambient lighting fixture offering a 3100° Kelvin light source for typical ambient lighting requirements and a second tube burning at 5000° Kelvin, during periods of the day when color-control work is in progress.

The installation of 5000° Kelvin lighting as the only ambient light source is not recommended because the blue cast to this synthetic light source reduces contrast, causes eye fatigue, and turns flesh tones and all of the interior finishes an unpleasant blue color.

Initial Deflection. The bounce or sag that occurs as soon as a structure is loaded with its own weight exists in all modern buildings and causes the floor slab to be uneven. While the floor may appear to be even to the eye, actually it has hills and valleys caused by deflection. These flooring variations may require evening-out, to locate office doors or workstations over a long expanse. Situations may occur in which the adjustment potential of office furniture glide feet or filing cabinets is simply not enough to compensate for the initial deflection. It may be impossible to preorder office doors cut to size at the factory, because the gap between the underside of the door and the floor might vary from a negative 2 inches to a positive 2 inches (the desired undercut is approximately ½ inch to ¾ inch).

Where the initial deflection is too great, the entire floor slab must be patched using flash patching, a process that is costly to achieve and is usually recommended so late in the construction process that delays in carpet and furniture installation typically occur.

For these reasons, the base building architects, engineers, and contractors should be consulted on the issue of initial deflection, and standards for initial deflection should be established and written into lead tenants' leases and all owner/user construction contracts.

Interdepartmental Circulation. An allocation of circulation paths and patterns is made between blocks of offices and workstations, and typically demarcates the various departments within an organization.

Interior Fit-Out Costs and Expenses. Exact amounts are difficult to specify, because costs vary from region to region, from urban centers to suburbs, and from year to year. Frequently, the costs to fit out a tenant's office facility will be included

FIGURE 3.21

Comparison of Footcandle Levels Provided by Continuous Rows of Single-Tube (T8) 3100K Fluorescent Fixtures Spaced on 8'-0" and 6'-0" Center Lines

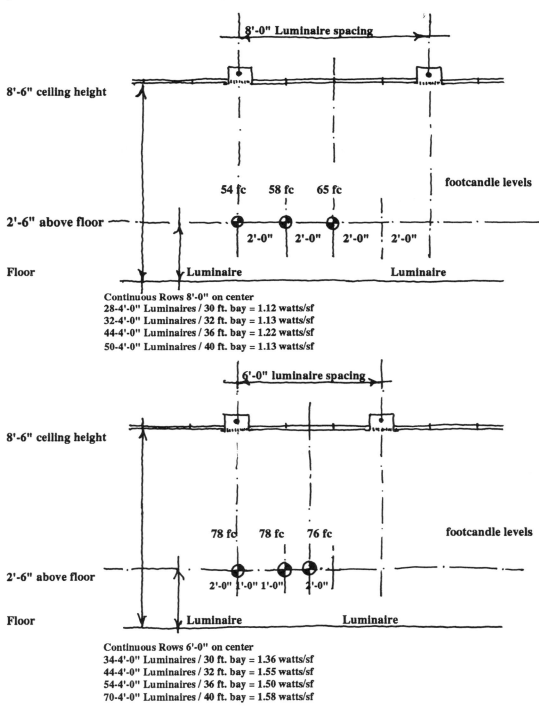

Continuous Rows 8'-0" on center
28-4'-0" Luminaires / 30 ft. bay = 1.12 watts/sf
32-4'-0" Luminaires / 32 ft. bay = 1.13 watts/sf
44-4'-0" Luminaires / 36 ft. bay = 1.22 watts/sf
50-4'-0" Luminaires / 40 ft. bay = 1.13 watts/sf

Continuous Rows 6'-0" on center
34-4'-0" Luminaires / 30 ft. bay = 1.36 watts/sf
44-4'-0" Luminaires / 32 ft. bay = 1.55 watts/sf
54-4'-0" Luminaires / 36 ft. bay = 1.50 watts/sf
70-4'-0" Luminaires / 40 ft. bay = 1.58 watts/sf

within the landlord's or developer's lease proposal on a "build-to-suit" basis. In other forms of lease negotiations, the landlord or developer may provide an assortment of products and features as a base building tenant's standard fit-out program. Typically, the program specifies the quantity of items available for the tenant's fit-out (i.e., within the 10,000 square feet of space, the tenant can install 6 outlets, 10 doors, and 45 fluorescent fixtures.) This method of defining the scope of the landlord's tenant fit-out obligations is known as a "workletter." In recent years, landlords and developers have begun to negotiate with larger tenants on a dollar-allowance basis: the parties agree to a certain dollar amount for tenant fit-out. The tenant is then assured that the developer or landlord will spend this sum to pay for improvements made using tenant-managed architects, contractors, and suppliers.

An alternate form of the dollar-allowance agreement positions the developer as the contractor or contract manager. In this scenario, the suppliers and subcontractors report directly to the developer, and the tenant's architect or design professionals report directly to the tenant.

Because the landlord's workletter or dollar allowance is frequently provided within the base building's mortgage financing, developers are reluctant to allow tenants to use these funds to purchase personal property that will not survive the term of the lease. For this reason, furniture, office equipment, certain finishes and materials, accessories, and other interior decor items are typically excluded from the workletter, dollar allowance, or other fit-out funding programs provided by the developer. These items are paid for directly by the tenant.

In lease agreements where the landlord or developer is managing the construction process, fixed asset items may be excluded from the construction agreement which otherwise requires a mark-up on costs for the construction management process. Frequently, these management fees add 20 to 25 percent to the actual invoice cost for certain goods and services such as carpeting, track lighting, movable partitioning and storage systems, kitchen appliances, and similar items that are delivered and installed by special subcontractors after the tenant construction process is completed.

This mark-up on actual costs is described using at least four terms, as follows:

1. *General conditions.* All of the overhead costs of administering and managing a construction project. These may include permits; insurance; demolition; clean-up; work safety and security; blueprints; temporary light, heat, and power; hourly fees for project managers and foremen, etc. Frequently, general conditions add 10 to 15 percent to the costs of the actual subcontractor's and supplier's invoices.

2. *Fees.* Direct payments to the contractor or construction manager for services rendered; may be either a dollar amount or a percentage of the individual costs and expenses associated with the project. Fees range from a few percentage points to as much as 10 to 15 percent of construction costs, depending on the scope of work covered by the fee agreement.

3. *Profit.* The mark-up on costs typical of certain types of construction agreements. Profit percentages range from a few percentage points to as much as 10 to 15 percent of the total costs of a project.

4. *Overhead.* Similar to the charges described above under "general conditions."

A tenant who decides to exclude certain "almost fixed" assets from the purview of the construction contract can save substantial costs, but the onus of managing the various subcontractors falls then on the tenant. However, many tenants have in place the purchasing teams required to manage these miscellaneous tenant fit-out purchases, and most tenant architects and design professionals offer these services to tenants who are unable to manage these purchases themselves.

The actual tenant fit-out costs and expenses for a typical office facility project are frequently presented using a "CSI [Construction Specifications Institute] format." (Readers who have copies of the Sweet's catalogs may be aware that the numbers from 1 to 16 on the covers of these catalogs correspond to the CSI format.)

The CSI sections are as follows:

1. General data
2. Site work
3. Concrete
4. Masonry
5. Metals
6. Wood and plastics
7. Thermal and moisture protection
8. Doors and windows
9. Finishes
10. Specialties

11. Equipment
12. Furnishings
13. Special construction
14. Conveying systems
15. Mechanical
16. Electrical.

A clear understanding of all project-related costs should be achieved prior to lease confirmation. One process for attaining a high degree of preliminary budget accuracy is called the "workbook approach." Marginal sketches and catalog photo presentations are prepared, to show each feature desired by a particular tenant. Preliminary tenant plans and documents are also provided, to indicate the likely location of each feature. A line-item budget is then prepared, listing each of these features according to the CSI format. The features illustrated on the plan are calculated and measured, and alternate features are offered which may be useful to test other available options. The line-item budget is then prepared, based on this "workbook."

The "workbook" process requires approximately four to five weeks from project initiation, depending on the degree of accuracy required by the tenant and on how many alternate features are to be reviewed. Implementation of this "workbook" approach prior to lease confirmation is strongly recommended for tenant project budgeting and for confirmation of the costs associated with the tenant fit-out.

Intradepartmental Circulation. An allocation of circulation paths and patterns is made between departments and the common spaces within the facility, such as core elements, elevator foyers and lobbies, reception and conference areas, coat closets, lunch areas, and toilets. This circulation includes the required means of egress to the fire stairs.

Layering. Since the advent of computer-aided drafting (CAD), architects, engineers, interior designers, and other project team professionals have begun to look at a building as a series of layers superimposed one over another. The CAD process drafts one layer at a time and then superimposes the various layers on top of each other within the computer or blueprinting machine. The completed (composite) drawings are then published, as required, for the various building trades to use during construction. (See Figure 3.22.)

As an example, the lighting fixtures, sprinklers, fire exit signs, and duct diffusers are all located on the ceiling plane. Each of these elements is installed by a different trade, and four separate contract documents could be published for bidding or construction use. Layering allows all four "layers" to be published together as one plan for general design review.

Because most architects and project team members use similar CAD systems, various professionals can design simultaneously within their area of specialization, at their own offices or design studios. Later, their efforts can be combined for design reviews, project presentation to the client, and construction documentation for bidding and building. This combining can occur electronically, if a layering system of drafting and overall modular design development is employed.

These layers should be separated from each other in vertical space. Workers can then construct the building using the same simultaneous methods that the design professionals used during the building's design phases.

For example, the space between 9 ft.-0 in. and 9 ft.-3 in. above the finished floor might be relegated to the sprinkler piping; the space from 9 ft.-3 in. to 9 ft.-6 in. might be relegated to the telephone and data wiring conduits and connection junction boxes. By establishing this physical layering, both trades could build at the same time without fear that one would negatively impact or otherwise conflict with the work of the other. Moreover, future additions and deletions can occur to either system without concern for subsequent conflicts in these overlapping but layered systems.

Although many of a building's systems are physically flexible, it is good design and construction practice to layer each element and to consider each as if it were fixed in three-dimensional space. CAD systems make such design efforts easier to achieve.

Length of Travel to Fire Exits. This distance becomes a critical planning factor, if the floor plate of any particular floor of an office facility exceeds 30,000 square feet.

Most building codes state that the maximum length of travel to any fire exit shall not exceed 300 feet for an office building with a fire suppression (sprinkler) system. Figure 3.23 gives an example.

Office partitions and workstation configurations could elongate the length of travel by their "maze" effect. It is necessary, therefore, to carefully study office facilities with larger floor plates, in order to position the fire exit stairs within this 300-feet rule.

Linear Feet of Window Wall. The number of linear feet varies substantially from one building configuration to another. Larger floor plates do

FIGURE 3.22

Concept of CAD Layering

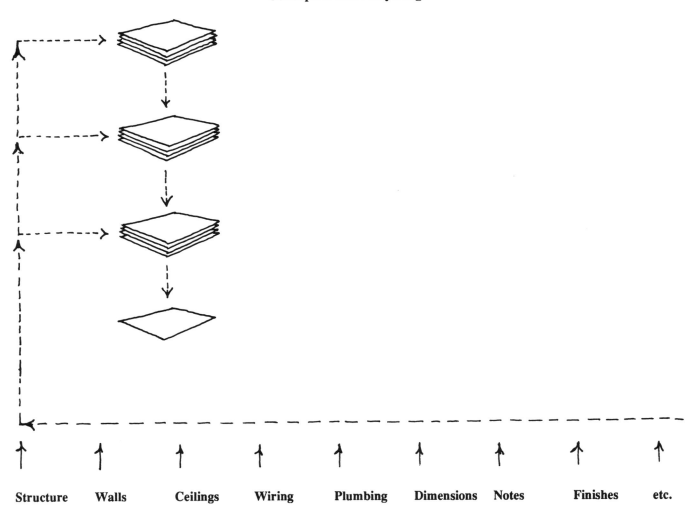

| Structure | Walls | Ceilings | Wiring | Plumbing | Dimensions | Notes | Finishes | etc. |

Each layer of information within the CAD database contains finite features (by combining layers into a composite plot and print, the "full picture" is published)

not necessarily mean more available window wall, as shown in Figure 3.24. An office tower of 25,000 square feet gross floor area could measure as follows, with the resulting amounts of window wall:

Width (Feet)	Length (Feet)	Window Wall (Linear Feet)
158	158	632
120	208	656
100	250	700
96	260	712

By employing "bites" or "re-entrant corners," additional window wall can be added to an otherwise rectangular office tower. As noted earlier, a central atrium will also add substantially more window wall to an office building.

Facilities planners are typically pressured to add more private offices at the window wall and to devote all available window wall to private-office occupants. Little, if any, window wall is available for the open plan workstation occupants to enjoy.

FIGURE 3.23

Distance to Required Means of Exit

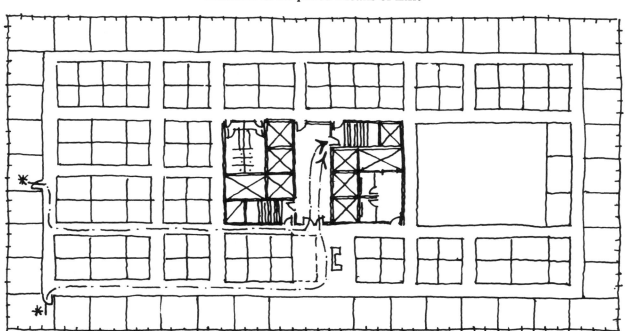

Illustration of code-required test of maximum travel route to fire exits stairs (for sprinklered buildings the maximum permitted travel distance is 300 feet). In this example 21,000 sq. ft. tenant floor, the maximum travel distance is 150 feet.

FIGURE 3.24

Four Floor Plates of Equal Gross Area, with Varied Linear Feet of Window Wall

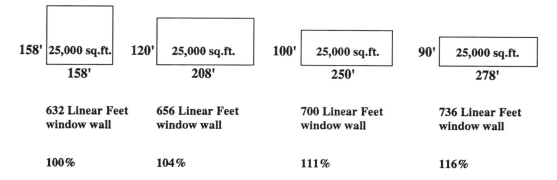

158' 25,000 sq.ft.	120' 25,000 sq.ft.	100' 25,000 sq.ft.	90' 25,000 sq.ft.
158'	208'	250'	278'
632 Linear Feet window wall	656 Linear Feet window wall	700 Linear Feet window wall	736 Linear Feet window wall
100%	104%	111%	116%

It is recommended that certain areas of the window wall be devoted exclusively for the use of the open plan workstation occupants, with the proviso that any glare conditions arising from the daylight at the window wall be managed with effective solar control. One method to achieve this goal is to develop a shell condition that prevents offices from being located along that particular portion of the window wall. Using this method, the subsequent pressure to place offices at this location is eliminated.

Tenants and owner/user developers are well advised to review available window wall and consider the overall shell configuration.

Live Load Deflection. Although this type of bounce and sag is typically not a problem with modern buildings. A tenant who is reviewing an adaptive reuse office facility, especially one built at the turn of the century, may find that the live load deflection is so pronounced that computer-intensive office activities will suffer from the constant bounce of the floor. Moreover, in such buildings, libraries and file rooms should not be concentrated over any one area of the building. They will need to be planned in a linear fashion, along a column and beam line.

Mail Distribution Systems. To send mail and interoffice memos from floor to floor and from receiving docks to various mail distribution points, lead tenants or owner/users frequently use mail distribution systems that reduce floor-to-floor elevator loads during off-peak hours. Mail distribution systems—such as electronically controlled horizontal conveyors and parcel delivery "dumb" waiters; electronically addressed robotic conveyance vertical systems; rolling mail carts guided along an electronic pathway; and the earlier pneumatic tube mail and message delivery systems—also avoid the use of clumsy mail carts, which detract from the otherwise businesslike experience of a modern elevator cab and can damage the cab interiors.

Mechanical Systems. A variety of engineering applications can provide the required quality, quantity, and velocity of acclimatized air and ventilation to the necessary locations, according to the occupancy plan of the facility.

Mechanical systems have no finite module or dimensions, other than the earlier design imperative that mechanical fittings, grills, diffusers, and sensors be located on a center of tile relationship. However, three major considerations require a coordinated design effort:

1. The duct system, above the ceiling or below the access floor, should travel in a reasonably uninterrupted path both horizontally and vertically. Sharp bends or jogs to avoid an obstruction created by another infrastructural or structural element may cause air turbulence, which will result in constriction of the flow of air. This, in turn, will reduce the efficiency of the system and cause the objectionable noise of rushing air.

2. A modular approach to the air supply is highly desired so that the flow of air will be evenly balanced throughout the space. Rushing-air noise and/or hot or cold areas indicate a lack of system balance. An evenly balanced air conditioning system with duct/diffuser noise levels below 35 decibels is critical to effective use and occupancy and to future flexibility. The tenant should be able to replan the space in the future without the need for revisions to the basic duct distribution systems or infrastructure of the facility.

3. Fresh air changes designed into the mechanical system have become increasingly critical to good mechanical design standards, as buildings have become tighter and more energy-efficient. In buildings with double-glazing and fully insulated skin and roof designs, there is little if any leakage of outside air into the facility. If the mechanical system is designed to limit the availability of fresh air throughout the system (a typical characteristic of post-energy-crisis, mid-1970s designs), the same air is circulating throughout the facility day in and day out. This may result in a condition described as the "sick building syndrome," which is further exacerbated during initial move-in by glues, solvents, plastic finishes, upholstery, and paints that leach their potentially toxic odors and chemicals into the environment. A 15 to 20 percent fresh air formula should be present for most office environments; as much as a 30 percent formula should be effected during the initial postoccupancy period. It is also beneficial to operate the mechanical system for at least 30 days prior to the installation of any carpeting or furniture. Approximately 30 days are required to dry out the newly constructed office facility to the point where the interior furnishings can be installed without fear that their hygroscopic textiles will become permanently damaged by the mixture of construction dust, debris, and moisture.

It is critical to the overall design effort of the proposed facility that the mechanical systems be engineered to correspond to the occupancy plan. In particular, special spaces requiring atypical mechanical ventilation or higher ceiling heights should be identified and appropriately located and engineered early in the design development process. If these early steps are not taken, the mechanical system may interfere with the intended use of the facility, rather than complement and support that intended use.

Multifloor Tenants. These tenants may require special consideration, whether in a high-rise office tower or in an owner/user low-rise office facility. Two principal circulation elements may require structural modifications to the base building; tenant monumental or utility stairways connecting floors, and tenant mail distribution systems, which may include dumbwaiters or other mechanical mail conveyance equipment.

In addition to structural considerations, if more than three sequential floors are to be connected by a stairway or opening, the section of the building code relating to atria should be given careful attention. Fire hazards, principally related to the smokestack effect of more than three sequential floors of stair wall or atrium, require smoke evacuation systems and additional sprinkler locations.

Generally, tenant stairways for high-rise towers must be limited to no more than three sequential floors. Where more than three floors are to be connected, two separate stairways are typically provided, each with its own fire and smoke envelope.

Multitenanted Floors. Special consideration is needed for these floors, because of the required means of exit (see Core Design Recommendations). The common corridors between tenant spaces and the core must reach the fire stairs. The corridors must be designed to avoid a dead-end corridor condition.

Careful core design and planning are required to meet the needs of the fire exit code while devoting the least amount of space to these nonhabitable

FIGURE 3.25

Typical Office/Workstation Panel Heights

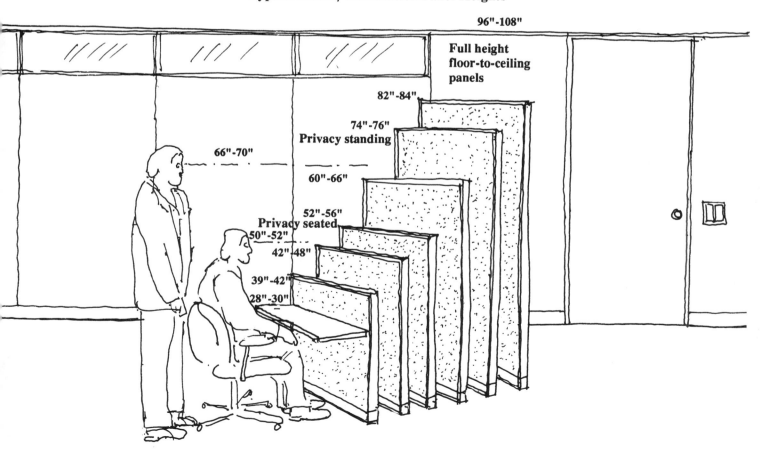

functions. Moreover, corridors typically reduce the effective core-to-glass dimensions, which may impact overall planning efficiencies of the remaining office space from corridor wall to window wall.

The width of the common corridor, when subtracted from the core-to-glass dimension of the base building, may render the net core-to-window-wall dimension so small that effective tenant planning of offices, workstations, and tenant circulation patterns cannot be accommodated with any degree of planning efficiency.

For this reason, certain office facilities with wider core-to-glass dimensions will be more suitable than others for multitenanted floors.

Owner/user developers who plan to sublease certain office areas should consider the effects of the core-to-glass dimension(s), both with and without the common corridor requirement, for means of egress by the subtenant(s).

Office and Workstation Circulation. Access space is needed directly adjacent to each office or workstation of the individual employees of the company. For ease of accounting, the space program includes fifty percent of the typical aisle width when calculating the square feet occupied by that office or workstation.

Office, Workstation, and Circulation Dimensions. The size and configuration of offices and workstations have a wide latitude. The set of decisions related to these critical elements should precede the design of the office facilities core and shell. (See Figure 3.25.)

For this reason, the interior designer should ideally be hired by the tenant or the owner/user prior to initiating schematic design efforts for the new facility.

Partitions. Office partitions may be located and fixed to a screw spline ceiling system at any place along a 2-foot module line or at any line perpendicular to the 2-foot module line. Partition locations placed either on the ceiling grid module line or on the center line between module lines offer the most efficient and structurally sound relationship. (See Figure 3.26.)

Private Offices. Typical widths for small private offices are 10 feet and 12 feet. Private offices are frequently planned along the window wall of the office building. American architects often design these window walls with either 5 feet or 4 feet between the vertical mullions framing the window glass. Because thermal action and overall esthetics discourage the physical connection of office partitions directly to

window glass, architects and space planners limit the location of office partitions to these window wall mullion partitions. The 10-foot width is usually employed when the architect uses a 5-foot window wall modulation; the 12-foot office width is used when the architect employs a 4-foot window wall modulation. (See Figure 3.27.)

The front-to-back ergonomic dimension of the smallest office measures approximately 11 ft.-4 in. and allows for a standard credenza, the occupant's chair space, a desk, and a visitor's chair space.

When possible, office layouts with 4-foot window wall modulations are preferred. In this plan, office occupants' space is positioned perpendicular to the window wall, allowing daylight to fall over the occupants' shoulders onto the reading matter on their desks, and permitting both the office occupants and their visitors to enjoy the exterior view.

In a 5-foot window wall modulation, the 10-foot office width forces occupants to sit with their backs to the window wall. This is less desirable because the occupants must work in their own shadows from the window and are prevented from enjoying the view.

Moreover, the occupants are backlit by the window wall and visitors must frequently squint when meeting with the occupants.

From both energy conservation and interior space planning points of view, the 12-foot office width is preferred for low-rise suburban office facilities and owner/user headquarters. When considering the many structural factors of an urban high-rise office tower, the typical 10-foot office width is still the most prevalent and the most cost-effective.

Programming. Architects and interior designers use this term to account for the current and future requirements of people, places, and items that will establish the guidelines for the interior space planning effort to follow. (Chapter 1 gives a detailed discussion of the programming process.)

To support modern computer usage, the typical array of offices and workstations requires units of varied sizes. Most workstations start at approximately 72 inches wide and they are between 6 and 12 feet long. Larger workstations are 96 inches wide, with various lengths. These dimensions have been generated by the office furniture industry, based upon collective studies of the people and equipment required to conduct modern office procedures.

Re-Entrant Corners. This design feature can be detailed to provide a continuation of the structural, ceiling, and window wall module at the corners, but

FIGURE 3.26

Typical Interior Fit-Out Panel Partition and Door Types

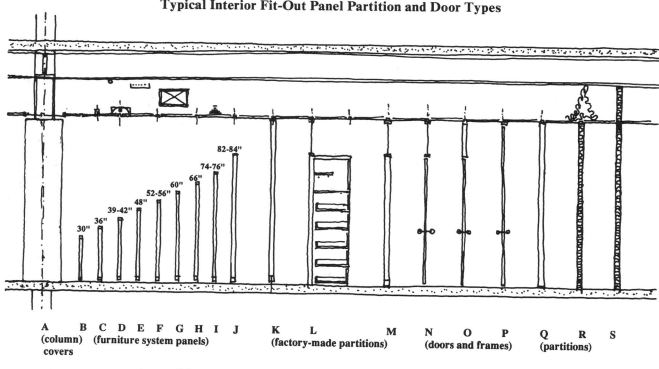

A - Column cover
B - J - Office workstation panels
K - Full height factory-made demountable partition
L - Storage wall with transom above
M - Partition with transom above
N - Door with transom above
O - Door with transom panel above
P - Full height door
Q - Full height partition
R - Acoustically insulated full height partition
S - Fire rated and acoustically insulated floor to underside of slab partition

it may thwart the interior designer's efforts to establish these modular relationships.

Screw Spline Ceiling Grids. This type of 2-foot ceiling grid is preferred for operations and headquarters facilities designs, because it not only carries the ceiling tiles but also provides a convenient and dimensionally rational method for attaching and supporting the tops of office partitions. (See Figure 3.28.) The screw spline ceiling support system is designed to accept from the partition a screw connection that will fix the head of the partition to the ceiling. This connection can later be removed and relocated, without damage to either the partition or the ceiling system.

Security. Any modern office facility must deal with the building's security. Many tenants and owner/

users have specific security needs that must be built into their office facility. Some are easy to accommodate; others involve more documentation. Fire safes, data security areas, file rooms, and library installations, which have fire and intrusion security specifications and other space planning requirements for special security, will need documentation and design development subsequent to the programming and date-gathering phase of the project. Early attention to security requirements will lower overall project costs by allowing security features to be built into the base building.

Overall building security is much more difficult to accomplish if the base building has been built with a complex plan or section. The more linear and direct the building's access and egress paths, the easier they are to monitor and secure. Nooks and crannies,

FIGURE 3.27

Typical Dimensions for Management Offices and Secretarial Workstations Within 4′-0″ and 5′-0″ Window Mullion Module Office

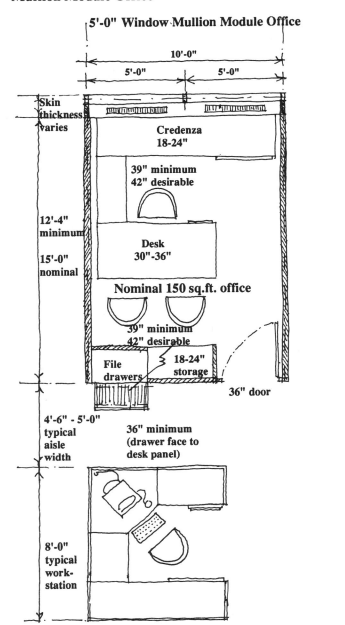

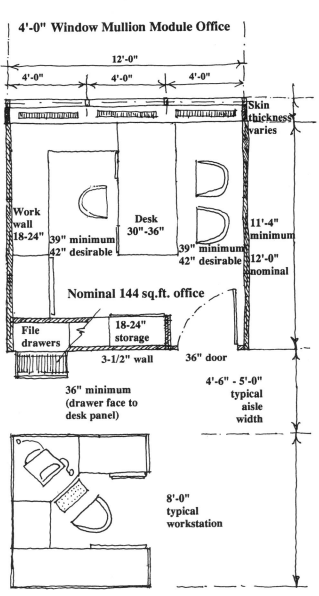

FIGURE 3.28

Fixing Demountable Partition to Ceiling Grid

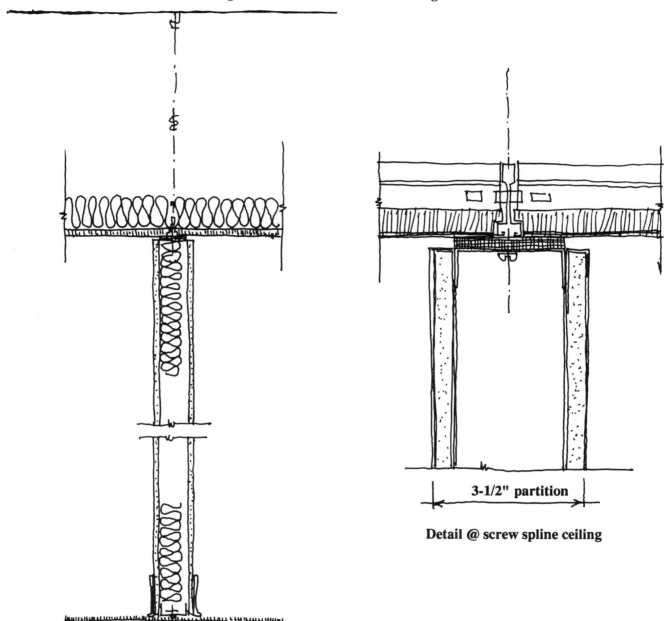

3-1/2" partition

Detail @ screw spline ceiling

dead-end spaces, and blind alleys can encourage theft or violence. Nondirect circulation paths should be avoided or properly monitored as part of the base building design development.

Sick Building Syndrome. This term is being used in the press to describe the unhealthy effect certain buildings are having on some of their occupants. The court system is reviewing many cases of claims of cause and effect for a variety of occupational health hazards and personal injuries. Pending cases will undoubtedly soon produce legal decisions that are likely to generate revisions to federal, state, and municipal health and occupational health standards and related building codes.

Prior to the energy crisis of the mid-1970s, many buildings lacked the full complement of insulation, twin or triple glazing, and energy conservation features that automatically limit the amount of fresh air coming into an otherwise closed-loop HVAC system. Operable windows and tenant-controlled dampers or ventilation grilles have all but been eliminated from modern office buildings, in an effort to improve energy conservation. In fact, many local and state building codes require these extremely "tight" and well-insulated building construction techniques.

While these conservation measures were being demanded by the building code, the furniture, carpet, and interior finishings industry continued to employ more plastic materials for office facilities. Almost every desk in a modern office facility has some type of plastic-housed computer terminal, telephone, or other piece of office equipment.

Many municipalities and corporations have tried to limit cigarette smoking by law, code, or corporate directive, but smoking is still common in the modern office.

The combination of an extremely tight, energy-efficient HVAC system, a growing quantity of plastic interior finishes, many plastic-housed office machines, and several individuals who still smoke at their workplace tends to yield a stuffy and, perhaps, unhealthy working environment.

One likely result of revised building codes and trade practices will be to increase the amount of fresh air introduced into the mechanical HVAC systems, thus increasing energy consumption as a cost for improving the health and occupational safety of the building's occupants.

Until these issues are resolved and codified, all parties to the office facility design and construction process are well advised to document their design decisions with a clear understanding that the state of the art is progressing quickly on this subject. Wherever possible, they are advised to provide for alternate means of increasing the fresh air entering the otherwise closed HVAC systems. Energy conservation guidelines may soon be relaxed, in an effort to reduce the sick building syndrome and the resulting legal claims.

Sound Masking. A recently developed audio system, employed in ceiling design, generates a type of noise known as "white noise," which masks or drowns out the audible portion of human speech and produces "speech privacy."

Too often, with the sole use of acoustic isolation techniques, small leaks occur that transmit clearly the sounds of one's neighbor. The concept of speech privacy does not try to eradicate sounds. Its goals are simply to eliminate specific sounds and to allow neighbors to conduct their individual business without interrupting the work of others. By using an electrical/mechanical speaker device, the vagaries of office ceiling and partition construction can be accepted while still providing the desired result of speech privacy.

Sound-masking speakers are typically placed on 15-foot center lines and tuned individually to provide the level of speech privacy required.

Where speech privacy is critical, a blanket of acoustic material is specified above the partition line from the ceiling to the underside of the slab above. Often, a more absorbent or more reflective ceiling tile will also be used for that particular area.

Sprinklers. To meet fire codes, sprinklers must form a module of no more than 15 feet on center in both directions. Each room must have at least one sprinkler head. Based on these requirements, the most efficient sprinkler system would be 15 × 15 ft., with partitions located on the half-module and a sprinkler head in the center of each room.

Storage Wall. A storage wall is a system of filing cupboards, storage elements, and office doorways, designed to be factory manufactured and assembled later on the project site.

These storage elements serve a dual purpose: they provide the necessary storage, and they serve as the partitioning system between offices and open office workstation areas, as shown in Figure 3.29.

The storage elements can be located for use by the office occupant, the open office workstation area, or

FIGURE 3.29

Storage Elements Employed to Create Demountable Storage Wall/Work Wall/Partition Wall Office Partition System

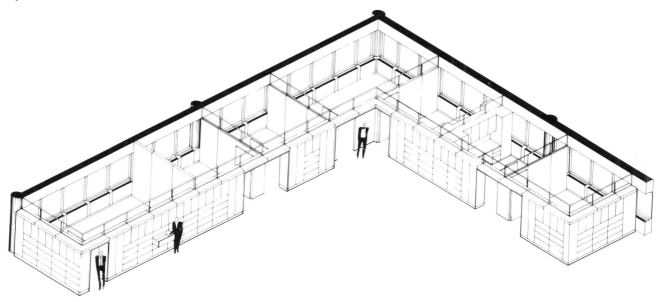

both. They can be relocated and fitted out with alternate filing and storage components, as required over the life of the project, and later removed and relocated to the next office facility.

The tax possibilities of depreciating a personally owned storage wall system at a quicker rate than other fixed asset elements of the office facility should be discussed with a knowledgeable accounting firm.

The major benefit of storage wall is that it offers appreciable savings in circulation patterns and consequently in square feet required. (The circulation path between the offices and the workstation areas of the facility usually serves as the access space for the files and storage elements.) In a typical facility, approximately 16 square feet of space can be saved per person by using the storage wall concept.

Storage wall costs more than an equivalent capacity of partitions, doors and frames, freestanding file cabinets, file rooms, and storage areas, but the substantial space saved more than compensates for the additional cost.

Storage wall is typically 2 ft.-0 in. deep and is located under the standard 2-foot ceiling grid, to accommodate a clerestory detail.

Structural Considerations. The base building is rarely a subject of design review, beyond the above-noted issues related to column bay sizes and core-to-glass dimensions. The actual structural integrity of the base building, because it is regulated by the building code, is usually not an issue for review. Only one structural issue substantially impacts on a facilities fit-out: the issue of deflection. (See *Deflection.*)

Structural Elements. As noted earlier, the core of most office buildings forms the basis for certain structural elements—stairs and elevators, and the wind bracing or sheer bracing that assists in making the building resistant to lateral forces of wind or earth tremors. The structure of the core does not typically affect the space planning effort, because the structural elements are within the core and are not exposed within the tenant's space.

The shell of the building includes other structural elements—columns and, for especially tall office towers, some form of lateral wind bracing, or other diagonal elements that may impact the loss factor (reduced usable space because of structural needs). A structure's location in an inconvenient place may affect the space planning. The overall number of offices or workstations possible in a particular building may be reduced.

Structural elements placed near the window wall may obstruct views. Some offices may then be more or less desirable and problems of hierarchy within the tenant organization may result.

Lateral bracing elements at the shell may prevent an otherwise usable office from being located in that specific area. If the window has been blocked by the structure, appropriate furnishings may not be usable.

A subtler effect occurs if the rhythm of the structure at the shell does not correspond to the other rhythms or "modules" within the space, such as structural elements, elements of the building shell, or commonly established building planning modules.

If the structure is sized and modulated solely on the basis of a structural and economic calculation by the structural engineer, the resulting structural module may not correspond to the other building and interior modules. The result will be an inefficient interior plan that will yield lower density and will increase the "costs per employee housed."

If offices, for instance, need to be 10 feet wide at the window wall, and the structural engineer determines

FIGURE 3.30

Structural and Window Mullion Modules

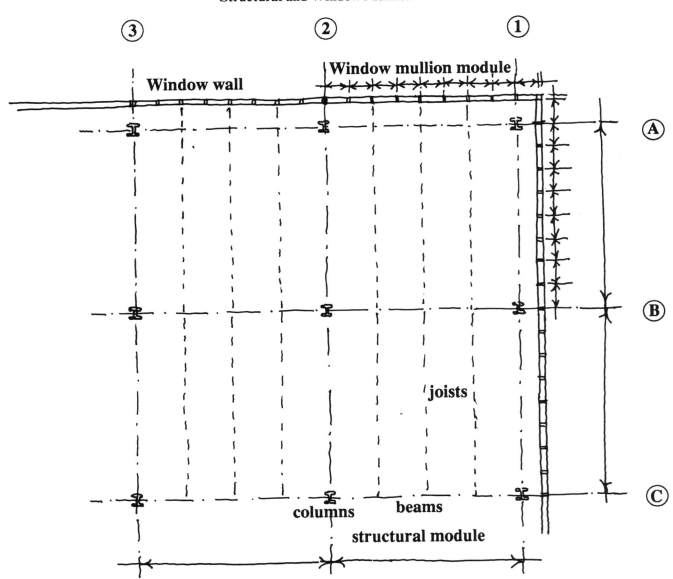

that the structural bay is least costly at 24 feet on center, every third office will have a column in the middle of its window wall. (See Figure 3.30.)

If these columns are large, 12-foot offices may be (resulting in a 20 percent waste of space) or some other compromise may have to be effected, to ensure that the third office can be furnished for its occupants' work tasks.

The compromise of a 30-foot structural bay would be easier to plan from the inside but might cost more to construct.

The calculation of the structural cost premium for the 30-foot module versus the density loss arising from the 24-foot module will establish the most accurate and cost-effective decision. (More than the cost of the steel or concrete structural elements will be evaluated.)

For certain types of buildings, principally those with substantial dimensions from the core walls to the shell walls (usually found in low-rise suburban office facilities), the architect and structural engineer will need to locate intermediate columns between the core and the shell.

The modulation of these intermediate columns becomes a critical determinant of the building's interior planning density. One must look at both the module that is parallel to the structural elements at the window wall and at the dimension from the core and window wall structural elements. The sum of office and workstation dimensions and circulation aisle widths must generate the structural bay dimension; otherwise, a column will disrupt a workstation

or aisle location, or prevent an efficient rhythm of aisles and workstations, which substantially reduces overall planning efficiencies. (See Figure 3.31.)

Inefficiencies result if incorrect compromises among architectural, structural, and interior planning requirements are not taken into account.

Of particular importance in low-rise suburban buildings may be the varied structural requirements of offices versus parking.

Frequently, parking, which has structural module requirements quite different from those of office space, is introduced below the building. To allow one element of a building's construction economic formula (such as parking) to become problematic to another element in the equation will likely produce a less efficient building overall and higher costs per employee housed.

Telephone and Data. Wiring for these facilities is required at convenient locations near each office desk and workstation work area, and throughout the office area, according to the occupancy plan.

Toilet Fixture. The necessary quantity becomes a critical element in the design of any core, if the base building architect has no knowledge of the tenants' use of the space. In addition to satisfying the ratio of men to women, and handicapped persons' requirements, certain floors may require special considerations. Some areas may be occupied by senior executives who desire higher quality toilet facilities; other floors may be heavily populated with

FIGURE 3.31

Core-to-Glass Dimension

| Office Space Core-to-Glass Dimension | Core | Office Space Core-to-Glass Dimension |

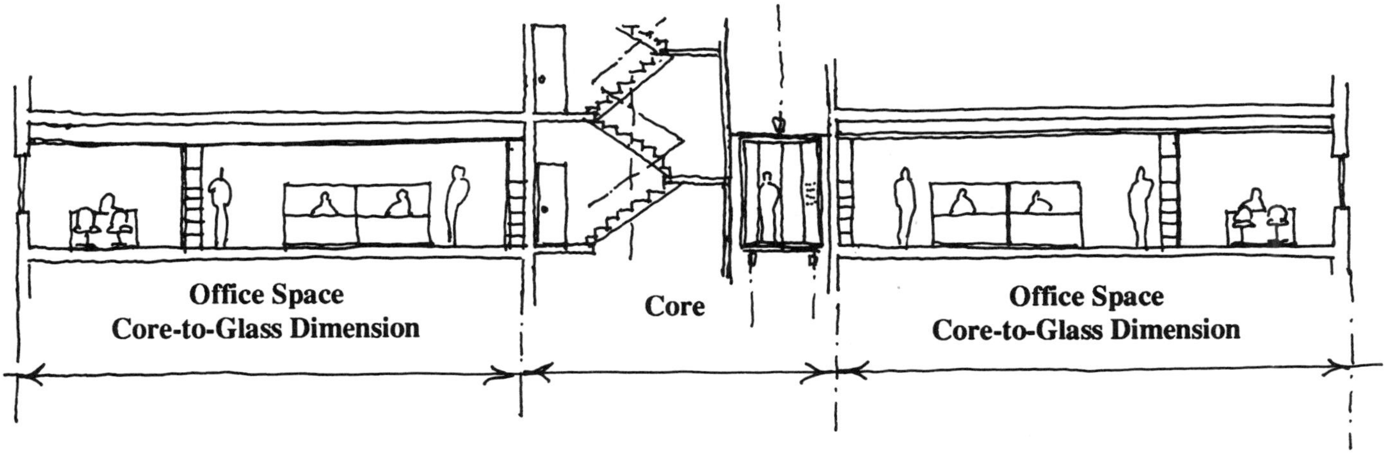

operational employees and a standard fixture count may be overloaded.

In general, the building code assumes an even ratio of men to women and provides for most tenants' requirements, but an evaluation of toilet fixture requirements should be undertaken soon after the programming process, which will produce the stacking of employees on each floor of the facility.

Twenty-Four-Hour Air Conditioning Systems. Many professional firms and key areas of other companies (telephone and computer areas, boardrooms, and private pantry kitchens) now need this service.

Without air conditioning, the use of office facilities with inoperable windows becomes nearly impossible during nonnormal business hours. Few evenings and weekends have average outdoor temperatures within the 65° to 75°F comfort range.

Ventilation alone will provide the required interior climate for the other days and evenings of the year, and air circulating over the fan coils that still carry refrigerated water after hours can provide comfort for an hour or so in the evenings.

During other times, the tenant will want to call upon the building's chillers to provide additional air conditioning.

It may be possible to plan a tenant's space so that the need for after-hours air conditioning is relegated to certain floors or to areas on a specific floor. This would minimize the after-hours air conditioning charges the landlord can bill back on a per-hour basis.

Some tenants (and many owner/users) will want to install their own air conditioning chillers for special spaces, for 24-hour use, or for auxiliary requirements of certain areas of their facility.

Under the building code, it is not possible to exhaust compressor air into the space between the ceiling and the slab above (the plenum). Most building inspectors will accept a few such conditions in a large project for a back-up system, but not for a continuously operating air conditioning system.

Accordingly, if a tenant requires its own auxiliary equipment for computer spaces, large conference rooms, and so on, it will also require a ducted air supply from the window wall or the top of the building. Both of these potential sources for fresh air are very difficult to achieve in an already constructed building.

Most tenants will need to negotiate after-hours air conditioning with the landlord. Their agreements should include a metered system of verification.

Typical Office and Workstation Dimensions. The dimension from the building's core to its shell or glass line should be at least 32 feet for a 4-foot window wall modulation building, or at least 35 feet for a 5-foot window wall modulation building. Preferred minimums are 36 feet and 40 feet, to allow for demountable partitions or a cost-effective storage wall concept. (See Figure 3.32.)

When considering a wider core-to-glass dimension for a suburban operations facility, these minimum dimensions would be increased in increments of 17 feet for either the 4- or 5-foot window modulation buildings.

Window Wall Design. A critical factor in achieving a lower level of illumination while avoiding glare, window wall design necessitates lowering the light transmitted from outside the building's window wall to approximately the level of the inside illumination.

Daylight on a north facade on a clear day registers approximately 275 footcandles on a light meter; direct sunlight registers 10 times that amount.

Architects typically employ tinted Thermopane® (glazed mirrored surfaces) to reduce the intrusion of daylight and direct sunlight and to lower the glare and solar heat gain inside the office area. Window treatments such as miniblinds, vertical blinds, draperies, or fixed solar shades are used to further reduce the intrusion of light to below the level of the ambient lighting provided for the office facility.

If the amount of light coming in through the windows is allowed to exceed the 50 to 60 footcandles of the interior illumination, glare will result. Increasing the level of interior illumination will increase energy usage above the corporate responsibility level of 2.5 watts per square foot and will require a pro rata increase in air conditioning to overcome the additional solar load and interior lighting levels. Adding 1 watt per square foot of lighting to overcome approximately 20 more footcandles of light transmission will cost approximately $1.25 per square foot per year in additional energy costs of operations (lighting plus the resulting additional air conditioning).

Solar-controlled window walls are modulated at either 4 ft.-0 in. or, more typically, 5 ft.-0 in. in width, with mullions between the window panels or panes. The mullions offer structure to the glazing and a convenient location to affix the partitions that typically demise one office from another.

With solar-control glazing, interior designers cannot locate partitions up to the glass, because the line

FIGURE 3.32

Efficient Core-to-Glass Dimensions (with Double-Loaded Corridors)

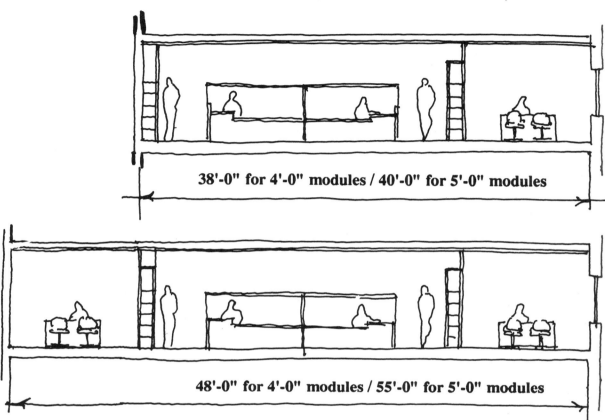

38'-0" for 4'-0" modules / 40'-0" for 5'-0" modules

48'-0" for 4'-0" modules / 55'-0" for 5'-0" modules

of a partition will cast a heat sink line into the glass and, under certain conditions, the glass will shatter. Accordingly, all partitions perpendicular to the shell of the building will be located coincidental to the modulation of the window wall.

The disadvantages of solar-control glazing are: an ongoing perception that the outside is dull and hazy, and an inability to provide a large, uninterrupted expanse of glass suitable for special spaces in typical office installations (i.e., the boardroom, major presentation or reception spaces, or the lunchroom).

In custom designed headquarters, these special spaces may be treated with customized window wall shell designs, or located on the north facade where solar control is not as critical, or otherwise provided with special design details. In general, in high-rise buildings, all elements of the window wall are consistent throughout the building's shell.

Wiring. A major design element of any office facility is its wiring. By code, the wires that carry 120- to 125-volt current must be in separate wireways from wires that carry low-voltage current for telephone, data, and signal wires. (See Figure 3.33.) Unions representing the telecommunications workers also prefer that telephone wires travel in wireways that are separate from the data and signal wires. Thus, three separate wireways or "septums" are typical: one for line voltage wires, one for telephone wires, and one for data wires. (See Figure 3.34.)

If wires are in a conduit, the wires themselves can be insulated with normal PVC (although this specification has become a major issue in recent fire cases). Wires that may be managed, or otherwise travel throughout the space between the ceiling and the underside of the floor slab above, must by code be either in a conduit or, if telephone or data wires,

FIGURE 3.33

Flush-Mounted Floor Wire Service Box, Engineered to Support Two or Three Workstations with Power, Communications, and Data Wiring

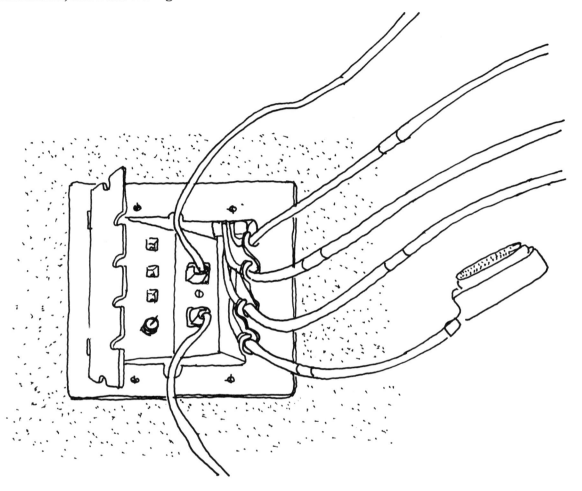

insulated with Teflon® and run in the ceiling chase space.

When the wires reach their destination, they must be managed within a junction box fixed to the architecture and tied off and connected with the appropriate plugs, amphenols, or connectors. The computers, telephones, and appliances (task lights and other office machines) are plugged in from the junction box.

In most speculative office buildings, the wiring travels in the ceiling and then down a column cover or partition to the base, where the appliances and equipment are plugged into junction boxes.

For facilities that have few walls and that use a substantial number of open office workstations, the wires may run down from the ceiling to a specified junction box and then to the workstations via a "flat wire" system (also using the three-septum concept). Flat wire installations are costly, are not fully accepted by facilities managers, and require the use of carpet tiles, because flat wire, by code, must be continuously accessible and, broadloom carpets would prohibit accessibility.

The usual alternative to flat wire installations is a poke-through system: the wires travel in the ceiling of the floor below, and penetrate the tenant's space, through the floor slab, at the location most appropriate to service the islands of workstations or equipment, as indicated in the tenant occupancy plan.

Certain concrete structural floor slabs and many turn-of-the-century masonry arch floor structures cannot structurally accept the poke-through method.

FIGURE 3.34

Three-Septum Wire Duct Floor Slab System

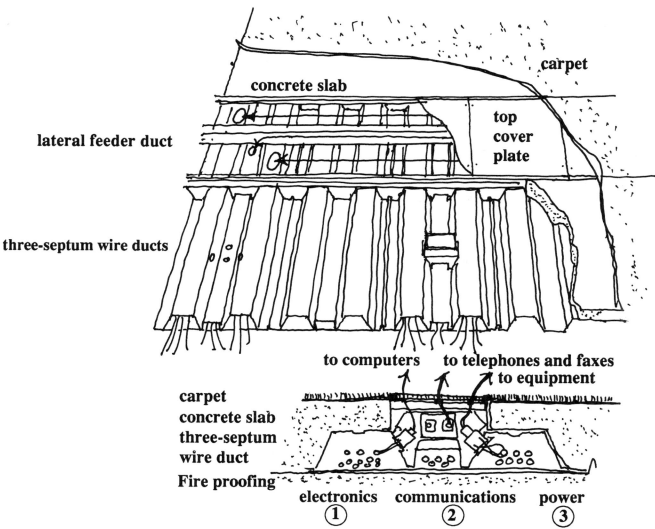

Poke-throughs are costly installations, and, if not done properly, they present a fire hazard from one floor to another. They are also difficult to install when the floor below is occupied, especially by a nonrelated tenant.

Poke-throughs will serve only one or two electric circuits at a time; each poke-through will serve only three to five workstations.

The ultimate architectural concept for wire distribution is within the slab itself. There are many competing systems, and each provides a three-septum wireway of steel within the floor slab. Some systems have access points "preset" on the floor slab, others offer a continuous trough of access along various lines across the floor slab, and others offer a matrix of access points throughout the floor slab.

Each of these architectural wire distribution methods is acceptable.

In some markets, "smart buildings" offer tenants the wireway features noted above, but in many cities these features have yet to become reality. Thus, most tenant facilities does not employ these methods, relying instead on a combination of poke-throughs, wires in walls and columns, and wires overhead in Teflon® and flat wire.

Access flooring systems, with wires distributed between the space of the raised floor and the concrete finished floor, are very practical wire distribution systems for major computer and machine-intensive office facilities. Access flooring has yet to prove cost-effective for either speculative office facilities programs or typical computer-intensive owner/user headquarters or operational facilities. The proliferation of local area networks (LANs) for personal computers (PCs) may prove access flooring's potential for cost savings.

Workstations. In most modern offices, the current ratio is approximately 30 percent private offices to 70 percent workstations.

A workstation can be any place an employee works, including a desk or office machine, but, more commonly, the term describes a series of horizontal work surfaces, vertical panels, and surrounding partition elements and storage components that can be assembled together to comprise an efficient workplace for an individual or group of individuals. Frequently, "office furniture systems" is used interchangeably with the term "workstations." Both terms indicate factory-made workplaces.

Interrelation of Elements

Individual elements of a typical office facility can be layered and designed to coordinate with the overall, inside-out, facility design goal of creating an efficient and cost-effective (using cost per employee housed criteria) office facility.

Each client's program of space requirements, project goals and objectives, image and esthetics, and other related project relocation opportunities and constraints will vary. Ultimately, the cost per employee housed should be used to test the results of each facilities design.

Through the diligent review and the layering of each of these elements, the most efficient and cost-effective facility will result within each individual project's goals, objectives, parameters, and constraints.

Individual Planning Elements

To allow the reader to test the concepts noted throughout this chapter, a series of critical planning dimensions has been prepared for the following construction and interior planning elements:

- Column grid
- Sprinkler grid
- Window mullion module
- Office and workstation planning
- Office and workstation planning with storage wall
- Ceiling grid
- Lighting grid.

By registering copies of the various sheets one on top of the other on a light table, it is possible to layer these various elements and to see how they relate to one another. For example, two basic best-case relationships are indicated in the cross sections: a 4-foot window wall modulation, with a 36-foot column grid and a 36-foot core-to-glass dimension; and a 5-foot window wall modulation, with a 30-foot column grid and a 40-foot core-to-glass dimension.

The reader should overlay copies of the following pages, to test various other options and combinations of the above-noted elements.

(Chapter 4 begins on page 167.)

BUILDING COLUMN GRID	CEILING GRID	LIGHTING GRID	SPRINKLER GRID
○ 28' 14WF/20"∅	○ 2'x2' GRID	○ 1x4 ON 6'℄	○ 14'x14' GRID
○ 30' 16WF/22"∅	○ 2'x4' GRID	○ 1x4 ON 8'℄	
○ 32' 16WF/22"∅			
○ 36' 18WF/24"∅			
○ 40' 24WF/24"∅			

BUILDING WINDOW MULLION MODULE	OFFICE & WORKSTATION LAYOUTS	OFFICE & WORKSTATION LAYOUTS W/ STORAGEWALL
○ 4' MULLION MODULE	○ 4' BUILDING MODULE	○ 4' BUILDING MODULE
○ 5' MULLION MODULE	○ 5' BUILDING MODULE	○ 5' BUILDING MODULE

MATCH LINE   1/16" = 1'-0"

BUILDING COLUMN GRID

● 28' 14WF/20"∅

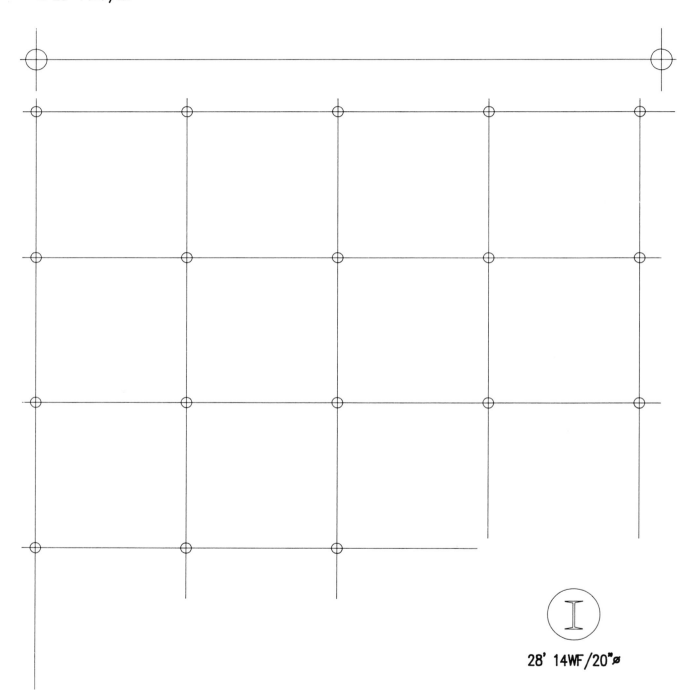

28' 14WF/20"∅

BUILDING COLUMN GRID
● 30' 16WF/22"∅

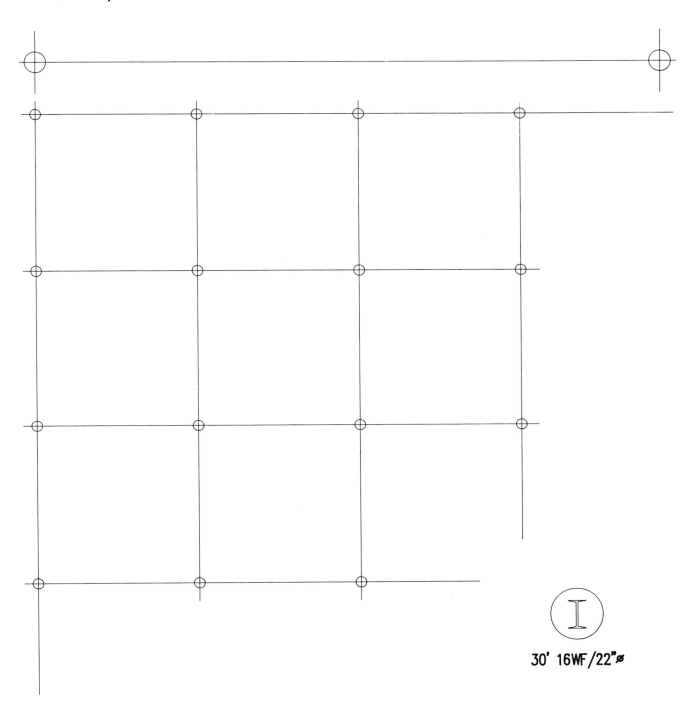

30' 16WF/22"∅

BUILDING COLUMN GRID

● 32' 16WF/22"⌀

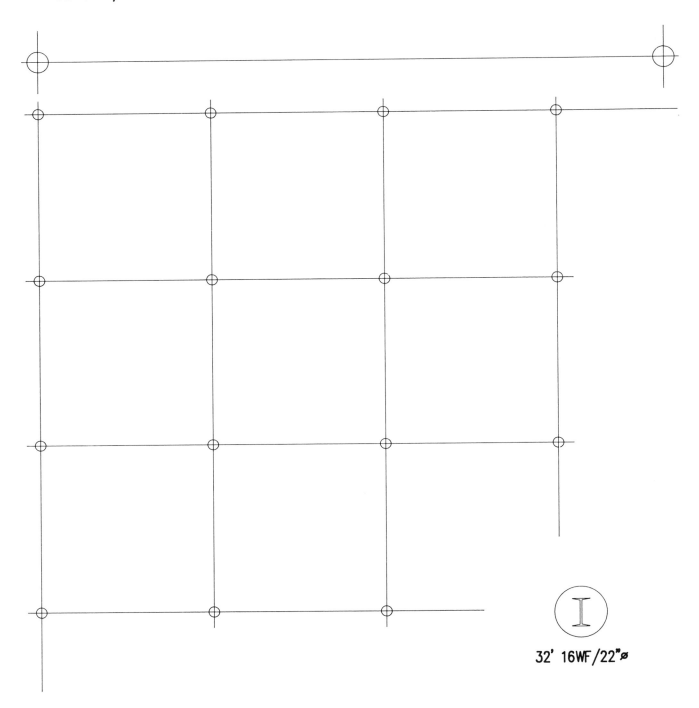

32' 16WF/22"⌀

BUILDING COLUMN GRID
● 36' 18WF/24"ø

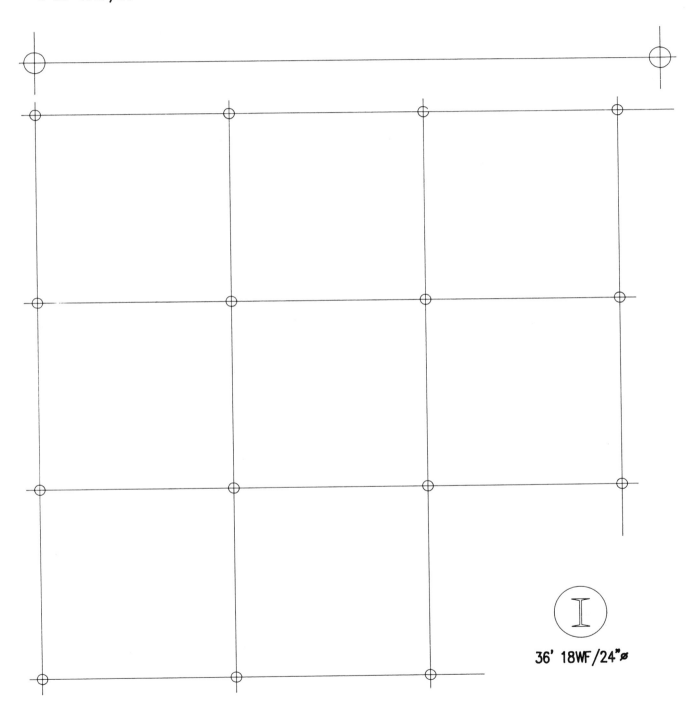

36' 18WF/24"ø

BUILDING COLUMN GRID
● 40' 24WF/24"⌀

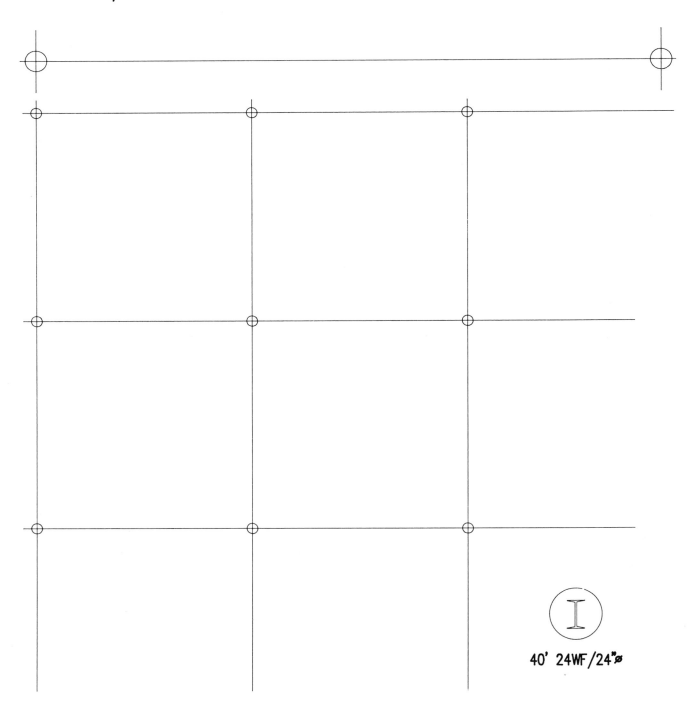

40' 24WF/24"⌀

BUILDING WINDOW
MULLION MODULE

● 4' MULLION MODULE

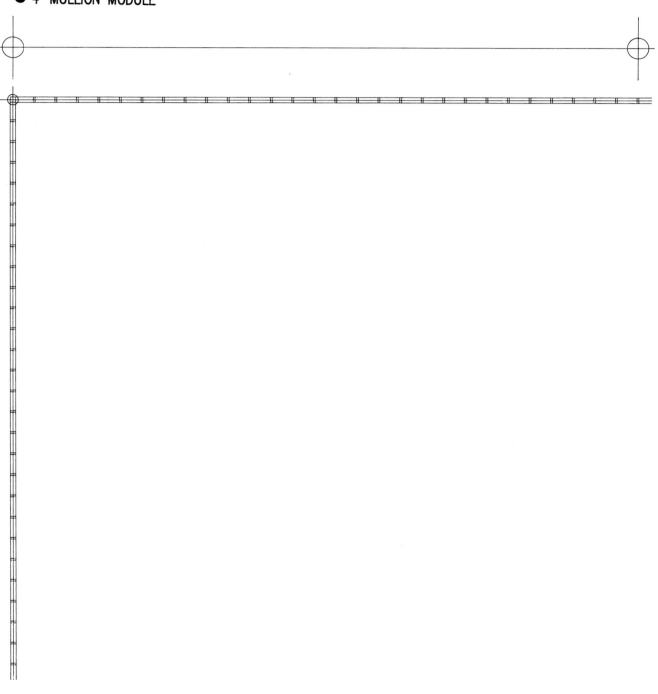

BUILDING WINDOW
MULLION MODULE

● 5' MULLION MODULE

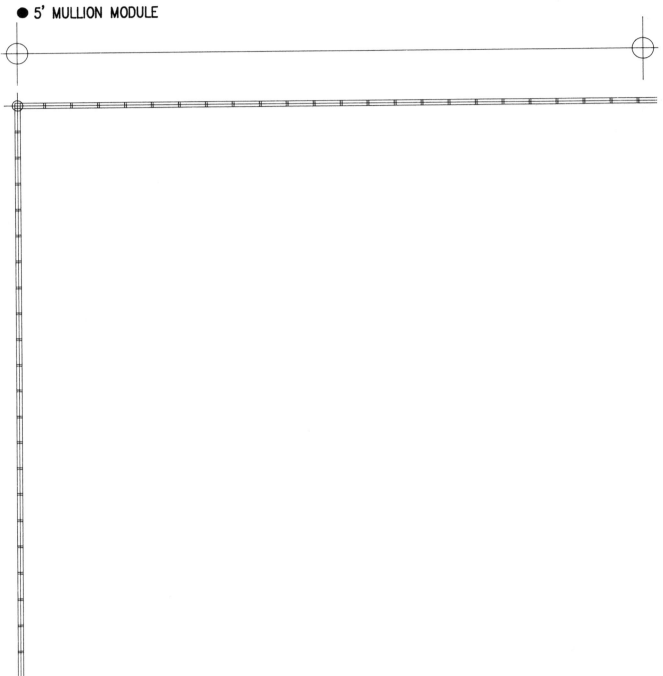

CEILING GRID
● 2'x2' GRID

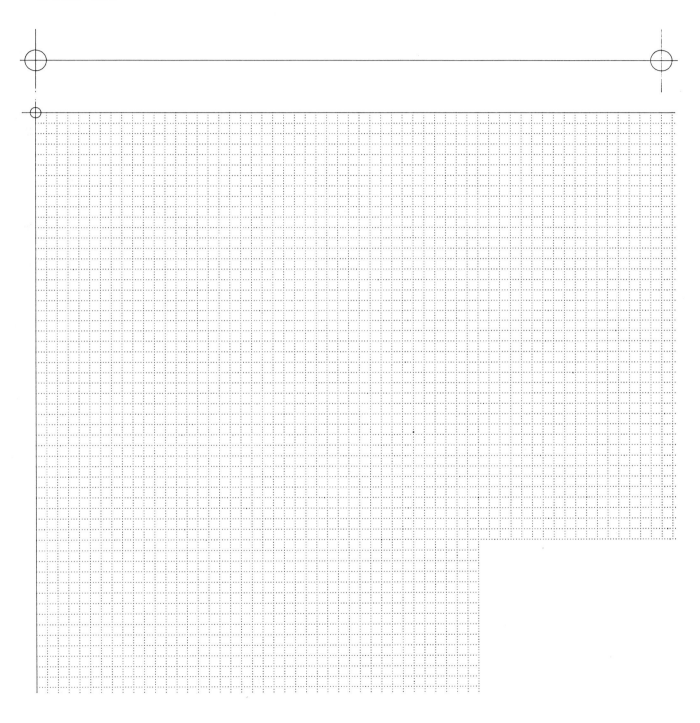

CEILING GRID
- ### 2'x4' GRID

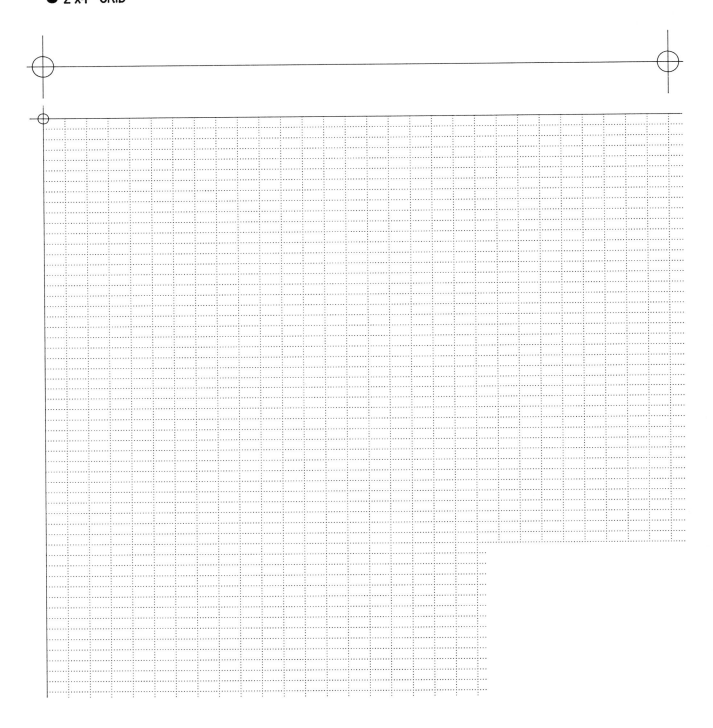

LIGHTING GRID

● 1x4 ON 6'℄

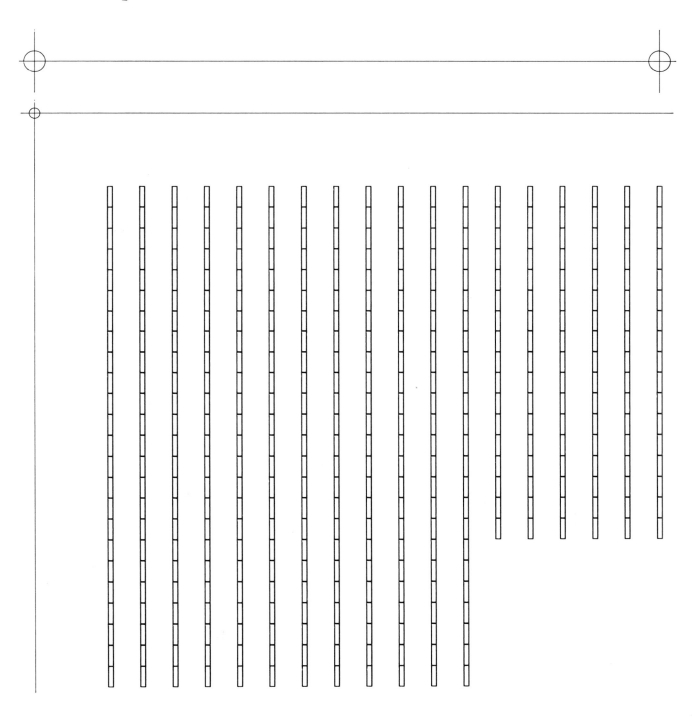

LIGHTING GRID
● 1x4 ON 8'℄

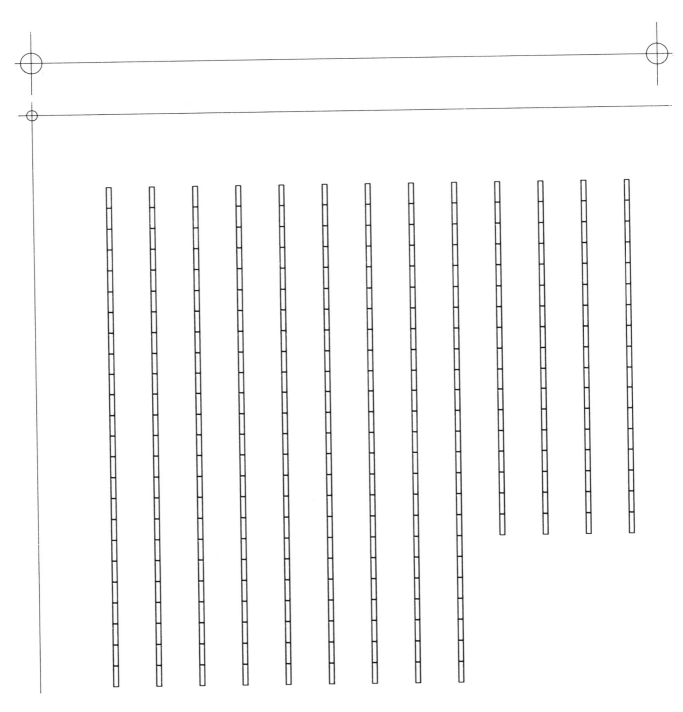

SPRINKLER GRID

● 14'x14' GRID

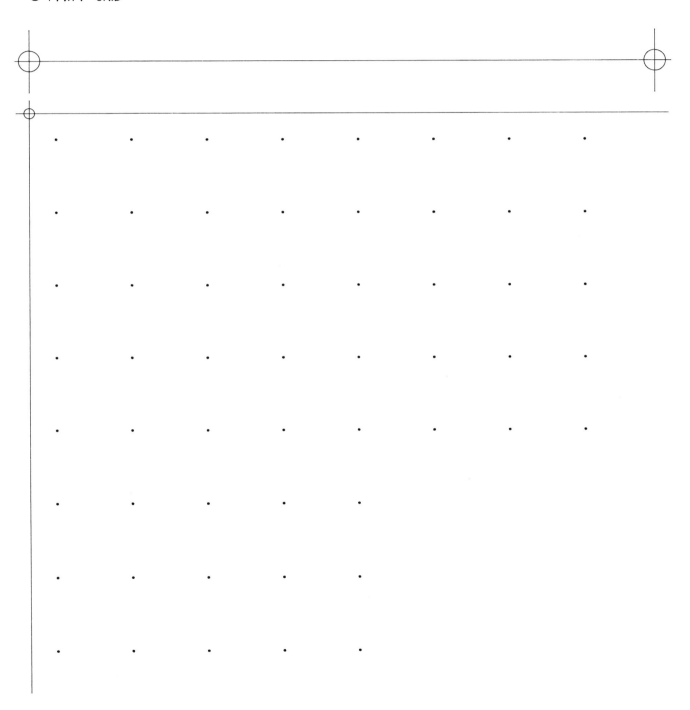

OFFICE & WORKSTATION LAYOUTS

● 4' BUILDING MODULE

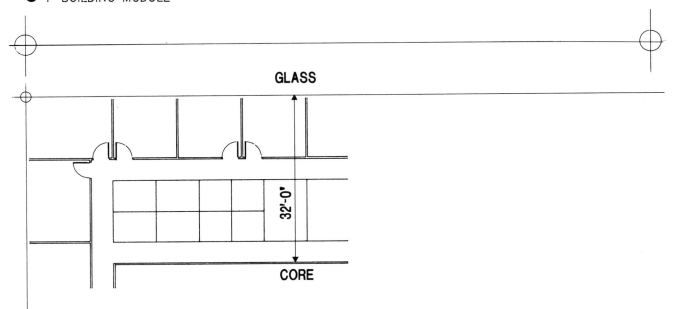

GLASS

32'-0"

CORE

OFFICE & WORKSTATION LAYOUTS

● 5' BUILDING MODULE

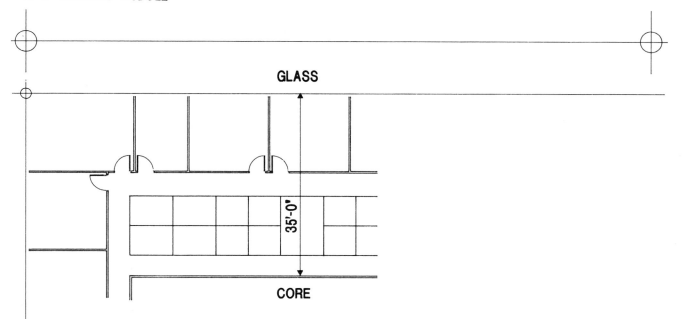

GLASS

35'-0"

CORE

OFFICE & WORKSTATION
LAYOUTS W/ STORAGEWALL

● 4' BUILDING MODULE

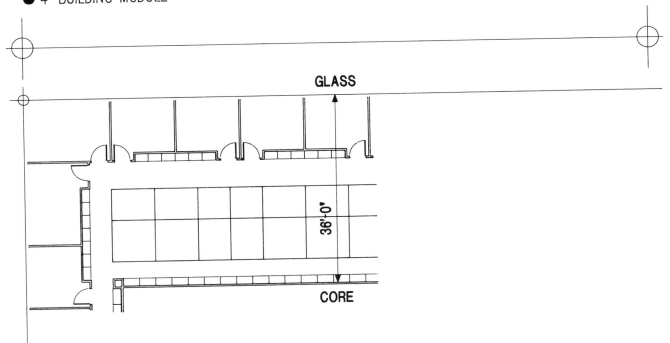

GLASS

36'-0"

CORE

OFFICE & WORKSTATION
LAYOUTS W/ STORAGEWALL

● 5' BUILDING MODULE

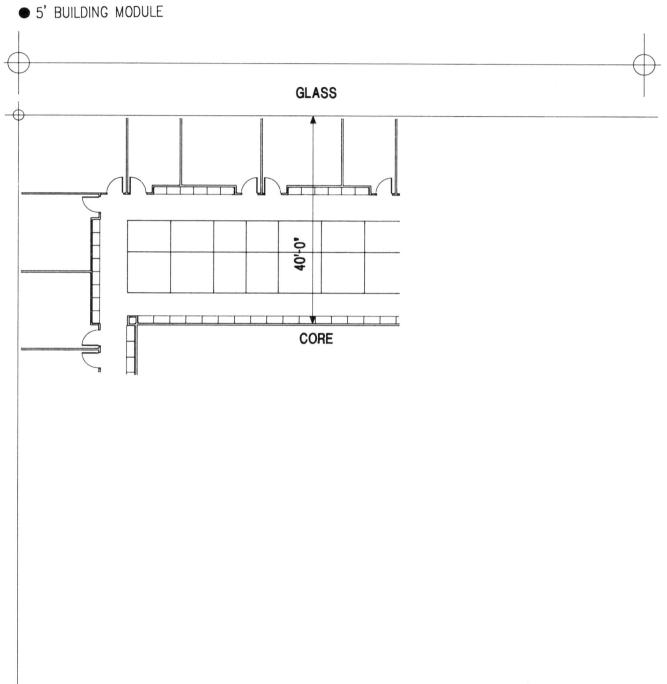

GLASS

40'-0"

CORE

CHAPTER 4

Inside-Out Design

Karen Daroff and James E. Rappoport

This chapter outlines the various owner/user and tenant requirements that can impact on the cost-effective design of an office building. Two distinct but interrelated design and project budget and construction packages are typical: (1) the base building core and shell package, and (2) the office facility's interior construction package referred to as the "tenant fit-out" or "tenant improvement" (TI) package. (See Figure 4.1.)

The design of an office building is frequently initiated by a developer or investment group that retains an architect to prepare designs for what is generally described as a speculative office building.

Many developers hope first to attract a major tenant who will "anchor" the financial success of the investment and, by a lease commitment, will allow the developers to confirm their mortgage financing and begin design and construction.

The anchor tenant's intended use and occupancy of the leased space can influence the developer and the developer's architect in their final stages of design of the building. The use and occupancy are documented (usually in a data base format), which architects, interior designers, and their consulting engineers refer to the documentation as "a program of space requirements."

The project management and design concepts outlined in this chapter are described by the authors as designing the office facility "from the inside out."

The authors recommend that all owner/users of office space, and any tenant large enough to be "courted" as an anchor tenant in a developer's new office building, prepare a list of specific design criteria to be used for the building's design from the inside out.

FIGURE 4.1

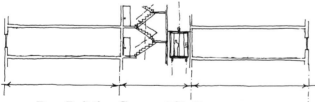

Base Building Core and Shell
- window wall (shell)
- structure
- core (elevators, stairs, toilets, etc.)
- mechanical, electrical, plumbing risers
- fire safety risers and controls

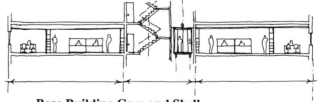

Base Building Core and Shell plus Tenant Fit-out
- window wall (shell)
- structure
- core (elevators, stairs, toilets, etc.)
- mechanical, electrical, plumbing risers
- fire safety risers and controls
- partitions
- ceiling systems
- furniture and equipment
- tenant finishes

Using the comparative analyses and checklist presented here, owner/users or major office tenants can begin the inside-out design process in preparation for design discussions with the project's architects, interior designers, consulting engineers, and development team. The design team members can use the same forms to prepare for discussions with an owner/user or tenant.

Each office facility design project developed following this inside-out design process is likely to be different, because no two office facility programs of space requirements and combined design and planning issues are exactly equal. By recognizing the variations and differences between an "average" speculative office building's design criteria and those of a specific facility, designers following the inside-out design process will attain a more cost-effective and efficient office facility for a prospective tenant's long-term use and occupancy.

The use and occupancy costs of office facilities represent a substantial percentage of overall corporate operating costs. (See Figure 4.2.) A more efficient office facility, therefore, yields substantially greater bottom-line profits.

Chapter 1, which detailed the programming process, presented an outline of the various interrelated office design elements. Chapter 3 provided an encyclopedic description of all these elements as a guide for those who must judge the suitability of an office space, using the criteria given in Chapter 2. This chapter unites these earlier presentations into an ultimate set of decisions that will yield a cost-effective office facility for an anchor tenant. The outline format used here is mutually useful for an owner/occupant and for an architect or facility planner preparing for or guiding initial discussions with the developer and owner/occupant. Those seeking to upgrade, renovate, or enhance an existing office building will find the outline helpful, whether they are presently occupying the building or intend to renovate or convert it for owner/user occupancy. Owner/users who plan to be their own developers can use the outline in their programming and design discussions with architectural, interior design, and engineering consultants.

The outline provides recommendations for the design and development of cost-effective, efficient office facilities using the "inside-out" design approach. Smaller tenants who are seeking to rent space in existing office buildings can use these recommendations to test the existing conditions in the various office buildings competing for their tenancy. Those who are about to begin an office facility design and development effort as an owner/user, or as a lead tenant at a newly designated headquarters or operational facility, should use this analysis to guide the design development of their new facilities.

The outline analyzes the various features of a typical office facility—the structural, mechanical,

FIGURE 4.2

Professional/Service Organization's Typical Operating Cost Budget

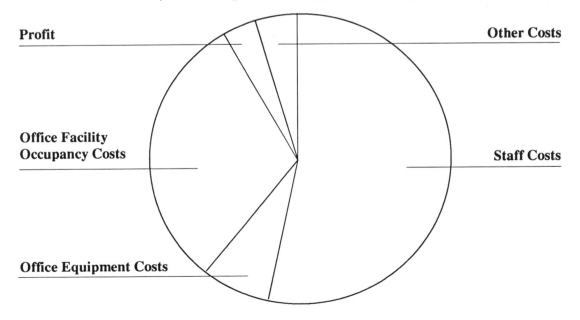

wiring, and infrastructural elements of the base building, as well as the interior planning elements typical of the finished interior layout, "fit-out," or tenant improvement (TI) package of the completed office facility. (See Figure 4.3.)

Each element of a construction project has a "best case" set of dimensions and planning criteria for each set of project-specific program requirements. The skillful combination of the various elements in this market basket of diverse components allows an overall cost-effective office facility to be planned, designed, constructed, operated, and later replanned for changing use and occupancy of the facility over time.

Operating Costs

The office facility management industry's trade association, known as BOMA (Building Office Management Association), maintains yearly records of the costs to operate various types and configurations

FIGURE 4.3

Composite of Base Building and Interior Fit-Out Planning Modules

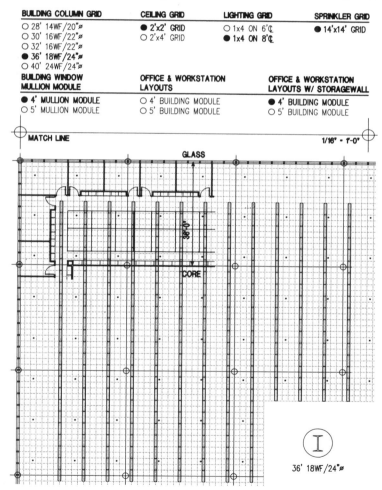

This plan illustration is a composite of the following modules: a 36' structure, 4' window mullions, 2' x 2' ceiling tiles, 8' luminaires spacing, 14' x 14' sprinkler heads spacing, 12' offices and 8' workstations.

FIGURE 4.4

Comparative Analysis: Office Building Operating Costs/Rentable Square Foot/Year

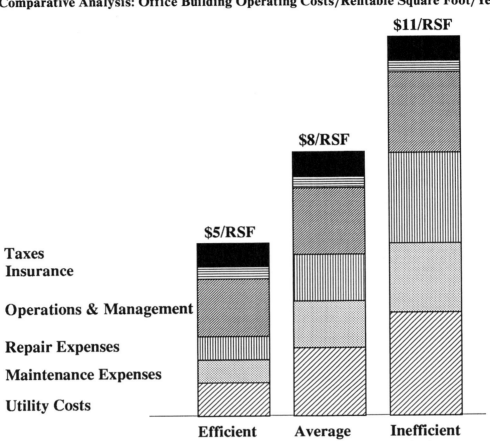

of office buildings throughout the country. BOMA calls this annual survey the "experience report." In recent years, with the advent of "smart," energy-efficient buildings standing side-by-side with relatively inefficient buildings, some of which were built as recently as the late 1970s, this experience report shows a dramatic difference in the costs to operate office facilities.

For instance, the raw data for the year 1988 indicate that very efficient office facilities can be operated at total operating costs of less than $5 per rentable square foot per year, while relatively inefficient buildings frequently cost more than $14 per square foot per year to operate. (See Figure 4.4.)

Operating costs include the landlord's costs for light, heat, power, maintenance, repairs, and operations, but they do not include the financial or capitalized costs to build or own the building. The sum of the operating costs, the costs to own the building,

and the profit, when considered together, form the basis for the rental value and the specific price of rental real estate.

The operating cost per square foot per year is, thus, only one statistic. Some buildings are designed so efficiently that, on average, the tenants can house their employees at a density of less than 175 square feet per person. Relatively inefficient buildings might require more than 250 square feet per person to house the same program of space requirements. (See Figure 4.5.)

When calculating operating costs or total use and occupancy costs (including rental values or actual rental costs), tenants should use a formula that includes both costs and the density of employees housed, to yield an average "cost per employee housed" per year. Using the above-noted square footage, substantial variations are evident in the operating costs per employee housed per year in various office facilities, as follows:

	Operating Cost ($ per sq. ft.)	×	Occupancy (sq. ft. per person)	=	Occupancy costs ($ per person per year)
Best-case costs	$ 5	×	175	=	$ 875
Next best case	5	×	250	=	1,250
Next best case	14	×	175	=	2,450
Worst case	14	×	250	=	3,556

The difference between the best case and the worst case is frequently caused by a lack of applying appropriate design criteria in the initial phases of a project. Following the inside-out design criteria presented in this chapter will lead to lower office facility operating costs. As the tabulation above indicates, it is clearly worth the effort.

Office Facility Design: An Integrated Approach

For better or for worse, the components of an office facility (furniture elements, ceiling systems, column and structural elements, air conditioning, lighting, fire protection, wire distribution systems, window wall conditions, and so on) are manufactured or built to various dimensions. By considering each element as a subpart of an overall building system, a designer ensures a building in which architectural, structural, mechanical, and interior planning elements fit together, benefiting the overall efficiency of the facility, defined as the *cost per employee housed.*

Background of Inside-Out Design

The inside-out design process reconciles available materials and methods of construction to a specific set

FIGURE 4.5

Relative Efficiency of Simple Rectangle vs. Complex "Organic" Shape: Employees Housed in Equal Area

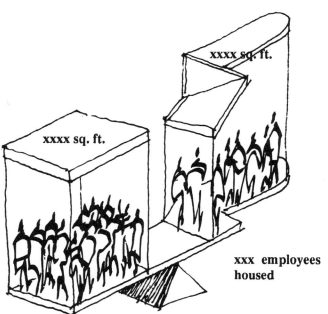

xxxx sq. ft.

xxxx sq. ft.

xxx employees housed

xxxx employees housed

of use and occupancy requirements and to particular construction, operating, management cost guidelines.

A later section of this chapter provides comparative analysis forms and a checklist of criteria for some aspects of the office building design process. Readers are encouraged to make maximum use of computer systems in gathering, storing, and updating these data. Yet, even the computer-literate must not abandon old-fashioned rules of reason, compromise, and discussion among members of a project development team, in determining the best set of office design criteria.

Designers are frequently asked by clients to review various planning concepts, to determine the cost effectiveness and efficiency of a particular office facility's base building core and shell. These reviews may be requested by developers who are seeking to attract tenants to their buildings through a more efficient use of space, by tenant facility managers who are comparing proposals from various developers seeking their tenancy, or by owner/users who are reviewing design concepts offered by their project architects and engineers. In all cases, *costs per employees housed* should be the determinant criterion; costs of the project should be related to the number of employees likely to occupy the completed facility.

Such evaluations are frequently based on initial project capital costs as well as the yearly operating costs of the resulting facility, because additional capital cost improvements can often be cost-justified by operating cost efficiencies.

The elements of the base building that affect the interior planning efficiency of the facility, and the relative advantages and disadvantages of the various resulting design decisions, should be analyzed for each client. Each element should be evaluated within the context of new building designs and existing building opportunities and constraints.

An efficient interior plan can be developed if attention is focused on use and occupancy of the office facility and the building's interior space planning needs. These should be priorities during the planning and designing phase of the base building core and shell or while reviewing renovation concepts for an existing building.

By neglecting the inside-out interior planning concepts during the building core and shell design phase, designers may find a building so difficult to plan that the resulting compromises will reduce overall efficiency and lead to substantial increases in overall costs per employee housed.

When these concepts are ignored in the review of an existing building, a building with a "bargain" rent may cause so many constraints to efficient planning that the total project costs will exceed those of a better designed facility with a higher rent.

Categories of Costs

The project costs to buy lands, build buildings, and fit out interiors for office use and occupancy are defined as the initial capital costs of the project. The costs associated with mortgage financing, land leases, real estate taxes, maintenance, utility, and other similar costs, and with the management, insurance, renovation, replanning, and repair of the facility over its useful life are considered operating costs. The tax effect when these costs are paid out versus the cash costs when these expenses are incurred, and the related issues of depreciation, amortization, and appreciation, affect the net after-tax operating costs of an office facility.

Many tenants believe that a lower first cost means a more cost-effective office facility. This conclusion is wrong. Those who lower their first costs by leasing and otherwise postponing first costs until a later payment date are likely to reach an inaccurate conclusion as to the aggregate costs of their facility. Moreover, those who rely on tax effect as the sole investment criterion are likely to overlook the mounting costs associated with use and occupancy of the facility over time.

Finally, those who look at costs per se, without regard for the relative ability of various building design options to efficiently house their intended use and occupancy, will frequently conclude that an inefficient facility costs less. However, on a cost-per-employee-housed basis, an inefficient facility may well cost more than a facility designed to respond to the criteria outlined in this chapter.

Present Value Cost Analysis

The most efficient and accurate method to calculate and analyze relative costs of various real estate options is the "present value" concept of cost accounting. As applied here, the basic steps for present value cost analysis are:

1. Determine the period of useful life of the project under study;
2. Determine each cost of the project, including its use and occupancy costs, over the period of useful life;
3. Estimate the inflation impact for each year of the useful life;

4. Bring each year's occupancy costs back to the first cost year by reducing the costs by the estimated cumulative impact of inflation for each year since the first cost year;

5. Add up each inflation-impacted cost item to yield a present value cost.

For example, the following analysis for a 1,000-employee office facility leads to the total present value cost for a project with a useful life of five years, based on a 5 percent per year estimate of inflation impact.

Inflation Impact Estimate
(000s omitted)

		Year 1: 5%	Year 2: 5%	Year 3: 5%	Year 4: 10%	Year 5: 10%	
Items:	A	$1,000					
	B	100	100	100			
	C		100	100	100	100	
	D			100	100	100	
Total costs per year (year to year)		$1,100	$200	$300	$200	$200	=$2,000
Less: Estimated inflation impact (5%)		$1,045					
Plus: Present value of projected $200 cost in year 2*		180	190				
Plus: Present value of projected $300 cost in year 3*		257	270	285			
Plus: Present value of projected $200 cost in year 4*		154	162	171	180		
Plus: Present value of projected $200 cost in year 5*		139	146	154	162	180	
Total present value cost		$1,636					

* Present value is computed by reducing each future year's dollar cost by the 5 percent estimated inflation impact for each year up to the present year.

Using the costs per employee housed as the basis of real estate decision making, and assuming 1,000 employees, the present value cost over the useful life of 5 years is divided by the number of employees housed. The present value cost per employee housed, over the 5-year useful life of the project in this example is $1,636.

Any analysis of the major elements affecting the overall cost and efficiency of an office facility should always seek to strike a balance between efficiency and esthetics, and between architectural design and the tenant's interior space planning requirements. This balancing has been proven to result in cost-effective and esthetically pleasing office facilities.

Costs Justification: Office Productivity and Employee Benefits

A growing body of data documents cost savings and improved employee productivity resulting from efficiently planned office facilities. A case in point following the concepts described by William Ouchi in his book *Theory Z: How American Business Can Meet the Japanese Challenge* is an office facility designed "from the inside out," to house a very specialized set of space requirements for a computer software firm. More than 300 identical, windowless, office cubicles had to be designed as individual workrooms for the computer software writers. The unique concept behind the facility was the ability to organize the computer software writers into specialized teams, to tackle a specific project of varied time duration. Once the project was completed, they would regroup and be relocated into new project teams. Because an office facility was created with identical offices, individuals could more easily relocate from one office to another by simply transferring files and personal effects.

The owners measured performance before and after relocating to this building (1) by the number of lines of computer software programs written per employee per year, and (2) by the number of errors and omissions (glitches or "bugs") later found to exist in the programs thus written. The company claimed a twofold increase in output and a 50 percent reduction in errors—a quadrupled productivity improvement. (See Figure 4.6.)

The present authors developed, for an office building client, an economic model to demonstrate that an investment of several million dollars to bring a bank of elevators down to street level could be cost-justified by improved employee productivity. The lost employee hours were determined by calculating the hours per year each employee spent using an existing second-floor sky lobby escalator transfer concept of building access. Because the building housed approximately

FIGURE 4.6

Productivity Improvement from Use of Helical Design Process

Using Linear Critical Path Process	**Using Helical Design Process**
XXXXXXXXXXXXXX XXXXXXXXXXXXGG	XXXXXXXXXXXXXX XXXXXXXXXXXXXX XXXXXXXXXXXXXX XXXXXXXXXXXXXG
X - Lines of software output developed/employee/year	**2X - Lines of software output developed/employee/year**
G - "Glitches"/Errors	**G/2 - "Glitches"/Errors**
	= 4X Productivity Improvement

FIGURE 4.7

Lobby Access: Second-Floor Elevator Sky Lobby via Escalator vs. Street-Level Elevator Lobby

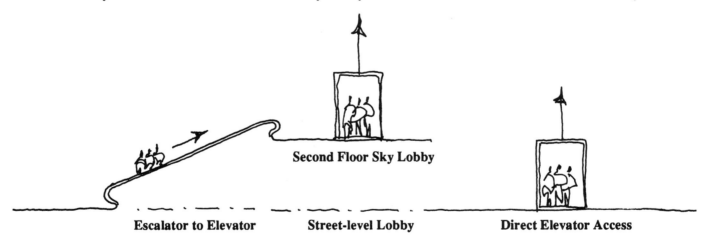

Escalator to Elevator   Street-level Lobby   Direct Elevator Access

Second Floor Sky Lobby

	5,000	**Employees**
(x)	240	Work days per year
(x)	5	Street-to-office trips per day
(x)	3	Additional minutes of travel / trip (due to escalator ride time)
(=)	18,000,000	"Wasted" minutes of travel time
(=)	300,000	"Wasted" hours
(x)	$20	Per employee hour opportunity lost value
(=)	$6,000,000	Lost employee value per year

5,000 insurance industry employees, a saving of 60 cumulative hours per employee per year amounted to no less than $8 million in additional productive employee time at work per year—a capital cost payback in less than one year! (See Figure 4.7.)

Another example involved a personal products company that had recently merged a number of product brands into a unified new company. The senior executives of this conglomerate desired a new office facility as the vehicle for creating a renewed and unified corporate culture. The relocation also was used as a catalyst for resolving employee redundancies after the reorganization. Approximately 15 percent fewer employees successfully managed the growing company one year after the relocation. These savings and productivity improvements resulted in substantial bottom-line profit improvement.

In his book *Corporate Facility Planning,* Stephen Binder (vice president of facilities at Citibank) reviewed another quantifiable aspect of office productivity—the use of the office facility as an employee benefit. Binder suggested that a cost-effective and efficient office facility:

- Enhances effectiveness and allegiance;
- Is used all day, every day;
- Has a direct and comparative value;
- Is visible all day, every day;
- Is tangible and, in general, offers many advantages over more abstruse and indirect employee benefits programs.

However one measures productivity, there is a growing body of proof that cost-effectively designed office facilities provide one of the major bases for improvements in productivity and corporate profits. Cost-effective and efficient office facilities might be cost-justified in terms of overall productivity improvement and human resource costs and benefits. However, because each office facility use and occupancy varies, and because each set of corporate management guidelines also varies, designers should avoid a blanket use of any productivity or employee benefit economic formulae or criteria as cost justification for an office facility project.

Space Measurement

Various methods of measuring office facility space exist within the real estate, architectural, and building

FIGURE 4.8

Gross Floor Area Calculations Out-to-Out (Less Shafts)

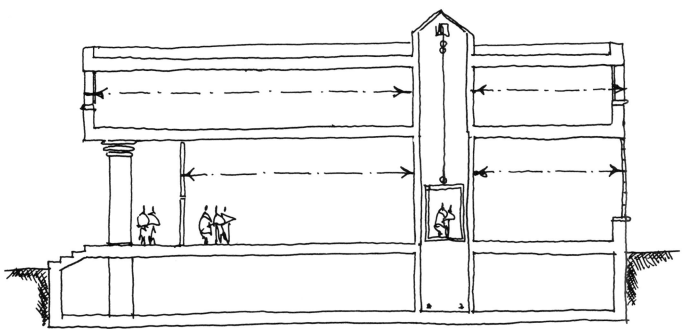

code vernacular. The most common methods of space measurement are discussed here.

Gross floor area is the measurement of a building required under most municipal zoning ordinances, which allow a specified amount of gross floor area on a specific project site. Following the general guidelines, gross floor area is typically measured to the most exterior portion of each floor of a building above grade and includes all space demised by the shell of the building, with the exception of mechanical rooms and penthouses with ceiling heights below 7 ft.-6 in. Basements, cellars, and other spaces below grade, and parking areas above grade, are usually not counted in gross floor area calculations. (See Figure 4.8.)

An interesting aspect of gross floor area as it relates to zoning calculations is found in the ability to not count space employed for mechanical, air conditioning, and other nonhabitable uses in areas with ceiling heights below 7 ft.-6 in. This language, found in almost every zoning code throughout the United States, has been frequently used to remeasure an existing building in an effort to gain "as-of-right" approval for an addition to an existing building that was built initially to the full extent of the allowable zoning ordinance. (See Figure 4.9.)

A remeasurement assignment requires seeking out and measuring tenants' interconnecting stairway shafts and bulkheads; telephone and computer data network mechanical and wire distribution rooms and closets; supplemental air conditioning, ventilating, and domestic hot water installations; and any other nonhabitable areas that might be defined as mechanical spaces or bulkheads with a low ceiling height.

In two recent office-tower remeasurement assignments, 12,000 to 15,000 square feet of such spaces were found within existing buildings measured earlier at approximately 1 million square feet of gross floor area. In both towers, new lobby entrances and related retail spaces were added to the building's first

FIGURE 4.9

"Found" Space

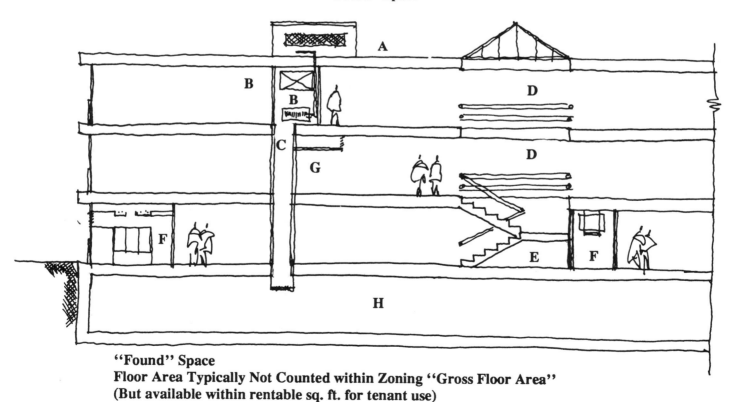

"Found" Space
Floor Area Typically Not Counted within Zoning "Gross Floor Area"
(But available within rentable sq. ft. for tenant use)

A - Roof-top equipment space
B - Tenant mechanical rooms
C - Duct and pipe shafts
D - Atrium floor cut-outs
E - Spaces below tenant stairs
F - Tenant equipment spaces
G - Areas with less than 7'-6" ceiling heights
H - Basement and cellar spaces

floor, within the zoning ordinance, using the as-of-right technique of remeasurement. The rental payback for the costs of these building additions averaged less than two years.

Rentable square feet is a marketing term used by real estate developers and brokers as the basis for lease negotiations. There is no clear definition of rentable square feet; however, it typically approximates the gross floor area. An industry standard formula (Figure 4.10) recommended by BOMA includes the gross floor area measured from the outside face of exterior walls, less certain shafts, plus a prorated apportionment of the building's common spaces (such as lobbies and landings), plus a factor added or subtracted from this sum to adjust the total to respond to marketing needs. In some real estate regional markets, stairs and elevator shafts may (or may not) be counted within the rentable square feet formula.

In building leases, rentable square feet are typically a nonnegotiable given, because they are used by the developer or landlord to present pro formas to the building's investors and financiers, and because the total (published) number of rentable square feet of a building is the basis for apportioning common maintenance and service charges among the tenants of the building.

The landlord's workletter (or tenant construction allowance) and the various architectural and other consulting fees are typically based on rentable square feet.

To illustrate the capricious nature of the terminology regarding rentable square feet, design firms are routinely asked to "remeasure" existing buildings and to provide a computer-aided data base that will support a revised number of rentable square feet, to be stated in the marketing and lease negotiation package after a building's renovation or upgrading.

Landlords of buildings built and measured prior to 1975 are likely to have used a more conservative definition for rentable square feet than landlords who measured their space in the 1980s. Frequently, the variation between an earlier measurement and a remeasurement can add 15 to 20 percent to the building's rentable square footage—without adding one square inch of actual architecture.

For this reason, if a facility manager, real estate consultant, or developer quotes a density or employee occupancy factor using rentable square feet, the definition used for rentable square feet should be questioned prior to reaching any comparative or analytical conclusion.

Usable square feet is the space actually to be fitted out by the tenant. This will include only the space within the demising walls and inside face of the skin of the building's facade, for a partial-floor tenant.

For a full-floor or multifloor tenant or owner, usable square feet will include areas of the core that must be fitted out under the tenant's workletter or construction allowance, including elevator foyers, service areas, telephone and electric switching rooms, tenant's mechanical spaces, and other similar areas of the tenant's full-floor or multifloor occupancy. (See Figure 4.11.)

Habitable square feet is the portion of usable square feet actually occupied by the tenant's employees—the pure office space. (See Figure 4.12.)

Loss factor is a term used to denote the amount of space devoted to building common elements, including the core and shell dimensions and thicknesses.

If the loss factor is applied to the ratio of usable square feet to rentable square feet, it is expressed as a percentage. A higher usable percentage indicates a more efficient base building.

If the loss factor is applied to the ratio of usable square feet to habitable square feet, it too is expressed as a percentage, with the higher usable percentage being the more efficient core and shell of the base building, as shown in Figure 4.13.

Loss factor alone, although important as a guideline in determining the efficiency and cost effectiveness of a base building core and shell, does not provide

FIGURE 4.10

Typical Computation of Leased Rentable Floor Area

Gross Floor Area (of tenant space)	(-) Shafts	(+) Pro-rata Share of lobby, building common spaces and shared multi-tenant corridors	(+/-) a "Marketing" Factor	(=) Rentable Floor Area Leased

FIGURE 4.11

"Usable" Floor Area

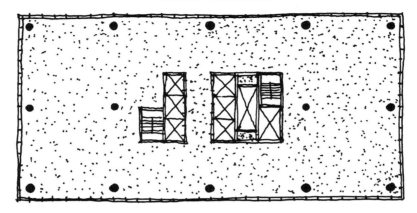

FIGURE 4.12

Floor Plate – Out-to-Out = Gross Floor Area

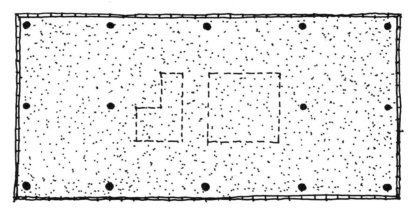

the prospective tenant or owner/user with the most important yardstick of building efficiency—cost per employee housed.

Cost per Employee Housed

The best benchmark judgment of the overall efficiency of office space is an economic evaluation based on a cost per employee housed. (See Figure 4.14.) All expenses to operate the office facility are included in the evaluation:

- Rent or mortgage payments
- Opportunity loss on initial down payments
- Taxes
- Insurance

- Consultants' fees
- Light, heat, and power utility costs
- Telephone and data switches, equipment, and wiring
- Construction, fit-out, furniture, and equipment
- Move-in expenses
- Repairs and maintenance
- Housekeeping
- Replanning and relocation costs (after move-in)
- Costs of down time during relocation
- Similar real estate and business-related costs associated with the occupancy.

Costs are typically accounted for in terms of current buy-out dollars (what it costs initially), as well as

FIGURE 4.13

Loss Factors: Rentable-to-Usable and Usable-to-Habitable

$$\frac{\text{Rentable Sq. Ft.} - \text{Usable Sq. Ft.}}{\text{Rentable Sq. Ft.}} = \text{Loss Factor}$$

$$\frac{\text{Usable Sq. Ft.} - \text{Habitable Sq. Ft.}}{\text{Usable Sq. Ft.}} = \text{Loss Factor}$$

(for example)

(for example)

$$\frac{\underset{\text{rentable}}{100,000 \text{ sq. ft.}} - \underset{\text{usable}}{90,000 \text{ sq. ft.}}}{100,000 \text{ sq.ft. rentable}} = 10\% \text{ loss factor}$$

$$\frac{\underset{\text{usable}}{90,000 \text{ sq. ft.}} - \underset{\text{habitable}}{80,000 \text{ sq. ft.}}}{90,000 \text{ sq. ft. usable}} = 11\% \text{ loss factor}$$

a carefully developed projection of the costs to use, occupy, and operate the facility over the term of the lease or useful life of the facility.

This "life cycle cost" analysis is first prepared year by year, and then restated as a "net present value" cost analysis. This brings the individual years' budgeted costs forward to the present value, in order to determine the overall effects of cost variations over time, as adjusted for inflation impact.

Employees housed is a constant in the calculation. Simply, it is a count of all office and workstation occupants and of shared offices, workstations, and computer workstations which, in sum, represent the employees housed or provided for when the facility is at full occupancy.

The goal of cost-effective facilities planning is to lower the cost per employee housed while designing a facility conducive to more productive corporate operations within the client's budgetary, quality, esthetic, and time constraints, goals, and objectives.

The coincidental interrelationship of the many planning, design, and engineering factors has a decisive influence on the *density of the facility* and ultimately on the cost per employee housed.

(Text continues on page 186.)

FIGURE 4.14

Average Cost per Year per Employee Housed

$$\frac{\text{Total Yearly Occupancy Costs } \$^1 + \$^2 + \$^3 + \$^4 + \$^{5 \text{ (year)}}}{\text{(N) years x Number of Employees Housed}} = \begin{array}{l} \text{Average cost per year} \\ \text{per employee housed} \end{array}$$

(for example)

	Year 1 costs $100,000		
+	Year 2 costs $120,000		
+	Year 3 costs $140,000	=	Total 5-year costs of $680,000
+	Year 4 costs $140,000		
+	Year 5 costs $170,000		

$$\frac{}{5 \text{ years x 40 employees housed}} = \begin{array}{l} \$3,400 \text{ average cost per} \\ \text{year per employee housed} \end{array}$$

COMPARISON OF ECONOMIC LEASE TERMS AND CONDITIONS

Report prepared for _____, dated _____

	Properties Being Compared		
	( )	( )	( )
A Rentable sq. ft.	____	____	____
B Measured usable sq. ft.	____	____	____
C Loss factor A/B	____%	____%	____%
D Population illustrated in sketch plan(s)	____	____	____
E Population density A/D = Sq. ft. per person rentable	____	____	____
1. Population density B/D = Sq. ft. per person usable	____	____	____
F Rental asking price (in dollars per rentable sq. ft.) for the base year(s)	$____	$____	$____
1. (in dollars per usable sq. ft.) for the base year(s)	$____	$____	$____
2. (in total dollars first year)	$____	$____	$____
3. (in total dollars all years of the proposed base lease)	$____	$____	$____
G Other occupancy costs foreseen in the base rental lease (in dollars per year) (base year):			
· Utilities	$____	$____	$____
· Overtime light, heat and power	$____	$____	$____
· Maintenance	$____	$____	$____
· Real estate taxes	$____	$____	$____
· Use and occupancy taxes	$____	$____	$____
· Cleaning service, rubbish removal	$____	$____	$____
· Add-on for landlord's increased operating costs	$____	$____	$____
· Other	$____	$____	$____
Total nonrental occupancy costs	$____	$____	$____
Occupancy costs estimated in:			
1. Year 1	$____	$____	$____
2. Year 2*	$____	$____	$____
3. Year 3	$____	$____	$____
4. Year 4	$____	$____	$____
5. Year 5	$____	$____	$____
6. Year 6	$____	$____	$____
7. Year 7	$____	$____	$____
8. Year 8	$____	$____	$____
9. Year 9	$____	$____	$____
10. Year 10	$____	$____	$____

*Use an inflation factor for known or estimated operating cost increases year to year

Properties Being Compared

(   )   (   )   (   )

H   Total costs in F-2, plus occupancy costs in G for:
1. Year 1 $____ $____ $____
2. Year 2 $____ $____ $____
3. Year 3 $____ $____ $____
4. Year 4 $____ $____ $____
5. Year 5 $____ $____ $____
6. Year 6 $____ $____ $____
7. Year 7 $____ $____ $____
8. Year 8 $____ $____ $____
9. Year 9 $____ $____ $____
10. Year 10 $____ $____ $____

I   Estimate of tenant's share of construction and tenant improvements costs (not including tenant's furniture and equipment) $____ $____ $____

J   Yearly allocation of this tenant's cost using the formula for present value; cost per year in:
1. Year 1 $____ $____ $____
2. Year 2 $____ $____ $____
3. Year 3 $____ $____ $____
4. Year 4 $____ $____ $____
5. Year 5 $____ $____ $____
6. Year 6 $____ $____ $____
7. Year 7 $____ $____ $____
8. Year 8 $____ $____ $____
9. Year 9 $____ $____ $____
10. Year 10 $____ $____ $____

K   Total costs in F-2, plus occupancy costs in G, plus cost per year in J for:
1. Year 1 $____ $____ $____
2. Year 2 $____ $____ $____
3. Year 3 $____ $____ $____
4. Year 4 $____ $____ $____
5. Year 5 $____ $____ $____
6. Year 6 $____ $____ $____
7. Year 7 $____ $____ $____
8. Year 8 $____ $____ $____
9. Year 9 $____ $____ $____
10. Year 10 $____ $____ $____

L   Total costs all ( ) years $____ $____ $____

M   Total costs per employee all ( ) years   (   )   (   )   (   )

N   L/D = Cost per employee housed $____ $____ $____

O   Ranking of cost per employee over ( ) years on a scale of 1 (highest) to 10 (lowest)   (   )   (   )   (   )

Note: Other terms beyond 10 years may be used, if the term of occupancy or useful life exceeds 10 years

ANALYSIS OF ISSUES RELATED TO CLIENT TENANT OCCUPANCY

Properties Being Compared

(   ) (   ) (   )

**Subjective Location Ratings
Using a Subjective Evaluation on a
Scale of 1 (worst) to 10 (best)**

Note: Items indicated by (N) require the actual number of items to be posted to the particular line.

Subjective Issues

1	Location quality (within the region)	(1-10)	____	____	____
2	Location quality (related to tenant's needs)	(1-10)	____	____	____
3	Actual floor number(s) available	(N)	____	____	____
	a. Location on the floor(s)	(1-10)	____	____	____
	b. Date of availability of space	(1-10)	____	____	____
4	Building's image for customers and clients	(1-10)	____	____	____
	a. Building's image for employees and consultants	(1-10)	____	____	____
5	Convenience to highways	(1-10)	____	____	____
	a. Convenience of parking	(1-10)	____	____	____
	b. Number of parking spaces in lease	(N)	____	____	____
6	Convenience to mass transit	(1-10)	____	____	____
7	Convenience to employees' homes	(1-10)	____	____	____
	a. Available labor pool	(1-10)	____	____	____
8	Elevator service quality	(1-10)	____	____	____
	a. Handicapped access	(1-10)	____	____	____
	b. Freight elevator service quality/ convenience	(1-10)	____	____	____
	c. Average waiting time to access elevators	(1-10)	____	____	____
9	Lobby image quality	(1-10)	____	____	____
	a. Lobby directory image quality	(1-10)	____	____	____
	b. Number of lines available for tenant on lobby directory	(N)	____	____	____
	c. Public toilet room quality	(1-10)	____	____	____
	d. Elevator image quality	(1-10)	____	____	____

**Subjective Location Ratings
Using a Subjective Evaluation on a
Scale of 1 (worst) to 10 (best)**

	Properties Being Compared		
	( )	( )	( )

10	Image of neighboring firms and businesses	(1-10)	___	___	___
	a. Existence of competing firms or businesses within building (10 = no competitors)	(1-10)	___	___	___
	b. Convenience of shops, restaurants and recreation	(1-10)	___	___	___
11	Convenience to firm's bank(s) and other support services	(1-10)	___	___	___
12	Safety/security (building location and proposed office facility or suite)	(1-10)	___	___	___
	a. Number of police and fire incidents reported last year (rank of 10 = no incidents)	(1-10)	___	___	___
13	Availability of after-hours heating and air conditioning	(1-10)	___	___	___
14	Quality of available office maintenance services	(1-10)	___	___	___
15	Reputation of the building's property manager	(1-10)	___	___	___
	a. Reputation of the building's developer	(1-10)	___	___	___
16	Potential for convenient subsequent expansion/ option space	(1-10)	___	___	___

Architectural and Tenant Workletter Issues

17	Typical office ceiling height (in feet and inches)	(N)	___	___	___
18	Ambient lighting level available (in footcandles)	(N)	___	___	___
19	HVAC offered in tenant's space (in tons)	(N)	___	___	___
20	Electric service (watts per sq. ft.)	(N)	___	___	___
	a. Quality of wire distribution	(1-10)	___	___	___
21	Acoustic index (STC) of proposed partitions	(N)	___	___	___
22	Number of linear feet of partition to be provided in workletter	(N)	___	___	___
23	Number of doors and frames to be provided in workletter	(N)	___	___	___
24	Number of ceiling lighting fixtures to be provided in workletter	(N)	___	___	___

Subjective Location Ratings
Using a Subjective Evaluation on a
Scale of 1 (worst) to 10 (best)

Properties Being Compared

(   ) (   ) (   )

25 Number of switches and outlets to be
provided in workletter   (N)   ___   ___   ___

   a. Number of electric circuits to be provided
in workletter   (N)   ___   ___   ___

26 Number of yards of carpet to be provided
in workletter   (N)   ___   ___   ___

   a. Value of carpet provided (in $/yard)   (N)   ___   ___   ___

27 Number of special computer or photocopier
outlet circuits to be provided in workletter   (N)   ___   ___   ___

28 Number of window blinds to be provided
in workletter   (N)   ___   ___   ___

29 Number of feet of window wall   (N)   ___   ___   ___

30 Number of toilet facilities (men's + women's)
designated (to tenant)   (N)   ___   ___   ___

   a. Number of drinking fountains
in tenant space   (N)   ___   ___   ___

Miscellaneous Workletter Issues
(from tenant's specific needs)

31 _____ (N)   ___   ___   ___

32 _____ (N)   ___   ___   ___

33 _____ (N)   ___   ___   ___

34 _____ (1-10)   ___   ___   ___

35 _____ (1-10)   ___   ___   ___

Final Tally

36 Total sum of all numbers noted above   (N)   ═══   ═══   ═══

37 Ranking of properties (first, second, third)
by total number in line 36   (1-10)   ___   ___   ___

38 Estimated number of days from today's
date _/_/_ until move-in   (N)   ___   ___   ___

39 Ranking of properties by move-in date
(10 = most appropriate from tenant's
point of view)   (1-10)   ___   ___   ___

CONCLUSION

Properties Being Compared

		(	)	(	)	(	)

I   Ranking of properties in this analysis
by cost per employee (from O)   (1-10)

II   Ranking of properties in this analysis
by subjective location ratings and architectural
tenant workletter issues (from 37)   (1-10)

III   Ranking of properties in this analysis
by move-in date (from 39)   (1-10)

IV   Ranking of capital cost relegated to tenant
for tenant's share of tenant improvements
(from I) (1 = most costly)   (1-10)

V   Overall evaluation ranking of properties
in this study   (1-10)

Report prepared for _____, dated _____

Leasehold Cost/Benefit Analysis

The line-by-line comparison format shown on pages 187–198 and the tenant fit-out checklist presented on pages 200-201 will assist tenants in the evaluation of various buildings seeking their tenancy. This self-paced evaluation method compares the objective, subjective, and financial aspects of the tenant's various options, yielding "best case" options from the facilities being compared.

Owner/users seeking to develop a new office facility will also find this comparative analysis format useful for studying various options proposed during the schematic design phases of their project, and for comparing those options to their current facilities and to various options offered by competing developers.

This comparative leasehold cost/benefit analysis is typically used to review various building locations, developer options, and/or offers proposed by various developers to a client/tenant.

The data base is usually compiled with the assistance of a tenant's architect or interior designer and real estate consulting firm or client-approved broker, who will conduct the ongoing negotiations with the various competing developers.

The analysis reviews both the economics of the proposed lease agreement and the effects of the lease on various tenant costs related to the leasehold, more commonly known as use and occupancy expenses.

The comparison report should illustrate economic terms and conditions, subjective image considerations, and various qualitative aspects of the architectural and interior space planning and design issues of the properties under study.

In addition to the standard issues encountered in most developer/tenant negotiations, tenant-specific issues can be added to the format.

Once completed, the summary of the alternative leaseholds offers a quantifiable and objective guideline for comparison.

Frequently, prospective tenants find that this analysis can assist their real estate brokers and attorneys in negotiating more effectively with developers. Subsequent to these negotiations, the format can be used to chart the changes in the developer's offer(s) during the lease negotiations, until the terms of the lease are finally confirmed.

(Chapter 5 begins on page 203.)

TENANT FIT-OUT CHECKLIST

This checklist is intended as a review of the landlord/tenant lease, the workletter and building rule(s) agreement, and the developer's base building core and shell designs. Each item has an effect on the overall tenant fit-out design, documentation, and project cost.

Lease Review Items

1. Name, address, and contact information for the landlord:_____

    _____

2. Landlord's designated professionals:

    ·   Leasing agent _____
    ·   Architect _____
    ·   Engineer_____
    ·   Structural engineer_____
    ·   Elevator consultant_____
    ·   Contractor_____
    ·   Major subcontractors_____

    _____

3. Description of the tenant's suite of offices:

    _____
    _____

4. Rentable square feet of these offices as stated in the lease: _____

5. Landlord's stated "usable" square feet of these offices with an explanation of the measurement system (BOMA, etc.):

    _____

6. Actual measurement of the "habitable" square feet (the amount of space to be fitted out) measured (from glass-to-glass, less shafts and core areas to be fitted out by the landlord (i.e. toilet rooms, closets, stairs, and elevators):

    _____

7. Conditions of the lease, related to who pays for the fit-out (check one):

    ·   Loft lease (tenant pays all costs)   ☐
    ·   Workletter (Landlord provides certain features on a unit basis)   ☐
    ·   Construction allowance (Landlord provides certain money)   ☐
    ·   Build to suit (Landlord constructs per tenant's plans)   ☐

8. Landlord's role in the tenant fit-out contracting process (check one):

    ·   Landlord builds to suit and takes full responsibility   ☐
    ·   Landlord acts as the tenant's agent to secure contractors   ☐
    ·   Landlord only reviews and comments on tenant's plans   ☐

9. Date when landlord proposes to turn over the base building core documents to tenant for tenant review:_____/___/_____

10. Date when base building core drawings will be substantially complete and coordinated so that tenant's architect can begin tenant planning design activity: _____/___/_____

11. Type of plans landlord will provide to tenant (check one):

    ☐ Mylars   ☐ Computer database on diskettes (CAD software type_____)   ☐ Blueprints

12. Date when tenant must turn over tenant plans to landlord for review: _____

13. Number of days landlord has to review tenant plans: _____

14. Date when existing tenants are to leave and/or when tenant work can begin: _____

15. Date when substantial completion of tenant work is to occur, and definition of substantial completion _____

16. Tenant's right to punchlist base building work prior to beginning tenant work (date of punchlist__/__/__) Yes ☐ No ☐

17. Tenant's right to punchlist tenant work prior to occupancy and rent initiation (date of punchlist__/__/__) Yes ☐ No ☐

18. Date of rent initiation: __/__/__

19. Provisions for tenant's change orders during fit-out construction:

   · How additional costs are evaluated

   _____
   _____

   · How delays are negotiated

   _____
   _____

20. If tenant is partial occupant of the building as a whole:

   · Tenant's share of common services and charges _____ %
   · Year-to-year increases in these charges _____ %
   · Cap on increases in these charges _____ %
   · List of these common services and charges

   _____
   _____
   _____

21. If electric service is a common charge built into the lease rent structure:

   · How tenant's electric consumption is calculated

   _____
   _____

   · How costs to tenant can be reduced through conservation

   _____
   _____

   · How landlord proposes to calculate electric usage changes in kwh where submeters are divided

   _____

22. Base building core and shell design criteria:

   · Floor loading capacity _____ lb./sq.ft.

   · Total occupancy capacity _____ persons

   · Plumbing fixture count _____/occupancy

   · Drinking fountain count _____/occupancy

- Barrier-free design criteria   Yes ☐   No ☐

- Available tons of air conditioning   _____ tons

- System of air distribution

  _____

  _____

  _____

- Air being distributed in tenant's space   _____ cfms

- System of window wall HVAC distribution

  _____

  _____

  _____

- If an air system, cfms at window wall   _____ cfms

- Base building HVAC distribution system provided as part of base building
  prior to tenant workletter fit-out work to distribute HVAC system

  _____

  _____

- Fire protection system criteria

  _____

  _____

  _____

- Base building sensors, controls, and annunciator panel system

  _____

  _____

- Fire protection system as part of base building prior to tenant
  fit-out dollars (main branches and feeds, etc.)

  _____

- Wiring types and capacity available for tenant use

       _____ amps
       _____ volts
       _____ total approximate watts

- Is 277-volt power available for tenant ambient lighting circuits?   Yes ☐   No ☐

- Distribution of wiring in tenant space:
  a. In floors _____

  b. In ceilings _____

  c. At window wall _____

  d. In risers _____

·   Telephone wire distribution, trunk (inches) capacity, and plans for landlord-supplied switch controls

_____

_____

_____

·   Provisions for:

Cable TV	Yes ☐ No ☐	Microwave	Yes ☐ No ☐
CCTV	Yes ☐ No ☐	Other specialties	Yes ☐ No ☐

_____

_____

23.   Tenant's right to remove prior tenant's fit-out before tenant's fit-out begins: Yes ☐ No ☐

·   Who pays for removal?_____

24.   Tenant's right to remove tenant's personal property when lease is ended:
Definition of personal property: Yes ☐ No ☐

_____

_____

25.   Length of initial lease and terms of option space, and lease extensions:

         initial lease   _____ yrs.
         option term   _____ yrs.
         extension term(s)   _____ yrs.

26.   Tenant's right to select tenant's architect, designers, engineers, contractor, and subcontractors   Yes ☐ No ☐

27.   Landlord's rules governing use of common loading dock(s) and freight elevators during normal business hours

_____

_____

28.   Tenant's cost to use loading dock(s) and freight elevators after hours

·   During construction   _____ \$/hour
·   During business hours   _____\$/hour
·   During overtime hours   _____\$/hour

29.   Description of any agreements with neighbors or code officials to limit demolition, construction, move-in, or other activities to certain hours of the day:

_____

_____

_____

30.   Winter/summer schedule for HVAC chillers and boilers:

·   Provisions for hot or cold transition days at midseason

_____

_____

_____

31. Normal operating hours for HVAC system

_____

_____

_____

32. Normal operating hours for tenant ambient lighting system

_____

_____

_____

33. Normal operating hours for lighting over parking lot(s)

_____

_____

_____

34. Costs to tenant and procedures for overtime use of:

· HVAC system

_____

_____

_____

· Ambient lighting and other use of electric current

_____

_____

_____

· Parking lot lighting and other safety features provided

_____

_____

35. Provisions for tenant's installation of supplemental HVAC systems: _____

_____

36. Potability of water serving tenant's pantry kitchens and drinking fountains: _____

_____

37. Does landlord or tenant change the tenant's bulbs, tubes, and ballasts?   Landlord ☐ Tenant ☐

38. If landlord is to provide, will landlord follow tenant's specifications for same?   Yes ☐ No ☐

39. Name and signage on the building:
Describe _____

_____

_____

_____

40. Type, size, and configuration of base building lobby directory; tenant's available space on same; point size of tenant's lettering; etc.

_____

_____

_____

41. Statement offering tenant comfort that subsequent additions to building by landlord will not obstruct tenant's light, air, views, etc.

_____

_____

_____

42. Assuming the base building is currently under construction, date prior to which tenant's plans for (a) supplemental HVAC, (b) structural reinforcement, (c) stairways and chase areas, (d) dunnage and poke-throughs can be incorporated within base building (as a bulletin) without cost implications to tenant: ___ / ___ / ___

43. Base building security system and concept for securing building during and after normal business hours:

_____

_____

44. Base building maintenance program including exterior maintenance:

_____

_____

45. Dollar amounts landlord proposes to provide tenant for:

- Consultants' fees $_____
- Fit-out construction $_____
- Moving expenses $_____
- Other tenant relocation costs $_____

46. Dollar amounts tenant is obligated to pay to landlord for:

- Administrative services during construction and fit-out $_____
- Contracting services $_____
- Fees $_____
- General conditions of the fit-out contracting activity $_____

47. Definition of general condition items:

_____

48. Who secures builder's risk insurance?   Landlord ☐   Tenant ☐
On base building during tenant fit-out: Landlord ☐   Tenant ☐
On tenant fit-out work in progress: Landlord ☐   Tenant ☐

49. Who must secure building permit for tenant fit-out work?   Landlord ☐   Tenant ☐

- Estimate of building permit cost $_____

- Estimate of building permit review and approval time   _____ weeks

50. Name, address, and contact of local building code agency:

_____

_____

_____

_____

51. Type and description of governing building codes:

_____

_____

_____

52. Special codes or rules landlord has imposed on tenant fit-out:

_____

_____

_____

53. Landlord's representation as to the presence (or absence) of asbestos and PCBs:

_____

_____

_____

54. Parking lot capacity and allowance of same for tenant's use: Car spaces available_____

55. Who maintains parking lot? Landlord ☐ Tenant ☐

56. Tenant's right to install thin set tiles and other hard surface flooring within tenant's space: Yes ☐ No ☐

57. Rules governing removal of waste:

· During construction_____
· During move-in_____
· During normal operations_____

_____

58. Description of base building lobby and common area design, details, materials, and finishes:

_____

_____

59. Description of base building toilet rooms, elevators and other special area design, details, materials and finishes:

_____

_____

_____

_____

_____

_____

_____

_____

60. Availability on site or near site for:

    · Food service   Yes ☐   No ☐
    · Shopping   Yes ☐   No ☐
    · Public transportation   Yes ☐   No ☐
    · Auto service shops   Yes ☐   No ☐

61. Building management concept and staffing:

    _____

    _____

62. Acoustic control and isolation between tenant's space and:

    · Other tenants' spaces_____(NCR)   (STC)
    · Exterior_____(NCR)   (STC)
    · Elevator machine rooms_____(NCR)   (STC)
    · Fan rooms_____(NCR)   (STC)
    · Toilet rooms_____(NCR)   (STC)

63. Other items of interest to specific tenants:

    _____

    _____

    _____

    _____

    _____

    _____

    _____

    _____

    _____

    _____

    _____

Inside-out Base Building Design Issues

1. Window wall mullion module size: _____inches

2. Condition of window wall module at corner(s):

    _____

    _____

3. Conditions at any atria, cuts, bites, angles, or other window wall features:

    _____

    _____

4. Glazing type and specification, and color and percent of opacity or mirroring:

    _____

    _____

5.   Window treatment details, solar control potential, and pockets for same:

_____

_____

_____

_____

6.   Typical structural bay size: _____ feet   x ___feet

7.   Size of typical columns in plan: _____feet _____ inches

8.   Floor-to-floor height: _____ feet _____ inches

      a.   Floor-to-ceiling height   _____ feet _____ inches

9.   Type, configuration, and size of duct loop, if provided within base building:

_____

_____

_____

10.   Type, configuration, and size of sprinkler loop, if provided within base building:

_____

_____

_____

11.   Condition of window sill; details and sizes; opportunity to distribute tenant wiring below window:

_____

_____

_____

12.   Elevator size, capacity, weight, and height (to confirm move-in and construction component sizes)
          cab size: ____inches x _____inches
          capacity: _____people
          cab weight: _____lbs.
          cab height: ____feet _____ inches

13.   Core-to-glass dimension   narrow side _____ feet
                                     wide side _____ feet

      a.   Interior column line dimension from center line to window wall: _____ feet

      b.   Interior column line dimension from center line to core wall: _____ feet

14.   Space between elevator(s) within elevator lobby core: _____ feet

15.   Width of common tenant corridor(s):   _____ inches

16.   Width of entrance doors:
     ·   Freight   _____feet

     ·   Lobby   _____feet

17. If landlord has workletter or base building standard, what specifications are given for the following?

· Ceiling grid type, color, configuration, installation procedure

_____

_____

· Ceiling tile type, color, acoustic quality, etc.

_____

_____

· Ambient lighting type, quantity, footcandles, watts per square foot, etc.

_____

_____

· GWB partitions, details at window wall and ceiling(s)

_____

_____

· Door types, sizes, and finishes

_____

_____

· Door hardware type, finishes, and locking features

_____

_____

· Door undercuts and provisions to flash patch as required

_____

_____

· Duct type and layout

_____

_____

· Air distribution type; layout and finishes

_____

_____

· HVAC control system, quantity and location(s)

_____

_____

· Sprinkler head type, finish and notation as to center of tile (or not)

_____

_____

·   Telephone, data, and electric wire distribution system and elements

_____

_____

·   Provision for access floor and depressed slab or ramp up

_____

_____

·   Condition of access floor at window wall

_____

_____

·   Floor leveling, deflection, and patching

_____

_____

·   Floor finish(es) type, installation, finishes, and materials

_____

_____

·   Base detail(s), materials, and colors

_____

_____

·   Paint specifications

_____

_____

·   Other workletter-supplied items

_____

_____

_____

18.   Tenant's corporate standards (if any) for office and workstation sizes, and any tenant construction or life safety corporate standards affecting layout:

_____

_____

_____

_____

_____

_____

_____

19.   Tenant's program of requirements for offices and workstations, by department:

	Dimensions (ft.)	Sq. Ft.	Number of Units Required*
Office types by size:			
A	_____ x _____	= _____	( )
B	_____ x _____	= _____	( )
C	_____ x _____	= _____	( )
D	_____ x _____	= _____	( )
E	_____ x _____	= _____	( )
F	_____ x _____	= _____	( )
Workstation types by size:			
G	_____ x _____	= _____	( )
H	_____ x _____	= _____	( )
I	_____ x _____	= _____	( )
J	_____ x _____	= _____	( )
K	_____ x _____	= _____	( )
L	_____ x _____	= _____	( )
Total tenant population*			( )

*Use a planning period of at least two years subsequent to the relocation date as the basis for the program requirements

20.   Tenant's "best case" stack and block planning requirements:

_____

_____

_____

21.   Prepare a forecast of the tenant program requirements in item 20, illustrating:

- Usable and rentable square feet of space required
- Bubble diagram of departments
- Block plan of departments
- Stack plan of departments

Describe the highlights of the forecast:

_____

_____

_____

_____

_____

_____

_____

22.   Prepare a preliminary tenant plan to test the forecast on the specific base building configuration proposed in the lease. (Attach the plan to this review.)

23.   Evaluate the preliminary tenant plan.

24.   Present findings to tenant for review.

Short-Form Building Comparison Spreadsheet

The less detailed spreadsheet that follows illustrates a methodology that may be used as a first-pass comparison, when many variations are being reviewed prior to serious lease negotiations.

It is recommended that tenants review a number of office buildings, and various floors within each building, to discover the many variations offered by these real estate options. The review should include preparation of a preliminary tenant plan matched to the tenant's program of space requirements.

This comparative analysis, conducted prior to substantive lease negotiations, is useful for narrowing the field and selecting those properties that warrant the more detailed evaluation methodology shown earlier.

COMPARATIVE OFFICE FACILITY EVALUATION (Short Form)

	Tenant's Prgm. Requirements A	Actual in Building B	Actual in Building C
1 Office facilities (B, C...) available for evaluation against (A) the tenant's program and forecast of requirements	_____	( )	( )
2 For floor(s) being reviewed, usable square feet as measured _____ floor _____ floor _____ floor	( ) ( ) ( )	( ) ( ) ( )	( ) ( ) ( )
3 Total gross usable square feet (all floors)	_____	_____	_____
4 Less: Sublease potential (if subleasing a portion for subsequent occupancy is a condition of the comparison)	( )	( )	( )
5 Total net usable square feet in this comparison	══════	══════	══════
6 Total rentable square feet indicated by landlord's proposal	_____	_____	_____
7 Less: Rentable square feet available in the sublease option space (if this is a consideration)	( )	( )	( )
8 Total rentable square feet of net option space which is basis of this comparison	══════	══════	══════
9 Ratio of usable square feet to rentable square feet (USF/RSF)	_____ %	_____ %	_____ %
10 Loss factor percentage Reciprocal	_____ %	_____ %	_____ %
11 Linear feet of window wall (in total linear feet)	_____	_____	_____
12 Window wall mullion module (in feet per window)	_____	_____	_____

13   Office and workstations by type (list the number
of units of each office type per the program in
column A and per the tenant plans in columns B, C...)

Type	Dimensions (ft.)	Sq. Ft.			
a _____	_____ x _____	= _____	_____	_____	_____
b _____	_____ x _____	= _____	_____	_____	_____
c _____	_____ x _____	= _____	_____	_____	_____
d _____	_____ x _____	= _____	_____	_____	_____
e _____	_____ x _____	= _____	_____	_____	_____
f _____	_____ x _____	= _____	_____	_____	_____
g _____	_____ x _____	= _____	_____	_____	_____
h _____	_____ x _____	= _____	_____	_____	_____
i _____	_____ x _____	= _____	_____	_____	_____
j _____	_____ x _____	= _____	_____	_____	_____
k _____	_____ x _____	= _____	_____	_____	_____

	Tenant's Prgm. Requirements A	Actual in Building B	Actual in Building C
14 Total square feet devoted to offices and workstations	_____	_____	_____
15 Total square feet devoted to support spaces, files, etc.	_____	_____	_____
16 Total square feet devoted to circulation	_____	_____	_____
17 Total all occupied square feet (usable)	_____	_____	_____
18 Total office and workstation occupants	_____	_____	_____
19 Ratio of circulation space (square feet) to total occupied space (usable square feet)	_____	_____	_____
20 Square feet (usable) per person housed	_____	_____	_____
21 Square feet (rentable) per person housed	_____	_____	_____
22 Total rental costs proposed by landlord in simple dollars, over the term of the lease	$_____	$_____	$_____
23 Estimate of other occupancy costs over the term of the lease (including estimated fit-out costs to be paid for by tenant)	$_____	$_____	$_____
24 Total costs of occupancy over the term of the lease	$_____	$_____	$_____
25 Costs per employee housed over the term of the lease (total $/employees housed)	$_____	$_____	$_____

26 Notes and comments (rank from 1 (lowest) to 10 (highest)):

· Fit of program within facility			
· Quality of resulting plan	_____	_____	_____
· Overall quality of building	_____	_____	_____
· Quality of facility's views	_____	_____	_____
· Evaluation as to desirability of floors in building under study	_____	_____	_____
· Evaluation of location of buildings in region	_____	_____	_____

Other notes and comments:

_____
_____
_____
_____
_____
_____
_____
_____
_____
_____
_____

CHAPTER 5

Retrofitting Existing Buildings for Office Automation

Piero Patri, Jay R. Hendler, and Richard Carl Reisman

Studies by the Department of Labor have determined that average clerical workers produce about 50 percent of their potential output; managers, about 65 percent of their potential. In the past 10 years, the federal government and the private sector have invested more than $25,000 per worker to improve the performance of factory workers across the country, and their productivity has nearly doubled. Over the same period, only $2,000 was invested per office worker, and the result was a correspondingly low (4 percent) rise in productivity. In the current shift from a manufacturing to a service-oriented economy, there is acute pressure to invest in the American office worker. Evidence of this is exemplified in how two giants of the office systems industry, IBM and AT&T, are spending more than $4.5 billion a year on product research and development, all targeted at the office marketplace. As a result of this and other research, better office automation systems with greater capacities and lower costs are entering the market daily. IBM added telephones to its terminals, acquired Rolm, and merged Rolm with Siemens; AT&T began selling computers and software; Wang expanded into data processing and telecommunications. At the same time, divestiture of the telephone industry and a lack of compatibility among competing office automation systems created confusion in the marketplace.

Today, a majority of office workers, at and below management levels, work at automated workstations; predictions for the year 2000 foresee a 100 percent saturation of computer workstations throughout the entire office facility market. Because the nation's developers add only a small percentage of new office facilities to the national stock of office facilities yearly, the vast majority of new computer workstations are being installed in existing buildings. Many of these existing buildings were designed and built prior to the invention of the computer, and most of these facilities require partial if not total renovation and upgrade, to support a modern, computer-intensive office environment. This chapter focuses on the retrofitting of existing office buildings to accept office automation and sophisticated building management systems. We will attempt to point out some of the critical issues that must be addressed and the potential impact of the solutions on construction costs.

In many respects, the greatest immediate impact of the "intelligent building" on the practice of architecture has not been in the physical design of the building. The technicalities of physically accommodating office automation are not unusually complicated. However, as chief representative for the client, the architect must take fiduciary and managerial responsibility for a design process that has been elevated to a new level of complexity, in efforts to create intelligent buildings. Architects must be able to seek out the right consultants, to obtain the technical advice necessary to protect their client's investment. They must be able to evaluate a consultant's proposal for expanded engineering, telecommunications, and office automation services for its appropriateness, and coordinate it with their client's needs. They must also successfully orchestrate the activity of the expanded project design and development team, to ensure timely completion of each team member's activity while maintaining the client's budget and schedule. Realizing that automation functions and equipment are constantly being updated within client organizations, we find that this broader responsibility of the architect includes such items as facilities management services to support ongoing

This chapter has been updated and edited by its authors since its original publication in *High Tech Real Estate,* edited by Alan D. Sugarman, Andrew D. Lipman, and Robert F. Cushman (Homewood, IL: Dow Jones-Irwin, 1985). Used with permission.

building operations. Within our own organization, we have introduced as integral parts of our services such automated operations as computer-aided design and drafting (CADD), space planning, and computer data bases for cost/benefit analysis of many intelligent building features.

Definition of an Intelligent Building

To paraphrase an article in *The New York Times* (1984), an intelligent building is one that has a computer for a brain and a nervous system of cables and electronic sensors that allows the computer to monitor and interact with building conditions and offers tenants access for telecommunications and for automated office services. Intelligent buildings have been around in one form or another for several years, but only the largest corporations have been able to afford the sophisticated technology involved. What is making headlines now is the fact that developers are beginning to offer their tenants these sophisticated capabilities, much as they once offered air conditioning or other amenities. The major impetus to this development has been the divestiture of AT&T and the subsequent deregulation of the telecommunications industry, which has made possible the bypass of the Bell System operating companies in the long-distance transmission of voice, data, and video signals.

Two major types of systems make up the intelligent building—building management systems (BMS) and communications/data processing systems. Building management systems form the operations core of a building: environmental controls, lighting controls, and elevator controls. The latest technology in BMS includes sensors distributed throughout the system that provide self-monitoring capabilities. BMS can result in reduced operating costs, better preventive maintenance, and increased equipment life. With a BMS, a smaller but more highly trained staff can monitor and maintain a larger building or several buildings from a remote location. The selection of the proper BMS systems, whether for new construction or renovation, involves programming and cost/benefit analysis by the architectural and engineering consultant team at the earliest stages of a project's development, in order to fully integrate the systems and thereby derive maximum benefit of their use. Rather than futuristic technology, BMS is a proven way of reducing the long-term costs of building ownership and is a necessary part of a building's structure in today's competitive leasing market.

Communications/data processing and related office systems, include local and long-distance voice, video, and data transmission; teleconferencing; and electronic mail—all supplied by means of a twisted pair of wires, coaxial cable, flat wiring, fiber optics, microwave, satellite, or a combination thereof. Data processing originates from desktop computers or terminals linked with a central processing unit; these may operate singly or in networks within the room, across the particular office facility, or throughout a multinational company's worldwide offices. Office systems include word processing, copying, and image transmission (such as telefax). All of these systems are packaged as the automated office and are the focus of most of the research and development and aggressive marketing of high-tech office product manufacturers.

Reasons to Consider Renovation

There are a number of reasons for considering renovation of an existing building as a real estate investment. With the recent revitalization of many city centers, there is a wealth of existing office buildings and other structures suitable for renovation or adaptive reuse. In selecting a potential site, the same considerations apply as for new construction—location, cost, time, function, and image. Price, access to transportation, public facilities, housing, and other amenities should be considered. Another consideration is the image of a company in its community, created through restoring an older building. Preserving a building helps to preserve the history of a city. The ambience, drama, and scale of materials of older buildings are not available through new construction.

There are financial reasons to consider renovation as well. Generally, rehabilitation, exclusive of automation, is 20 to 35 percent cheaper than new construction. One of the reasons for this is that renovation avoids many of the expenses of materials associated with new construction. Rehabilitation is, by its nature, labor-intensive; most of the materials are already on the site. The construction time is shorter and, in many cities, the approvals process for a renovation project is much quicker than for new construction, which accelerates the project and reduces carrying costs. Some tenants can even remain on-site during construction, avoiding loss of revenues. Ultimately, the costs in renovation depend on a multitude of conditions. In general, however, the additional costs of preparing a building to accept intelligent features during renovation are higher than for new construction, which runs $2 to $5 per square foot. This is just the cost for preparing the building to accept the intelligent features, and does not include the cost of the intelligent feature equipment, wiring, or other related items. Because of the rapidly improving technology and the variety of services available, planners should not rely on rules of thumb. A case-by-case analysis is required.

During the Carter Administration, the federal (and some state) tax codes were rewritten to provide tax incentives for the renovation of older buildings. Additional tax incentives were offered for energy conservation measures, and additional assistance was made available through grants and loans from the federal Housing and Urban Development (HUD) agency and its associated municipal and state job development authorities.

Owing to this "pump-priming," the construction and development industry initiated systems and procedures to cost effectively renovate older buildings, even those requiring the removal of asbestos and PCB perils. When the Tax Reform Act of 1986 limited these tax incentives, the process of renovating older buildings for modern computer-aided office operations proceeded on its own economic "steam," and because there are so many buildings requiring renovation, this process is likely to continue well into the next century.

Defining Development Goals

Before any final decision can be made regarding selection of a building for renovation, one should define the goals and objectives of the investment. For a developer considering renovation of an existing building into an intelligent building, this would involve the following: (1) defining the leasing market the project will ultimately seek to attract, (2) determining what communications/data processing systems are appropriate to that market and what building management systems are suitable to the building's operations, and (3) deciding when to provide and how best to structure the details of telecommunications and office automation features in the building—that is, owner provided or through a third-party provider. This process should involve the developer, the architect, leasing agents, operations staff, and special consultants for the engineering disciplines, telecommunications, and office information systems. The tenant mix is also important. Smaller tenants may not need sophisticated office services, and larger ones may own or lease such

equipment. The most likely potential users are those businesses with relatively heavy telecommunications and office automation needs, such as large accounting firms, law firms and other consulting groups, banks, and stockbrokers.

The same tenants that require the most sophisticated office automation systems also require the most sophisticated office security systems. At this writing, there seems to be a built-in negative bias against shared office automation systems from a security point of view and, moreover, as the price of local area network computer systems (LANs) continually spirals downward, the financial cost/benefits of sharing sophisticated office automation systems is further reduced.

For these reasons, each project will have its own criteria for office automation systems; there will be no standard operating procedure.

Office Automation and the Corporate User

Setting goals is somewhat different for the corporate user considering housing company operations in a renovated structure. It begins with an internal audit to determine automation usage in the company, both at current levels and at levels anticipated for the next three to five years. Questions to ask include: What benefits will be gained by using these technologies? Who should use them—executives, professionals, clerical staff? Which equipment is most appropriate? How much system integration is required? The dialogue should involve data processing staff, financial officers, appropriate departmental and facilities managers, architects, and specialized telecommunications and office automation consultants. Involving a broad base of staff in the goal-setting process prevents data processing personnel from forcing solutions on other departments and develops increased commitment within the organization to the program developed.

Historically, information systems were installed to solve internal problems so that key individuals would be free to focus on making business decisions. The ability of top management to understand the potential of office technology to achieve organizational results is critical to its success in effecting productivity gains. These gains range from supporting existing processes to creating new operational functions, and to using technology as a strategic tool in developing new business opportunities. The challenge to executive management is how to experiment with this new approach to information systems—how much control is needed, how to encourage innovation in the use of different technologies, and, while doing this, how to keep costs at a reasonable level.

According to the recently completed Buffalo Organization for Social and Technological Innovation, Inc. (BOSTI) study undertaken by Michael Brill and Westinghouse Corporation, 28 percent of office workers relocate once or twice a year, and 9 percent relocate three to six times a year. Statistics such as these illustrate the need for top corporate management to set policy on the issue of flexibility versus adaptability in their facility's design.

Basically, flexibility in building design translates into structures capable of accommodating changing operations and office technology requirements by quickly reconfiguring basic service systems. This versatility carries with it increased initial costs and is characterized by total reliance on such systems as raised access floors or flat wiring with carpet tiles, full-height removable partitions, and sophisticated HVAC-zoning capabilities, among other technologies. Adaptability, on the other hand, seeks to establish basic system configurations that allow expansion and contraction of functional areas, but always within established fixed constraints. An example is the use of a series of L-shaped, fixed walls in a large space, to access cabling systems from the ceiling plenum. Expansion of the department would be accomplished by growth out from the fixed wall into shrinking areas of adjacent operations and would only require additional cabling, which could be accommodated through the furniture systems. Adaptability may cost less initially for the facility, but it makes a greater demand on the employee to make do with what is available. For instance, newly promoted managers may find no suitable size office available to match that of their peers in the corporate culture, and other, perhaps financial, rewards may have to substitute for the more traditional recognition.

The Go/No Go Decision

Whether for the developer or the corporate user, once the programming phase is completed, the architect and consultant team can undertake a detailed analysis of the existing building systems and services and can recommend the amount and type of additional structural, technical, electrical, and telecommunications infrastructure required. Meetings with the city's planning and building department staff should be conducted at this stage, to ensure that building

renovation plans are within zoning and other code guidelines. This feasibility study is best accomplished before any financial commitments to the property are made. The critical product of this phase of project development is a preliminary cost estimate to accomplish the program. With this information, a pro forma can be generated, life-cycle costs calculated, and a go/no go decision made. The financial importance of this decision reinforces the need for early involvement of the right consultants, to provide sound and complete professional advice. At this stage, selecting a qualified general contractor to serve as a construction manager during the preconstruction/design process provides the entire project team with a valuable monitor for cost, schedule, and construction suitability. The contractor serving as construction manager should be engaged on a fee basis with no guarantees to take the project into construction. Incidentally, if microwave or satellite transmission is part of the program, a site analysis for technical suitability and the regulatory constraints of local public utility commissions should be part of the feasibility study to support the go/no go decision.

For corporate users of office automation, the earlier in the design process the automated office and telecommunications equipment can be specified, the simpler it is for the architect to design for its dimensional, electrical, acoustical, and heat dissipation requirements without costly change orders and construction delays. Developers, on the other hand, may be better advised to delay selecting their office automation offerings until a major tenant is signed up whose needs can then be more specifically accommodated. This approach avoids purchase of unnecessary or incompatible equipment. For the architect, the approach dictates a design strategy of preparing the renovated building to accept intelligent features without necessarily implementing them initially.

Contingencies for cost overruns and design changes are especially important in renovation projects. Generally speaking, during early stages of design, a 15 percent contingency is advisable; even at the end of the construction documents phase, the contingency should not drop below 8 percent.

Description of the Existing Building Stock

Before proceeding further, it might be helpful to categorize and describe the basic types of building stock available for renovation into intelligent buildings.

The first group consists of buildings constructed from the late 19th century to just before World War II. These may have originally been office buildings, lofts, warehouses, or factories. Most likely, if an office building, the structure has been renovated at some time previously in its history, but there are likely to be problems of power distribution and a need for other updated base support services. Whatever cabling system there is through the building is likely to be overcrowded with antiquated cables, which may be unidentified and perhaps cannot be reduced in bulk. Structural bay sizes will be small by today's standards, but greater floor-to-floor heights may provide the possibility of plenum or raised-floor approaches to new cabling, and the many columns allow for easy cable drops. Elevators, if present, are probably outdated, and energy conservation and life-safety systems, nonexistent.

These buildings may also have been designed with single-glazed windows, energy-inefficient roofing, and window wall details without insulation. They will not offer accessibility to the handicapped and are likely to contain asbestos and PCB perils. In a worst case, the existing duct work may contain a high level of bacteria and even the Legionnaire's disease bacteria. All of these perils are routinely remedied, but each must be reviewed prior to project initiation.

While on the subject of perils, many states now require an exhaustive review of all potential environmental hazards prior to obtaining permission to renovate older structures, especially those used earlier for industrial processing. Some of these older buildings simply cannot be sold, renovated, or even destroyed because of the hazards involved.

In the second category of buildings are those constructed after World War II. These buildings were wired originally by the telephone company and were in fact overwired. This wiring might be reused for many of today's automated applications, provided that adequate wiring plans exist and the insulation is still in good condition. Frequently, this older telephone wiring will be insulated with PVC plastic material which, in a smoldering fire, gives off poisonous gases. All PVC wiring must be removed from the ceiling plenums of such buildings. Typically, the ceiling plenum is utilized for mechanical systems. Main electrical cable distribution is through walls, from the ceiling plenum, or through service boxes coming from in-floor electrical ducts.

There is another unique problem associated with these post-World War II buildings: the use of the "soft touch" elevator button which, in a fire emergency, causes the elevators to home in on the floor where the fire is present. All such elevator buttons must be replaced as part of a renovation process. Moreover, energy conservation measures now required by some state laws mandate additional insulation, the replacement of single-glazing windows, and improvements to the heating and air conditioning systems of the buildings. Those buildings will not provide life-safety systems, sprinklers, or handicapped access as now required by many local building codes.

The final category is buildings built in the past 10 to 15 years. Many people would be surprised that such recently constructed buildings are candidates for rehabilitation into intelligent buildings. However, many of the speculative buildings completed only a few years ago are unable to accept the extensive office automation systems required by many tenants. Buildings from this period are characterized by HVAC in the ceiling plenum and overhead recessed fluorescent lighting. They may have underfloor ducting for wire management and outlet boxes built into the concrete floor. Power is probably adequate for some automation users; however, the problem lies in the distribution of power to meet current office space layout and special equipment needs. Many of these buildings may have elements of a building management system already in place. Some of the more current buildings will lack sprinklers and features for the handicapped, because those requirements are just being added to many local building codes.

Cabling

Perhaps the greatest demand the new office technology makes on a renovated building is how to accommodate the complex cabling requirements—how to handle all the spaghetti. Existing buildings were designed for cabling to enter at the ground level and then to be distributed upward. Microwave and satellite dishes on the roof upset the traditional bottom-up approach, wherein the riser system narrows dramatically as it goes up through the building. In addition, telephone closets were previously built to the specifications of AT&T, but now, in multitenant buildings, they must accommodate a variety of potential telephone equipment or service providers. Larger telephone closets may also be required because video and data transmission require access to cable of larger diameter, and many local area networks (LAN) will require computer software equipment associated with these wiring closets. At least a doubling in the size of these areas seems inevitable, with special air conditioning support likely for the LAN equipment.

The status of existing wiring can have a significant impact on the cost of renovation. As stated earlier, the telephone company often overwired older buildings, and much of this cabling may possibly be used to meet the needs of office automation. Moreover, the wiring raceway represents the greatest portion of the cost of wiring (not the wire itself). Given a situation with an existing in-floor duct system filled with unidentified or unusable cables, it may be more economical to salvage the duct system by removing all the wires and starting over. Many codes and good design practice require that power cables be separated from data lines, to avoid signal interference.

Even simple personal computers require three power connections: one for the VDU, one for the computer, and one for the printer, and the power may need to be stable and "clean." Beyond distribution of power, the automated office requires voice, data, FAX, and sometimes video cabling. A variety of cabling distribution systems are suitable for use in renovations, including ceiling plenums, poke-through systems, raised-floor systems, flat wire, and wiring in furniture systems, as well as combinations of each.

Ceiling Plenums

In older buildings with high floor-to-floor intervals, both ceiling plenums and raised-floor systems can be used. Ceiling plenums can economically accommodate a vast array of wiring, HVAC, sprinklers, and lighting. Delivering the wiring to the workstation can be somewhat of a problem. Using fixed walls is one solution. Although they are not flexible, they do provide privacy and would be appropriate in some instances, such as private offices in a law firm. Another alternative is full-height, movable partitions. These are not as acoustically private as fixed walls, but they do have the advantage of depreciating as pieces of office furniture or equipment. Power poles, although a somewhat unsightly solution, are probably the cheapest means of carrying the wiring down from the ceiling in open office design.

Poke-Through Systems

Ceiling plenums are also utilized in poke-through systems of cabling. Feeder lines are run through cable trays or brackets in the ceiling plenum. Floor penetration brings the services close to where they are needed

and has the capability to deliver power, telephone, and data through a single service fitting. Relatively low in cost at $2 to $4 per square foot, this system cannot be used in renovated buildings with thick concrete floors or those of post tension construction, because of resultant structural problems. The floor penetration requires other special considerations, because most floors are a part of the fire-rated protection of the building. This rating must be maintained, and all through-floor service fittings should contain fire-stopping material. The poke-through method has disadvantages in its inflexibility, and the structure is increasingly weakened when moves are made. Therefore, floor outlets must be placed carefully.

Raised-Floor Systems

Raised access floors were originally developed for areas where mainframe computers were located, but they are increasingly used throughout buildings in both new construction and renovations. The system is made up of pedestals or stanchions installed on the structural floor upon which modular floor panels are placed, creating a plenum underneath. This floor plenum can accommodate conventional cabling and, although an unusual application, it can also act as a void for return air from heating and air conditioning. The system requires no structural adjustments to the renovated building, but interfacing with nonraised areas—such as elevators, stairs, hallways, and bathrooms—must be dealt with. With a high initial cost of $6 to $10 per square foot, the raised-floor system provides maximum flexibility and minimal disruption to accomplish later changes. For a corporate client, we recommend this system in areas where significant operational changes occur, for projects where fiber optic cabling is to be installed, and in mainframe computer areas. For a speculative developer, allowance in the building design for a raised floor can provide a leasing advantage: new tenants are not as restricted by former tenants' layouts.

Flat Wire

Flat wire, used for cabling in both new construction and renovation, is taped directly on the structural floor and then covered with carpet squares. Building codes do not yet allow its use with broadloom carpet, but carpet tiles, although somewhat more expensive, have many advantages in their own right. Flat wire can carry power, voice, and data signals. For retrofit designs, permanent walls and structural columns can be utilized for transition boxes, to convert from conventional wiring in existing raceways to flat wires. A combination of this sort costs slightly more than poke-through. Flat wire's benefits include the fact that future moves and additions can be made with minimal physical impact and only very localized operational disruption. Because of its potential to wrinkle over a long run, it does require the floor underneath to be perfectly flat.

Furniture Systems

Most furniture systems on the market today have cable raceways integrated within the panels and partitions. Although such systems are higher in cost than nonelectrified furniture, they are extremely flexible and a good choice in renovations, as part of a strategy to retain existing wiring in fixed walls. If the tenants are to employ office furniture systems with wire troughs and other electrified wireways in the furniture panels, placing redundant wiring within the architectural floors, ceiling, and walls will not prove cost-effective. For owner/users, the selection of the most appropriate wiring system may include an almost total reliance on wired furniture panels; for a speculative office developer, such a reliance may prove detrimental to subsequent leasing success.

Wire System Maintenance

Whatever system is implemented, cable should be tested before and after installation of the lines and before hookup of equipment, to ensure that the loop is good. In large, highly automated operations, this can become a significant but necessary expense. Service people have in the past added new wires without pulling out the old, resulting in overcrowding and much useless wire in place. With increasing wiring loads, this cannot be done in the future. Owners should assume responsibility for maintaining building wiring diagrams and schedules.

Power Supply

Power supplies and distribution in existing buildings are usually inadequate for a heavier user of office technology. An energy audit by a qualified electrical engineer should be an integral part of the feasibility study undertaken before a final go/no go decision is made. For general budgeting purposes, assuming a routine renovation, one should allow $5 to $10 per square foot for electrical costs.

Automated offices require conventional electrical power and interference-free, "clean" power for both computers and telecommunications switches. In most situations, clean power simply means that, by using special equipment and dedicated grounding lines, circuits are protected from power fluctuations that can cause serious damage to electronic equipment. Backup generators and an uninterrupted power supply (UPS), although expensive, may also be required to protect valuable data bases. The UPS consists of a reserve electrical supply stored in batteries; it provides enough power to run backup diesel generators until they come up to full power or until computer operators can safely shut down the system without a loss of data. In addition, public utility power can be cleaned using the UPS, in conjunction with other equipment, to absorb fluctuations in the power. Because of the danger of potential acid leaks from batteries, the UPS should be stored in an isolated area. If electrically wired furniture systems are used, the UPS, in conjunction with the backup power system, constitutes a power source that is separate from normal utility power. The National Electrical Code requires each power source circuit to be housed in a separate raceway. If the extra circuit is required and it is not present in the furniture system, either an additional conduit must be provided or some other solution must be implemented at the user's expense. This wiring cost, as well as backup generators and UPS, is not included in the $5 to $10 electrical cost quoted earlier.

Structural Adjustments

The first step in assessing whether structural adjustments are needed is to understand the capacities of the existing system, which in the case of an older building can involve research and load testing. In California and some other states, there is the additional requirement of seismic retrofit. Many buildings today are designed with an 80- to 100-pound live load capacity to accommodate office automation equipment. Many of the older buildings that are candidates for renovation were originally intended in part for warehousing, and live load capacities of 100 to 150 pounds are not unusual, although many post-World War II speculative office towers were constructed with minimum allowable 40- to 60-pound live load capacities. If a building is a sound concrete and steel structure, with concrete floors and diaphragms in good condition, an allowance of $5 to $15 per square foot for seismic work is appropriate.

However, for a structurally sound building, several aspects of intelligent building renovation design may tax the structural integrity—including weight loads on the roof, imposed by microwave and satellite dishes; extra chillers; and other mechanical equipment. Within the building, there can be extreme weight loads from automation and telecommunications equipment, large banks of central files, or legal or business libraries, or from required supplemental air conditioning support systems or the UPS batteries. In addition, cutting holes in the floor to accommodate the increased size or number of risers and the chilled water lines from HVAC equipment can compromise the structure and may require mitigating measures.

HVAC

Many older buildings are excellent candidates for developing energy efficiency programs, because they were originally designed to function well in their climate—to keep their occupants as comfortable as possible without air conditioning. They generally have thick exterior walls and smaller and fewer windows than recently completed buildings. These aspects, when combined with a few additional passive features and active energy systems, can produce substantial energy savings in a building.

Sophisticated computers and related equipment generate substantial ambient heat into the workspace—as much as 15 to 20 percent average load increase over traditional offices. The impact of this increased heat load on mechanical systems varies, depending on such criteria as climate, building location, building materials, energy costs, and types of occupants and activities in the building. Other than in the renovation of the most recently completed buildings, one can assume that additional air conditioning and sophisticated energy management will enhance user comfort and operating efficiency. Based on a thorough listing of energy needs, a mechanical engineer can do an energy audit during the feasibility study and then give recommendations and prices for steps that may be appropriate. An allowance for upgrading the HVAC in an existing building should range from $5 to $15 per square foot.

Chiller capacity and the ability of the system to handle discrete zones where heat loads may be greater become more important with office automation. In many instances, mainframe computers require a jacket of chilled water or pipes running through the equipment to provide adequate cooling. Special computer utility closets in highly automated operations also require extra cooling. Air conditioning of these special areas should operate 24 hours a day, year round.

Lighting

As with energy-efficient mechanical systems, technology currently exists for several energy-saving lighting controls suitable for retrofits, most of which have payback within the first few years of operation. Some of these include infrared motion detectors that turn lights on and off as a person enters or leaves, and photocells that measure daylight contributions and adjust the levels of artificial light accordingly.

Glare on the VDU screen, which creates eye fatigue, is the greatest lighting problem in automated offices. Positioning the VDU away from windows or using blinds or shades helps. The wall behind the VDU screen should be a midtoned or medium color if possible. Light levels in general need to be lower in areas of heavy VDU usage. Where there is a mix of automated and nonautomated workstations, some combination of lighting is advisable. According to the General Services Administration (GSA), an even, glare-free blanket of 30 to 40 footcandles of ambient light is desirable for computer-intensive operations. This can be accomplished most easily with parabolic fluorescent fixtures mounted in the ceiling, with the remaining lighting within the office space provided by task lights directly on the work surfaces. The latter are more effective and more appreciated if they can be user-adjusted. Incidentally, static is one of the worst enemies of electronic equipment. Someone walking across a room in a building without humidity control and antistatic carpet could generate an electrical discharge strong enough to seriously harm both worker and machine.

Office Furniture Systems

Herman Miller first introduced modular office furniture with acoustic panels in 1968. Today there are more than 100 manufacturers of these systems. They have redefined modern space planning and are an integral part of the automated office.

Open Plan Limitations

The BOSTI study mentioned earlier revealed some interesting statistics on workers' attitudes and productivity in open plan offices. In spite of the fact that computers and printers can take up one third of the available horizontal space at a workstation, the dimensions of individual offices are currently shrinking because of economic pressures. Managers now generally are allotted an average of 115 square feet; professional and technical employees, 82; and clerical employees, 43. Space planners have tried to compensate for this shrinking space by lowering partition heights so that employees psychologically share their work areas. BOSTI discovered that workers actually favor offices with a high degree of enclosure and that their preference is reflected in their productivity levels. The study also found that, up to a point, this reduced-size office does not negatively affect job satisfaction. Extremes in crowding, noise, light level, and temperature, however, do have the expected detrimental effect on performance.

Selecting an Office Furniture System

As mentioned earlier, selecting an office furniture system designed to accommodate the new automated technologies can in some cases reduce the cost of installing cabling systems, facilitate future network changes, and improve the esthetics and productivity of the modern office and its maze of cabling. Acoustical panels and full-height relocatable partitions can significantly reduce the cost of reconfiguration over dry-wall construction. Beyond that, panels and modular office systems move when the tenant moves and allow for quicker occupancy in the new space.

Rather than moving to a file cabinet and back for information, VDU operators are confined to the screen for both input and output. As a result, they are much more stationary, and the workplace chair assumes a major role in worker comfort. Furniture companies are responding to this need with an array of new designs capable of a variety of adjustments to satisfy users' needs. Anyone preparing to purchase a large quantity of any office equipment would do well to work-test various options in actual in-office experiments.

Case Studies

In the past few years, the authors' office has been involved in several significant building renovations that included large amounts of office automation. Three of these renovations are described here.

Major Stock Brokerage Firm

The client for the largest of our smart building renovations is a major stock brokerage firm that had selected a newly constructed 28-story building in the heart of a downtown financial district. The building is typical of current speculative office building design and had not been specifically designed for their highly automated operations. One hundred percent of the clients' employees use either IBM terminals or Quotron, an electronic stock quotation system. Three floors of special computer rooms were required for the mainframes and related equipment. The Quotron system requires a home-run configuration, as opposed to a local area network (LAN), to provide maximum protection from tampering with the integrity of the financial data. The client also rejected flat wire as being too experimental for its conservative, highly security-conscious operating standards. Originally, the client anticipated leasing only the lower 16 floors of the building and the 28th floor, but initial programming and space planning studies showed that the entire building would be required.

RG62 coaxial cabling was used throughout the building, distributed by means of cable trays using a poke-through method in combination with electrified Herman Miller office furniture to reach the individual workstations. Quotron actually requires an RG59 cable; transformers were attached at the terminal end of the run to accommodate these specifications. This was done because the IBM equipment required RG62 cable, which is generally more common for automated needs. Extensive cable testing and wire management records were provided.

Each floor included a 140-square-foot telephone room. The telephone room on every third floor included Quotron processing equipment, which requires extra cooling to relieve heat loads. Because the four 4-inch risers originally in the building were inadequate for telephone and data lines, eight risers were added. However, their addition necessitated structural reinforcement to maintain the integrity of the floor slab.

The three-floor computer center was designed with a raised floor. Located in the central levels of the building, it was served by special chiller units located on the roof. This HVAC required additional structural support. Two 8-inch-diameter water lines were run from the chiller to the central computer area. In addition to extra air conditioning, some of the computer equipment required chilled water piped directly through it. Halon® fire extinguishing equipment was installed in the computer center, to avoid water damage from normal sprinkling systems. Extensive electronic security was installed to protect the center and other sensitive areas. A UPS and backup power generator were also installed to provide emergency power to the computer; four dedicated 4-inch conduits were required, to span from their locations to the computer center. According to the National Electrical Code, the UPS and emergency system would have required a separate raceway in the workstations that was not provided by the manufacturer. To avoid this extra expense and meet the code requirements, all power was run through what is technically the emergency circuit. The "regular" power circuits were few and were found only in areas without any VDUs or electronic equipment, such as lobbies and storage areas.

Advertising Agency

An advertising agency client had leased space in an office building completed in the previous five years. The building provided an in-floor cable duct system with "knock out" access points every five feet. Lack of reliable wire management records meant much of the cable was unidentified and unusable. Sophisticated building energy monitors had to be coordinated with the new interior construction. Renovation began with demolition of the three floors of space; only part of the HVAC ductwork was retained.

The client's program stipulated numerous private offices with fixed walls. These areas had wall outlets, which had to accommodate closed-circuit television on coaxial cable. The clerical areas used a Steelcase furniture system. Each station was designed to include a word processing unit with a printer. Cabling in these areas was accomplished through the in-floor duct system. All the existing cables in the ducts were removed and new wiring was installed. Clusters of six stations were served by a single electrical, telephone, and data floor monument; cable was run through the furniture system, which was prewired. Data from the word processor were transmitted through the duct system to central processing units located in a separate closet. A Donovan Data System was used for accounting; it had a similar layout, but it linked with a modem in the telephone closet to access the agency's East Coast headquarters. The overall space was very dense, with approximately 180 square feet per person. The preset knockouts did not work well with the layout, and numerous outlets had to be specially core-drilled to access the cable trenches in the needed locations.

Computer Training Center

A large corporation's computer training center was undertaken several years ago. Floor-to-ceiling heights were not great enough for a raised floor, and the client did not think such expense was justifiable. We attempted an unusual solution. A thin, wire duct system, two inches in depth, was laid out on the existing slab. Sleepers were used to provide additional support for a plywood subfloor, which was then covered with carpet. This solution was used before flat wire was on the market. The client has used the facility for some time now, and the limitations to accommodate the extensive cabling are becoming apparent.

Conclusion

The impetus behind making buildings "intelligent" is the desire of American business to become more efficient, more productive, and more profitable. Leading companies have targeted office automation technology as one of the key vehicles to increase clerical and management productivity. These companies recognize that their profit potential will be directly affected by worker productivity gains.

Building owners are beginning to ensure their tenants' success, and thereby their own rent structure, through direct support of these office technologies. Building management systems further enhance the owner's investment by reducing operating costs. As architects, we advise our clients to consider the following steps toward achieving their goals:

1. If a corporate user, define the objectives and goals for office automation. How will it assist current operations? How will it allow the business to remain competitive? How will it help to create new markets for products and services?

2. If a developer, define the leasing market. What kinds of tenants does one hope to attract? What communications/data processing systems will be needed? How can they best be provided—through the developer or through a third-party vendor/provider? Which systems are needed now, and which will be needed in the future?

3. Be willing to expand the traditional consultant team to include involvement of office automation and telecommunications consultants, and seek their early advice before firmly committing to any site, whenever possible. If microwave or satellite transmission is part of the program, a site analysis for technical suitability and regulatory constraints should be part of the feasibility study.

4. Consider renovation as the attractive alternative it is. When considering renovation, remember that it is cheaper to provide the ability for a building to become intelligent at the same time that traditional renovation work is done.

Architects are prepared to advise their clients as to the best technical, financial, and esthetic options for accommodating office automation technology in their buildings. Yet, in the end, the best advice they can give to clients is to remember to design for people as well, because that is the ultimate focus of productivity gains.

CHAPTER 6

Recruiting, Selecting, and Contracting with Design Professionals

Karen Daroff and James E. Rappoport

Overview

The Design Profession

Recruiting, selecting, and contracting with design professionals is a critical aspect of any corporate relocation project. By using the process recommended in this chapter, the corporate client will be able to quantify, qualify, form, and shape the project, establish its project management format, and build the internal organization necessary to maximize the benefits of the corporate relocation.

The term "design professional" is being used in this chapter rather than architect, interior designer, space planner, or any of the other professional trade titles various individuals and firms use to describe themselves and the services they provide for an office facility relocation.

Readers should be aware that a number of states and the many design professional trade associations in the United States have had ongoing discussions regarding various legislation to distinguish the legal criteria and professional ethics associated with the practice of architecture as it relates to interior design and associated office facility relocation professional services.

The professional liability insurance carriers also continually review the distinctions between the risks associated with the design of new office buildings by registered architects as compared to the risks associated with the design of office facilities within these existing base building core and shell structures.

There is some body of thought that a definition of "structural" improvements can distinguish what an architect does from the services an interior design professional is qualified to provide.

Because there are many variations in the services required for office facility relocations, and because there are various types of professionals and firms offering these services, the industry frequently uses the term "design professional" when referring in contracts to those engaged in the professional practice of office facility relocation design.

Readers are advised to determine which professional qualifications are required from a legal point of view, prior to further defining the term "design professional" for their particular project.

The office facility design profession has experienced significant growth and has become much more technically and fiscally proficient. The specialty of office facility design dates its origins to one of the first examples of a distinct functional separation from design's architectural parentage—the Chase Headquarters Plaza project, designed in the early 1960s by Architect Gordon Bunshaft. The interior fit-out was designed and managed by Bunshaft's interior design associate, Davis Allen of Skidmore, Owings & Merrill's New York office.

Many earlier corporate relocations, notably the Johnson Wax Tower by Frank Lloyd Wright and the Perelli Tower by P. L. Nervi, provided the clients with the architecture in which to set up their offices. In the Chase project, the headquarters facility was designed by Allen "from the inside out." The space program for this facility and its operations formed and shaped the architectural shell, and the facility was so well designed that it has met the needs of Chase for the past 30 years!

The modern office facility is most often tasteful, and sometimes elegant or even beautiful to view and work in; the inside-out designed facility works as a business tool to improve employee work flow,

This chapter has been updated and edited by its authors since its original publication in *The Commercial Real Estate Tenant's Handbook,* edited by Alan D. Sugarman, Robert F. Cushman, and Andrew D. Lipman (New York: John Wiley & Sons, 1987). Used with permission.

productivity, and interaction. The marketing needs of the company's image are enhanced and its spirit (or "corporate culture") has been created, nurtured, and displayed for its employees, customers, and clients, and for the public at large.

In the best of projects, this metamorphosis occurs within the time and budget constraints negotiated between the client's office facility manager (and/or project manager) and the selected interior design consultant. In the best of all possible worlds, the senior executives of the client company are pleased with the resulting new office facility and reward the facility manager in the time-honored corporate custom—with promotion, bonus, and salary increases.

This chapter is devoted to the authors' recommendations for medium to large corporate and professional firms that are about to recruit, select, and contract with design professionals to provide the variety of services required for a new office facility relocation project.

Appendix 1 of this chapter illustrates what the authors believe to be a typical 12-week time schedule for a major corporate project relocation, from the client's project initiation until the selection process recommended in this chapter has yielded a letter of intent between the client company and the selected design professionals.

These initial 12 weeks will be critical to the overall success of the project.

Trade Journal Statistics

One measure of the economic vitality of the office facility industry is the article, "The 100 Interior Design Giants of 1991," edited annually by Andrew Loebelson, in *Interior Design* magazine. For the 1990 calendar year, the 100 largest interior design firms, taken together:

- Employed 6,747 professionals
- Earned $665 million in fees
- Specified $12 billion in interior fit-out, furniture, and equipment
- Designed more than 265 million rentable square feet of office space.

In the process, they provided their services to more than 5,000 of the nation's major corporations, financial institutions, and professional firms and organizations.

Loebelson has computed a 32 percent per annum growth rate for the industry (or a 24 percent inflation-impacted growth rate) over the 17 years he has prepared his statistics.

A Unique Time in Real Estate

This is a unique period of time in the history of urban real estate in the United States and in the evolution of the real estate requirements of medium to large office facility users, to whom this chapter is addressed.

We define a medium to large user as one whose corporate staff is a minimum of 50 employees and whose real estate space requirement in a new facility will be at least 15,000 to 20,000 rentable square feet, when all of the space program requirements are analyzed and forecasts for expansion through the initial term of the lease are developed.

We believe that the recommendations suggested in this chapter are valid for company sizes beginning in the 15,000 to 20,000 rentable square feet range and extending to 1 million rentable square feet, the area of many of the major corporate relocation projects we and our peers design annually.

We make this distinction because the majority of office relocations in the United States are typically less than 3,000 rentable square feet of space for a staff size of 10 to 20 employees. Portions of this chapter may be appropriate for small space users, but most of our recommendations will be directed toward medium to large users' project requirements.

Some convergent background issues that have contributed to the uniqueness of urban office real estate in the United States in the 1990s are described in the following sections.

The 1981 Tax Act

The Economic Recovery Tax Act of 1981 (ERTA) provided the basis for five boom years of real estate development, from 1980 to 1985. By 1986, there was an excess supply of new, high-quality (A-level) office buildings and an even larger stock of renovated older office buildings, resulting in an excess supply of office building rentable square feet in most urban markets of the United States. By 1986, the office facility market had clearly become a tenant's market. These lingering market conditions have reduced the number of owner/developer/user office facilities, because it has become less costly to lease than to build. Most real estate economists believe that this phenomenon will continue in most markets well into the 1990s. Accordingly, the leased office facility will predominate in the years ahead.

The Mid-1970s Energy Crisis

The effects of the energy crisis of the mid-1970s had been on the wane, both because of the post-crisis fuel price reductions, which resulted in a slackening of cost increases for all types of energy, and because the post-crisis technical inventions produced highly energy-efficient office buildings. These buildings were constructed not only with an eye toward cost-effective initial development, but with the marketing requirement of clearly demonstrating to prospective tenants the energy-efficient and operating-cost containment features built into the new facility—the life-cycle cost features of intelligent (energy-efficient) buildings.

Owners of pre-energy crisis buildings have been renovating their buildings to add the energy-efficient features employed in new buildings, so that the marketing of renovated B-level office buildings can be said to be competitive, for life-cycle costs, with the newer energy-efficient A-level buildings.

Many tenants have learned the benefits of energy conservation and cost containment. Examples of the technical improvements they can employ include insulation, lower lighting levels, automatic heating and air conditioning setback controls, energy-efficient windows and roofs, fewer private offices and more open office planning, plug-in wiring and other details designed to ease office and workstation relocation after move-in, and many other office facility design features that affect operating costs.*

The Computer

The computer is now commonplace. Most companies are in or have already made the transition from manual to computer accounting, management, and word processing functions. Many companies are converting to PC networks, rather than continue

*Editor's Note: While this text was in preparation, a major disruption to oil supplies occurred as a result of hostilities in the Persian Gulf. For a few days, the cost of oil skyrocketed, which encouraged renewed political and technical discussions about conservation. After this short period of hostilities, oil prices returned to their former rates. It remains to be seen whether those parties encouraging conservation can maintain their political force in merit.

with their larger and less convenient mainframe configurations, and many new office buildings have prepared wiring configurations that will accommodate both the new PC networks and the local area networks (LANs) needed for telephone connections and data switches and controls.

Open Office Planning/Ergonomics

Most United States corporations have, to some degree, endorsed and implemented the technical, health, life-safety, and productivity improvements initially promulgated in West Germany in the early 1970s and known in this country as open office planning and ergonomic office product design (see Chapter 3).

Many tenants have responded positively to office furniture and computer support workstations that are designed to be configured in open office planning, and to office seating that meets ergonomic standards. These tenants are seeking further flexibility of use, improvements to productivity, and the health and occupational safety of their employees. In their search for new office facilities, their selection of new furniture and equipment, and their decisions regarding their existing inventory of equipment, they will be influenced by those goals.

They are also mindful of the "sick building syndrome," caused in part by a reduction in fresh air intake in highly energy-efficient mechanical systems, and they demand sufficient fresh air changes to avoid the toxic effects of a sick building.

The real estate, architectural, engineering, interior design, office products, and office equipment manufacturing industries are aware of these major changes in patterns of use and requirements for modern office facilities, and they are responding to the growing demand for superior office facilities that can offer the basis for further productivity improvement.

In sum, an adequate stock of both new and renovated high-quality office facility real estate is available to lease, to own through equity participation, or to otherwise develop. The majority of these facilities have been renovated or recently designed to meet the most stringent energy efficiency standards and the most advisable life-cycle costs containment. The facilities can be wired for the current and future needs of most tenants' data and voice communications requirements. They can be fitted out with the most up-to-date furniture, finishes, and equipment, and can meet tenants' expectations for further productivity improvement—all as a consequence of the office relocation.

A Tried and Tested Market Basket

These design concepts, economic factors, and technical forces have been at work since the early 1970s and have produced a market basket of ideas and products that most companies can employ in their office facility design and relocation in the 1990s and beyond.

Access to this market basket of ideas and products requires a design consultant who can assist in defining a client's precise requirements while utilizing the most effective and efficient set of design decisions and product specifications. Only then will the project's specific needs, program of space requirements, budgets, time constraints, and esthetic aspirations be realized. Moreover, clients require a design consultant who can prepare the various contract documents and specifications that control investment in a new facility, and who can manage the project within appropriate legal and fiscal constraints, at minimum risk.

The New Office Facility Project

Among the readers of this book will be corporate executives who are entrusted by their company with the management of a new office facility project. These executives may already be facilities managers, or they may recently have been pressed into service as a facilities manager for a new office facility project. In either case, the process of contracting with design professionals presupposes that a decision to seek a new office facility has been reached by the company.

The company then is a prospective client to the office facility design consulting firms in the region of the project. As word of the pending project spreads, there will be ongoing interaction between the company and a myriad of consultants, contractors, and suppliers who will recognize a potential opportunity to participate in the new office facility project.

During the initial stages of a project, little will be known about the exact size and scope of the proposed new facility. Usually, some corporate strategic requirement causes a relocation decision to be made. Once this has occurred, the organization will begin to consider what operational efficiencies, technical improvements, and corporate image issues need to be addressed as a product of the relocation.

The project will require almost full-time attention from at least one corporate executive, from its earliest beginnings until the move-in date, which is likely to be at least one year in the future. For a major relocation, the adaptive reuse of an existing facility, or a new development project, a two- to three-year project period is not uncommon. Accordingly, the selection of an appropriate in-house corporate project manager is critical for the company, and acceptance of this role can be important to the career of the selected executive.

Once the corporate decision has been made to seek a new office facility, and discussions occur as to how the project should be scoped out, staffed, and managed, the process of dealing with design professionals begins.

Preparing for the Selection Process

Who Should Join the Project Committee?

Initially, the client company's project committee will determine the strategic aspects of the project and will recruit and contract with the appropriate design consultants, real estate consultants, lawyers, and others who will be selected to provide the technical assistance and consultation required to develop the new office facility project.

Because preparing and negotiating contracts is one of the major skills required of this committee, those in the organization currently entrusted with similar responsibilities are typically selected to join the committee. The financial officer, the legal or contract officer, perhaps the purchasing officer, and the human resources executive would be likely candidates for the selection committee. Many chief executives want to head the selection committee, and many committees are joined by operational executives who have the most to gain from and to contribute to the project's success.

Once the committee is established, the first order of business should be to block out a weekly meeting day, time, and place, so that the work of the committee can proceed according to a time line to be established by the committee, and will not be hampered by day-to-day corporate responsibilities that might otherwise interrupt the committee's timely discharge of its responsibilities.

Appendix 1 of this chapter offers a typical project time line for a medium-size office relocation project, from the date of the first project committee meeting until the project is entrusted to the client company's project manager and the selected interior design consultant. This 12-week period will require at least one committee meeting a week, to proceed as indicated.

The ultimate timely completion of the project will limit the overlap of facilities and the resulting double rent and related costs associated with the worst-case scenario of operating both the old and the partially completed new facility at the same time. A timely relocation will also meet the overall corporate goals and ensure a positive response from the company's senior executives. Time is clearly of the essence in any corporate relocation.

If the assembled committee cannot select a peer to serve as the project manager for the corporate relocation project, then a project manager from within the company or from the community at large must be selected.

The company may wish to recruit a facilities manager who has managed a similar relocation for a peer company and has been trained to assume the responsibilities of a facilities manager.

There has been a growing body of knowledge since the early 1970s in the newly emerging corporate profession of facilities management. Facilities management is a new course of study in a few business and architectural universities, and the American Management Association and other similar management training organizations routinely offer courses in this new corporate management technique.

Reviewing corporate year-end statements, one finds substantial corporate assets invested in office facilities and related equipment, and most facilities management courses stress the methods to improve overall productivity by cost-effective investment in and ongoing operational management of new office facilities.

We do not view the facility manager's responsibilities during the design and construction process as being solely project management. The ongoing operational management of the new facility—including subsequent warranty management of the new furniture and equipment, departmental and office and workstation relocations, life-safety issues, risk avoidance and insurance relationships, energy conservation, relationships with the various public utilities and the data and telephone voice network suppliers, care and maintenance of the myriad of office equipment products, and ongoing maintenance and repairs in the new office facility—requires day-to-day management after move-in.

If a peer is selected from within the company, the selection process can proceed as indicated in Appendix 1. If recruiting from the community at large is required, the process will be delayed because the facilities manager must, in our opinion, lead the selection process. According to our timetable, this process begins in the sixth week, on the occasion of the pre-bid conference for interior design consultants.

Once the facilities manager has been selected, the project committee should be chaired by this manager, and thereafter the facilities manager should issue to each member of the committee weekly updated reports that outline the progress of the project and set the agenda for the next week's meeting.

Once the process proceeds into design phases, the weekly meetings might be reduced to biweekly meetings, but this decision should remain with the facilities manager, who will quickly learn how to manage the project and keep the selection committee informed, while allowing the other members of the committee to resume their day-to-day corporate responsibilities.

Who Will Make the Final Decisions?

One of the questions asked by Andrew Loebelson in his *Interior Design* magazine research is concerned with the relationships between the interior design consultants and the senior corporate executives of their client companies.

Fifteen years ago, when Loebelson's research began, most major office facility decisions were made by the senior executive(s) of the client company. Recently, the project committee led by the facilities manager has emerged as the final decision-making team, and, in some corporations, especially service organizations, the committee has included representatives from all aspects of the company, including nonexempt and industrial operative employees.

In theory, one of the goals of any office relocation is improvement of employee morale. By involving a wide range of company employees in the various project-related decisions, many companies have assured a high degree of improvement in employee morale during, after, and as a result of the office relocation process.

The facilities manager will need to establish early in the project how final decisions will be made, because the process of selecting, contracting with, and managing the work of the interior designer requires that the client company make timely and final decisions at various key dates during the process. The project will simply not meet its budget and time goals, if timely and effective decisions cannot be made by the client company.

In our experience, the best project result occurs when the facility manager has been entrusted with the decision-making power, authority, and responsibility to directly manage the relocation process.

What Services Are Required?

The project committee's major task is to establish the overall strategic goals of the project, including the qualification of the services required of the interior design consultant; the scope of work; budgets; the likely project size; and the selection of the relocation.

Many of these issues will be developed and confirmed by the interior design consultant after the consultant has been recruited. A decision made by many project committees is to hire an interior design consultant to provide only the services identified as being in Phases I through III of Appendix 4 of this chapter: programming, site selection, and technical lease assistance.

At a minimum, however, all of the following items should be tentatively established by the project committee, pending confirmation by the selected interior design consultant; otherwise, it is difficult to contract with the consultant for services unknown to either party. These essential concerns are:

- The type of corporate organization to be housed in the new facility
- The client's company's relationship to the new facility
- The company's overall project goals and the reasons behind the new facility
- The present location of the employees to be relocated
- The approximate rentable square feet of space occupied presently by the employees to be relocated
- Why the existing facilities are inadequate
- The approximate number of employees to be relocated to the new facility (current employees plus newly hired employees)
- The approximate date of the proposed relocation and the various critical deadlines in the process
- The approximate rentable square feet of space required in the new facility at move-in and/or at various periods of time subsequent to move-in
- The number of departments to be relocated
- The approximate make-up of these departments as to

    —private office occupants
    —open office workstation occupants
    —back office staff

- The number of senior executives to be relocated and some description of their individual expectations regarding custom office design and features
- Any especially elegant or highly detailed rooms required in the facility
- Key project dates
    —data gathering
    —move-in
    —full occupancy
    —acquisition of additional space
- The geographic location of the proposed new facility
- How many office buildings are to be tested and evaluated
- A full checklist of special features that the company knows may be required in the new facility.

Each of these items is itemized and presented in the Project Fact Sheet in Appendix 4.

When this information has been outlined by the committee, the selection process for the interior designer can proceed, in a format that gives both the company and the designer a reasonable idea of what each expects of the other.

To establish a firm contract with the selected interior designer, a project budget and more precise timetable will likely be required. The budget analysis could proceed parallel with the selection process, or could be established subsequent to the selection process but prior to the contract negotiations, or could be a first scope of service to be provided by the interior design consultant prior to contract signing. In any case, the company will be called upon by contract to establish a project budget, and the sooner this process begins, the more effective the project manager will be in negotiating and contracting with the interior design consultants and other consultants and suppliers associated with the project.

What Scope of Service Is Required?

After the basic goals and features of the project are outlined, and with a project budget in mind, the next step is to determine the scope of service required of the interior design consultant.

Most of the major interior design consulting firms follow approximately the same delineation of scope of service. Some years ago, these services were euphemistically described as: programming/data collection, schematic design, design development, contract documentation, and contract administration.

Appendix 4 of this chapter gives an expanded outline of the tasks associated with 13 phases of a typical corporate office facility relocation project. Each task is defined so that the client company's facilities manager and the project committee can clearly understand what services to expect from the interior design consultant. Our 13 phases are as follows:

    I. Programming
   II. Site selection
  III. Technical lease assistance
  IV. Assistance in recruiting engineers
   V. Space planning and schematic design
  VI. Design development
 VII. Revisions
VIII. Contract documentation and specifications
  IX. FF&E supervision
   X. Construction field observation
  XI. Punch listings
 XII. Occupancy
XIII. Postoccupancy evaluation

Not all projects require all of these aspects of the scope of service, and some projects may require specialized services not listed here. The project committee should review the scope of work and determine, in as precise a manner as possible, the basis for the interior designer's fee proposal and ultimate contract for services.

Why an Interior Design Firm?

The scope of services clearly indicates that most corporate office facilities will require the services of a design consultant trained in interior design and space planning. Several types of professional firms provide interior design and space planning services for corporate relocations. A brief description of each type follows.

In-house staff in major corporations may be able to design and manage the internal relocation of departments and of office and workstation occupants, once the facility has been created by an outside interior design consultant. Few major corporations maintain highly skilled interior design consultants on staff; most corporations that formerly employed in-house designers have found it much more cost-effective to contract with an outside interior design consultant for a specific project.

In some major corporations, the *in-house interior design team* will join with the project facilities manager to assist in the recruiting, selecting, and contracting of the interior design consultant. They will typically assume day-to-day management of the joint effort of the consultants and the in-house staff.

In addition to cost determinations, the *outside interior design consulting firm* will have a wide breadth of professionals able to cover a variety of the services required during a corporate relocation. The firm will approach the project from a fresh, objective, professional viewpoint that is free from corporate politics and policies, many of which may have created the present desire to relocate the corporate facility.

The *office building developer's designers,* whether they are on staff or consultants to the developer's project, may be eager to prove that a particular office building meets with the client company's intended use. They will offer an initial tenant plan based upon a quick programming effort, and, for many smaller office relocations, the resulting standard "workletter office space" will indeed meet the intended use within the budget and time goals the client company has established.

For larger corporate relocations, however, the client facilities manager will likely want to test various developers' office facilities against one another on a features and benefits basis. Together with the company's real estate consultants, the facilities manager will examine the costs of various facilities in several interpretations: cost per rentable square feet; cost to operate over time; and costs per employee housed. This latter efficiency analysis is sure to indicate the vagaries of the various office facilities being investigated.

Client companies cannot rely simply on the various individual developers' designers to provide this comparative analysis, because each designer is assisting in an effort to market a particular office building.

The *furniture dealer* presently selling office supplies and furniture to the company will typically have on-staff designers who are trained to lay out the furniture the dealer sells to the company. Many of these designers are highly trained to offer a full service for smaller office relocations.

Comparative analysis services are rarely provided by the furniture dealer's designers, and they will not be able to assist with the technical aspects of the project's engineering or architectural requirements. For some smaller projects, however, these services may not be required.

Many client companies will want to bid the interior design specifications among various competing dealers, to test available sources and prices for the goods and services required to fit out the new facility. In order to establish a competitive bidding process, a design professional who is independent of the organization(s) offering the goods and services is typically employed.

If a company wants to reuse existing furniture and add other components to fit out the new facility, the present furniture dealership will be able to provide invaluable service. Working with the independent design professionals, the dealership can assist in the furniture specifications, manage the purchase of new parts or components, and plan for the physical relocation of the existing furniture into the new facility.

A *decorator or small interiors firm* may have enjoyed a successful relationship with the company's senior executives or may even have provided interior design services to decorate some aspect of the existing corporate facility. These individual practitioners are typically not prepared to offer the scope of service required for a medium or large corporate relocation requiring thousands of hours of professional talent over an extended period of time.

In some special cases, corporate facilities managers will employ a decorator to offer assistance for a special area of the facility. Most major interior design consulting firms offer similar service with a higher degree of project management and reliability, and for similar fees.

The *interior design department of a large architectural firm,* or of the firm that has designed the office building, is technically able to offer a full scope of services, and these firms are frequently invited to submit qualifications for corporate relocation projects.

If the project is (for example) a computer or data center, where the base building engineering equipment must be modified to accept the client's intended use, then the architect's design professionals might be an effective choice.

The growing trend in the industry is for architects' interior design departments to create fiscal and legal entities that are separate from their architectural partners. This has occurred as a result of the recent professional liability premium inflation, because design professionals have fewer risks than architects and pay lower premiums. This separation of responsibilities was an outcome of the Economic Recovery Tax Act of 1981 (ERTA), whereby interior fit-out was described as personal property and was treated to rapid depreciation and investment tax credits not extended to the fixed asset work of the architects.

The interior design profession has developed its own specialties. Interior design consulting services added in the past few years include data base management, programming facilities management consultation, and furniture implementation and supervision services. Many of the most qualified interior design consultants have joined together to form the major interior design consulting firms researched annually for Loebelson's article in *Interior Design.*

Daroff Design Inc. is an example of a *full-service interior design consulting firm.* Staff size is approximately 50 interior design and architectural professionals. Specialization in major corporate, financial, and professional organization relocations is combined with similar service to the hospital, health care, hotel, and conference center industries. The firm is fully computerized, with computer-aided programming, planning, project management, and drafting equipment.

We believe that, for most corporate relocation projects, interior design consulting firms are the most qualified to provide the scope of service required within the client company's project goals, budgets, and time constraints.

The Selection Process

Even if the company or one of its senior executives has worked with a design professional in the past, or the company has determined that a particularly talented designer or design firm is uniquely qualified to design the proposed office facility relocation, the company will almost certainly want to investigate various sources for the interior design services required.

The company may not typically follow formal bidding practices. Nevertheless, we recommend that the selection process for the interior design consultants proceed in the formal manner of competitive bidding of goods and services.

Interior design consulting firms have substantial experience in this method of competing and, we believe, would unanimously join in a recommendation that a clear, precise, competitive evaluation of each firm's merits will produce the best project result with the most "goodwilling" client/consultant relationship.

To prepare for a formal competitive selection process, the client company must provide certain project-related information, which will require substantial project management and clear presentation of the results of this management effort.

From the consultants' point of view, a client's clearly presented "request for proposal" and "form of pricing proposal" offer the basis for a clear competitive presentation of qualifications. The consultants' feeling that professional ability, understanding of the client's requirements, and interpersonal compatibility with the client will be the bases for selection will usually produce the best responses to the client company's request for proposal and ultimately the best project.

Selecting Firms to Submit Qualifications

The interior design consultants will be entrusted with the design and project management of a substantial amount of the client company's budgeted costs for the project. In addition to creating a new corporate identity, the design professionals will be responsible for designing the features that will establish the operating cost containments and productivity improvements the client company expects from the new facility.

Using proper project management, the design professionals can become the catalyst in relocating the company, within the stated time constraints and budget allocations; plan effectively for the known requirements of the growing company; and consult with the company's managers, to prepare the organization for its space and equipment requirements in the years ahead.

Interior design consultants will assist in establishing a new image for the client company (or updating the present image)—an important aid in marketing efforts. They will also assist in recruiting new employees and monitoring the care and comfort of the existing staff. As a result, overall operating costs per year per employee in the new facility can be reduced. In the process, the interior design consultants will advise on the most efficient and cost-effective use of the space being leased and the capital resources to fit out this space, and they will meet the client company's goals for reducing utility bills, maintenance costs, and other ongoing operational expenses.

Moreover, the interior design consultants will design the new facility so that it provides a high level of occupational safety for the client company's staff, customers, clients, and visitors. They will make recommendations to resolve chronic complaints of employee eyestrain, noise pollution, backache problems (caused in part by improper seating posture), and a myriad of related health and safety issues.

This relationship between a client company and its interior design consultants is likely to be long-term. Even a one-floor installation requires 8 to 10 months from start to finish. A multifloor headquarters could require 20 to 30 months of consultation, and the best managed projects provide the basis for an ongoing client/consultant relationship in the years following the initial project installation.

Each major urban market has a handful of highly qualified and competitive full-service interior design firms available to respond to requests for submission of qualifications, and ultimately to provide the scope of services required within stated budget and time constraints. Some of these firms may be too large or too small for a particular client company's needs or project requirements; some firms may be too busy to respond when the services are required; and some may be specialized in certain aspects of the profession that do not match with a specific project.

The first step in the process of selecting an interior design consultant is to ask several firms (as appropriate for the project requirements) to submit a qualifications brochure.

Client companies can learn which firms to approach from consulting Andrew Loebelson's annual *Interior Design* article; from discussion with peers, friends, associates, real estate agents and consultants, developers, architects, mortgage bankers, and building managers. Other sources of references are the local chapter of the American Institute of Architects (AIA) and the Institute of Business Designers (IBD). Client company purchasing managers may also learn of qualified interior design consultants by consulting with the major furniture dealers and the local sales representatives for the major office furniture systems and related products in use in the existing facility.

The resulting list of likely firms is known in the trade as a "long list." Eventually, this list is reduced to a group of competing firms that the client company's selection committee feels is manageable under the particular circumstances of the project.

For most office facility relocation projects, the initial list should be pared down to no more than eight to ten firms, prior to issuing a request for qualifications.

The Request for Qualifications

The request for qualifications could take the form of a letter to the chief executive of each firm on the long list, asking the firm to submit qualifications for the project. An example of such a letter is shown in Appendix 2 of this chapter.

The same result can be achieved with a telephone call to each firm's marketing manager, requesting that a qualifications brochure be sent to the attention of the client company's project manager.

The federal General Services Administration (GSA) has prepared two qualifications forms—Form 254 (general) and Form 255 (project-specific)—which all design firms have completed and updated from time to time. The forms, available from any GSA office, make qualifications presentation uniform and concise and may be useful to evaluate design firms for certain types of projects. However, the free-flowing marketing prose of the typical interior design consulting firm's qualifications brochure is more likely to offer the insight required to preselect the firms most likely to understand the client company's specific requirements and to allow the client the best opportunity to understand which firms can produce the design quality required.

Because most design firms follow the GSA format in their qualifications brochures, a client company will probably learn more about the relative strengths and weaknesses of various firms by specifically requesting their qualifications brochures rather than the GSA forms.

Selecting Long-List Firms to Submit Proposals

Once these qualifications brochures have been received, the firms that best meet the project requirements will become obvious. We recommend that no fewer than three and no more than five of these firms be asked to submit a formal proposal for the project. This list of three to five firms is known in the trade as a "short list."

Each of these firms will be asked to invest substantial time and energy in the competition for the project. If the list is too long, the most qualified firms will simply not submit. An average cost to respond to a formal request for proposal is approximately $5,000; many firms only submit proposals where at least a one-in-three chance of being selected is believed to exist.

We recommend the following checklist for evaluating the qualifications brochures of firms that respond to a request for qualifications.

- Response illustrates projects similar in scope, type, and size to the proposed project.
- Response illustrates a capacity to provide the services the project requires, in the time frame in which the project is to be designed and built.
- Professional staff is sufficient to provide the project team required.
- References seem to offer confirmation from former clients (a formal check of references is required in the final stages of the selection process).
- Location is in the general geographic area, or a project team can be located in the geographic area.
- Printing quality of the brochure and overall graphic content illustrate the firm's ability to present itself graphically.
- Reprints and photographs included illustrate the quality of the firm's work on specific projects.
- Brief history of the firm defines the firm's staying power and assists in understanding its financial strength.
- Statement of design philosophy assists in understanding the firm's culture and its fit with the client company's as well as the firm's language and writing skills.
- Staff résumés offer insight into the professional qualifications of the firm's principals and key staff members and illustrate length of service, an indication of the firm's management stability.
- Rate sheet assists in an overall understanding of the firm's pricing policy; average hourly rate allows comparison with other firms' fee requirements.
- Fee income and present backlog assist in understanding the firm's ability to take on the project and present level of success.
- Statement of design philosophy assists in understanding the firm's culture and its fit with the client company's.
- Overall writing skills assist in understanding the ability of the firm to efficiently communicate.

The Pre-bid Conference

After the short list has been established, the firms' representatives meet formally for the first time. This is typically accomplished by calling for a pre-bid conference. Appendix 3 to this chapter shows a simple form of invitation.

Typically, the meeting will begin with introductions of the client team to the assembled competitors. A sign-in sheet for the pre-bid conference can be designed to identify who is attending from each firm and to gain acknowledgment that the attendees received the formal request for proposal and understand when the formal proposal is due back. The competing design firms' representatives will then introduce themselves. Knowing who the competition is nurtures a competitive spirit and may sharpen fee pricing competition.

Drafting the Request for Proposal

We have provided a draft form of a request for proposal (see Appendix 4), which includes many of the features most office facility relocation projects will require and outlines most of the scope of service phases that are typical in the interior design industry.

The client project manager is invited to review this recommended form of request for proposal and to edit this form as required to suit the needs of the client's specific project.

Later in the process, the request for proposal form will become the scope of service attachment to the contract for interior design services. By using the same language in the request for proposal, bid proposal, and contract, the client facilities manager is assured a reasonable degree of clarity and continuity between the offer and the accepted offer, confirmed by the ultimate contract.

We recommend that, prior to the pre-bid conference, the formal request for proposal form be distributed and that any questions posed by the various competing firms be responded to both at the conference and as a written addendum to the request for proposal.

Addendum to the Request for Proposal

The questions the competing firms will ask at the conference may be divided into two basic areas: honest requests for clarification, requiring clear and concise replies and subsequent addenda issuance, and marketing diatribe that is ill served to highlight the questioner. The latter should be noted as part of the subsequent evaluation process.

If any substantive questions raised at the pre-bid conference, or in subsequent individual interviews

or telephone conversations with individual bidders, require clarification to all bidders, the clarification should be issued in the form of an addendum to the request for proposal. An example is presented in Appendix 5.

In this manner, all bidders have the benefit of each other's questions and the responses given, and all will understand that a fair and even-handed competitive process has been used.

Any addenda should be distributed to all competitors no less than five working days prior to the due date of the proposals. Generally, all questions received within the five-day period prior to the bid's delivery should be refused, but if a deal-breaking question is raised in the eleventh hour, a telephone call to each competing firm may be required, with a written follow-up.

Meeting with Each Firm

As an agenda item during the conference, the client representatives should establish the date(s) for individual interviews conducted at the various competing firms' studios. These private interviews will require at least 90 minutes each and should be arranged back-to-back over one or two days, to maximize the comparative understanding of the interaction of each of the firms with the client representatives.

We recommend that the agenda for the individual meetings be set by the design firm(s), so that the client selection committee can learn first-hand how the would-be consultant organizes project meetings. The meeting might take the form of an informal walk-through of the offices, to observe the size and type of organization and its working environment. The firm might then show slides of its prior work, introduce proposed key project team members, conduct a tour of the work areas, to view the stages of other projects in progress, and show off the prowess of its computer-aided drafting and facilities management installations.

The firms will need to discuss each of these issues in the request for proposal. An informal studio walk-through will serve as confirmation and clarification of the significance of their responses on the form.

We recommend that the client selection committee limit each visit to no more than 90 minutes and avoid asking for precise information about work in progress for other clients. Any information gathered should be considered confidential by both the host-firm and the visitor-client.

The key goals of the office visit are as follows:

- Verification of the information supplied in the qualifications brochure
- Confirmation that the proposed project team is technically qualified to provide the scope of service required
- Evaluation of whether the proposed project team members can communicate in harmony with each other and with the client company's project team and other related project consultants
- Estimation of whether the consultant's studio space and layout are sufficient to provide for the comfortable management of the proposed project
- Direct response to any points of clarification raised by the consultant(s) and issuance of any necessary formal addenda
- Review of project documentation (drawings and specifications) of recent projects of similar scope, to verify the quality of the firm's documentation process.

By holding these interviews back-to-back and, if possible, by scheduling the two best firms for first and last, the client selection committee will gain the needed insight into which firm or firms can best provide the scope of service required.

The committee must then learn the relative equation of the service proposed versus the cost of the service proposed.

Selecting from the Firms that Submit Proposals

We view the selection decision for an interior design consultant as a matrix of price/quality expectations. No two projects are alike, no set of project teams functions the same way, and each project seems to offer a unique set of opportunities and constraints.

The interior design consultant's response to the formal request for proposal, and the qualifications and understanding derived from the studio visits, should provide for the objective evaluation of the competing firms.

A matrix evaluation form for determining the most qualified firm is provided in Appendix 6.

If, in reviewing each firm's responses, the selection committee determines that certain information is missing or unclear, the committee should request, in a telephone call, verbal clarification followed by a written confirmation from the would-be consultant.

The written follow-up is important; the ultimate contract for service will be based on the response to the request for proposal plus all of the addenda and these final points of clarification.

By following the matrix in Appendix 6, a clear winner will usually emerge. The next step is to actively enter into an acceptable contract with the selected interior design firm.

The Contracting Process

The 1980s were marked by a skyrocketing increase in all types of professional liability insurance premium costs. Interior design firms have little, if any, architectural risk, because their profession is limited to fitting out buildings built under architects' plans and specifications; yet their insurance premiums increased during the 1980s from less than $5,000 yearly to more than $50,000 yearly. For multidisciplinary firms, premiums increased at an even greater rate.

Many of the contract forms approved and printed by the American Institute of Architects (AIA) are dated as "revised in 1974 and 1980," before professional liability insurance premiums skyrocketed. (These contract forms are copyrighted and cannot be reprinted in this text, but are readily available from AIA bookstores in most major urban areas, or by mail from the AIA, 1735 New York Avenue, N.W., Washington, DC 20006.)

These contract forms, specifically Forms B141, B141CM, and B707, are, in our opinion, still viable as agreements to wrap around the expanded and clarified scope of interior design service recommended in the request for proposal. However, both the client and the selected consultant will want to make major modifications to this form agreement, to accommodate the consultant's professional liability coverage and related new codes of professional practice.

The AIA forms are used almost universally in the industry, because they tie the language and scope of service in the agreement with the design professionals to similar language found in parallel agreements between the owner and the project engineers, contractors, construction managers, other project team members, and various other consultants.

The client's goals should be, in our opinion, to negotiate a complete scope of service and set of responsibilities with the various members of the ultimate project team, and to be assured that one or more of the project team members has taken on and been contracted to provide each of the areas of responsibility and scope of service required for the specific project.

It is far easier to use the AIA forms for this purpose than to begin to create a series of agreements to cover each responsibility or scope of service requirement.

Negotiating with the Selected Consultant

In negotiating with the selected interior design consultant, the first step is to be assured that the scope of service itemized in the request for proposal is matched in the consultant's response to the request for proposal. Through fact finding, in the initial contract negotiation, the client must ascertain that these scope issues are covered within the proposed fee, and, if not, that each scope item required is documented and assigned a fee.

Even if some scope items are not foreseen, it is wise to outline the likely scope and determine a method of fee compensation. As the project progresses, there should be little, if any, need to recontract for services.

These unforeseen issues are typically negotiated as add−deduct alternates at stated fees or in stated methods of payment. Dollars per staff hour, per diem fees, or percentages of itemized construction or fit-out costs are typically employed.

After the scope of service is agreed, the fee is set as either an upset fee or a not-to-exceed upset fee of a fixed fee. Each of these methods of fee determination has a different legal meaning, as follows:

Upset fee means that the total fee shall not exceed the upset agreed upon without both parties' revising the agreement.

Not-to-exceed upset fee has a similar meaning; however, in practice, if the project requires a lower fee to complete than contracted for, the client has no obligation to pay more than the fee required to complete the project to the client's satisfaction.

Fixed fee is a sum certain for the stated scope of service, and any savings that occur in the management of the project become additional profit to the design firm.

For some unknown items, a fixed fee per hour or per phase might be useful, and these additional fee agreements state the dollar amount for each item being priced.

Finally, the open-ended fee agreement may be required for items that cannot be contracted for at the project's initiation. These are referred to as time and materials (T&M) agreements and are the most difficult for clients to manage against a stated overall project budget.

Some design firms develop fees as a percentage of the contract costs; others use markup on the costs of various furniture and related interior fit-out items. The majority of projects discussed in this chapter will not use either of these fee structures. Our firm is not familiar with the resulting contract points, and we prefer to limit our discussion to the other forms of fee compensation noted above.

All projects generate a substantial amount of reimbursable expenses. These should be budgeted for within the contract, as either a fixed amount or a percentage of the fees, and clients should not be surprised to learn during the negotiations that 6 to 10 percent of project fees are required to pay for reimbursable expenses. When computer-aided drafting, facilities management computer software, critical path method (CPM) project tracking, flat-bed printing processes, and other labor-saving project management techniques are employed, these expenses increase above the average because each technique requires specialized materials that are typically reimbursable.

Many firms are asking for reimbursement for computer time beyond normal drafting techniques. FAX, express mail, couriers, modem and telephone line charges, and other aspects of the "I must have it yesterday" project management requirements all add to the growing list of reimbursable expenses. Marketing renderings, samples, mock-ups, photo services, and other reimbursable expenses will vary for each type of project.

In sum, reimbursable expenses require management by the client, and it is recommended that their management begin with a clear understanding during the contract negotiations.

After the scope and money issues of the contract are settled, the following items should be amplified beyond their present inclusion in the AIA form contract(s).

1. Is the contract between an owner and an interior design firm or an architectural firm that is providing interior design services? This needs to be determined, to understand the scope of service related to the legal filings with the local building and planning departments, and the client's expectations as to the appropriate professional liability insurance coverage for the project. If

the project is a typical interior design project, the word "architect" should be removed in each instance and "interior designer" substituted.

2. Regarding professional liability, the limits of coverage and the track record of the firm should be discussed, and certain aspects of the insurance coverage should be inserted in the contract.

3. If the client's landlord or developer is providing the base building architectural documents upon which the design professionals are to base the design and documentation scope of service, the ownership of these original documents and the ability for the project team to use these documents must be settled in the contract negotiations; otherwise, claims may develop involving the owner, the design professionals, and the original creator of the base building documents.

4. If a project budget is being established at the time of the contract negotiations, and if the client is interested in negotiation with the interior design firm to design (or redesign) to meet this budget, the specific project budget must be included in the contract negotiations and the terms for revising this budget must be defined.

5. If further budget negotiation is required by the client, there might be a need to state specific areas of the overall budget in a line-item fashion and to include a contingency line at the bottom. In our opinion, it is unreasonable for a client to require specific line-by-line budget compliance, but a statement up front of how the overall budget is to be spent is a typical guideline. Many project types, especially in mixed-use facilities, such as headquarters buildings with an operations center, a computer center, and a conference and training center, have various budgets, based on cost per rentable square foot.

6. The costs to reproduce the resulting documents, drawings, and specifications should be negotiated into the contract. If a construction manager (CM) is employed, the designer's responsibility is to prepare and transmit a reproducible set to the CM for distribution to various subcontractors.

   In other forms of project contracting, the design professionals may be called upon to issue documentation, in the forms of prints of the originals, to the various contractors and subcontractors. The additional paperwork and reimbursable expenses should be negotiated in the scope of service of the contract.

7. Many professional liability insurance carriers are requiring that their clients contract for a limit of professional liability for any one project. These limit of liability clauses limit only the liability of the design professionals to the owner/client—not to third parties—and, for many interior design firms, these limits are the only method for securing professional liability coverage.

8. The design professionals are relying on an ongoing project team and an ongoing project. If the project is suspended for some time, or if a project team member is replaced and a new team member must be oriented to the project, there will need to be a period of reevaluation, which will incur additional printing expenses and additional project team orientation meetings. These eventualities require negotiation in the contract.

9. Of major importance to both parties is the ownership of the resulting documents. The AIA calls the documents "instruments of professional service," which have specific legal definitions. In practice, the client will want the use of the documents for the specific project, without restraints from the design professionals, and the design professionals will want assurances that the documents will be used only for the specific project for which they were prepared.

   If computer-aided drafting has been used, many of the details and documents being prepared will probably be revisions to documents prepared for prior projects, and many of the details prepared for the present project may later be revised and reused on subsequent projects.

   Designers' insurance carriers insist that drawings should not be reused for another project, because that project would not be covered by the professional liability insurance without the designer's full professional process.

   In some recent legal cases, clients have objected to the reuse of certain design features and details in subsequent projects. Architects and designers have claimed that it is too risky, and far too costly, to create all new details for each project, even if one could invent new details for each project.

   Thus, the ownership of documents, and their use and reuse, is a point of negotiation in the contract form, and the resulting negotiated clause will likely vary from the older AIA form.

10. In many urban areas, private mediation consultants are available to adjudicate claims against

owner/designer contracts (and many other types of contracts). Some professional liability insurance carriers require mediation as a form of settlement, rather than the earlier arbitration or court process outlined in the AIA form contracts.

Mediation allows for the forms of evidence admissible in courts, but offers the parties a more cost-effective and timely resolution of claims and counterclaims than either the courts or arbitration.

How disputes are to be settled is a key provision of the contract negotiations.

11. Many projects directed toward the adaptive reuse of older structures may become involved in hazardous waste material and/or asbestos disposal. A design professional is not qualified to offer consultation in these areas of the construction industry and must decline responsibility for such project scope.

   If the client believes that these perils may impact the specific project, they should be spelled out in the contract negotiations and a suitable specialist should be hired to provide this scope of service.

12. The client may wish to negotiate "time is of the essence" or liquidated damages clauses within the contract. In our experience, most major projects are managed as a team effort, which, while not eliminating individual project team members' specific responsibilities, makes subsequent claims for specific performance and/or liquidated damages difficult to sustain. When such clauses are required, a bonus system is usually established, to reward advanced delivery of the documents. A very detailed CPM chart for the project is required to manage these negotiated clauses.

   We do not recommend contract negotiations that include "time is of the essence" or liquidated damages provisions.

Contracting with the Selected Consultant

The client's lawyers should be asked to prepare a first draft contract form. From this first draft, both parties will begin the contract redlining process that will ultimately produce the final signed contract.

In the interim, the project begins with a letter of intent, which should state at least the following points:

- Project name, location, date of project initiation, and principal contact

- Interior design firm, principal contact, and upset fee
- Staff rates per hour, monthly billing cycle, and terms of the invoicing
- Limited scope of service to be performed prior to formal contract signing
- Project timetable during that limited period of time
- A seven-day cancellation clause.

With the letter of intent, the design firm can begin its service, knowing that it will be paid on a monthly basis until the project's formal contract has been prepared and finalized. The client can proceed, knowing that a limited scope of work will be underway while the contract is being drafted and redlined, and that, in a worst case, the letter agreement can be rescinded within one week's time.

The actual legal responsibility of providing the contract between the owner/client and the design professionals rests with the client's attorneys.

The Contract Management Process

After the letter of intent is issued, and while awaiting the drafting and redlining of a formal project contract, the client and other project team members (who may also be working under letter agreements) will typically join the interior design firm to kick off the project and will proceed to define project goals and guidelines.

The first phases of any project—project team orientation to each other, to the project, and to the client's project goals and guidelines—are critical to the ultimate success of the project.

Initial Project Scope Clarifications

Most design professionals begin their fact finding with what is called a programming phase (Phase I in Appendix 4). Some scope of service issues can be expected to surface. For example, in interviewing the marketing manager, the team may learn of a new audiovisual presentation process that must be added to the scope of service; or, while interviewing the chief financial officer, the team may learn of the impending consolidation of two units of the company into one, and thus a reduction in scope of service.

As these initial assumptions are tested and clarified, their impact on the contracted-for scope of service and fee must be managed and accounted for.

Upset Fee Clarification

For most office facility relocation projects, this fact finding will occur in a shorter length of time than it will take for the lawyers to prepare the contracts. This benefits all parties: the fee can be clarified as part of the final contract negotiations, and not subsequent to contract signing. Fee negotiation takes the form of a pro-rata analysis on an hours-required basis, a per capita analysis, or a per rentable square foot calculation.

Minutes and Memos

We believe that effective project management depends on establishing project guidelines and goals and thereafter monitoring them with written documentation. As noted earlier, even medium-size projects result in almost a year of effort, and larger jobs might require 15 to 20 consultant professionals' working for 20 to 30 months. With such a major commitment of professional time, and with the resulting product being a set of contract documents, the written minutes and memos, and related drawings and specifications, become the basis for project management tracking.

CPM is typically used to develop a time line for the project. A fast-track project might have many critical paths occurring at the same time, rather than sequentially. In either case, managing the project goals and guidelines and documenting the milestones of the project are tried and tested project management techniques.

If the client project manager discovers errors in the minutes or memos, or if the time line of the project falls behind the schedule, it is critical to the success of the project to resolve these discrepancies before they result in problems for which no time or money has been provided.

Contractually, minutes and documents issued at key milestones of a project should be signed by both the consultant and the client project manager, and work should not proceed beyond milestone dates without written authorization from the client project manager to proceed.

This process may seem cumbersome for many smaller projects, but it has been our experience that only in this manner can later claims and disputes be avoided.

Client-Authorized Extras

The Waterloo of most client–consultant relationships is a result of improper management of extra services.

The client project manager(s) can reasonably assume that the consultants are experienced and are willing and able to provide the scope of work within the contracted-for fee and within the project's time and budget constraints. The interior design consultant also has ample experience with client project managers who try to demand additional services without agreeing to increased fees.

Every project can be subject to changes, and many of these changes are foreseen within the initial scope of service and fee proposal. However, each project and each consultant firm will have its own threshold beyond which one of the principals will call for a meeting to discuss claims for additional services required.

If it is possible to manage these claims forthrightly and to establish a process for managing similar claims in the future, the project will proceed in a "good-willing" manner. If at any time in the process either party feels taken advantage of, the project spirit will dwindle to a constant barrage of project minutes documenting in great detail each minor claim or demand of one party upon the other.

These same cautions apply to the ultimate contracts between the client and the various suppliers and contractors, which are drafted by the interior design consultant. Clear initial direction and clear changes in direction yield the best projects and the best relationships between the project team members and their respective contractors and product suppliers.

The Invoicing Process

The request for proposal form shown in Appendix 4 provides for a built-in understanding between the client and the interior design consultant as to the expected schedule of events and the amount of work expected to be completed at various points in the project. Generally accepted accounting principles (GAAP) require an analysis of the percent completed: percent billed ratio, if the firm believes that the billing exceeds the actual completed work.

The client project manager's major charge under the proposed form of contract is to maintain a reasonable equation of completed work to percentage of the fee billed. The worst managed projects find the entire fee expended in the design phases, with little if any documentation from which to reconstruct the expenditures. At this point, even the drastic measure of firing the consultant will not result in meeting the project's time and budget goals.

Careful scrutiny of the monthly invoices of time expended and of the developing data base of information and documentation, and comparison of the work in progress against the CPM time line forecast are the only methods available to ensure meeting cost and time goals within the contracted-for fees.

The interior design consultant will invoice monthly, either against time card records or using a self-imposed percent-completed analysis. Consultant-prepared data bases are available, under contract, for audit or review by the client, and periodic presentations of work in progress are advised, to track actual compliance with the expected time line goals.

All monthly invoices should include the following data:

- Initial contracted-for upset fee
- Any additional authorized extras agreed to as of the date of invoice
- Revised contract total
- Amounts billed in prior billings
- Amounts billed in the month of billing
- Remaining billable amount available (to project completion), expressed as a percentage of fee and as a percentage of the total work.

In addition, the interior design consulting firm's project manager or project principal should be required to provide the client project manager with a monthly covering-letter statement of the project's progress in the month of billing and the predicted progress during the next month.

Typically, monthly invoices are dated the first day of the month following the work performed but, owing to computation time, are not received by the client project manager until day 6 through day 12 of that month.

If the client's project manager finds fault with the invoice or the covering letter, it is the manager's responsibility to offer comment and revised direction, in writing, to the interior design consultant. Without such written comment, the work will proceed according to the consultant's project manager's letter.

Claims and Disputes

As noted above, claims and disputes will surface in even the best managed projects. *Any claim or dispute should be managed and resolved immediately.* Waiting for the next major project meeting, or for a group of claims to pile up, or for the client's or consultant's principals to return from vacation, or in any other way delaying timely resolution, will materially affect the working relationship and substantially delay the project.

Arbitration and Mediation of Disputes

We favor the current preference for mediation rather than arbitration or litigation. With effective project management, most disputes can be avoided or resolved in a timely manner.

Firing the Consultant

If the claims and disputes cannot be resolved in due time, the only course of action available for the client project manager is to give the contracted-for seven-day notice and fire the consultant. The client project manager will be well advised to seek legal counsel prior to issuing this notice, because counterclaims, including the issuance of liens on the project property, may be forthcoming from the consultant, in the event that fees are not paid or bonded to be paid subsequent to arbitration or mediation.

Firing the consultant is clearly a drastic step, especially with much work in progress and with the consultant's having control of the original project files, records, and documentation.

To facilitate an orderly transition, the few consultant firings that have occurred in the industry have usually provided for the consultant to remain on for a limited period of time, while a new consultant is recruited and oriented to the project.

These delicate negotiations require substantial skill and courage. If carried out in a spirit of rancor, they result in chaos to the project.

The Reselection Process

Few interior design firms will want to "bail out" a peer whose project has failed for any reason. Major corporate facility managers can dangle the next new project as an incentive to assisting with the failed project, but they will need to either accept some redesign from the new designer or select an interior design consultant who has limited design interest.

Our best recommendation is to interview the remaining firms on the original short list, to determine which firm is the most willing to take over the project with minimum amounts of start-up cost and overlapping redesign, and the highest amount of overall interest in offering the assistance required, in a cost-efficient and timely fashion.

The Second Hiring and Contracting Process

Client project managers will need to retrace the contract negotiations process if a second hiring negotiation and contract process becomes necessary.

A major issue that will surface in this renegotiation is project credit: Who will ultimately share (or not share) the credit for the project in publicity notices and trade magazine releases?

The transition agreement with both the initial and the second consultant should include a statement on ultimate project credits. Even in a firing mode, the client project manager has substantial negotiating strength to cause an orderly transition. The initial interior design consultant will want the firing to appear to be a mutual and amicable parting, and will seek participation in the project credits when and if the project is published in a trade magazine.

All parties to the contract with the second consultant will want a clear understanding of the scope of work to be completed and the form and substance of the professional liability that the second firm is willing to undertake.

If specifications have begun, one of the transition points should be acquisition by the second interior design consultant of the first consultant's data base and specifications diskettes, as well as any original Mylar® drawing documents that may have been created. For a full CADD project, the transfer would logically include the diskettes of the entire project.

A decision to fire the first consultant carries with it an understanding that the required period of transition will delay the project and add a significant premium to the overall project cost. Such a decision should therefore not be taken lightly, and every effort should be made, by both sides, to resolve claims through effective project management and to avoid a firing and reselection process.

Final Payment

Establishing the interior design consultant's upset fee is as much a marketing exercise as it is a finite estimate of the work to be provided. For the client project manager, knowing when to authorize claims for contract extras is as much good project management as it is good public relations with the interior design consultant.

While these divergent forces are at work on the fixed fee dollar amounts, the fee is typically dwindling down because the project is reaching its conclusion.

The scope of service and fee proposal (see Appendix 4) specifies the amount of fee that should be available and allocated for field supervision of the construction work in progress and for the related project management and contract administration services that the client typically requires. These services follow the completion of the contract documentation and agreements with various contractors and furniture and equipment suppliers.

The most effective time for measuring how the estimated upset fee has met the test of the real project is the moment when the contract documents are prepared and distributed to the construction manager (or directly to the bidding contractors and suppliers). At this time, the bulk of the work has been completed and a known amount of work, quantified (in our proposed format) in worker hours on the job site, remains. Both parties should know reasonably well whether the resulting bids and contracts will meet the initially established budget. If alternate documentation, or cuts in the documentation, or even redocumentation is required to meet the budget, the time to make these revisions should be taken into consideration when reviewing the invoice for the month of contract documentation issuance.

The monthly billing at this date of contract document issuance is then the most critical invoice to audit, and payment should not be made until the client project manager has reasonable assurances that the remaining fee will support the required redocumentation to meet the budget, and the contract administration and field supervision phases of the scope of service foreseen in the contract.

For the interior design consultant, this is also a critical point in time. The project can be built from the documents being issued, and all outstanding claims for extra service should be settled at this time.

The final payment (per se) is, therefore, not the final payment; the payment made in the month when the documents are issued has much more finality. Both parties should examine carefully the financial aspects of the relationship at this point, so that the construction supervision and contract administration phases can proceed in an orderly fashion.

Post-Contract Issues

Trade Journal Publicity and Credit(s)

The interior design consultant will want to interest one of the trade journals in publishing the finished work. The use of trade journal articles in qualifications brochures requires a constantly updated portfolio of these articles. Architectural and interior design trade journals are eager to publish significant projects, in their ongoing efforts to compete with each other in publishing the best projects and to give marketing support to the furniture, fixtures, and equipment manufacturers who are the source of their advertising revenues.

Candidate projects are reviewed from both the client's point of view (suitability for the intended use) and the designer's point of view. If significant manufacturers' involvement yielded new product offerings, these results will also be discussed.

The project credits will list each of the project team members, and his or her responsibility or title, and, in most trade journals, the major product manufacturers.

To receive this publicity, it is universally recognized that the design firm and/or the client must arrange, direct, and pay for the photography. There are only a few highly qualified interior design photographers in the United States, and their daily rates range from $1,500 to $2,000 plus. To achieve publishable quality prints, these photographers use 4 × 5-in., 5 × 7-in., or 8 × 10-in. plates, and typically set up no more than two to three shots in a day. A typical trade journal article might require five to ten photographs, or a $5,000 to $10,000 photographic investment.

If the client company can use the trade journal article in its own marketing effort, or if the photographs can be used elsewhere to the benefit of the company, the client may wish to share these expenses with the design consultant. Otherwise, the design consultant will typically make this investment on its own account.

The best trade journal editors pride themselves on their professional integrity and objective viewpoint. Most articles are complimentary, but others are critical of some design feature or concept. The journal will frequently allow the clients and designers time to review the article prior to publication, so that facts can be verified, but there is always a risk that the final version may not exactly meet with one's expectations.

Regardless of the expense and editorial risks, trade journal publicity benefits both the client and the design firm.

Prior to initiating a contract with trade journal editors, the client and design firm must clearly understand:

- Who pays for the photography
- Which magazines to apply to
- The form and content of a publicity release
- The form and content of the resulting interview(s)
- How to edit the journalist's work
- How to assist the journalist in properly listing the project team involvement
- Which manufacturers to list
- The use of the resulting magazine reprints
- The use of the resulting photographs

Future Project-Related References

A prospective client will want to check at least three project-relevant references for each design firm on its short list. However, each project has its own individual circumstances and results, and its ultimate project team relationships are interactive and mutually inclusive. It may be difficult for an existing or prior client to accurately judge the suitability of the interior design consultant for another client's project.

The following checklist is offered to assist in the initial reference check for the client's project and in subsequent responses to reference requests from the interior design firm's prospective clients.

- Verification of the project statistics:
  —Client's project manager
  —Consultant's project manager
  —Consultant's designer
  —Consultant's principal
  —Date(s) of the project
  —Size of the project in usable square feet
  —Size of the project in rentable square feet
  —Size in number of employees
  —Size in overall project budget
- Subjective evaluation of the project's design quality
  —Suitability for the intended use
  —Relative balance of creative solutions to errors, in design decision making
  —Overall efficiency of resulting space plan
  —Overall feel and spirit of the resulting facility
  —Match of project feel and spirit to client's corporate culture

- Objective evaluation of the project's design quality
  - —Project met the time constraints
  - —Project met the budget constraints
  - —Project met the expected density of rentable square feet per employee
- Overall evaluation
  - —Would work with firm again (if not, why)
  - —Would recommend firm to others (if not, why)
- Overall rating
  - —Superior
  - —Good
  - —Acceptable
  - —Unacceptable

Conclusion

This chapter has outlined our recommendations for the cost-effective and timely recruiting, selection, and contracting of an interior design consulting firm for a medium to large corporate facilities relocation project. Each project will require its own form of agreement, and the scope of services required will vary. We have provided a series of documents in the following appendices. When edited for the client company's specific project requirements, these documents should provide a clear understanding between the parties entering into a contract for professional interior design services.

These recommendations are not meant to be the final legal word on the contractual relationships, but rather a process whereby the scope of services required and the business aspects of the agreements can be presented and negotiated prior to or parallel with the legal advice required to formulate the actual contract document.

(Chapter 7 begins on page 267.)

APPENDIX 1

Interior Design Consulting Firm Recruiting Selection/Contracting Process Time Line
Typical Medium to Large Size Office Relocation Process

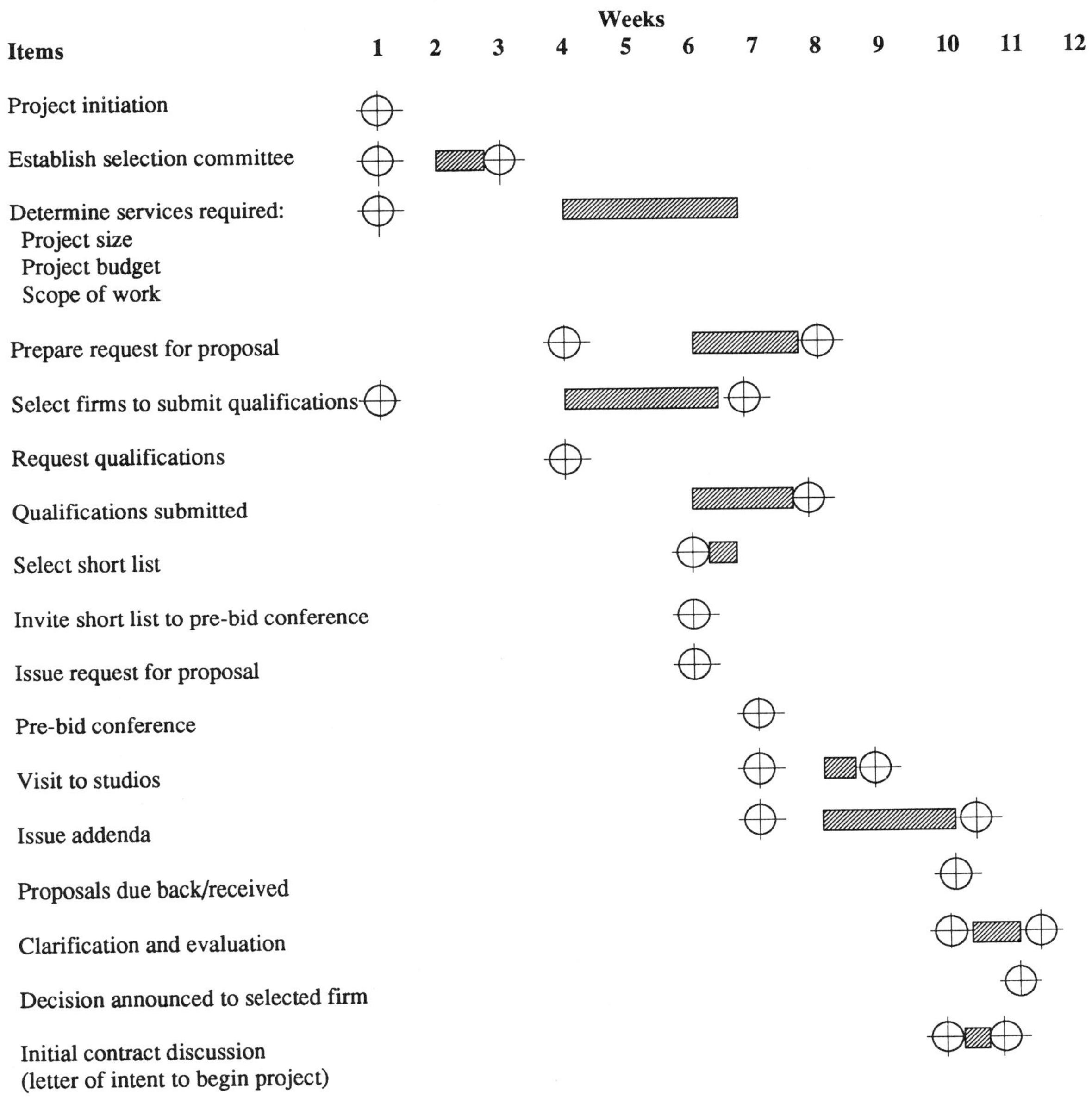

Items	Weeks

A timeline/Gantt chart with week columns numbered 1 through 12 across the top, and the following items listed down the left side with corresponding markers and bars:

- Project initiation
- Establish selection committee
- Determine services required:
  - Project size
  - Project budget
  - Scope of work
- Prepare request for proposal
- Select firms to submit qualifications
- Request qualifications
- Qualifications submitted
- Select short list
- Invite short list to pre-bid conference
- Issue request for proposal
- Pre-bid conference
- Visit to studios
- Issue addenda
- Proposals due back/received
- Clarification and evaluation
- Decision announced to selected firm
- Initial contract discussion
  (letter of intent to begin project)

APPENDIX 2

Date_____

Request for Qualifications Brochure

Re XXX Project

Dear XXX,

(Company) is (describe briefly company's business). We plan to relocate our office facilities of approximately ( ) employees requiring approximately ( ) rentable square feet on or about (date of expected relocation) within (state geographic location). (Choose one) (A) We have employed (real estate consultant's name) to assist us in selecting our new office facility location or (B) We are presently investigating various alternate locations for our new office facility or (C) We have tentatively selected (state selected office building facility and floor numbers)

We would appreciate reviewing your firm's qualifications to serve as our interior design consultant for this project. Please deliver to the attention of the undersigned by (due date) your firm's qualifications brochure. We would like you to include the following information:

- A covering letter listing your interest in our project and your firm's ability and capacity to provide the scope of service in the time frame we require

- A statement of your firm's design philosophy

- Professional resumes of your principals and key staff members

- Your current hourly rate information for relevant project staff members

- A list of relevant projects, stating in each case
  - Name of project
  - Client company
  - Size of project in rentable square feet, client staff size, and project interior fit-out budget

- Three recent project references, stating in each case:
  - Name of project
  - Client company
  - Size of project in rentable square feet, client staff size, and project interior fit-out budget
  - Client contact
  - Telephone number

- A list of your firm's major work in progress, stating in each case:
  - Name of project
  - Client company
  - Size of project in rentable square feet, client staff size, and project interior fit-out budget
  - Client contact
  - Telephone number

- Estimate of your firm's fee income for (state the year)

- Estimate of your firm's design projects in rentable square feet of space for (state the year)

- Trade magazine reprints or photographs of recently published projects.

We look forward to receipt of this information, following which we will invite qualified firms to a pre-bid conference to be held on (state the date).

Prior to the pre-bid conference, we will issue to the qualified firms a request for proposal and outline the scope of service we believe is required for the project and further explain our selection process.

Please feel free to call with any questions you may have.

Very truly yours,

Client Project Manager

APPENDIX 3

Invitation to the Pre-bid Conference

Re XXX project

Dear _____.

We have received your qualifications submitted on (date) and (choose one):

(A) would like to invite you and your proposed project team to a pre-bid conference of those we have short-listed to be held (time, date, and place).

At this conference, we will further describe the project, issue a formal request for proposal, set a date to meet with you in your studio, and outline the other key dates in our selection process.

(or)

(B) wish to advise you that your qualifications do not meet with our specific requirements for this project. Accordingly, we are returning to you the information you sent us and look forward to calling upon you again when our future project requirements may correspond to our understanding of your firm's qualifications.

(Choose one):

 (A) We look forward to meeting with you at the pre-bid conference; (B) We thank you for participating in our search for an interior design consultant.

Very truly yours,

Client Project Manager

APPENDIX 4

(On Client Stationery)

Date_____

A Proposed Form of:

Request for Proposal for Interior Design Services
(To be mailed to the short list prior to the pre-bid conference)

Dear XXX,

Your firm has been selected as a qualified bidder to provide interior design services for (Client).

We have already prequalified your firm and a number of your competitors to provide us with the information requested in this request for proposal. Accordingly, your proposal shall consist of only items specifically requested in this form of proposal.

Prior to submitting this proposal, we would like you to meet with us at a pre-bid conference on (time, date, and place). Please come prepared to ask any questions or points of clarification you feel is required for your firm to make a competitive bid proposal.

Subsequent to the pre-bid conference we would like to meet with each firm in their studio for a one hour interview, where we will question you on your qualifications and further discuss the project. You will be given an additional 30 minutes to present recent projects you believe are relevant to our decision to select our interior design consultant.

These interviews will occur during the week of (date).

Your proposal must be delivered and received at the offices of (Client, (address), attention (Client representative) on or before (time and date) in order to be considered.

Please call me no later than (date) to confirm that you have received this RFP and to advise us if you intend to meet with us at the pre-bid conference and submit a bid.

Our decision and selection of our interior design consultant will take place during the week of (date). We will advise all parties to this RFP of our selection decision by (date).

The enclosed project fact sheet, scope of service required, and form of fee bid proposal shall be used by all bidders to submit their proposals and will be used as an exhibit to the contract (client) will negotiate with the selected interior design consultant.

We thank you for your interest in our project, and we look forward to meeting with you at the pre-bid conference, visiting your studio, and receiving your bid proposal.

Sincerely,

Client Project Manager
(Direct Tel#)

PROJECT FACT SHEET

The following project fact sheet has been prepared to provide the basis for the interior design fee proposal.

Actual requirements may vary from those indicated below, and in that event, the contract for services will be adjusted on a prorated basis, once actual requirements are known.

Some items are left blank pending additional information from (Client). This information will be provided by (   ) date to assist in the fee proposal.

(Client) operates a (   ) business which serves (   ).

(Client's) customer base consists of (   ) some of whom may visit the proposed new (   ) facility.

(Client) requires new office facilities (describe the reasons and goals behind the proposed relocation).

(Client) is presently located on (number of floors) of (   ) Building(s) consisting of xxx rentable square feet.

(Describe why these premises are inadequate for present requirements thus prompting the relocation).

(Client) intends to relocate approximately (   ) employees to the new facility on approximately (   ). It is expected that this new facility of (   ) rentable sq. ft. will house the company until at least (state date) at which time the complete (   ) rentable sq. ft. facility is expected to be fully occupied by (Client) when (Client) will likely require additional expansion space.

The employees to be relocated operate within (state number) departments and consist of approximately:

(state number)   ____   of private office occupants
                    ____   of open office workstation occupants
                    ____   of back office staff

(Client) expects to receive approximately (state number) visitors and customers at the new office facility daily.

Regarding the private offices (a) only the following senior executive offices will require custom individualized design treatment, _____ and _____ and (b) there will be a standards program throughout the other various sized private offices with no custom designs required for individual offices on this project.

Regarding the open office workstations, assume that (___%) will be required to support EDP, word processing, or PC equipment.

The interior design consultant is expected to verify all of these assumptions and to set out a facilities programming report for (Client) review itemizing the expected requirements at the following key dates (select the key dates as indicated):

_____   dates of data gathering
_____   move-in dates
_____   date when the initial premises is filled and fitted out
_____   date at which time the optioned space contiguous with the initial premises is filled and fitted out

In sum, (Client) estimates that (Client) shall require approximately (   ) usable square feet of space which at an average of a (   )% building loss factor will compute to approximately (   ) rentable square feet of space on (   ) typical (   ) sq. ft. floors in a building of approximately (   ) rentable sq. ft.

(Client) is presently working with (real estate consultant) who is assisting in reviewing a number of available office facilities and sites in (location).

Regarding the scope of work related to testing various available (likely new building) office facilities and site configurations, the interior design consultant (a) will be asked to test (state number) such facilities and sites or configurations (or) (b) will be asked to test the site (client) has been selected, it is (describe site).

(Client) recognizes that the special requirements for space utilization will in large respect require a majority of the interior design professional design talent and time. Accordingly, (Client) has outlined the present understanding of the special requirements for this project:

(Select applicable special items)
001 Customer contact space in the building's lobby or store front (   ) sq. ft.
002 Below grade truck docks (   ) sq. ft.
003 Below grade warehousing of (   ) sq. ft.
004 Below grade vaults (   ) sq. ft.
005 Below grade central filing
006 Private area of building lobby at street level
007 Private security area at building lobby at street level
008 Main office facility lobby and reception area
009 Visitor's coat closets
010 Employee coat closets
011 Employee lockers
012 Central mail distribution space of approximately ___ square feet (with telelift)
013 Central file area above grade of approximately ___ square feet
014 Central law or business library above grade of approximately ___ square feet
015 Power file rooms with heavy filing requirements of approximately ___ square feet
016 Central supply room of approximately ___ square feet
017 Central computer room of approximately ___ square feet with raised floor
018 Central photocopy room(s) of approximately ___ square feet with a capacity of approximately __ pages of copied text per day
019 Employee cafeteria seating approximately ___
020 Executive dining seating approximately ___
021 Coffee kitchens throughout the office area which in total ___ square feet
022 Vending areas of approximately ___ square feet
023 Private toilet room(s) of approximately ___ square feet
024 Private shower room(s) of approximately ___ square feet
025 Exercise room(s) of approximately ___ square feet
026 Parking requirements for approximately __ cars within the office building or nearby
027 Two-hour fire secure file area(s) above grade of approximately ___ square feet
028 Custom built in vault(s) of approximately ___ square feet
029 Standard vault(s) placed on reinforced floor slabs of approximately __ x __ in floor plan size
030 Any other heavy equipment requirements which may require revised structural design including ___ mail distribution systems, mail lift and robot systems, mail opening machinery, mail sorting machinery, computer output burster stuffers, and check processors.
031 Conference and training rooms with the following seating capacities:
  Boardroom(s)   ___ seats total
  Conference room(s)   ___
  Training room(s)   ___
  Auditorium room(s)   ___
  Conference rooms (s)   ___ (with audiovisual equipment built in)
032 Space which may require special acoustic control, either owing to noise being created within the space, or especially quiet requirements for the work to be performed within the space. If so, please itemize these requirements_____
033 Photo darkrooms of approximately ___ square feet
034 Paste-up areas of approximately ___ square feet

035 Other areas requiring special HVAC or plumbing design services (please list them):

_____

_____

036 Teleconference room(s) of approximately ___ square feet
037 Telephone switch room(s) of approximately ___ square feet
038 Sound masking throughout the space
039 Security system(s) throughout the space
040 Video monitoring of security throughout the space
041 Day care facility for __ children
042 Full PC data network wiring
043 U.P.S. for the computer center
044 Halon protection for the computer center
045 Private tenant stairs between floors (how many ___)
046 Private tenant elevators
047 High quality executive/boardroom floor
048 Cellular deck wire distribution system
049 Energy efficient task/ambient lighting system
050 Name and logo on and within building
051 Art program
052 First aid station
053 Factory made relocatable partition systems
054 Various audiovisual marketing installations requiring an AV Consultant

To further assist in the interior design consultant's fee proposal, (Client) notes the following:

(Client's) overall project budget for interior fit-out is approximately \$____ per rentable square foot, including moving costs, the refurbishing of existing furniture for the reuse of approximately ___% of the office occupants and ___% of the open office workstation occupants, new furniture and related equipment, the relocation and up-grading of the telephone switch(s), the construction fit-out costs (above the building developer's workletter or above the base building construction budget of \$____) and other related expenses including interior design fees and those of the other consultants that will be required to assist us in this project.

This overall budget includes an allocation of approximately \$____ for art and antiques and approximately \$___ for signage and graphics required to provide orientation systems for the facility.

This budget does not include any new computer or operational equipment that may be required in the new facility, but the electrical wiring of this equipment and its voice and data network wiring should be considered as part of the overall project budget noted above.

Regarding the contracts to implement the interior design consultant's specifications, (Client) understands that the (Client) corporate policy is to provide no less than _% of contracts to minorities and an additional _% to Woman-Owned Businesses. Each bid package will be bid to no fewer than ____ competitive bidders.

(Client) (a) plans to employ a construction manager for this project, or (b) plans to bid the construction package competitively using general contractors.

Regarding FF&E items, (Client) presently maintains national accounts with the following major furniture manu-facturers:

· _____

· _____

· _____

The scope of service required by this request for a proposal includes the following phases of work.

PHASE I

Programming

Meet with each of ___ department managers and with their assistance develop and verify current staffing projections for the key dates of the project and assist in establishing a corporate wide space standards program.

Prepare computer aided facilities reports illustrating in data base and in bubble diagram the required functional and adjacency requirements, the support spaces and special space requirements and assumptions related to circulation factors and planning factors to yield a required rentable square feet of space.

Review private office requirements to forecast window wall requirements.

Verify the special requirements presented as part of this RFP.

Verify the project budget assumptions.

Verify the fee proposal related to the data you have developed and enter into a standard form agreement to provide the balance of the services required on a not-to-exceed upset fee basis.

Gain approval for each of these items.

PHASE II

Site Selection

Assist in the review of the opportunities of the ___ sites to allow (Client) employees easy access via various transportation means and up and into the office facility in a safe and secure manner.

Illustrate approximate blocking and stacking plans for the distribution of the various departments within each of the ____ buildings.

Evaluate the programming requirements against each of the ____ building's opportunities to meet the stated requirements.

These evaluations will take the form of a review of the (offered workletters and facilities' related lease terms and conditions,) (or) the developer's (or) Architects plans and operating features related to move-in, security and after hours access and use of HVAC equipment and the overall base building plans and specifications.

Prepare tenant plans for each of the buildings (or configurations), illustrating how the program of space allocation might fit within the building and its window wall and planning module and overall building systems.

Present the findings on the ____ buildings studied in a pros and cons method, comparing the ___ buildings item by item, and recommend which building best meets the stated criteria.

PHASE III

Technical Lease Assistance

Assist the project team in the review of the selected building's terms and conditions of the lease related to the fit-out and building operations.

Present the tenant plans to the building's architects and engineers and project team for their review and comments.

Review the building's construction schedule and advise how the project schedule relates to the overall building's schedule.

Prepare a detailed timeline for the project to be included in the lease (fit out schedule).

Prepare tenant plans revised as required to be included as the basis of the lease (fit out schedule).

Review the developer's workletter analysis and architects comments on the approved tenant plans for quantity take off and related information.

Recommend improvements to the base building that may be required to better meet (Client) requirements and stated criteria and goals.

PHASE IV

Assistance in Recruiting Engineers

Assist in the recruiting of the other team members that will be required to complete the project.

These may include (state those that are appropriate for the project) interior fit-out, mechanical, electrical, plumbing and structural engineers. It may also include security consultants, telephone and data wiring consultants, fine art consultants, lighting consultants, graphic design and signage consultants, landscaping consultants, materials testing consultants, and others.

Participation will be to assist the project management team in the drafting of RFP's for these consultants and in attending interview meetings and reviews of their subsequent fee proposals.

(Client) (a) will select the consultants and contract with them directly, but Interior Designer will be required to attend scheduled project team meetings to review the work of all of the consultants during the course of the project, or (b) the design professionals will be responsible for contracting with and coordinating the work of the following consultants: _____

and working with the other project consultants that will be contracted with directly by (client).

PHASE V

Space Planning and Schematic Design

Refine the program data and determine specific interior design solutions, including defined adjacencies, efficient circulation, work flow and space standards for all levels of office and workstations required by the program.

Present these plans and building stacking sections for approval prior to proceeding to develop the designs.

Present a revised project budget to verify that the initial project budget can support the schematic design recommendations.

As part of the schematic design phase of the project, review the Client's FF&E inventory documents and assumptions that certain items can be refinished and relocated to the new facility.

Interior Designer (a) will not be required to provide the inventory or the documentation of this existing equipment, but will be required to evaluate this furniture and assist the Client in preparing bid packages for the removal, refinishing and relocation of this existing equipment, or (b) will be required to inventory and document (client's) existing furniture and equipment inventory.

PHASE VI

Design Development

Prepare design studies for review and approval, including plans of all furniture, equipment, partitions, ceilings, lighting, electrical and telephone outlets, furniture and furnishings selections and textile and finish specifications including materials, colors, finishes, window treatment and carpet recommendations.

Present these designs to the project management team, and gain approvals to proceed to document these recommendations.
Solicit preliminary pricing quotations from manufacturers and reconfirm the project budget assumptions.

Assist in evaluation of various furniture and carpet options using showroom visits and/or mock-up presentations of competing product lines.

PHASE VII

Revisions

Review these designs with the building's architects, engineers, the project team engineers, and other consultants to reach consensus that the designs can be built to meet the Client's budget and criteria, goals, and gain approval from the various building code agencies that have jurisdiction over the project.

Revise the designs as required to meet the consensus of the project team and prepare a record set of documents and meeting minutes to gain approval to proceed into contract documentation.

PHASE VIII

Contract Documentation and Specifications

Prepare contract documents required for the general construction of all partitions, ceilings, lighting, telephone and electric outlets, doors, hardware, fixtures, and all of the special features required to fit-out the facility.

Review and coordinate the contract documents of the other project team engineers and other team members so that their documents correlate with yours.

Package these documents for a unified competitive bidding process subsequent to the Client's authorization to proceed into the contract administration phase of the project.

Prepare contract documents and specifications required for the purchasing and installation of all furniture, furnishings, carpeting and equipment, including the refurbishing of our existing furniture to be relocated.

Provide a list of potential bidders for each scope of the work and assist in the evaluation of potential bidder's qualifications.

Publish (a) one original set of bid documents for the (Client) or (construction manager) to copy and distribute to the selected bidders, or (b) bid packages as required to facilitate the competitive bidding process for each contract required to implement the design package.

Attend the various pre-bid conferences and assist the bidders in their understanding of the contract documents.

Issue addendums as required to clarify the bidding process.

Attend the bid openings and assist in bid evaluation.

Assist in preparing contracts with the selected bidder/contractors.

Assist in filing the documents with the various building code agencies that have jurisdiction over the project.

PHASE IX

FF&E Supervision

Review the various FF&E order confirmations for conformity with the specifications.

Review the samples and shop drawing submittals.

Assist in testing the quality assurance issues indicated in the specifications via factory or field visits and/or assisting in contracting for outside independent testing.

Periodically inspect the items as they are delivered and bring to (Client's) attention items that are not in conformity with the specifications.

PHASE X

Construction Field Observation

Review the various general construction activities for conformity to the specifications.

Review the samples and shop drawing submittals.

Assist in testing the quality assurance issues indicated in the specifications via periodic on site visits and/or assisting in contracting for outside independent testing.

PHASE XI

Punch Listings

Review the installed furniture and equipment and construction items on the project site and issue punch lists to assist in completing the project according to the specifications.

Prepare appropriate final authorizations to pay the various suppliers and contractors according to the terms of the contracts.

PHASE XII

Occupancy

Assist (Client) in the orderly and staged move-into the facility. Provide a field superintendent fully familiar with the specifications and (Client) move-in schedule to offer technical assistance on an as needed basis during the move-in.

PHASE XIII

Post Occupancy Evaluation

Assist in the relocation and re-layout of various individuals and their offices and workstations as required revisions from the approved occupancy plans, assist in preparing additional or revised contract bulletins and purchase orders to facilitate these required revisions.

Periodically inspect the facility during the warranty period(s) of the various contracts and file periodic reports in sufficient detail to meet (Client's) responsibility of due notice to the contractors of defects in workmanship, materials, and claims against the contracted for warranties provided by the contractors.

ADDITIONAL SERVICES

(Client) understands that some of the following additional services may be required.

These services may be required during the course of the project, and if they are required, the Interior Design firm will be asked to provide these services (a) on a time and materials (or) (b) fixed fee basis.

Survey Existing Conditions

Survey all existing conditions at the current (Client) headquarters site(s) and produce accurate architectural and mechanical construction drawings of the "as-built" condition of the existing facilities.

Verify through detailed measurements the available usable square feet of the new facility to assist us in negotiating the rentable square feet.

Furniture Inventory

Provide a complete furniture inventory listing, identifying all furniture for reuse and refurbishment.

Art

Program, budget and select all art, oriental rugs, and other one-of-a-kind art objects for designated private offices and public areas.

Signage

Design and document the interior and exterior identification and directional architectural signage.

Lighting

Program and select all lighting elements throughout the facility. Prepare presentations and mock-ups of selected lighting elements. Document quantity and quality of lighting being specified. Prepare energy utilization studies and related lamping and relamping cost evaluations. Inspect lighting elements during and after installation and aim and correct installed lighting to meet the specifications.

Architectural Services

In in the event that the interior design consultant is required to file the occupancy plans with the local building authorities, sign and stamp the occupancy plans and provide the full service of code review and approval (as architect of record for the interior fit-out).

Additional Interior Design Services

(Client) understands that the programming effort may revise the project scope and to that extent, the interior design consultant may be called upon to provide the following additional services:

Programming

The programming effort as described in Phase I may involve more or less employees than indicated, or it may involve the reprogramming of employees whose jobs or assignments will change during the course of the project.

Indicate in the fee bid form the cost per employee for the additional programming service, if required.

Upgrading Base Building Standards

(Client) has indicated in this request proposal an estimate of the special spaces and features required. If in fact, (Client) requires additional special features, the Interior Design firm will be required in each instance to prepare a fee proposal for those special feature designs.

No work shall be charged for work on any additional special features absent written authorization from (Client) to proceed.

There shall be no retroactive claims for contract extras.

Special Furniture and Millwork

(Client) may require the design of personalized furnishings for certain senior executive private offices and the design and documentation of custom millwork in a boardroom and other items beyond those indicated which shall require additional services.

If in fact additional special features are required, the Interior Design firm will be required in each instance to prepare a fee proposal for those special features.

No work is to be charged for work on any additional special features absent written authorization from (Client) to proceed.

There shall be no retroactive claims for contract extras on this project.

Additional Services

There may be additional consulting services required in the areas of:

- FF&E procurement and/or supervision
- Construction observation
- Warranty management subsequent to punch listing

The Interior Design consultant shall provide in this fee proposal fees for these additional services when and if required on a dollars per hour basis.

Proposed Form for (Client)
RFP for Interior Design Services
Form of Bid for Fee Proposal

Date of proposal   _____
Firm making this proposal   _____
Address of Firm   _____
Tel. #   _____
CEO's name   _____
Contact to discuss proposal   _____
Year Firm started   _____

Firm size information:

Total number of employees   _____

Total number of employees
in (city of project)   _____

Ranking in *Interior Design* Giants   _____

Value of (last year's) specifications $ _____

Square feet designed in (last year)   _____ sq. ft.

Reference List:
(Three recent office projects)

1.   Client   _____
     Contact   _____
     Tel. #   _____
     Date of move-in   _____
     Sq. ft. designed   _____

2.   Client   _____
     Contact   _____
     Tel. #   _____
     Date of move-in   _____
     Sq. ft. designed   _____

3.   Client   _____
     Contact   _____
     Tel. #   _____
     Date of move-in   _____
     Sq. ft. designed   _____

RFP for Interior Design Services
Form of Bid for Fee Proposal/2

Computer Capability:

    CAD hardware in use   _____

    CAD software in use   _____

    Facilities hardware   _____

    Facilities software   _____

    # employees trained on CAD software   _____

    # employees trained on facilities software   _____

Proposed Key (Client) Project Team:	**Name**	**Years with Firm**
Principal	_____	_____
Project Manager	_____	_____
Project Designer	_____	_____
Project Architect	_____	_____
(licensed in [state of project]?) Yes ☐ No ☐	_____	_____
Field Supervisor	_____	_____

Client project manager to fill in all (blanks) prior to issue to the competing interior design consultants

Form of Pricing Proposal assuming (   ) rentable square feet of space

PHASES		**PRICE PER PHASE**
I	Initial data gathering, programming budgeting and needs analysis (assume ( ) employees to be relocated)	$ _____
II	Site selection assistance, tenant planning and landlord lease and workletter analysis (assume ( ) site(s) to be analyzed)	$ _____
III	Technical assistance during lease negotiations (assume ( ) hours of consulting time required)	$ _____
IV	Assistance in recruiting project team engineering, telephone and data system wiring consultants	$ _____
V	Space planning and schematic design for selected site	$ _____
Subtotal		$ _____ ____hours
VI	Design development of approved scheme	$ _____
VII	Review and revision to meet building criteria	$ _____
VIII	Contract documentation and specifications	$ _____
IX	Assistance in supervision of FF&E packages (assume ( ) hours)	$ _____
X	Assistance in field observation of construction packages (assume ( ) hours)	$ _____
XI	Assistance in punch listing and produce warranty management (assume ( ) hours)	$ _____
XII	Assistance in occupancy move-in (assume ( ) hours)	$ _____
XIII	Assistance in post-occupancy evaluation (assume ( ) hours over a 24-month period of time)	$ _____
Subtotal		$ _____ ____hours
Total Fee Proposal		$ _____ ____hours

Form of Pricing Proposal/2

Additional Fee Proposal:

Programming		$_____/person programmed
FF&E procurement and supervision	Average	$_____/hour
Field observation	Average	$_____/hour
Warranty management	Average	$_____/hour

Based upon the scope of service and fees indicated above, please estimate the reimbursable expenses required to provide the service proposed:

Reimbursable expenses estimate: $_____

Signature of responsible bidding party: _____

Date: _____

As an alternate form of proposal, the Client company project manager may wish to receive two sets of fees: the above-noted fee proposal format for the operational aspects of the project, and the following fee proposal format for the special area features of the project. In this manner, special features which are priced separately can be backed out of the final contract if their costs are prohibitive, or if the resulting project site will not provide the required space or appropriate conditions for these special features.

The preceding fee proposal is intended for the operational and administrative spaces of the proposed project, which total approximately (   ) rentable square feet of space.

Interior Design Consultant bidders are requested to provide not-to-exceed upset fees for each of the special features outlined on pages 3, 4, and 5 of this Request For Proposal, stating in each case:

			Fees for Phases:		
Item #	**Item**	**Sq. Ft. Est.**	**I - V Design**	**VI - VII Production**	**Total Fee**
001	Lobby space	00,000	$00,000	$00,000	$00,000
___	___	___	___	___	___
___	___	___	___	___	___
___	___	___	___	___	___
___	___	___	___	___	___

Please list here any consultants that are required by the bidding firm to provide specialized service, either for the operational and administrative spaces of the proposed project, or the above-noted special features of the project, including at least the following specialized services foreseen:

Service	Consultant's Firm	Contact	Telephone #
Engineering			
Lighting design			
Acoustic design			
Audiovisual design			
Kitchen planning			
Art consultant			
Signage design			
Graphic design			
Security consultant			
Data consultant			
Telephone consultant			
Procurement consultant			
Other			

The interior design consultant shall prepare the following key project dates for this project with a starting date of (   ) and an expected move-in date of (   )

		(Dates)		(Dates)
1.	Initial data gathering	_____	-	_____
2.	Site selection/Building configuration decisions	_____	-	_____
3.	Technical lease assistance/Fit-out scheduling	_____	-	_____
4.	Recruiting interior fit-out construction manager	_____	-	_____
5.	Schematic design	_____	-	_____
6.	Design development	_____	-	_____
7.	Approval process with Client, building owner and building code agency	_____	-	_____
8.	Contract documentation and specifications packages	_____	-	_____
9.	Bidding period	_____	-	_____
10.	(Client) review and decision to proceed	_____	-	_____
11.	Construction activity	_____	-	_____
12.	FF&E installation activity	_____	-	_____
13.	Punch listing	_____	-	_____

The interior design consultant shall attach here a chart of organization for the firm.

The interior design consultant shall attach here an abstract of the firm's professional liability policy.

The interior design consultant shall attach here a copy of a form of contract proposed for the project.

(Please use as the basis AIA Form (   ), adding, deleting, or modifying clauses the interior design firm and its professional liability insurance carrier suggest.)

The interior design consultant shall attach here resumes of the key project staff proposed for this project.

The interior design consultant shall attach here the present staff list and their present billing rates in dollars per hour.

The interior design firm shall attach here any addendum to this request for proposal that have been received as of the date of this proposal submission and included in this fee proposal.

APPENDIX 5

Form for Addendum to Request for Proposal

To: All competing interior design firms

From: (Client) project manager

Date: 10 September 19xx

This is Addendum __ of __ to the request for proposal dated _____ .

Subsequent to our issue of the previous Addendum # ( ) on _____ (date), the following points of clarification have been received and responded to as indicated:

1.   Issue:

        Response:

2.

3.

You are requested to sign a copy of this addendum indicating your receipt of same and attach this addendum to your response to our Request For Proposal, due (time and place).

Received by: _____ on _____ (date)
                        Consultant firm

Signed: _____ Date _____

APPENDIX 6

Evaluation of the Responses to the Request for Proposal and Interview Process

Evaluating various responses to a request for proposal, no matter how formal and exacting the request may have been, requires a combination of objective and subjective judgments.

In order to lead a selection committee through the process of selecting the most qualified interior design consultant for the project, we recommend a checklist format.

Each response to the request for proposal should be logged in and read with the checklist beside it, and each member of the selection committee should fill out a checklist for each response.

The chairman of the committee would then receive each member's checklists and correlate the various checklists into a composite checklist document used to determine the statistical winner.

With this statistical winner determined, the chairman should call a meeting of all members of the selection committee to discuss various divergent opinions. These divergent opinions may have skewed the statistical result, and if the weight of peer opinion in the selection meeting causes a revision in some statistics, then a revised tally should be made at the meeting and a revised winner determined.

The result of the selection meeting should be a ranking in order of preference, with a resolution that one of the members of the selection committee meet with the selected consultant in an effort to prepare a contractual agreement. If, within a specified number of days, a suitable agreement cannot be negotiated, then one would go on to the second on the list, until an agreement can be reached with the most qualified firm willing to enter into an agreement suitable to the selection committee.

There may be certain issues of fact-finding and clarification which the committee may request the contract negotiator to determine prior to entering into final contractual agreements with the selected consultant, and there may be the necessity to reconvene the selection committee to discuss various points of fact or contract negotiating problems which may require group participation and authorization.

The ultimate result of these discussions and negotiations should be a draft agreement suitable to both the selection committee and the consultant, and subject to final documentation and confirmation by both parties' legal counsel.

If time is of the essence, the project might begin with a letter of intent, based upon the negotiated contractual terms and conditions, and pending final approval by both parties' counsel and signatures. In the meantime, the letter of intent might spell out certain tasks and estimated fees that could proceed within a limited framework of time.

Individual Checklist Request for Proposal Evaluation Form
(to be filled out by each member of the selection committee having read the individual consultant's response to the request for proposal

Person completing this form

Date

Firm Being Evaluated

Item of Evaluation		Raw Score 0 - 10	Weight	Weighted Score (Raw Score (x) Weight

1. Price calculation formula ___ x 300 = ___

   Total fee proposed for
   Phase I - XIII for
   (   ) rentable sqft
   of operational space $_____

   Total fee(s) proposed for
   all special spaces itemized
   in the proposal of total
   (   ) rentable sqft of
   space $_____
   Total bid price $_____
   Total bid price $/sqft $_____/sqft $_____
   Less any proposed and acceptable
   price reduction concepts ($_____/sqft)
   = basis of bid comparison ($_____/sqft)

   Basis of budget is $_____/sqft
   If bid is equal to or less than budget = 10 points
   If bid is 0 to 15¢/sqft more than budget = 8 points
   If bid is 16¢ to 25¢/sqft more than budget = 6 points
   If bid is 26¢ to 35¢/sqft more than budget = 4 points
   If bid is 36¢ or more/sqft than budget = 2 points

2. Scope of work required = scope of work proposed ___ x 10 = ___
   Scope of work required = 100%

   Score
   If scope of work proposed = 100% of scope required = 10
   = 95% = 8
   = 90% = 6
   = less than 90% = 0

   Outline of missing scope items to be negotiated back into contract with
   selected consultant:

   •
   •
   •
   •
   • _____
   • _____
   _____
   _____
   _____

Individual Checklist Request for Proposal Evaluation Form (continued)

Item of Evaluation	Raw Score 0 - 10		Weight	Weighted Score (Raw Score (x) Weight	
3. Ability of consultant to begin work as required Yes = 10 No = 0	____	x	10	=	____
4. Ability of consultant to complete work according to schedule Yes = 10 Maybe = 5 No = 0	____	x	10	=	____
5. Consultant understands the quality expectations of the project Score 0 - 10 subjectively	____	x	20	=	____
6. Consultant has demonstrated in prior projects for other companies the ability to provide the quality level expected for the project Score 0 - 10 subjectively	____	x	30	=	____
7. Consultant understands the budget constraints of the project Score 0 - 10 subjectively	____	x	20	=	____
8. Consultant has demonstrated in prior projects for other companies the ability to provide the required quality level at the expected budget Score 0 - 10 subjectively	____	x	10	=	____
9. Consultant understands the expected project management methods to be used and is able and willing to work within these guidelines and constraints Score 0 - 10 subjectively	____	x	20	=	____
10. Consultant's typical construction contract documents, working drawing details and specifications meet with the requirements of the project Yes = 10 Maybe = 5 No = 0	____	x	20	=	____
11. Consultant's CAD capabilities are compatible with the requirements of the project Yes = 10 No = 0	____	x	20	=	____
12. Consultant carries sufficient liability and professional liability insurance to meet the needs of the proposed project Yes = 10 No = 0	____	x	20	=	____

Individual Checklist Request for Proposal Evaluation Form (continued)

Item of Evaluation	Raw Score 0 - 10		Weight		Weighted Score (Raw Score (x) Weight
13. Consultant's subcontracting consultants and engineers are acceptable for this project Score 0 - 10 subjectively	___	x	20	=	___
14. If consultant's response outlined cost saving or project management strategies which might provide for a more cost effective and efficient project, evaluate these concepts for their appropriateness to the project Score 0 - 10 subjectively	___	x	30	=	___
15. Consultant is familiar with the office furniture system currently being used by the company and likely to be reused in the new facility Yes = 10 No = 0	___	x	20	=	___
16. Consultant has worked for the company before and is familiar with the workings of the company and its project management techniques and style Yes = 10 No = 0	___	x	20	=	___
17. Consultant's written style, as expressed in their response to the request for proposal, illustrates report writing and language skills sufficient for the requirements of the project Score 0 - 10 subjectively	___	x	10	=	___
18. Consultant's proposed project team, evaluated as to continuous length of service with consultant Average length of service of proposed project team ___ years If 5 or more years = 10 points If 4 to 5 years = 8 points If 3 to 4 years = 6 points If less than 3 years = 0 points	___	x	20	=	___
19. Subjective evaluation of proposed project team Score 0 - 10 subjectively	___	x	50	=	___
20. Objective evaluation of proposed project team If project leader has managed a similar successful project = 4 points If not = 0 points If project team includes the architects and other specialists required = 4 points If not = 0 points If consultant's owner/manager(s) (principals) proposes to participate in project = 2 points If not = 0 points Add up these points for the score	___	x	30	=	___

Individual Checklist Request for Proposal Evaluation Form (continued)

Item of Evaluation	Raw Score 0 - 10		Weight	Weighted Score (Raw Score (x) Weight)

21. Objective evaluation of consultant's staff average billable hourly rate
If 1991 average billing rate as calculated by the sum of all staff rates divided the number of technical staff
listed is $65 or less/hour = 10 points
     $66 to $70/hour = 8 points
     $71 to $75/hour = 6 points
     $76 to $80/hour = 4 points
     $81+/hour = 2 points
	____	x	20	= ____

22. Proposed staff hours to complete the project Budgeted staff hours was ____ hours If bid is = to or less than budget = 10 points If bid is 1 to 500 hours more than budget = 8 points If bid is 500 to 1,000 hours more than budget = 6 points If bid is 1,001 to 1,500 hours more than budget = 4 points If bid is 1,501 to 2,000 hours more than budget = 2 points If bid is 2,001+ more than budget = 0 points	____	x	20	= ____
23. Consultant's enthusiasm for the project Score 0 - 10 subjectively	____	x	10	= ____
24. Size of firm If firm size is at least 40 = 10 points If firm size is at least 35 = 8 points If firm size is at least 30 = 6 points If firm size is at least 25 = 4 points If firm size is less than 25 = 0 points	____	x	10	= ____
25. Results of reference checks Checking three references with the following results: Good + Good + Good = 10 points Good + Good + Acceptable = 8 points Good + Good + Unacceptable = 6 points Good + Acceptable + Unacceptable = 4 points Good + Unacceptable + Unacceptable = 0 points	____	x	30	= ____
26. Level of interest consultant demonstrated to the selection committee during the RFP process Score 0 - 10 subjectively	____	x	20	= ____
27. Subjective evaluation of the ease with which a contract can be negotiated with consultant Score 0 - 10 subjectively	____	x	10	= ____

Individual Checklist Request for Proposal Evaluation Form (continued)

Item of Evaluation	Raw Score 0 - 10		Weight	Weighted Score (Raw Score (x) Weight
28. Level of consultant's owner/manager (principal) involvement in this project If owner/manager proposes to be project principal Otherwise	____ = 10 points = 0 points	x	30	= ____
29. Subjective evaluation of consultant's design ability, based upon references and prior project review Score 0 - 10 subjectively	____	x	100	= ____
30. Subjective evaluation of consultant's ability to maintain confidences during the consulting effort Score 0 - 10 subjectively	____	x	10	= ____
31. Subjective evaluation of consultant's proposed project team's "performance" during the interview process Score 0 - 10 subjectively	____	x	30	= ____

Total weighted score items 1 through 31

Maximum score being   10,000

Composite Checklist Request for Proposal Evaluation Form

(To be filled out by the selection committee chairperson and returned to each of the committee members for review prior to the selection committee decision-making meeting)

Note to members of the selection committee: If, after reviewing the responses of the other members of the committee, you wish to revise any of your scoring, please make the revisions on a copy of this form, and bring these revisions with you to the selection committee decision-making meeting.

Selection committee chairperson to post to this form the average score* of the various selection committee members for each of the five consultants' proposals being reviewed and evaluated

Items of Evaluation	Consultants Being Evaluated					Average Score of All Five Proposals*	Maximum Score Possible
	1	2	3	4	5		
1. Price calculation	___	___	___	___	___	___	3,000
2. Scope of work required	___	___	___	___	___	___	100
3. Ability to begin work	___	___	___	___	___	___	100
4. Ability to complete work on time	___	___	___	___	___	___	100
5. Understands quality expectation	___	___	___	___	___	___	200
6. Prior project's quality	___	___	___	___	___	___	300
7. Budget understandings	___	___	___	___	___	___	200
8. Cost benefit of prior projects	___	___	___	___	___	___	300
9. Understands project management	___	___	___	___	___	___	200
10. Documentation quality	___	___	___	___	___	___	200
11. CAD capability	___	___	___	___	___	___	300
12. Liability coverage	___	___	___	___	___	___	200
13. Subcontractor's acceptability	___	___	___	___	___	___	200
14. Consultant's strategies	___	___	___	___	___	___	300
15. Familiarity with existing equipment	___	___	___	___	___	___	200
16. Familiarity with company	___	___	___	___	___	___	100
17. Written style	___	___	___	___	___	___	100
18. Team length of service	___	___	___	___	___	___	200

Items of Evaluation	Consultants Being Evaluated					Average Score of All Five Proposals*	Maximum Score Possible
	1	2	3	4	5		
19. Project team compatibility	__	__	__	__	__	__	500
20. Project team professional ability	__	__	__	__	__	__	300
21. Average billing rate	__	__	__	__	__	__	200
22. Staff hours estimated	__	__	__	__	__	__	200
23. Enthusiasm	__	__	__	__	__	__	100
24. Size of firm	__	__	__	__	__	__	100
25. Reference checks	__	__	__	__	__	__	300
26. Level of assistance during RFP process	__	__	__	__	__	__	200
27. Ability to negotiate contract	__	__	__	__	__	__	100
28. Level of owner participation	__	__	__	__	__	__	300
29. Design ability	__	__	__	__	__	__	1,000
30. Maintain confidences	__	__	__	__	__	__	100
31. Interview process	__	__	__	__	__	__	30
Total score							10,000

Ranking by total score 1 to 5, with 1 being
the statistical winner, having the highest
score in the evaluation

*To calculate average score, assume, for example, four selection committee members with a score for subjective evaluation for item 5 as follows:

Committee member 1 score for consultant #1 of 200	and for consultant #2	200
Committee member 2 score for consultant #1 of 180	and for consultant #2	100
Committee member 3 score for consultant #1 of 180	and for consultant #2	100
Committee member 4 score for consultant #1 of 160	and for consultant #2	40

The average score to be posted to this form would be180 for consultant #1 and110 for consultant #2

**Average score of all five proposal evaluations to be used as a ranking guide, item by item, and against the maximum possible score

Consultants Being Evaluated

	1	2	3	4	5

Items of Evaluation

List of items to consider in negotiating contract(s) with various consultants being evaluated (place a (●) under each consultant's column where this item is applicable)

Item	1	2	3	4	5
· (For example) Did not include ABCDEF	—	●	—	●	—
·	—	—	—	—	—
·	—	—	—	—	—
·	—	—	—	—	—
·	—	—	—	—	—
·	—	—	—	—	—
·	—	—	—	—	—
·	—	—	—	—	—
·	—	—	—	—	—
·	—	—	—	—	—

CHAPTER 7

Interior Design Contracts

C. Jaye Berger

Editors' Note: In writing this chapter, the author has been guided by two interrelated assumptions:

1. That the readers of this book include present or prospective members of a major tenant relocation or development team and/or students aspiring to join one of the various disciplines associated with the real estate development process;

2. That, for the foreseeable future, most, if not all regions of the United States will recognize that licensed or registered architects and engineers (a) are uniquely and legally qualified to draft certain life-safety features encountered within most major office facility design projects and (b) by law must prepare or supervise the preparation of the documentation in order to legally employ their respective professional licenses and seals on the documents that they present to the local building departments having jurisdiction over the particular office facility construction project.

The United States has a national building code, but it does not have a national building code review process. Some states have established statewide code review departments to assist smaller municipalities that could not otherwise afford to support a code review team of professionals. However, most major municipalities in the United States (and elsewhere) employ their own building code officials to review the plans for all office facilities prior to granting construction permits, and any construction that proceeds without these legal permits is subject to violations and fines.

Some municipalities rely on the national building code, and associated national plumbing and electrical codes, as the basis for their review process. Other municipalities with particular histories of construction-related casualties (e.g., San Francisco, from earthquakes; Miami's Dade County, from

hurricanes; Chicago and New York, from high-rise tower construction) have written their own building codes in response to local technical and political goals and objectives.

Legally, the professional practice of providing interior design services for major office facilities is currently in a state of turmoil in many regions of the United States. Architects, who are registered or licensed by state regulators, maintain that they have certain legal and professional qualifications that non-registered or nonlicensed design professionals may not possess. Interior design professionals routinely provide "interior architectural" services when, for instance, they design an interconnecting stairway, or simply plan an office corridor or aisle that must be used as the legal means of exiting during a fire emergency. To respond to this quasi-architectural professional practice, the American Institute of Architects (AIA), the National Society of Interior Designers (NSID), and the Institute of Business Designers (IBD) have recently joined together to recommend to the various state legislatures the licensing of all design professionals engaged in the design and specification of various aspects of the construction building trades.

Many state legislatures are reviewing these issues.

The professional liability insurance industry, which serves architects and interior design firms, is also attempting to resolve the liability aspects of this overlapping professional responsibility. The industry is proposing increased insurance coverage for interior designers who are in fact qualified to provide quasi-architectural services, and are insisting that these design professionals purchase this insurance coverage and pass a series of nationally recognized standardized tests of professional practice and qualifications.

Recently, the AIA issued a restatement of its professional code of ethics, in support of licensing interior designers and to clarify the overlapping roles of architects and interior designers. The term "design professional" is currently being used instead of "architect," "designer," or "interior designer" in a variety of contracts, insurance policies, and state legislation governing these allied professions.

Since the legal foundation of the design profession is currently in such a state of turmoil, design professionals and their clients are well advised to carefully consider all aspects of their contractual relationships prior to entering into a contract for design services.

On projects where an interior designer has been contracted to provide services involving architecture and has hired a licensed architect to stamp the drawings, major legal questions have arisen as to whether, just by taking on such a project, the designer is practicing architecture without a license. Clients frequently raise this issue in lawsuits against interior designers in which they are trying to recover fees. There may also be a question regarding the propriety of the architect's stamping drawings that he or she has not prepared or supervised. For these reasons, legal advice should be sought within the jurisdiction of the project site, before any contracts involving architectural interior design services are signed.

As of this writing, the legal position throughout the United States remains that only licensed architects may sign drawings for major office facility construction projects, and, by the act of signing these drawings, the licensed or registered architect is certifying that he or she actually supervised the preparation of the drawings being signed and presented for plan review and permit.

Owners and tenants are well advised to assure themselves that the design professional they seek to employ for their office facility project is either a licensed or registered architect or is associated with an architect who will certify that he or she has prepared or supervised the preparation of drawings.

* * *

Only a handful of lawyers in the country concentrate on legal issues involving architectural and interior design contracts and litigation. For this reason, many people rely on printed, form contracts published by the American Institute of Architects (AIA), the Institute of Business Designers (IBD), and the American Society of Interior Designers (ASID). Clients and designers feel safe with these forms of agreement because they have been endorsed by these national professional organizations. These contracts are very good for covering the important areas, but they do not always meet the parties' special needs for their particular project. In addition, in response to recent recommendations from the professional liability insurance industry (in the post-asbestos era), even the standard forms of agreement published a few years ago must be modified with riders and with sections crossed out, to comply with current professional practice and to address current issues. The resulting messy "standard" contract can be very difficult to read and understand and may create ambiguities if a rider conflicts with the printed contract.

Design professionals who do not use these forms tend to make up their own contracts by combining a variety of resources—provisions from prior agreements, sections from books they have read, clauses provided by their insurance companies, form contracts, and their own made-up language. These practices can result in poorly drafted contracts that do not provide adequate legal protection or address either party's interests in the agreement. Similarly, owners and their attorneys, who often do not understand the construction industry, sign "form contracts" without understanding the ramifications of the documents.

As more and more people work with interior designers and spend huge sums of money on major office facilities, these contracts become more and more important. A well drafted contract is critical, in case any litigation should result from the project. Form contracts cannot be blithely signed without understanding their provisions. A project-specific form of agreement is often more appropriate than a marked-up form contract.

Every design professional performs different services and works in a unique way with each client. Some provide decorating services and purchase furniture for clients with modest budgets. Others are involved in multimillion-dollar office facility renovations requiring coordination with architects and various other professional consultants. Some designers use rough sketches to show the placement of furniture; others prepare elaborate computer-aided architectural drawings. Every designer has a different style of working. Therefore, every designer has different contractual needs. Clients have various ways in which they can negotiate the contract, but first they must understand what the document is all about. The contract that is ultimately signed should be a document that reflects what both parties have agreed to.

Form versus Nonform Contracts

Many people like to use form contracts because they believe that the provisions reflect industry standards and have been tested in court cases. This is not necessarily true. No matter how many times a form contract is used, should a dispute arise, the facts of the particular case will have to be litigated just like any other contract dispute. Expert witnesses will be required to explain what the standards are in the industry, whether the designer was in compliance with these standards, and what the contract language means within the context of how the industry operates. Unfortunately, using form contracts does not necessarily lessen the likelihood of litigation.

Form contracts are recommended if:

1. They suit the specific project;
2. The parties cannot afford to have a contract drafted;
3. The parties do not have access to the kind of expertise needed to draft such a contract.

One of the worst aspects of form contracts is that, because they are printed, people do not bother to read them. Consequently, neither party knows what he or she is signing until an issue is raised in a lawsuit. These documents also tend to be very long, which makes the parties and their attorneys less than enthusiastic about reading them cover to cover.

An architectural or interior design contract should be easy to read, understandable to lay people, and long enough to cover the essential points. It can be in the form of a letter agreement on either the design professional's or the client's letterhead, as long as it is clear that it is a contract, that it contains all the essential terms, and that both parties must sign it.

Some interior designers prepare proposals describing their services and the terms of the arrangement before the actual contract is signed. This is fine, as long as a contract is eventually signed before work begins. Some clients mistake the proposal for a contract and never bother to sign a formal contract. Naturally, this becomes a major problem when a dispute arises, because many important issues have not been addressed. A *signed* contract is a must.

Not having a contract can be an expensive mistake—usually more so for the design professional than the client. Such extensive testimony is needed to prove the designer's entitlement to fees, that it becomes economically impossible for the designer to pursue such a claim. Invariably, the designer will forego many dollars in design fees.

How long should the contract be? Length is not as important as thoroughness. Many design professionals feel that long contracts will scare their clients away. No contract should scare a serious client away; a scared-away client may be having second thoughts about committing to the project because of budget constraints and would have been problematic anyway. Clients should *want* to have a signed contract. They are spending a lot of money and they should know how it is being spent.

Project-specific contracts vary in length according to the size and complexity of the project. The content of the contract is important, not its length.

An attorney who knows this area of the law can draft a contract for interior design services, and it can be reused with appropriate modifications by the design professional or by a client who is frequently involved with office facility renovations or design projects. A freshly drafted contract avoids the awkward appearance of crossed out provisions in printed contracts (which the client will be able to read anyway) and of having lengthy riders attached. Another major benefit to the design professional who invests in a customized form of agreement is that the agreement itself can assist in the marketing of design services and related fees. For instance, many design professionals now seek to charge for their computer-use hours, an issue not addressed until recently. The customized contract allows them to approach these issues and, ultimately, to include only those points to which both parties agree.

The major aspects of a basic form of agreement between a client and a design professional are addressed in the sections that follow.

Project Description

The project description should state what work is going to be performed by the design professional. This is different from describing how it will be done. How the project will be done is described under project services. One example of a project description provision is the following:

> Interior design of a 10,000-square-foot office facility on the 30th floor of the XYZ Building, located at _____ ("the Project").

If the space is difficult to describe or is part of a larger floor, a drawing can be attached to show the area involved.

Some would-be contract drafters incorrectly combine the project description and the project services, as in this example:

> Working with the client to determine a budget and select fabrics and colors for the conference room.

It is also a mistake to describe work that the parties do not intend to perform in the near future. For example, if ". . . and possibly the 31st floor" were to be added to the above description, it would create confusion about payment for services. Additional new work can be addressed in a written amendment to the contract or in a separate contract.

The project description should be very detailed. If a design professional was asked to give a flat fee for services and, thinking that the work was to be done only on offices in a client's suite, simply identified the services as "interior design for your office," major problems could result if the client had actually requested the redesign of the entire office facility at the stated fee. The designer would have contracted for more work than was intended for the stated fee. The contract's language must reflect both parties' thoughts and expectations. Imprecise contract language leads to lawsuits.

A client or a client's attorney should not rejoice in such poor contract drafting or feel that he or she has received an irrevocable bargain; the expense of an inevitable lawsuit will not be worth it, even if the client prevails. The contract should be fair to both sides and should correctly state what both parties have agreed to.

Design Services

A thorough description of those services being provided by the design professional is essential because it is directly tied to the professional fee. Only the services listed will be included in the designer's fee. Any extra work or services will be billed as additional services. The language of the description will be scrutinized if the client feels that the project did not turn out correctly or seeks to claim that the designer was in breach of contract.

Design work is usually done in six phases:

1. Programming;
2. Schematic design;
3. Design development;
4. Contract documents and bidding;
5. Contract administration;
6. Furniture and equipment implementation or purchasing.

Occasionally, phases are combined or one or more may be deleted, depending on how the designer works and what the client's needs are. For example, some clients want the designer to have a very limited role, if any, in the contract administration phase. This phase may then be abbreviated or deleted entirely.

Prior to the revisions to the standard forms of agreement, it was considered good practice for clients and design professionals to reach an agreement to proceed from one phase to another. Each of the standard forms of agreement now calls for client approval prior to proceeding from one phase to the next.

Since the mid-1970s, design professionals have been asked by their clients to speed up the design process through implementation of "fast track" project management procedures. In effect, fast tracking necessitates the overlapping of project phases. Documentation of client approvals proceeds issue-by-issue in the form of meeting minutes and follow-up letters and memos.

Contracts covering fast track project management should state how approvals are to be documented and might include for reference a project time line or other form of schedule so that both parties understand clearly and agree to the scheduling of the various phases of the project.

Programming Phase

The programming phase is the period in which the design professional meets with the client to determine specific project goals and objectives. Does the client want to have two conference rooms? How many offices or workstations will be required? Where will various departments and individuals' offices be located in relation to one another? What sort of seating arrangements are required? These goals are then written up in a space utilization program for the project, which should be approved by the client in writing before proceeding to the next phase. Some projects may require the preparation of adjacency diagrams and of stacking and blocking diagrams that show the functional relationships among department, personnel, and offices. Clients should indicate approval of these documents by signing them. The endorsement helps to ensure that the designer and the client are in agreement on each design step along the way.

Standard contract language for programming is as follows:

1.1 Programming Phase

1.1.1 The Designer shall consult the Owner and other parties designated in this Agreement to ascertain the applicable requirements of the Project and shall review the understanding of such requirements with the Owner.

1.1.2 The Designer shall document the applicable requirements necessary for the various Project functions or operations, such as those for existing and projected personnel, space, furniture, furnishings and equipment, operating procedures, security criteria, and communications relationships.

1.1.3 The Designer shall ascertain the feasibility of achieving the Owner's requirements identified under Subparagraphs 1.1.1 and 1.1.2 within the limitations of the building or buildings within which the Project is to be located.

1.1.4 Based on a review, analysis, and evaluation of the functional and organizational relationships, requirements, and objectives for the Project, the Designer shall provide a written program of requirements for the Owner's approval.

This language is adequate. Although there is little cause for the client to negotiate or revise this language, it is lengthy.

An example of a simpler, project-specific way of describing these services would be to say:

The Designer shall consult with the Client to determine the Client's requirements, and shall provide a written program of requirements for the Client's approval and prepare a schematic design of the Project showing the general relationship among personnel, sales, and display areas.

Schematic Design Phase

The schematic design phase starts when the designer begins to sketch the layout of the project. Rough drawings may show, for example, where offices will be in relation to conference and supply rooms. At this point, preliminary reflected ceiling drawings of the lighting and ceiling grid will be prepared. Other drawings will show the preliminary location of telephones. The designer may become involved during this phase with helping the client to determine what the budget should be or how much renovation can be accomplished for the amount the client has allocated. The designer may also prepare boards showing samples of colors and finishes available.

Standard contract language for this phase reads as follows:

1.2 Schematic Design Phase

1.2.1 Based on the approved written program, the Designer shall prepare for the Owner's approval preliminary diagrams showing the general functional relationships for both personnel and operations.

1.2.2 The Designer shall review with the Owner alternative approaches to designing and carrying out the Work.

1.2.3 Based on the approved adjacency diagrams, the Designer shall prepare space allocation and utilization plans indicating partition and furnishings locations and preliminary furniture and equipment layouts. The Designer shall provide an evaluation of the program and the project budget, if one has been established by the Owner, each in terms of the other, subject to the limitations set forth in Subparagraph 4.2.1.

1.2.4 The Designer shall prepare studies to establish the design concept of the Project indicating the types and quality of finishes and materials and of furniture, furnishings, and equipment.

1.2.5 The Designer shall submit to the Owner a preliminary Statement of Probable Project Cost, based on the recommended design concept and on current costs for projects of similar scope and quality.

These responsibilities on a commercial project can be condensed into a simpler statement:

The Designer shall consult with the Client to determine the Client's requirements, and shall provide a written program of requirements for the Client's approval and prepare a schematic design of the Project showing the general relationship between personnel and operations.

Clients will generally want to include language requiring the designer to submit statements of probable cost:

The Designer shall provide sufficient information to the Client to assist in defining the Project budget.

Many designers are comfortable taking on such responsibility, but for those who do not have the expertise or desire to calculate costs, this language should not be included in the contract. On very large projects, it may even make sense for the client to retain a consultant known as a cost estimator, who specializes in this field.

Budgets and statements of probable cost often lead to litigation. If the designer and the client are working with and designing for a $200,000 budget and find, when bids are taken, that the project will cost $300,000, the client will be understandably angry. The client will assume that the bids are high because the designer failed to design for the agreed-upon budget. Major changes in the design will be required and the designer will not necessarily be paid for the time spent in revising the design. Often, at such junctures, a rift develops between the designer and client, and the designer's contract may be terminated. Therefore, designers should be cautious about taking on this responsibility.

Design Development Phase

Before beginning the design development phase, the client will have approved the schematic design drawings. It is best if all such approvals by the client for each phase are done in writing. The client can also sign a set of drawings that are stamped or titled "Approved" and are dated.

The schematic design drawings will be further refined during this phase, to show details of work being done to floors, walls, and ceilings. For example, custom-built furniture would be shown in detail on these drawings. If the designer has agreed to work on the budget, it too would be refined at this point.

An example of language for this phase might be:

> Based on the approved program and schematic design, the Designer shall prepare drawings and other documents to fix and describe the interior construction, and furniture, furnishings, and equipment ("FF&E"), colors, materials, and finishes of the Project.

Contract Documents and Bidding Phase

The contract documents and bidding phase is extremely important. During this phase, the designer will prepare detailed drawings and specifications showing the contractor exactly how the project will be implemented. These drawings and specifications are incorporated into the documents given to the contractors or suppliers, such as millworkers and carpet suppliers, for their bids.

The absence of important specifications or details could result in incomplete bids or unsatisfactory work. When these omissions become apparent during construction, the client will be asked by the contractor to pay for them as extras, under change orders. Once the general contractor and the subcontractors are physically working on the project site, introducing third-party contractors becomes impractical, as does requesting competitive bids for change orders. Thus, the client may be faced with higher unit costs for these change orders. One technique frequently employed to limit the price inflation of change orders is to negotiate a schedule of unit prices for many of the individual items in the overall "market basket" of the contract (e.g., dollars per outlet, dollars per door, dollars per yard of carpet). However, some change orders are likely to occur, and items of construction that are not documented even in the most detailed schedule of unit prices will be required. Although change orders may be expensive, the client has little negotiating power at this point and will probably pay more than he or she might otherwise have paid. The client will no doubt be angry, believing that the extras were included in the contract with the contractor. Thus, it is crucial that these documents be thorough.

Once again, the client will have approved the design development drawings before this phase is started and the budget will have been readjusted if necessary.

The designer will prepare the package of documents and drawings that will be given to the contractors bidding on the project. The designer may recommend one or more contractors to the client and help the client locate recruiting and negotiating agreements. This service is usually not mentioned in contracts. Designers should, in fact, avoid recommending contractors, so that the designers are not blamed or held responsible if something goes wrong. If the client wants such a provision, the designer may agree to "assist the client in selecting a contractor."

The client should negotiate directly with the contractor, which means performing an examination of the contractor's background and qualifications. The contractor's business structure should be ascertained (whether it is a corporation, partnership, or sole proprietorship). The length of time in business, the kinds of projects worked on and how they turned out, the company's financial status, and its ability to obtain the required insurance and bonding should all be investigated.

Some designers contract directly with contractors. They feel this gives them more control over the quality of the work. Some designers also do contracting as part of their own businesses. If they are hiring an independent contractor, this can be a risky way of doing business. The client will have no choice but to sue the designer if the contractor's work is poor. There are also some licensing issues involving contractors, which the parties should be aware of; these are discussed later in this chapter.

If a designer is working in conjunction with the client's architect, there should be language describing how they will work together. The client should agree in the designer's contract to have a provision in the architect's contract stating that the architect will advise the designer of any changes to the project which may affect the designer's work.

Contractually, it is usually the client's responsibility to obtain building permits and file drawings, even though the designer may assist in the process. In most jurisdictions, only a licensed or registered architect or engineer who has supervised the contract document process can sign and stamp the drawings presented to the code officials for the issuance of the required permits.

The contract language for this phase reads as follows:

1.4   Contract Documents Phase

1.4.1   Based on the approved Design Development submissions and further adjustments in the scope or quality of the Project or in the Project budget authorized by the Owner, the Designer shall be responsible for the preparation of, for approval by the Owner, Construction Documents consisting of Drawings, Specifications, and other documents setting forth in detail the requirements for the interior construction work necessary for the Project. The Work described by such interior construction documents is intended to be performed by the Owner or under one or more Contracts between the Owner and Contractor for construction.

1.4.2   Based on the approved Design Development submissions, the Designer shall prepare, for approval by the Owner, Drawings, Schedules, Specifications, and other documents, setting forth in detail the requirements for the fabrication, procurement, shipment, delivery, and installation of furniture, furnishings, and equipment necessary for the Project. Such Work is intended to be performed under one or more Contracts or Purchase Orders between the Owner and Contractor or supplier for furniture, furnishings, and equipment.

1.4.3   The Designer shall advise the Owner of any adjustments to previous Statements of Probable Project Cost indicated by changes in requirements or general market conditions.

1.4.4   The Designer shall assist in the preparation of the necessary bidding and procurement information, bidding and procurement forms, the Conditions of the Contracts for Construction and for Furniture, Furnishings and Equipment, Purchase Orders, and the forms of Agreement between the Owner and the Contractors or suppliers.

1.4.5   The Designer shall assist the Owner in connection with the Owner's responsibility for filing documents required for the approval of governmental authorities having jurisdiction over the Project.

1.4.6   The Designer, following the Owner's approval of the Contract Documents and of the most recent Statement of Probable Project Cost, shall assist the Owner in obtaining bids or negotiated proposals, and assist in awarding and preparing contracts for interior construction and for furniture, furnishings, and equipment. All bidding and negotiating activities shall be coordinated by the Designer.

Designers who do not differentiate among bidding, construction documents, and contract administration phases may feel comfortable having the following language:

> (a) The Designer shall assist the Client in obtaining bids or negotiated proposals and assist in awarding and preparing contracts for interior construction and for FF&E, if requested.
>
> (b) The Designer shall assist the Client in connection with the Client's responsibility for filing documents required for the approval of governmental authorities having jurisdiction over the Project, if required.
>
> (c) The Designer shall assist the Client in coordinating schedules for delivery and installation of the FF&E, and the issuance and pursuance of the punchlist to the completion of the work. However, the Designer shall not be responsible for any malfeasance, neglect, or failure of any manufacturers, contractors, or suppliers of FF&E to meet their schedules for completion or to perform their respective duties and responsibilities, including but not limited to delays or mistakes in delivery and defective or unsatisfactory FF&E.
>
> (d) The Designer shall visit the Project premises on a periodic basis, at intervals appropriate to the stage of construction, to become generally familiar with the progress and quality of the work and to determine in general if the work is proceeding in accordance with the contract documents, but shall not be required to make exhaustive and continuous inspections of the Project. The Designer shall review all contractor submittals such as shop drawings, product data, and samples, but only for conformance with the design concept of the work.

If the designer will not have any responsibility for assisting the client in filing with governmental authorities, because, for example, the contractor is responsible for this task, then that language should be deleted from the contract.

Another very important issue can arise at this time. Assume that a client has given all the necessary approvals up to this phase but, during the preparation of the construction documents, decides to change the design. Does the designer have to do this work or can it be billed as additional services? The form contracts do not address this issue and therefore imply that this work would be part of the designer's regular fee—an obvious benefit to the client.

The designer who wants to be paid extra for this unforeseen work might want the following language in this phase of the agreement:

> The designer will make up to two major changes in the Contract Documents as part of the Fee. Any changes requested by the Client thereafter shall be billed as Additional Services.

Contract Administration Phase

In the contract administration phase, the renovation or construction work is actually done. The walls are put up, the paint is applied, and the furniture is delivered. The extent of the designer's involvement in this phase is often the subject of intense negotiations between the client and the designer. For the client's part, he or she would like the designer to visit the project every day and oversee the construction and installation from start to finish. For the designer's part, he or she would like to only be required to visit the site periodically, to make sure that the work is progressing and looks like what he or she designed. The resolution of this issue in the contract will have a major impact on any litigation that might occur later.

The standard language for this phase is very lengthy. The portion pertaining to site visits reads:

1.5.6 The Designer shall visit the Project premises as deemed necessary by the Designer, or as otherwise agreed by the Designer in writing, to become generally familiar with the progress and quality of the Work and to determine in general if the Work is proceeding in accordance with the Contract Documents. However, the Designer shall not be required to make exhaustive or continuous inspections at the Project premises to check the quality or quantity of the Work. On the basis of such on-site observations, the Designer shall keep the Owner informed of the progress and quality of the Work, and shall endeavor to guard the Owner against defects and deficiencies in the Work of the Contractors.

Clients may want the designer to have a higher degree of contractual responsibility and oversight. They may want the designer to agree to "provide daily supervision of the contractor" or to "observe the work being performed by the contractor." The words "supervision" and "approval" connote a higher degree of involvement by the designer and greater potential for legal liability. Designers should be careful about signing an agreement with such language, and most professional liability insurance policies require that design professionals "observe and comment" rather than "supervise and approve."

A balance must be struck between each party's interests. Most designers are not paid enough to be on-site every day and should not be taking on the role of a construction foreman or construction manager. The contractor has a supervisor on staff, and construction management involves different responsibilities. Some designers unwittingly sign contracts in which this type of language appears and are therefore more likely to be involved in litigation if something goes wrong with the construction. Many clients believe that if anything goes wrong with the project, it must be because the designer failed to supervise the work. This is another reason why all contracts in this area should be drafted only by attorneys who know this area of the law and should be reviewed by an attorney before signature.

Standard contract language requires the designer to "endeavor to guard the Owner against defects and deficiencies in the Work of the Contractors." This is fine from the designer's perspective. The client might want to add some extra language such as: "The designer shall use his best efforts to guard the Owner against defects and deficiencies in the Work of the Contractors."

Standard contract language makes the designer the interpreter of the Contract Documents and the "impartial judge of performance" by the Owner and the Contractors. In other words, if a question arises as to whether some work is part of the contractor's contract or should be billed as an extra, the designer's decision will be final. The designer is also required to "endeavor to secure faithful performance by both the Owner and the Contractors . . . ."

Surprisingly, this language may place more of a legal burden on the designer than he or she wants. Some designers argue that they have met their contractual responsibility if they bring any problems to the attention of the client and help the client decide how to handle it. In this particular instance, the standard form language may be more favorable to the client than to the designer, and some designers might want to delete it.

In a similar vein, some designers might not want to be involved in preparing change orders. The contractor should do this. Designers should also require the client to put language in their contract with the contractor stating that no change orders will be valid and paid for unless delivered in writing and signed by the client, and the contractor will not be able to claim fees for this work *in quantum meruit* (the fair value). If the contractor does extra work without change orders, there may be a claim that it was done with the designer's written approval. If the designer feels that he or she needs authority to order minor changes, a dollar limit can be placed on the changes, in the contract.

Furniture and Equipment Implementation or Purchasing

In this phase, the designer, with the client's assistance, will specify which furniture will be reused and which new furniture, furnishings, and equipment ("FF&E") will be purchased. The designer will also prepare drawings and specifications for any custom work, such as cabinets, bookcases, and tables. Drawings will be prepared showing the location of these items in the space.

Large companies often order their own FF&E, using the designer's specifications. If this is done, the designer usually agrees to coordinate the preparation of these requisitions and to assist the client in the management of any bidding that may take place.

The designer will also help by coordinating the relocation and installation of the client's furniture. Although the designer will not take responsibility for accepting and rejecting FF&E, he or she will prepare a punchlist for the client. (A punchlist is a list of all the fine points, such as scratches and loose screws, that need to be attended to, in order for the project to be complete.)

Design professionals following the AIA code of ethics will not act as furniture dealers or otherwise buy and resell furniture and equipment to their clients. They are permitted to provide professional procurement or implementation services such as expediting or order processing, but their remuneration must be in the form of a fee for services rendered. Most clients agree that design professionals should not directly profit from purchases of goods and services made according to the design professionals' recommendations and specifications.

Additional Services

If the description of the project services is thorough, only a brief statement of additional services should be required. Additional services include anything that was not mentioned in the statement of services.

The standard contract language is fine, but if brevity or succinctness is of concern, all that need be said is:

> If the Client requests services not included within the scope of services provided in this Agreement ("Additional Services"), they shall be paid for by the Client as provided in this Agreement, in addition to the compensation for Services, at the following rates: [describe rates].

For certain clients, a list of some of the anticipated additional services may be useful, to avoid any claims of surprise. The list might include:

> Meeting with the landlord of an office building to explain the work or doing extensive revised drawings.

Reimbursable Expenses

Many people like to make exhaustive lists of all the types of reimbursable expenses there are on a project. Generally, these lists are not necessary. If the list says ". . . including, but not limited to . . ." and gives some representative examples, that language should be sufficient. Special items might be listed, such as the cost per page of local and international facsimile (FAX) transmissions, blueprints, models, trucking, storage, and insurance. Some designers mark up the cost of these items; the mark-up should be specifically stated.

Designers frequently use taxis and rent cars for local work on behalf of the client. Clients may not consider these costs reimbursable. If there is any possible question about their being reimbursable, their status should be specifically listed.

Owner's Responsibilities

Having someone in the owner's camp who has authority to make decisions can sometimes mean the difference between a successful, on-time project and a failed and delayed one. On a commercial project, a person in authority is essential because the designer will be dealing with many people from the company and only one or two will have authority to issue orders.

The standard contract language only requires the owner to designate a representative "when necessary."

On commercial projects, a number of people usually contribute ideas toward what the client wants, and achieving a consensus is difficult. The designer has to pull all of these ideas together. A restaurant may have a managing partner and several investors. A corporation will have several executives and many personnel who have to work in the space being designed, and each is likely to have a different idea. The only way to assure that proper authorizations are given is to provide for them in the contract. The designer should make that an affirmative obligation.

In practice, the designer's project manager will establish a weekly project team meeting schedule so that even the busiest executive can plan to attend or can appoint a surrogate. An executive officer in a corporation who knows that he or she will be frequently out of town or busy at meetings should also want such a contract provision. Nothing can delay a project more than a situation in which the client's approval is needed and the client is unavailable.

If the renovation work is being done in an office building, approval may be needed from the landlord. This should be the client's responsibility, although the designer should be contractually obligated to assist the client in providing necessary information and drawings.

It may be important for the designer to have access to the "existing condition" drawings for the floor or building. It should be the client's responsibility to provide these.

Compensation

Types of Fees

There are three main ways in which the designer can be compensated:

1. Hourly;
2. By a flat fee;
3. Using a percentage of the costs of construction and of furniture, furnishings, and equipment (FF&E).

Billing based on a multiple of direct personnel expense is a variation on hourly billing, but some designers prefer it to a plain hourly fee because it more easily gets the client's approval. Billing based on square footage is another variation of a flat fee.

Designers may charge differently for each phase and, in a typical contract, more than one type of compensation will be used. For example, some designers look at all the design work as a unit and bill for it on a flat fee or hourly basis. For visiting the project, administering the work, and ordering FF&E, they bill on an hourly or percentage basis.

Clients want predictability and certainty when it comes to expenses on a project. For many clients, this means negotiating the entire project on a flat fee basis, or on an hourly basis with a not-to-exceed amount. A certain number of site visits and revisions to drawings would be factored into that fee. This arrangement eliminates the possibility of having to pay the designer additional fees if bids are high (requiring additional design services) or if there are numerous revisions to the designs.

Such a contract might read:

For Services in phases 1 through 5, the designer shall be paid a fixed fee of $_____. This Fee shall include two revisions in the Design Development Drawings and one site visit a week for six weeks. Any additional services shall be billed by the Designer as Additional Services.

A slightly different contract might read:

For services on phases 1 through 4, the designer shall be paid at the following hourly rates:

Designers $_____

Draftsman $_____

For Services in Phase 5, compensation shall be computed as follows:
_____% of Construction Cost as defined herein.

A client might agree to this language but might want to add a "not-to-exceed cap" on the hourly billing, to put a little more control on how much the designer can bill. The definition of construction cost should be carefully drafted, to avoid problems when a particularly expensive contractor is used. If a contract is negotiated with a contractor who is much less expensive than the other bidders, the design professional may lose fees.

Amounts of Fees

Hourly rates can vary tremendously from one design firm to the other. These differences relate to the designer's general level of experience, reputation, and experience with the particular type of project. The fact that one designer offers to do the project at $90 per hour and another quotes $45 per hour does not mean that the more expensive designer is overcharging. The client should meet with several designers, before signing a contract.

The certainty in flat fees or hourly fees with a guaranteed maximum makes them popular with clients. However, most designers cannot predict accurately how much time a project will take because the work always takes more time than anyone expects. The project may greatly exceed the predicted number of hours and the designer may be left working essentially for free. This is not a desirable result, and both parties should carefully think about the flat fee amount before agreeing to it.

An effective method for managing the cash flow of client fees to the design professional is to agree in advance to the percentage of the total fee to be allocated to each phase of the project. In this manner, if the client or the designer sees the actual project time commitment exceeding the basis of the fee calculation, either party can give an early warning signal that too much time is being spent at this point.

Fees for Furniture

As stated earlier, most designers working on large-scale office facility projects adhere to the AIA code of ethics and will not buy and resell furniture and equipment. They will provide implementation services to assist their clients in the purchasing of these goods and services, but the client will remain the ordering party and the design professional will act only as agent. Fees for this additional service are typically negotiated on an hourly or fixed fee basis. They should not be negotiated as a percentage of the costs of the goods and services, because this form of payment presents a clear conflict.

Retainer

The designer should obtain an initial retainer before starting any work. This should be roughly 10 to 15 percent of the total fee. Areas of controversy come into play during negotiations on how the retainer should be credited to the client. The designer will want the retainer to be credited to final payment, creating some security for the last payment. The client will want the retainer credited to the first or second payment so that less money has to be paid out of pocket in the early phases.

Generally, retainers are nonrefundable if the project terminates prematurely. Depending on the size of the retainer and on which phase the project is in when the termination occurs, the client may want to negotiate a sliding scale for refunding the retainer (assuming that neither party is in breach of contract).

Payment

Payment is usually made on a monthly basis. If fees are based on a percentage of cost of construction, the designer will be entitled to different percentages of the total fee for each phase. The designer bills each month until payments reach the allocated percentage for that phase.

A flat fee will be paid as earned against time card billing or in equal monthly amounts, except for the last payment. Hourly fees are very straightforward and can be billed monthly as earned. Fees can be apportioned to each phase of the project, to assist both parties in the effective management of the agreed-to fee dollars over the entire duration of the project.

Various penalties can be inserted, in the event that the client does not pay on time. These can vary from interest on late payments, to stopping work, to being able to collect attorney's fees if the designer has to bring legal action to collect fees.

Publicity and Photographic Rights

Publicity is very important to any designer. When projects are published in magazines, the recognition helps generate new assignments. Therefore, a provision should be inserted in the contract in which the client agrees that, if the project is published, the designer will get credit as "the designer." This provision might read:

> In the event the Client publishes or causes to be published photographs or other representations of the Project after completion of the Services under this Agreement, the Client agrees to include reference to the Designer as the designer for the Project in any such publication.

The designer should also get the client's permission to take photographs for the designer's own purposes. Occasionally, the client may have certain confidentiality requirements. These should be set forth in the contract.

Arbitration

Provision for arbitration appears in most printed (AIA) form contracts. It is recommended that this provision be left in the contract as the method of resolving disputes. Litigation in this area can be very time-consuming and expensive. The fees paid to the designer on most projects are not enough to justify or pay for the expense of a protracted lawsuit. For this reason, many designers avoid litigating for their fees. Also, when a designer sues for fees, there is invariably a counterclaim for negligence and breach of contract.

Arbitration provides a less expensive, relatively fast method of resolving disputes. A client might not want this provision, wishing instead to exert economic pressure on the designer if a dispute arises.

Those who do not like arbitration feel that arbitration awards tend to be split down the middle. All things considered, arbitration works well for resolving design disputes because the construction arbitration panel is comprised of people who know the industry.

Mediation is somewhat similar to arbitration in the way it is conducted, but the important difference is that it is nonbinding. It can be performed by a private mediation company or through the American Arbitration Association. The parties may agree to hold a mediation hearing. If they do not like the outcome, they can proceed to arbitration or litigation. However, many parties who have gone through a mediation proceeding decide to accept the decision rather than continue the dispute. Some insurance companies actively promote mediation; others prefer to have the courts decide disputes.

A major difference between arbitration and mediation is the ability under mediation to bring together all parties to a dispute, in an effort to arrive at a complete resolution. The arbitration rules require that only the party to the particular contract can arbitrate, and other parties cannot be brought in. If, for instance, a particular project involves a dispute among a client, an architect, a designer, and a subcontractor or two, mediation may clearly be a path to a more cost-effective resolution of the dispute, because all of those parties can be brought into one hearing. This can be done with arbitration only if the standard language is modified.

Termination

Design industry contracts usually provide for mutual termination only in the event of a breach of contract. Both parties may want to have the right to terminate for any reason, after giving the required notice. The client may want to terminate the contract if the project is abandoned.

Industry form contracts usually have a provision for termination expenses to the designer, if the termination is not the designer's fault. Termination expenses compensate the designer in part for the profit that would have been made if the project had been completed. The client will usually argue in favor of deleting the provision for termination expenses. The basis for this argument is the notion that, if the designer is paid to the date of termination, adequate compensation has been given for the services received.

Signature

The client should be sent two originals of the contract for signature and asked to return one to the designer with a retainer check.

If the contract is in the form of a letter, the signature section should look something like this:

AGREED AND ACCEPTED:

ABC Corporation, Inc.   XYZ Design, Inc.

By: _____   By: _____
        President   President

Dated: _____   Dated: _____

Conclusion

No one should ever sign a contract just to get a project started. Parties sign printed contracts for services they never intended to buy. When this happens and a dispute arises, the parties are always surprised when they go back and finally read the contract. Invariably, one party will say in shock, "I agreed to that?" A lot of money is involved in interior design projects and a little time spent in the beginning, negotiating the terms, can mean less money spent in litigation later on.

CHAPTER 8

Effective Leasing

Larry C. Baucom and Barry M. Nealon

Leasing is often viewed as the simple matching of available space and potential users' requirements. Today, however, this process has become one that requires some of the most sophisticated skills in real estate.

Investors compare investment yields in real estate to those that can be achieved in alternative investments. Leasing success is the determinant factor in the yield of any income-producing real estate investment. Investors are not generally buying bricks and mortar. Instead, they are buying an income stream. Critical issues in the quality and durability of that income stream are determined in the leasing process.

From the tenant's point of view, the bottom-line cost of its space and facilities resulting from a poorly negotiated lease can drastically affect its profitability and, in the extreme, even its business survival.

While the usual goal of both the landlord and the tenant in the negotiation process is to achieve the most favorable position possible, it is well to remember that a lease is a long-term arrangement. If either party is seriously disadvantaged, then the relationship may not withstand the test of time. Examples of this include a landlord's reduction in the quantity or quality of services provided to a tenant, poor property management, deferred maintenance, little or no capital improvements to the property, or simply walking away from the property. On the tenant's part, its business may not only be adversely affected by the quality of the landlord's services and property management, but also by rents escalating above the level at which the tenant can profitably carry on its business operation. Thus, the landlord may be left with a bankrupt tenant in a period of poor market conditions in which to negotiate a lease with another tenant.

This chapter has been updated and edited by its authors since its original publication in *Property Management Handbook,* edited by Robert F. Cushman and Neil I. Rodin (New York: John Wiley & Sons, 1985). Used with permission.

A well-negotiated leasing transaction is one that is ultimately fair to both parties. The relative negotiating strength has frequently favored the landlord. However, there is currently a buyer's (or tenant's) market. This is due to many changes in our economic environment over the past decade, particularly the inflationary spiral. In the late 1970s, high rates of interest curtailed office building construction; in the mid- to late 1980s, as interest rates were reduced, the market rebounded with a flood of new office buildings which have come onto the market, substantially exceeding the yearly absorption rate. Tenants have had to become much more sophisticated in analyzing real estate decisions in this highly competitive and complex market, especially since office facility costs affect their business position over the long term.

This chapter outlines some of the broad areas that should be considered in developing and implementing marketing strategies to attract the best match of tenants to the space, negotiating the business deal parameters, negotiating the lease and tenant fit-out package, and discussing issues that affect the negotiation process to achieve an effective leasing transaction.

Developing Marketing Strategies

One of the areas most often overlooked or simply given a minimum of attention is that of developing a marketing strategy for an effective leasing program. The usual emphasis is on "flogging" the property to as many potential users as can be reached and on getting deals started as soon as possible. That may not be the best strategy for maximizing the owner's total profit.

Market research is a must, for planning an effective leasing campaign. The market, which is made up of users and suppliers of space, must be carefully analyzed. Then, the subject property must be analyzed to determine salient features and amenities that can be used to appeal to this market. From these factors, a marketing strategy can be developed to position the property to this market in a way that will achieve the best use and ultimately the highest value.

Analyzing the Market

Competition (Supply). First, the total market must be studied, to determine competitive supply and demand conditions.

From a supply viewpoint, the total number of existing competitive buildings in the marketplace should be carefully surveyed. A profile of each building should be prepared. This profile should include:

1. Locations of the competitive buildings within the region;
2. "Curb appeal," design features, amenity package, and overall qualitative image of the various buildings in the marketplace;
3. Relative efficiency of the various buildings in the study, frequently expressed as a ratio of net usable floor area to gross rentable square feet calculations;
4. Space available directly from the owner;
5. Space available on a sublease from tenants;
6. Listing of key tenants;
7. Size and configuration of the building, including the size and number of floors;
8. Floor plate size, core-to-glass dimensions, and other architectural features that provide the basis for efficient space planning;
9. Age of the property;
10. Condition of the property, including fire- and life-safety features, asbestos abatement, and accessibility to the handicapped;
11. Parking spaces (generally not a factor in cities with mass public transportation systems, but important in cities dependent on automobiles and in suburban areas);
12. Quality of the management;
13. Competence of the leasing agents;
14. Flexibility of the lease proposal(s).

This survey should include building-by-building and overall current market vacancy factors, the quality of the competing offerings, and a profile of the tenant structure in the marketplace. Frequently, in cities where office leases are recorded public documents, lease termination dates for major tenants can be added to the survey, to discover the dates when prospective tenants will be in the market for a stay/ relocate decision. If this survey is continually updated over a prolonged period, take-up rates and market absorption patterns can also be determined.

A thorough survey of buildings under construction or planned for construction, and of sites potentially available for construction, should also be made. A best-case/worst-case analysis should be made as to the timing of their completion. These future potential availabilities should then be merged with the current availabilities and average annual absorption rates, to forecast the potential supply and demand patterns over future years.

These studies are critical in analyzing the timing of new building construction as well as in developing leasing and pricing strategies that will maximize the profitability of a property.

Users of Space (Demand). From a demand viewpoint, a detailed analysis should be made of the key industries within the market. The survey should include how these industries are doing currently and how they are projected to do in the future. The individual companies in the market within these industries should be studied to determine their relative growth within the industry. From an effective leasing standpoint, it may be advantageous to the owner to make a more competitive deal for a company that is fast growing and may need more space within the property. Higher rents can usually be achieved on additional space requirements because the tenant can avoid the cost of moving its entire operations to another location.

The size of the companies in the marketplace is also important, particularly as to floor-size requirements. For example, if large corporations or institutions are the prevailing users, then floor sizes of 30,000 square feet and greater may be preferred. Horizontal space may allow more efficient use for larger operations than vertically stacked space. On the other hand, if the market is a central business district with a heavy concentration of service firms such as law firms, accounting firms, public relations firms, and so on, then there may be a good market for smaller floor sizes. These smaller floors will allow a firm the prestige and image of being located on an entire floor as opposed to a partial floor. If a tenant has an entire floor, its business guests can step off the elevator directly into the firm's lobby area, thus giving an impression of being a larger organization. A full-floor user also has a more efficient utilization of space. Even if the price is higher, this utilization factor may make this space more cost-effective to the tenant.

Other leasing issues that are highlighted by a study of the users in the market are the relative needs for back-office versus front-office operations, preference patterns for net versus gross leases, parking requirements, and transportation patterns. Front-office needs generally require more services, higher-quality tenant installations, and higher-quality space with a greater ratio of window area to floor area. Back-office needs may require better mechanical, electrical, telephone, and data wiring; support facilities for operational efficiencies; and good public transportation networks to attract clerical staff.

Larger tenants that require an entire building may prefer to own or net-lease the building. With a net lease, the tenant provides and pays for all operating services and taxes above the net rent. This gives the tenant the operating control of the building, which may be preferable for security or special operations. Smaller tenants usually prefer a gross lease (the landlord provides full services).

Analyzing the Property

After a study of the market is completed, it is fundamental to an effective leasing program to carefully analyze the property to determine features that can be highlighted in the leasing campaign. Special property features are discussed in the following sections.

Location. If the property is a 100 percent location, this factor should be a special theme in the campaign. It is hard to get away from the old real estate adage that the three best determinants of property value are "location, location, and location." If it is not a 100 percent location, the campaign should center on other amenities, such as the quality of the building; key location for back-office or other special use; excellent location to public transportation, shopping, or other public amenities; or excellent rental value.

Quality of the Building. Tenants are attracted to well-maintained, well-managed properties, whether old or new. The best leasing programs are achieved in those properties where (1) the facade, lobby area, and structure have been maintained or refurbished to their best condition; (2) the space has been modernized to provide amenities for new office requirements such as (a) central heating, ventilation, and air conditioning (HVAC); (b) suspended ceilings with

recessed lighting; (c) adequate electrical power and wire distribution systems for modern computing equipment, and capacity for installing modern communications facilities ("smart building"); (3) building services are well-maintained; and (4) modern fire, security, and elevator systems are in place. Capital improvements and modernization programs should be considered as part of an effective leasing campaign. They can provide an excellent return to the owner through increased rents.

Floor Sizes. Floor sizes of 25,000 to 35,000 square feet are preferred by the widest range of tenants. If there is a center core area, the floor can be easily divided to accommodate multiple tenants, thus reducing the leasing risks by increasing the number of potential candidates for the space.

If the floors are smaller than 15,000 square feet, the leasing campaign should focus on smaller tenant-users. For example, if a tenant requires 150,000 square feet in such a building, the tenant would need 10 or more floors of inefficient, vertically oriented space. In addition, the tenant would place heavy wear and tear on building elevator services and inconvenient internal traffic would be created. For a large tenant, this property would not compete well with properties that have larger floor sizes.

Floor Configuration. In older office buildings, floor configuration can be in various shapes, such as an X, H, L, U, and so on; or it can be square, with a courtyard which, before air conditioning, allowed tenants to be close to windows for ventilation. Many of these older buildings are ideal for marketing space in small units, with a high proportion of windowed offices on a multitenant floor. Newer office buildings have square, rectangular, or designed shapes that have modern, more efficient layouts. These layouts can vary substantially in design from center core to side core and differ in column structure, bay size, and window module—all of which can affect a specific tenant's utilization of space. Studies should be made to show the most efficient layout patterns for both full-floor and partial-floor rentals and for varying types of users requiring space designs ranging from extensive open planning to heavy private-office density.

Loss Factor. One of the most important, yet often misunderstood, selling factors from a comparative marketing standpoint is the building's relative efficiency—its "loss factor." The loss factor is the difference between the net rentable square feet on which rent is paid and the usable square feet which the tenant actually occupies for functional purposes. To simplify this problem, the Building Owners and Management Association (BOMA) has issued a standard form of measurement, which has been further clarified by the real estate board of New York in their standard form of measurement, to try to establish a common interpretation. (See Figure 8.1.) Many local real estate boards have also issued standards for the measurement of space, some of which vary from the BOMA standard. If a building has a higher efficiency, that is, a more favorable or lower loss factor than other competing buildings within the marketplace, this is a comparative advantage that should be highlighted in the marketing campaign.

Window Size. The size of the windows and their perimeter location determine the size of the typical standard windowed office. In buildings where the perimeter wall is substantially glass, the mullions and columns that separate the glass panels are used to locate the walls of the perimeter offices. Generally, window widths are between 4 feet and 5 feet. This allows the design of a two-window standard office of between 8 and 10 feet in width. Offices of less width cannot easily accommodate standard size desks, chairs, and other office furniture without overly cramping the space. Window widths larger than these dimensions result in standard offices of greater than 16 feet in width, which accommodate fewer personnel on the perimeter and reduce the flexibility for efficient layouts of the space.

Ceiling Heights. Standard building ceiling heights average 8 feet, with many superior-quality office buildings providing 8 ft.-6 in. or 9 ft.-0 in. Suspended ceilings, recessed lighting, and air conditioning supply and return ducts are isolated in the plenum (area between the suspended ceiling and the floor slab above). If the height between the floor slab of a given floor and the floor slab of the floor above is great enough to give a suspended ceiling height of greater than 8 ft.-6 in., this can be a marketing plus. This feature is particularly important where a raised floor system is needed for computer facilities or to accommodate wiring requirements for heavy communications users.

Floor Loading. The average floor loading specification for space accommodating standard office use is 50 pounds per square foot live load, with 20 pounds per square foot additional rating for interior partitioning. If the building has a higher floor load

specification, that fact should be highlighted in the marketing campaign, because it would be an important feature for special uses such as accommodation for library facilities, computer and other equipment requirements, special file storage, and so on.

Air Conditioning and Heating Systems. The efficient functioning of air conditioning and heating systems has become especially important to tenants. Many tenants, particularly law firms, accounting offices, and other professional operations, require after-hours facilities. Twenty-four-hour tenant control of the air conditioning facilities supporting the tenant space has become very popular in the design of new office buildings. It is an important feature and should be highlighted in the marketing campaign.

Fire Safety and Security. Regardless of whether the building is located within a downtown or a suburban market, fire-safety and security systems are extremely important and are part of the overall selection parameters considered by tenants in today's marketplace. These features do not have to be highlighted in the marketing campaign, but they should be part of any substantive package of promotional materials on the property.

Positioning the Property to the Market

After the market and property have been carefully studied, it is important to determine the target group of users to which the property should be presented.

The qualification of the types of users to which the marketing program will be addressed is the concept of market segmentation. For example, if the property is a new, prime property located in the heart of a major city's business district, with floor sizes of 5,000 square feet, it will not be well-suited for a tenant who requires a large block of space. Furthermore, it will not be especially attractive for tenants who are looking for a low-priced transaction. Thus, the marketing campaign should be aimed at corporations, banks and financial institutions, law firms, accounting firms, and other prestigious service-oriented businesses requiring a presence in the downtown area. This type of tenant is generally looking for image, address, and quality, as opposed to a low price.

Few properties appeal equally to a wide range of users. Thus, it is important to properly position the property to its market. This can be achieved by a
(Text continues on page 287.)

FIGURE 8.1

Standard Method of Floor Measurement for Office Buildings
Effective April 1982

In order to facilitate a comparison of the cost of space among buildings, The Real Estate Board of New York, Inc., recommends that owners use standard definitions of gross area and usable areas, and clearly explain how the definitions are used to calculate rentable area. Architectural plans and calculations should be displayed to the tenant, if requested.

The Real Estate Board of New York, Inc. recommends the following definitions and methods as the Standard Method of Floor Measurement in office buildings.

GROSS AREA OF BUILDING

The gross area of the building shall be all the floor area within the exterior walls of the building and enclosed by a roof and, in addition, free-standing power plants or other utility structures to the extent that they service the building.

GROSS AREA OF FLOOR

Determine the gross area by measuring all the space on the floor to the inside finished surface of the exterior walls. Where the exterior walls contain windows, fixed clear glass, or other transparent material, the measurement should be taken to the inside surface of the glass or other transparent material.

USABLE AREA, SINGLE TENANT FLOOR

Subtract from the gross area of the floor the following, including the finished enclosing wall:

- Public elevator shaft and elevator machines and their enclosing walls
- Public stairs and their enclosing walls
- Heating, ventilating, and air conditioning facilities (including pipes, ducts, and shafts) and their enclosing walls, except that shafts serving a floor in question shall not be subtracted
- Fire tower and fire tower court and their enclosing walls
- Main telephone equipment rooms and main electric switch gear rooms, except that telephone equipment, and electric switch gear rooms serving the floor exclusively shall not be subtracted

USABLE AREA, MULTIPLE TENANT FLOOR

- First, calculate the usable area as if for a single tenant floor
- Then deduct the corridor area, including toilets, supply rooms, etc., but excluding the enclosing wall of the corridor
- Measure the net usable area of each space on the floor by measuring each enclosing wall which is a building exterior wall to the inside finished surface of the exterior wall, or to the inside surface of the glass as the case may be. Measure demising walls to the center and walls which abut corridors to the corridor side of the finished surface of the corridor wall.
- To determine the usable area on a multiple tenant floor, apportion the corridor area to each space by multiplying the corridor area by a fraction, whose numerator is the net usable area of the space and whose denominator is the total of the net usable areas of all the spaces on the floor, and add the result to the net usable area of the space.

BELOW-GRADE, CELLAR AND SUB-CELLAR SPACE

To determine the usable area of below grade, cellar, and sub-cellar areas, follow the same procedures as are appropriate for single or multiple tenant floors except, that, in addition, the following should be omitted from usable area:

- Machine rooms and pump rooms and their enclosing walls
- Electric switch gear rooms and their enclosing walls
- Telephone equipment rooms and their enclosing walls
- Steam and water meter rooms and their enclosing walls

(Continued)

FIGURE 8.1 *(Continued)*

- All space devoted to servicing the operation of the building, i.e., cleaning contractors, storage, building maintenance shop, building engineer's office, etc.

FULL DISCLOSURE PROVISION

The variations in location of mechanical equipment, in the zoning regulations under which they were built, and in structural design among buildings of different ages require different methods of calculating rentable space. In view of this, The Real Estate Board of New York, Inc. recommends that owners fully disclose their method of calculating rentable area in a building.

Stores

1. The term "store" as used herein shall mean only that space at ground-floor level suitable for commercial use.
2. The rentable area of a store shall be computed by measuring from the building line in the case of street frontages, and from the inside surface of other outer building walls to the finished surface of the corridor side of the corridor partition and from the center of the partitions that separate the premises from adjoining rentable area.
3. No deductions shall be made for columns and projections necessary to the building.
4. Rentable area of a store shall include all area within the outside walls, less building stairs, fire towers, elevator shafts, flues, vents, stacks, pipe shafts, and vertical ducts with their enclosures.

STANDARD METHOD OF FLOOR MEASUREMENT FOR OFFICE BUILDINGS
For Guidance of Owners and Managers, Appraisers, Architects, Lending Institutions and Others

The purpose of a standard is to permit communication and computation on a clear and understandable basis. Another important purpose is to allow comparison of values on the basis of a generally agreed upon unit of measurement. The Building Owners and Managers Association International has sponsored a Standard Method of Floor Measurement for more than fifty years. The BOMA Standard has also been the one accepted and approved by the American National Standards Institute for many years. The result is a unit of measurement that can be used by owners, managers, tenants, appraisers, architects, and lending institutions, among others.

It should also be noted that this standard can and should be used in measuring office space in old as well as new buildings. It is applicable to any architectural design or type of construction because it is based on the premise that the area being measured is that which the tenant may occupy and use for furnishings and people.

The Standard Method of measuring office space as described in this publication measures only occupiable space, undistorted by variances in design from one building to another. It measures the area of an office building that actually has rental value and, therefore, as a standard can be used by all parties with confidence and with a clear understanding of what is being measured.

The Building Owners and Managers Association International urges all its members and others in the office building industry to use this method in measuring office space. This publication also includes the approved methods of measuring street-level store space.

The New Standard

Area measurement in office buildings is based in all cases upon the typical floor plans, and barring structural changes which affect materially the typical floor, such measurements stand for the life of the building, regardless of readjustments incident to tenant layouts.

In the case of buildings designed for divided or multiple tenancy, this typical floor plan must permit subdivisions to accommodate usual tenant requirements with corridors that reach every reasonable office subdivision. The definition of "Rentable Area—Multiple Tenancy Floor" applies to this typical floor, designed for tenant subdivision.

In the case of buildings designed for whole-floor tenancy, where corridors are omitted, the definition of "Rentable Area—Single Tenancy Floor" applies.

BOMA STANDARD

In 1915 the Association adopted the first Standard Method of Floor Measurement for office buildings. This was readily accepted as a "National Standard," serving the industry more than thirty-five years without occasion for amendment. With the advent of "block type" building design, a revised Standard Method was adopted by the Association in 1952. This was further revised (three years later) to conform to the new "American Standard," of which the Association was co-sponsor. At the Miami Convention in 1971, the Standard was again revised to reflect modern leasing concepts and practices.

FIGURE 8.1 *(Continued)*

AMERICAN STANDARD

The "American Standard" for measuring office areas in buildings is the result of joint action by participating organizations under the auspices of the American National Standards Institute. Our Association, as a sponsoring organization, is represented by the Chairman of our Rental Committee, Leonard J. Adreon of St. Louis, who serves as ANSI Committee Chairman. The new BOMA Standard has been unanimously approved by the ANSI Committee and was submitted on February 18, 1972 to the parent body for adoption as the new "American Standard."

Originally adopted September 15, 1915—Reissued (without change) December 1, 1925—Revised and reissued December 8, 1952—Revised and readopted December 6, 1955, and reissued January 10, 1956—Reprinted April, 1963; April, 1966; April, 1970—Revised and readopted June, 1971 and reprinted April, 1972; February, 1973; August, 1976.

AMERICAN NATIONAL STANDARD
Z65.1-1972Areas in Office Buildings, Method of Determining (revision of ANSI Z65.1-1956 (R 1964) Approved August 14, 1972)

Copyright © 1977 by Building Owners and Managers Association International

OFFICE SPACE

RENTABLE AREA—MULTIPLE TENANCY FLOOR

The Net Rentable Area of a multiple tenancy floor, whether above or below grade, shall be the sum of all rentable areas on that floor.

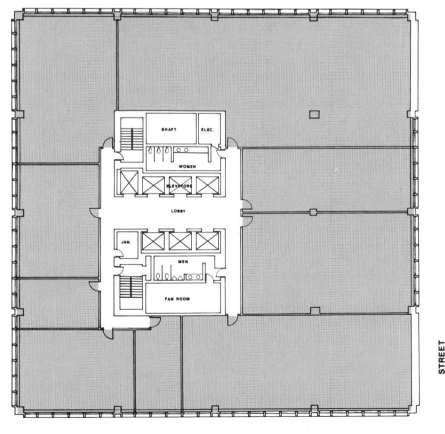

(Continued)

FIGURE 8.1 *(Continued)*

The rentable area of an office on a multiple tenancy floor shall be computed by measuring to the inside finish of permanent outer building walls, or to the glass line if at least 50 percent of the outer building wall is glass, to the office side of corridors and/or other permanent partitions, and to the center of partitions that separate the premises from adjoining rentable areas.

No deductions shall be made for columns and projections necessary to the building.

RENTABLE AREA—SINGLE TENANCY FLOOR

Rentable area of a single tenancy floor, whether above or below grade, shall be computed by measuring to the inside finish of permanent outer building walls, or from the glass line where at least 50 percent of the outer building wall is glass. Rentable area shall include all area within outside walls, less stairs, elevator shafts, flues, pipe shafts, vertical ducts, air conditioning rooms, fan rooms, janitor closets, electrical closets—and such other rooms not actually available to the tenant for his furnishings and personnel—and their enclosing walls. Toilet rooms within and exclusively serving only that floor shall be included in rentable area.

No deductions shall be made for columns and projections necessary to the building.

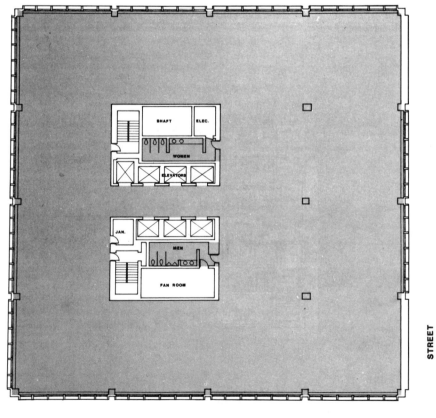

FIGURE 8.1 *(Continued)*

STORE SPACE

STORE AREAS IN OFFICE BUILDINGS

To determine the number of square feet in a ground floor rentable store area, measure from the building line in the case of street frontages and from the inner surface of other outer building walls and from the inner surface of corridor and other permanent partitions and to the center of partitions that separate the premises from adjoining rentable areas.

No deduction should be made for vestibules inside the building line or for columns or projections necessary to the building.

No addition should be made for bay windows extending outside the building line.

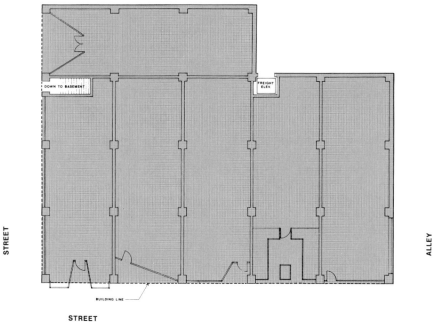

careful analysis of the property and the types of users in the market, as discussed above.

Implementing Marketing Strategies

After the conceptual design of the marketing program, an implementation package of promotional materials, support advertising, direct mail, and other solicitation campaigns must be prepared.

Promotional Materials

Rental Brochure. A quality brochure should be printed. It can range from a one-page flyer to a package containing a number of pages, depending on the size of the project and whether it is a new building under construction or an established, existing building. The brochure for a new building should be more elaborate, because the initial phase of the marketing program will be selling an intangible. Until the building is completed, the brochure has to take the place of an existing product that can be seen and physically reviewed. If an existing property is being extensively modified, a more descriptive brochure would again be a better marketing tool. If the building is well-established, a simple one-page flyer detailing the specific space available for lease may be enough.

In any case, it is important that the brochure sell the property. To make a proper sales presentation, the brochure should contain descriptive details of the building's architecture, location, special amenities, overall advantages, and specific space availabilities.

Presentation Folder. A presentation folder designed to hold all of the promotional materials as well as specific offering proposals should be considered. This folder should incorporate the same graphic design as that used in the brochure.

It is as important to establish the proper image in the marketing campaign as in the completed building being marketed.

Rental Plans. To aid tenants in visualizing how the space can be utilized, hypothetical layout studies should be prepared for typical floors, showing various office facility configurations. Some of these layout studies should show different ways in which the floor can be subdivided for smaller tenant installations.

In addition, the rental plan package should include ⅛-inch scale plans showing only the perimeter walls, columns, and core areas. The tenant or its space planner will need these plans to develop individual layout studies. Recently, developers have begun to provide these plans in computer-aided design (CAD) format so that the tenant's space planner can proceed in a more efficient, accurate, and timely manner.

Standard Installation Booklet. Details of the standard building installation are often not included in the rental brochure, except in summary form. A good technique is to develop a separate booklet describing the details of the building's standard installation workletter and interior amenities. This would allow a fairly detailed summary of the workletter. The workletter itself, which is a legal document generally attached to the lease documentation, describes a full legal specification of all of the construction work to be provided for the tenant by the landlord.

Advertising

Some owners rely heavily on advertising in newspapers and other media for their entire rental program. Other owners feel that advertising is not necessary. From a marketing point of view, advertising is a support tool that is helpful in establishing the proper market image for the property being promoted. Even if few direct calls are received as a result of the advertising, it is important in the positioning of the property to the market. It sets the base for property recognition when individual canvassing calls are made.

It is possible to overadvertise, thus giving the image of a property that is having rental problems. Therefore, it is extremely important that the advertising program not be ad hoc. It must be carefully planned and executed, to establish the desired image and results.

Direct Mail

If the target markets can be carefully defined, an extensive direct mail campaign can be developed. A high-quality rental brochure is usually too expensive to utilize in a mass-mailing campaign. An auxiliary one-page rental flyer that is designed to summarize some of the key features in the rental brochure can be used instead. In direct mail campaigns, a response level of one to two per 100 mailings is average. When these inquiries are followed up, the full brochure and presentation packages should be used for maximum impact.

Canvassing

Regardless of how well the marketing program and strategies have been planned, the effective leasing of space requires a strong support program of direct canvassing. This means extensive telephone follow-up of all direct mail campaigns and appointments arranged for personal interviews.

If the direct mail campaign is small, the telephone follow-up program should include calls to each firm that received a mail package. In general, however, the direct mail campaign should cover a large volume of companies. The follow-up telephone campaign can then be designed on a sample basis. In the immediate surrounding market where the building is located, a systematic program of direct canvassing of target companies should be implemented through personal interviews.

Agent versus "Doing It Yourself"

The main issue here is market coverage. Even if the owner has a leasing staff, it may be well to consider hiring a marketing and leasing agent to augment that staff and broaden market coverage.

The key concept is that there is no shelf life on space; for example, a month's rent loss can never be regained. The broadest possible market coverage increases the likelihood that the highest rental values can be achieved by developing more market activity and active candidates vying for space, together with a shorter lease-up period with tenants paying rent in advance of that which might be achieved with a more limited leasing program.

It is important to have a dedicated team of leasing professionals acting on the owner's behalf to generate this extensive market activity and work with the myriad of details necessary to set up and implement an effective leasing program. This task is people-intensive. It is particularly important that the owner or his or her agent have an effective canvassing team for the implementation and follow-up of the marketing program. Furthermore, in today's environment, with considerably more national and international business being done from both suburban and city locations, an agent having extensive links beyond the local market environment should be considered.

Whether the marketing and leasing program is implemented directly by the owner or through a leasing agent, full cooperation should be extended to outside brokers, thus giving the broadest possible local market coverage.

Negotiating the Lease

Nominal Price versus Effective Price

The first issue generally addressed by most tenants and landlords is the price quoted for the space. The focus for effective leasing transactions, from both the tenant's standpoint and the landlord's, should be the effective price per square foot—not the nominal or quoted price per square foot. For example, the landlord can frequently achieve a quoted price by concentrating on other concessionary points, thus allowing the tenant to achieve a lower effective price. By keeping the nominal price higher and by selecting front-end concession patterns, the landlord can still maintain a target asset value for the property, which

may be advantageous for refinancing, sale, or other disposition.

Issues in Determining the Effective Price

Efficiency of the Space. Very seldom are two buildings designed entirely alike. As a result, the floor layout patterns, loss factors, floor size, and core factors vary. From a marketing standpoint, a less efficient building with a higher loss factor and lower nominal quoting rent may, upon first inspection by a tenant, be the best transaction to consider. As shown in Figure 8.2, it is only later, when proper analysis is done on a comparison basis, that the effective rent is judged.

Thus, to maximize rental levels, the landlord must carefully consider pricing levels. If loss factors are considerably lower than competing buildings, that factor must be clearly highlighted when any pricing is quoted. In that way, the tenant is given more immediate estimate of value and favorable effective price.

Costs per Employee Housed. Frequently, a prospective tenant's space planner will prepare tenant plans for a number of office building floor plates from offerings proposed by competing developers and landlords. From these preliminary plans, the tenant can

FIGURE 8.2

Cost/Efficiency Comparisons

	Building A	Building B
Rentable area	10,000 sq. ft.	10,000 sq. ft.
Rental rate	$20/sq. ft.	$20/sq. ft.
Total rent	$200,000	$200,000
Usable area	8,200/sq. ft.	7,900/sq. ft.
Rent per sq. ft. usable area	$24.39/sq. ft.	$25.32/sq. ft.
Usable	8,200	7,900
_____(Efficiency)	_____ = .82	_____ = .79
Rentable	10,000	10,000
Rentable	10,000	10,000
_____(Add-on factor)	_____ = 1.22	_____ = 1.26
Usable	8,200	7,900
Rentable – Usable	10,000 – 8,200	10,000 – 7,900
_____(Loss Factor)	_____ = 18%	_____ = 21%
Rentable	10,000	10,000

Space in building B costs $0.93 per square foot, 3.8 percent more than space in building A. For 10,000 usable square feet, this would be $9,300 per year.

better visualize the actual layout variations among the competing offerings, and can calculate the number of offices and workstations that can be housed in the space being offered. By dividing the number of employees to be housed into the costs of each proposal, a calculation of the costs per employee housed can be computed.

This cost per employee housed becomes a major criterion for the selection of prime office space for many sophisticated tenants. In some real estate markets, competing landlords offer to pay for these preliminary tenant plans.

Escalations. Most U.S. leases in multitenanted office buildings are on a gross rental basis. This gross rental includes a base number for real estate taxes and operating expenses. As real estate taxes and/or operating taxes increase above the base amount, they are generally passed through to the tenant on a pro-rata basis determined by: the total square footage the tenant occupies, over the total square footage in the building.

For real estate taxes, it is common for the actual increases in the real estate tax rate and/or assessment value of the property to be passed through to the tenant on a pro-rata basis. For the operating expenses, the formulas can vary extensively. The fairest to both tenant and landlord is a formula designed to pass through actual increases in operating expenses on a pro-rata basis. However, many other formulas have been designed as alternatives to a direct pass through expense formula.

In some cases, an alternative formula is used because the owner would prefer not to have an open set of books showing all expenses and increases for the tenant to review in verifying the pass through charges. Formulas such as the penny-for-penny clause pass through increases in operating expenses, using the porter's wage as a proxy variable. This formula is sometimes easier for both the tenant and landlord, because it is tied to a specific, verifiable, porter's wage rate, generally subject to union contract negotiations. However, most tenants view it with a strong sense of suspicion, even when the ratio can be favorably negotiated. According to this formula, when the porter's wage goes up by one penny, the price per square foot to the tenant goes up by one penny. Variances on this formula have been 1½ to 3 cents per square foot per one penny increase in the porter's wage.

It is generally better, from a marketing strategy point of view, to keep the escalation formula as straightforward as possible, usually by having a direct pass through clause.

Rent Concession/Free Rent. This is a powerful concession to use in closing a lease transaction. It allows a higher nominal rent, yet achieves a lower effective price for the tenant. Particularly in a weak market, if the transaction did not close, it could be a matter of months before another completed transaction could be achieved. Thus, in effect, it may not be as much of a concession as it first appears.

From a tenant's point of view, a move in any one year frequently causes budgetary problems for capital to cover moving and other relocation costs, additional costs for tenant work above building standard, furnishings, and so forth. Many tenants are as concerned about these budget items as they are about the lower term rental patterns. Free rent helps offset these capital budgeting problems. Frequently, from the owner's point of view, the present value cost of free rent and other up-front concession patterns is less than the present value of the future benefits created through a higher rental pattern for the term of the lease.

Term. In today's inflationary environment, owners should consider pressing for shorter-term leases, rent reviews every 5 years, or annual consumer price index (CPI) adjustments to the rental level. Most larger corporations negotiate hard for 10-year flat deals, with fixed-price, 5-year term options beyond that period. Smaller tenants are more willing to consider shorter-term leasing patterns. Where longer-term flat leases are considered, the base rental level should be higher than that in shorter-term leases, to offset the financial risk associated with time; or, step-up leases should be considered, with the base rental automatically stepping to a higher rental at the end of each 5 years of the term. From the owner's point of view, shorter-term leases, market rent reviews in 5-year or shorter increments, CPI escalation clauses, and so on, will greatly increase the investment value of the property, should sale or refinancing be considered.

Options. Options that protect the tenant from having to relocate—because of a lease expiration or a requirement for additional space, for example—are a way of making concessions. Options make lease administration more difficult, but they can be favorable to the landlord by reducing tenant turnover. The key here is to make sure the options are not at a fixed rent, but are subject to a fair market value negotiation. Furthermore, an existing tenant may be willing to pay the landlord a small premium in rent over market, to save moving costs and disruption of business activities. For the tenant who has an option to expand, even though the tenant is paying a premium rent on the new space in the building, an effective rental package below market levels generally prevails. This is because the high rent level for the additional space is averaged with the low contract rate on the existing space.

Takeovers. Many landlords are unwilling to consider taking over a prospective tenant's current lease obligation. However, a takeover can be an effective marketing ploy, because most tenants are not willing to be obligated to two leases—nor do they want to be in the real estate business of trying to dispose of present facilities.

The financial leasing and legal exposure can be quantified and amortized over the term of the new lease as additional rent which, in many cases, is a much more palatable situation to a prospective tenant.

Services Provided. If special building services, such as tenant electricity, special cleaning after standard hours, heating and air conditioning, concierge services, special security, and so on, are being included in the base price and are provided above those being offered by competing buildings, then they should be quantified into value and presented at the same time that any nominal rental values are discussed.

Developers seeking smaller tenants may wish to consider including a central telephone and data network package to be shared by all of the tenants in the building. These sophisticated "switches" offer smaller tenants all of the features of highly sophisticated local area networks (LANs), at a substantially lower cost of operation than the smaller stand-alone systems applicable to the needs of individual tenants.

Construction Work or Allowances. Construction work or allowances for construction may be provided by the landlord in the effective leasing and marketing of a property. Until well along in negotiating, however, many tenants do not take into account the relative values of different workletter or dollar allowances included as part of the price. Therefore, the landlord should quantify the value of any tenant construction work provided as part of the overall lease price.

Tenant Covenant. Because a lease is a long-term transaction and rental markets can vary considerably, lack of a substantial tenant covenant and/or security

deposit can adversely affect lease values. If an owner is considering leasing to a weaker tenant, a significant security deposit or letter of credit may be required. Also, a higher pricing level can be justified as a rental risk premium.

Other Major Lease Clauses to Negotiate

Use. It is important for the owner to carefully define the specific use which the tenant will be allowed in the space. A tight use clause will not only aid in controlling the prime tenants' activities, but will assist the landlord in controlling the utilization of the space by any subtenants.

Sublease/Assignment. The owner should control the tenancy of the entire building as carefully as possible. In addition, because the landlord is in the real estate business and the tenant is generally not, the owner should endeavor to restrict subleasing rights as much as possible.

Even if subleasing is allowed, the lease should contain qualitative factors that allow the landlord to require the subtenants to maintain the quality of the tenants originally selected for the building. The landlord should also attempt to require the tenant to first allow the landlord the option of taking the space back or, if a subleasing is approved, to take any profit rents over and above the rent the tenant is paying out.

Alterations. Careful control needs to be designed into any lease clauses allowing the tenant to make alterations to the space. Plans and documentation of any alterations, and selection of any contractors or subcontractors being used by the tenant for alteration, should first be approved by the landlord. Furthermore, all appropriate bonds, insurance, and similar requirements must be supplied by the tenant.

Workletter Issues

Value of the Workletter. In an effective leasing and marketing campaign, the work provided by the landlord for any particular portion of space being marketed should be carefully considered. If an existing unit of space is small and cannot be configured in any other layouts, the landlord may want to offer only minor alterations when releasing this space. However, in large units, the existing tenant installation generally has to be substantially demolished to suit a new tenant. In such spaces, as well as in a new building where a tenant fit-out has not been completed, the landlord should consider offering the space with a building standard tenant installation. This building standard specification of work, which is provided as part of the overall pricing of the space, is generally outlined in an addendum (the workletter) attached to the lease document.

In considering the amount of work to be provided, a careful analysis should be given to workletters being offered by competing properties within the marketplace. This workletter will generally include basic air conditioning, floor tile or carpeting, acoustic ceiling tile, venetian blinds, initial painting, and 4 to 5 watts per square foot of available power. Usually, sheetrock partitioning, closets, doors, and basic hardware are included as well, although sometimes these are limited. Usually included, but always with limits, are thermostats, electrical wall and floor outlets, fluorescent lighting fixtures, outer door locks, and some automatic door closers on entry doors.

Electrical Power Consumption. Prior to the energy crisis of the mid-1970s, electrical power utility costs were typically included within a building's operating costs and expenses and thus within the lease terms and rents. With ever-escalating utility costs, and with tenants' increasing interest in energy conservation measures, many new leases are being written to provide each tenant with a submeter and a pay-as-you-go calculation of utility costs on a monthly basis. Meters and similar cost accounting measures have been offered for 24-hour air conditioning and the use of landlord-provided LANs of telephone and data services.

Substitutions/Credits. If a tenant chooses not to use building standard materials, a credit in the amount of the cost of the building standard materials may be requested to offset the price of new materials to be used. Generally, a landlord can resist any credit for these substitutions, because a fixed-quantity purchase may have been necessary to get economic pricing. If the tenant does not use the materials, an excess supply will be left on hand. Where substitutions are allowed, care should be taken to ensure that the quality of the materials substituted is equal to or exceeds that of the materials specified for the building standard workletter.

Additional Work over Building Standard. Many tenants require additional tenant work, above building standard, to fit out their spaces. Their landlords may want to consider some dollar allowance over building standard as an effective, up-front concession to close the lease transaction. This can be an effective tool; the landlord can generally build at a lower cost than the tenant can. Thus, the value passed along to the tenant is greater than the cost to the landlord and can appear to be a greater concession than its cost.

Dollar Allowances. Landlords seeking larger, more sophisticated tenants will realize that each major tenant will retain its own architects and space planners. These professionals will guide the tenant in designing and constructing the tenant's office facility to be uniquely suited to that particular tenant's intended use and occupancy. Marketing to these larger tenants typically requires a dollar allowance for tenant fit-out construction. Frequently, the landlord or developer will also agree to accept the builder's risk of bringing the project in on time and on budget, by preparing a lease and a construction management agreement side-by-side.

Construction Timing. It is extremely important that the workletter or construction management document attached to the lease contain the dates on which tenant plans and construction drawings are to be furnished to the landlord. The landlord has more control over the construction process than over the tenant design and planning process. Generally, rent does not begin until the space is substantially completed and the tenant can take occupancy. Therefore, the landlord should exercise careful monitoring and control throughout this period. Slippage (any time beyond the dates on which the tenant should have delivered completed plans) should be paid for by the tenant; that is, if the plans are delivered to the landlord two weeks beyond the dates specified, causing the space to be completed for tenant occupancy two weeks beyond schedule, then the tenant pays rent for this two-week slippage period.

Requests for Additional Work. Very few tenant fit-out projects are built according to the plans and specifications. Most tenants will desire additional features and enhancements to the plans, once the project's construction is in progress. Among the reasons are the fact that all businesses change their space requirements frequently, and the extended period between lease negotiation and relocation, which frequently exceeds one year in duration. Workletters and construction management agreements should spell out the process of documenting tenant requests for additional work, how these requests will be budgeted and paid for, and what effect the resulting delays in project completion will have on the rent and rental period.

Project Delays beyond the Tenant's Control. On many new office building construction projects, the base building core and shell will simply not be completed on time. Consequently, the tenant fit-out construction and resulting relocation date may slip beyond target. Developers of new buildings will want to write into their leases a grace period to cover these eventualities, and tenants will want a "drop dead date" for their relocation, beyond which the lease agreement may be cancelable.

Summary

In today's marketplace, the myriad of details associated with an effective lease transaction, including the pricing and promotion of the space, tenant prospecting, lease negotiation, and tenant fit-out construction process, must be carefully planned and executed through a concentrated professional effort. Successful landlords and developers concentrate their talents in the design, development, and implementation of effective leasing and marketing programs that add significant values to their real estate asset, while promoting ongoing superior tenant relationships.

CHAPTER 9

Tenant's Lease Negotiation Checklist

Gary Goldman

The origin of most commercial leases ensures their unfairness. Typically, the commercial tenant finds space in a building that meets the tenant's business needs (e.g., market and location). The tenant and landlord discuss items such as rent per square foot, the availability of space, the term of the lease, and build-out costs. After indicating approval, the tenant is handed the landlord's 20-page lease form, which must be signed to close the deal.

This lease form covers dozens of issues never discussed by the parties. Yet, within these never discussed issues lurk the following:

Unreasonable risks

Hidden costs

Ambiguity running amok

Legal rights and obligations of the parties.

Landlords' commercial lease forms throughout the United States are remarkably similar in their format. Each lease contains approximately 36 standard provisions. The essential differences lie in the treatment afforded those provisions: changing one or two words can be the difference between a fair or unfair provision.

This chapter raises the questions a tenant will find useful and necessary to negotiate a fairer deal, minimize risks, and understand the real cost of the lease and its other terms. The 36 provisions appear in approximately the same order as they do in a typical

Adapted from *The Practical Real Estate Lawyer,* January 1986. Copyright 1986 by The American Law Institute. Reprinted with the permission of *The Practical Real Estate Lawyer.* Subscription rates $22 per year; $5.75 a single issue.

This chapter has been updated and edited by its author since its publication in *The Commercial Real Estate Tenant's Handbook,* edited by Alan D. Sugarman, Robert F. Cushman, and Andrew D. Lipman (New York: John Wiley & Sons, 1987). Used with permission.

lease. The heading of each provision is followed by a series of pertinent questions.

01 Date and Parties

01-1 Is the lease correctly dated for reference purposes?

01-2 Are the parties accurately described with full legal names, correct states of incorporation, and principal business addresses?

01-3 Are the parties and the lease given shorthand references (e.g., "Lease," "Tenant," "Landlord") and are the references consistently applied throughout?

02 Premises

Description

02-1 Are the leased premises given a shorthand reference, such as "Demised Premises," consistently applied throughout?

02-2 Are the Demised Premises fully and accurately described, including the suite number, street address, municipality, state, and zip code?

02-3 Are exhibits referred to and attached showing the legal description and the location of the Demised Premises within the building?

02-4 Is a plan drawing provided as an exhibit to illustrate the Demised Premises?

Square Footage

02-5 Is the square footage of the Demised Premises specifically and correctly stated?

02-6 Is the square footage stated as rentable square feet (includes portion of common areas) or usable square feet (limited to space within four walls of Demised Premises), by referring to various points within the building (such as from the outer walls to the center of some point), or by referring to the Building Owners and Managers Association International (BOMA) standards?

02-7   If the Demised Premises cannot be measured because the building is still under construction, what standard of measurement will be used?

03   Term

03-1   Is the term specified by the number of years from the commencement date to the termination date?

03-2   If the commencement date is not specified because the building is under construction, does the Tenant receive adequate advance written notice when the Demised Premises are to be ready?

03-3   Are the parties obligated to sign a letter confirming the commencement and termination dates—especially when the commencement is estimated?

03-4   What triggers the Tenant's obligation to move in and pay rent: substantial completion (e.g., is substantial completion defined as the time when the Tenant is able to use the Demised Premises for its intended purposes without material interference); issuance of the certificate of occupancy; completion of the premises in accordance with specifications and plans as certified by the architect; or as when only minor details of construction, interior design, or mechanical adjustments remain to be completed?

03-5   How is a dispute decided as to whether the Demised Premises are ready: by negotiation; by mediation; by arbitration; by Landlord's sole, reasonable, judgment; by Landlord's architect; by Tenant's architect; or by an architect chosen by both parties?

04   Delayed Possession

04-1   If possession is delayed through no fault of the Tenant, what remedies does the Tenant have: rent abatement; money damages; cancellation; reimbursement for prepaid moneys, such as the security deposit and the first month's rent; or all of these remedies?

04-2   Are the commencement and termination dates extended in a time period equal to any delay?

04-3   If the Tenant has the right to cancellation after a "drop dead date," who is obligated to pay for the Tenant's project costs and expenses to date and who is obligated to pay the real estate broker's commissions and other lease documentation costs and expenses?

04-4   Must the Landlord provide a Certificate of Occupancy for the building prior to the Tenant's occupancy date?

05   Rent

05-1   Is the agreed-upon rental amount specifically stated for each year of the lease term?

05-2   If the rent is stated in more than one way—for example, monthly, annually, per square foot, for a full term—are the different amounts consistent?

05-3   Is the monthly rent prorated for the first and last months if occupancy is less than a full month?

05-4   Is there a reasonable grace period, such as 10 days, before a penalty is charged for late rent?

06   Additional Rent

Method

06-1   Does the rent increase periodically by the increased operating expenses (pro-rata share), by the consumer price index (CPI), or by a fixed percentage?

06-2   Is the increase by more than one method, or by the greater or lesser of the three methods?

06-3   Does the increase start immediately, on the first day of the calendar year following the lease commencement year, on the first anniversary of the commencement date, or at some later point in the lease term?

06-4   Is there a maximum cap on the increase year to year and/or over the term of the lease?

Operating Expenses

06-5   Does the Tenant pay a pro-rata share of the increase in operating expenses over a base figure or a pro-rata share of the total operating expenses for the operating year (net lease)?

06-6   Is the base a calendar year or an expense stop ($x per year or $x per square foot)?

06-7   If the base is a calendar year, is the base year specified?

06-8   What was last year's base-year amount?

06-9   Are the base-year expenses based on full tenant occupancy or are they properly adjusted (e.g., are base-year real estate taxes low because they are based on an unfinished building or a tax abatement situation)?

06-10   Was the expense stop computed by actual dollar costs of a particular year or based on an estimate of operating costs (e.g., in a new building)?

06-11   If the expense stop is an estimate, how was the estimate made and is it reasonable (e.g., is it based on the costs of operating a similar office building in the area)?

06-12   Is the Tenant's pro-rata share of the increase specified as a fraction and as a percentage, for example:

$$\frac{\text{Tenant's square footage}}{\text{Total square footage}} = \frac{1,000}{100,000} = 1\%$$

06-13   Is the computation of the increase based on the Tenant's usable or rentable square footage?

06-14   Is the total square footage the total usable, rentable, or leasable area in the building and how are those terms defined?

06-15   Must all expenses be reasonable and directly related to the building's operation?

06-16   Are the following expenses excluded: any payments (such as salaries or fees) to the Landlord's executive personnel; costs for items that, by standard accounting practice, should be capitalized (such as heating, ventilating, and air conditioning (HVAC) replacement), unless those costs reduce operating expenses and are amortized over the reasonable life of the capital item in accordance with generally accepted accounting principles and the yearly amortization does not exceed the actual cost reduction for the relevant year; depreciation or interest (unless it is related to allowable capital item); taxes on the Landlord's business (such as income, excess profits, franchise, capital stock, estate, inheritance); leasing commissions; legal fees; costs to correct original construction defects; expenses paid directly by a tenant for any reason (such as excessive utility use); costs for improving any tenant's space; greater than a 5 percent increase in management fees, or employees' salaries or benefits, or both; any repair or other work necessitated by condemnation, fire, or other casualty; costs exceeding those obtainable through competitive bidding; services, benefits, or both provided to some tenants but not to you, the Tenant; and any costs, fines, and the like due to the Landlord's violation of any governmental rule or authority?

06-17   Must the Landlord keep books and records in accordance with sound accounting practice or generally accepted accounting principles?

06-18   Must the Landlord provide a reasonably detailed list of expenses to support the increase prepared by a certified public accountant?

06-19   Does the Tenant have the right to audit the Landlord's books and records and is the Tenant given adequate time to decide to ask for and perform the audit?

06-20   If the audit reveals a discrepancy of a certain percentage, e.g., 2 percent or more, must the Landlord pay for the audit?

06-21   How are disputes over increased operating expenses settled: by negotiation, by mediation, by arbitration, by lawsuit, by the Landlord's list which is conclusive and binding unless tenant objects in (x) amount of days, or by the Landlord's CPA's certification, which is conclusive?

06-22   Is the increase prorated for the first and last years of the term if occupancy in those years is less than 12 months?

06-23   Does the Tenant receive a credit if the operating expenses are reduced or if the paid estimated monthly amounts exceed the actual incurred expenses?

CPI Increase or Fixed Percentage

06-24   Is the CPI index defined?

06-25   Is an alternative index selected, in case the original index is no longer published?

06-26   What is the base index period?

06-27   Is the increase 100 percent of the CPI increase over the base or some lesser percentage, such as 50 percent?

06-28   Is the fixed percentage reasonable, based on inflation, market rates, and the like?

07   Security Deposit

07-1   Under what circumstances and when is the security deposit returned, and is the security deposit held in a segregated escrow account?

07-2   Is interest earned on the security deposit and does the Tenant receive this interest upon lease termination?

08   Use

08-1   Can the Tenant use the Demised Premises for any lawful purpose?

08-2　If not, do the restrictions on use limit in any way the type of business the Tenant intends to conduct at the Demised Premises?

08-3　Can the use be changed (with the Landlord's consent)?

08-4　Are the Tenant's specific uses described (e.g., installation of a photostat machine requiring a ducted exhaust)?

08-5　Does the Landlord represent that the Premises is suitable for the Tenant's use and occupancy?

08-6　Does the Landlord represent that the building is accessible to the handicapped?

08-7　Does the Landlord represent that the building is asbestos- and PCB-free?

08-8　Does the lease limit the Landlord from leasing to third parties who may damage the Tenant's business or reputation?

09　Compliance with Laws

09-1　If the Tenant must comply with various laws, does the Landlord warrant and guarantee that the Demised Premises are in compliance with those laws at the commencement date?

09-2　Is the Tenant's obligation limited to those laws that pertain to the manner in which the Tenant will use the Demised Premises?

09-3　Is the Tenant obligated to make structural repairs?

09-4　Is there a dollar limit on the Tenant's obligation?

10　Services and Utilities

10-1　Which party provides and pays for such services as: HVAC, electric lighting, water, security, fire-safety equipment, janitorial services, and snow removal?

10-2　If the Landlord pays for and provides the aforementioned services, are the services provided during normal business hours only, during specified hours (such as from 6:00 A.M. to 7:00 P.M.), or during weekends and holidays? Are any excluded holidays specifically listed?

10-3　Does the Landlord mark up or otherwise profit on the purchase and resale of those costs and expenses, or does the Landlord provide a submeter or otherwise document and audit the Tenant's usage and charge the Tenant the pro-rata share of the actual costs of those services?

10-4　What standard governs the Landlord's provision of HVAC: the standard for first-class office buildings in the area; the Landlord's sole discretion, as the weather warrants; in sufficient (or reasonable) amounts and at temperatures sufficient for the Tenant's comfortable use and occupancy or specific engineering criteria, such as 72° F and 60 percent relative humidity with 20 percent fresh air changes per hour?

10-5　How does the Tenant request, receive, and pay for after-hours HVAC service?

10-6　What standard governs the Landlord's provision of janitorial services: five days a week, during or after work hours, the standard for first-class office buildings in the area, or a degree deemed sufficient by the Landlord?

10-7　Are particular janitorial services specified, such as emptying wastebaskets, vacuuming, and washing windows?

10-8　What remedies does the Tenant have if the services are interrupted? Can these remedies include money damages, rent abatement, and lease cancellation?

10-9　Is the Tenant automatically entitled to its remedies or is it entitled to them only if one or more of the following occurs: the interruption is caused by the Landlord's negligence or intentional act, the causes were not beyond the Landlord's reasonable control, or the Landlord failed to use its best efforts (or reasonable efforts, due diligence, reasonable diligence, diligence) to restore the services promptly (or with reasonable dispatch)?

11　Repairs and Maintenance

11-1　Is the Tenant's liability for repair, maintenance, or both, any greater than keeping the Demised Premises—but not every part—in good order and condition, and returning the Demised Premises at lease termination in the same condition as received at the commencement, except for ordinary wear and tear, damage by the elements, fire, and other unavoidable casualty?

11-2　If the Tenant's obligation is greater than that stated in question 11-1, does the obligation include responsibility for the structural portions of the building, roof, exterior walls, and systems (HVAC, electrical, mechanical, plumbing, and water), even if the Tenant does not have access to them?

11-3 If the Tenant's obligation includes part or all of the items listed in question 11-2, has the Landlord assigned any warranties to the Tenant, and is that assignment legally effective?

11-4 If the Landlord has an obligation to repair, is the obligation to repair with reasonable promptness or in a reasonable time after receiving written notice?

12 Alterations

12-1 May alterations be made with the Landlord's consent or without consent if the alterations cost less than $x? If the Landlord's consent is required, is the Landlord's decision conclusive?

12-2 In addition to alterations, does the provision also cover changes, improvements, additions, installations, and decorations?

12-3 At the Lease's termination, does the Landlord have the option of keeping and owning the alterations and the like made by the Tenant or of having the Tenant remove the alterations and repair the damage?

12-4 Does the Tenant have the right to remove (or, at its option, abandon) trade fixtures, all alterations, or alterations owned or paid for by the Tenant, such as improvements made at the commencement of the lease and paid for by the Landlord and Tenant?

13 Insurance

13-1 Do the Tenant's policy coverage and limits meet the minimums required by the Lease?

13-2 May the Tenant use a blanket or umbrella insurance policy that covers, in addition to the Demised Premises, other premises owned or leased by the Tenant?

13-3 If the Landlord is named as an additional insured, is the Landlord's interest under the insurance policy specifically limited to the Landlord's interests under the Lease?

13-4 May the Tenant supply a certificate of insurance rather than an original or copy of the insurance policy?

14 Waiver of Subrogation

14-1 Is the waiver mutual, that is, is the waiver by the Landlord and Tenant?

14-2 Does the Tenant's insurance policy permit the waiver?

15 Indemnity and Hold Harmless Provision

15-1 If the Tenant must indemnify and hold the Landlord harmless from claims, damages, or injuries arising out of the Tenant's occupancy of the Demised Premises, what is the degree of the Tenant's responsibility? Is the Tenant responsible for any and all claims; for any and all claims except those arising from the Landlord's intentional (willful acts, willful misconduct, wanton misconduct, and unlawful acts) or negligent (any negligence—primary, sole, gross) acts or omissions; to the extent of the Tenant's fault; or except for consequential, special, and indirect damages?

16 Landlord's Liability

16-1 Under what circumstances is the Landlord not liable to the Tenant? (See the related issues in question 15-1.)

17 Casualty

17-1 If the Demised Premises are damaged by casualty, is the Landlord's obligation to repair and restore them as soon as reasonably possible or to use due diligence?

17-2 Does the Tenant's rent obligation abate from the date the Demised Premises or access thereto are damaged or impaired and remain abated until the damage is repaired?

17-3 Is the rent abated in proportion to the nature and extent of damages, impairment of the use (diminution of value) that the Tenant can reasonably make of the Demised Premises, or in proportion to the amount of unusable square feet?

17-4 May the Tenant cancel the Lease (see question 18-4) if the Landlord fails to repair and restore the Demised Premises within a reasonable time, such as 90 days?

18 Condemnation

18-1 Is this provision limited to a taking of part or all of the Demised Premises and access thereto, or does it also include a taking of part or all of the building, common areas, and parking lot?

18-2   Is rent abated from the date of the taking? (See question 17-3 for the abatement basis.)

18-3   May the Tenant terminate the Lease if, as is reasonably determined by the Tenant: all (or any part) of the Demised Premises is taken or access is impaired; a substantial part or a specified percentage, such as 25 percent, of the Demised Premises is taken; use of the Demised Premises is materially impaired or materially interfered with; or the Demised Premises are no longer suited for their intended use?

18-4   If the Lease is terminated, is the Tenant reimbursed for prepaid rent and other prepaid expenses?

18-5   Is the Tenant entitled to a condemnation award for the Tenant's trade fixtures, other property, moving expenses, business dislocation damages, and the unamortized cost of leasehold improvements?

19   Assignment and Sublease

19-1   Is the Tenant prohibited from assigning or subleasing the Lease without the prior written consent of the Landlord?

19-2   What standard governs the Landlord's decision to consent: the Landlord's sole discretion; consent shall not be unreasonably withheld or unduly delayed; or objective reasonable criteria, such as the subtenant's financial strength (e.g., a net worth greater than $100,000) and the nature of its business (in keeping with the building's commercially reasonable standards)?

19-3   Must the Tenant obtain consent for an assignment to an affiliated company, and is "affiliated" defined?

19-4   Must the Tenant obtain consent for an assignment under a merger or acquisition?

20   Default

20-1   Is vacating and abandoning the Premises a default even if the Tenant continues paying the rent?

20-2   Is the Tenant's failure to pay the rent a default only after the rent is more than 10 days overdue and the Tenant receives written notice of the failure to pay?

20-3   Is the Tenant's failure to comply with the other material terms in the Lease a default even if the Tenant cures the material breach within 30 days of

receiving written notice of the breach, or if, because of the nature of the breach, more than 30 days are needed to cure and the Tenant began curing within 30 days and is diligently pursuing the cure to completion?

20-4   Are the following events—bankruptcy, receivership, seizure of assets, assignment for the benefit of creditors—automatic defaults or defaults only if those events are not vacated, released, dismissed, or otherwise corrected within a reasonable time, such as 60 days, after those events occur?

21   Remedies

21-1   Before exercising its remedies, must the Landlord give the Tenant notice or make a demand for cure?

21-2   Is the Landlord entitled to unreasonable remedies, such as "confession of judgment," "acceleration of rent," or "cumulation of damages that exceeds total rent payable absent a default"?

21-3   Must the Landlord mitigate damages, such as by making reasonable efforts to relet?

22   Brokers' Fees

22-1   Has the Tenant dealt with any broker other than the broker specifically mentioned in the Lease, whose fee is payable by the Landlord, and has the Landlord indemnified the Tenant from any brokers' claims?

23   Estoppel Certificate

23-1   Does the Tenant, considering internal corporate organization, have sufficient time to respond to an estoppel certificate request, for example, within 10 days?

23-2   Is the Landlord authorized to sign the estoppel certificate for the Tenant only if the Tenant fails to sign the certificate within a reasonable time, such as 30 days?

23-3   Is the Tenant obligated to certify to "true, accurate, and ascertainable facts" only?

24   Subordination

24-1   Can the Tenant's possession be disturbed by a mortgage foreclosure even if the Tenant is not in default, and is the Landlord to procure a nondisturbance clause from current and future mortgagees?

25 Quiet Possession

25-1 Does the Landlord warrant the Tenant's "quiet possession" and the Landlord's right to execute the Lease? (See also question 24-1.)

25-2 Does the Landlord warrant or represent that the Premises are suitable for the Tenant's intended use and occupancy?

26 Rules and Regulations

26-1 Do any current rules or regulations promulgated by the Landlord, or the Landlord's right to promulgate future rules and regulations, interfere with the Tenant's intended business use, such as the use of storage outside the building?

26-2 Do any current rules prevent the Tenant from securing the services of the Tenant's choice of suppliers or contractors (e.g., to supply towels or bottled water)?

27 Renewal/Holdover/Options

27-1 Is the Lease automatically renewed unless either party gives notice of termination?

27-2 Does the Tenant have one or more options to extend the term for one or more years on the same terms and conditions, with the exception of rent, as those found in the original Lease?

27-3 Is the rent during the option term renegotiated or increased by a fixed percentage, the CPI amount, a fixed dollar amount, or the current market rate?

27-4 If the Tenant holds over with the Landlord's consent, is the rent increased by an unreasonable amount?

28 Improvements

28-1 Are all of the proposed improvements itemized on the blueprints and specifications and attached as exhibits?

28-2 If the Tenant will pay, after receiving invoices, part of the improvement costs, what portion will the Tenant pay (e.g., the excess over a fixed

dollar amount) and how will the Tenant pay (e.g., 50 percent at commencement and 50 percent on completion; over the first 12 months of the lease; amortized over the lease term)?

28-3 If the Tenant pays part of the improvement costs, does the Tenant have the right to remove a portion of the improvements at the end of the Lease?

28-4 If the Landlord selects the contractor and the Tenant pays part of the costs, what control does the Tenant have over the cost (e.g., is competitive bidding required)?

28-5 Who pays for the Tenant's architectural and space planning fees?

28-6 Who pays for the Tenant's moving and relocation costs?

28-7 What are the terms and conditions of the Tenant's agreement with the Landlord regarding build-out costs and expenses, including requests for additional work during construction?

29 Entire Agreement

29-1 Is everything the Tenant bargained for, such as free rent concessions and parking, referenced in the Lease?

30 Attorneys' Fees

30-1 Is each party entitled to have its attorneys' fees paid if it is the prevailing party in any litigation, or in a dispute settled short of litigation, to enforce the Lease?

30-2 Is the prevailing party also entitled to other reasonable expenses and court costs?

31 Force Majeure

31-1 Is the general catchall phrase (e.g., "any other cause beyond the Landlord's control") or any specifically included item (e.g., the inability to obtain fuel) a risk that the Landlord ought to bear?

32 Mechanic's Liens

32-1 Does the Tenant have a reasonable time to discharge the lien before the Landlord is able to pay the lien and bill the Tenant?

33 Right to Enter

33-1 Exclusive of emergencies, must the Landlord give the Tenant reasonable advance notice of entry?

33-2 Exclusive of emergencies, can the Landlord enter the Demised Premises at any time, any reasonable time, or only during—or after—business hours?

33-3 May the Landlord enter to inspect, make repairs, construct improvements, or show the Demised Premises to prospective tenants (such as in the last three months of the lease term only)?

33-4 During the Landlord's entry, is the Tenant entitled to damages, or rent abatement, for injury caused by the Landlord's negligence or unreasonable interference with the conduct of the Tenant's business?

34 Right to Cancel

34-1 May the Tenant cancel the Lease at any time, or after x months, with or without a penalty charge?

34-2 Is the Tenant entitled to reimbursement of part of the penalty charge if the Landlord rents the Demised Premises within a fixed time period?

35 Right to First Refusal

35-1 Is the space sufficiently identified?

35-2 Is the Tenant given written notice of the proposed terms and conditions and a reasonable time, such as 30 days, to respond to the offer?

36 Tenant's Personal Guarantee (Lien or Security Interest)

36-1 Does the Tenant's financial strength and size negate the Landlord's need for this provision?

Conclusion

Most tenants are simply handed the landlord's lease form, a document that often contains unreasonable risks, hidden costs, and enormous ambiguity. By this time, wise tenants will have consulted a lawyer who has questioned the tenant about the nature of the deal and the tenant's plans for the premises.

If the tenant's lawyer does not fold, spindle, and interlineate the landlord's lease form, then the form is unusually fair, or the landlord is unreasonable and will not negotiate, or the lease form lacks sufficient margins to make changes, or the lease was revised on a word processor—or, worst of all, the tenant's lawyer did not use this checklist.

CHAPTER 10

The Ten Major Mistakes Most Often Made by Tenants in the Negotiation of Office Leases

Robert F. Cushman and Joel J. Goldberg

Introduction

The leasing of office space may well encompass the most important decisions made by a business manager. The location of the office building and the design of the leased space can affect employee attitudes, efficiency, and productivity. Most important, however, the office lease represents a significant financial obligation and liability for most businesses.

Some of the financial terms and responsibilities, such as the obligation to pay base or minimum rent, are commonly stated in a lease as an initially fixed and determinable sum. Tenants must not, however, overlook provisions that impose other financial obligations or affect the productive and efficient use of the leased space. For example, tenants are typically responsible for variable additional rental payments over and above the base or minimum rental payment. These additional rental payments typically compensate the landlord, in whole or in part, for the cost of real estate taxes, operating expenses, and insurance. Tenants may also be responsible for performing substantial repair and maintenance obligations.

The purpose of this chapter is to draw attention to mistakes made by prospective office building tenants who overlook or do not adequately address certain important issues while negotiating a lease. These mistakes can increase substantially a tenant's financial obligations and liabilities under a lease and affect the ability to use the leased premises to promote business objectives.[1]

This chapter has been updated and edited by its authors since its original publication in *The Commercial Real Estate Tenant's Handbook,* edited by Alan D. Sugarman, Robert F. Cushman, and Andrew D. Lipman (New York: John Wiley & Sons, 1987). Used with permission.

[1] The issues discussed in this article are not presented in any order of importance. Moreover, such issues are not the only aspects of a commercial office lease that must be addressed by a tenant.

The Mortgage Lender's Interest

In addition to the landlord and tenant, the landlord's mortgage lender has a considerable interest in the provisions of a tenant's lease. In some cases, the mortgage lender examines and negotiates the form of lease to be used by the landlord when the lender initially underwrites the loan prior to construction of the office building.

Prior to final confirmation by the landlord and tenant, lenders often examine leases as credit instruments, to determine whether the revenues payable to the landlord pursuant to the leases will enable the landlord to meet its debt service obligations, establish reserves, and meet other operating requirements. Moreover, lenders typically require landlords to assign all tenant leases to the lender as collateral security for such loans. Because a lender that takes possession of an office building in connection with a default under a mortgage loan would be forced to operate and manage the building in accordance with the terms of existing leases, lenders typically negotiate with landlords to minimize the lender's prospective obligations and responsibilities in the event that the lender assumes the role of a landlord under tenant leases.

Types of Leases

Under a net lease, a tenant is responsible, in addition to its obligation to pay base or minimum rent, for all (or its proportionate share, in the case of a multitenant building) costs and expenses attributable to real estate

Recognition and resolution of these issues, however, will reduce the financial liabilities of a commerical office tenant and promote the efficient and productive conduct of a tenant's business in the leasaed space.

taxes, insurance, maintenance, repair costs, and other operating expenses of the office building. Under a net lease, the landlord has no financial obligations for such costs and expenses, and rental payments received by the landlord are "net" of any expenses (other than income taxes and brokerage fees and similar charges unrelated to the maintenance and operation of the office building) payable by the landlord. Ground leases[2] and leases of entire freestanding commercial or industrial buildings are often net leases.

In some areas of the country, a "net" lease refers to a lease under which the tenant is responsible for the payment of real estate taxes, a "net-net" lease refers to a lease where the tenant is responsible for the payment of real estate taxes and insurance costs, and a "net-net-net" lease refers to a lease pursuant to which the tenant is responsible for all financial obligations associated with the leased premises.[3] Tenants should avoid the use of any of these terms in leases without clarifying and defining the exact meaning thereof. For purposes of this chapter, the term "net lease" will be used to mean a lease (as described in the preceding paragraph) under which the landlord has no financial obligations.

Under a gross lease, the tenant's sole financial responsibility is the payment of base or minimum rent and the landlord is responsible for payment of all real estate taxes, insurance payments, maintenance, repair costs, and operating expenses. Although the landlord remains responsible for the payment of these items, the base or minimum rent payable by the tenant may include the landlord's projected cost of such items. Gross leases are rare in commercial office lease transactions.

Because of the many possible allocations of financial liabilities, responsibilities, and risks between landlords and tenants, there can be a vast number of variations between a pure gross lease and a pure net lease. For example, each tenant in a multitenant office building may be responsible solely for its proportionate share of any annual increase of real estate taxes and operating expenses above a certain base figure, rather than its proportionate share of the total cost of these items to the landlord. In addition, in connection with repair obligations, tenants may only be responsible for nonstructural repairs or may be responsible for structural repairs only in the event of damage caused by the tenant's negligence.

The Landlord's Printed Form Is Not Sacrosanct

The landlord's lease is usually a preprinted form; it may have been approved by the landlord's lender. Landlords use preprinted lease forms to maintain uniformity of obligations from tenant to tenant, to simplify administration and management of the office building, and to avoid the time and expense of negotiating the form of lease proposed by each new tenant.

Many business and legal matters that are negotiated between the landlord and tenant do not require the lender's approval or disrupt the management of the building. Moreover, in certain instances, landlords may be willing to seek lender approval of certain changes. Tenants, therefore, should not be intimidated by the landlord's preprinted lease form and should aggressively seek to revise the landlord's form, especially in accordance with the suggestions of this chapter. Needless to say, tenants can be most successful in negotiating changes in a soft rental market.

The following sections list the 10 major mistakes made by tenants in the negotiation of office leases.

The Failure to Require the Landlord to Deliver the Premises Ready for Occupancy by a Specific Date

A tenant that is relocating its offices may bear considerable costs, if its new offices are not ready for occupancy on the specific date agreed to. For example, if a tenant's old lease expires and the new premises are not ready for occupancy, the tenant may have to vacate its old premises and discontinue or drastically reduce its business operations. A tenant could be forced to pay excessive rent to remain in its old premises or to relocate its offices on an expensive, short-term, interim basis until the new premises are ready for occupancy.

---

[2] A ground lease frequently takes the form of a transaction in which the landlord and tenant enter into a long-term lease of vacant real estate, real estate with obsolete improvements that will be demolished, or real estate with improvements requiring substantial rehabilitation or remodeling. The ground lease tenant may be obligated to construct a building or other improvements such as a hotel or commercial building according to specific terms contained in the lease.

[3] See C. Smith & H. Lubell, *Leases: Net And Not So Net,* 8 Real Estate Rev. 14 (Winter 1979), for a discussion of the concept of a net lease and the various types of leases that are mistakenly referred to as "net" leases.

There are two general ways in which the premises may not be "ready for occupancy." First, the landlord may fail to complete (or "substantially" complete, depending on the terms of the lease) the construction of or improvements to the premises. Second, a prior tenant of existing office space may fail or refuse to vacate the premises by the expiration date of the prior tenant's lease.

New Construction

Office leases requiring new construction or substantial improvements commonly provide that the term of the lease shall commence on a certain date, provided that the premises are "ready for occupancy." If the premises are not ready for occupancy on such date, the commencement of the lease terms is often delayed and rent will be abated until the landlord notifies the tenant that the premises are ready for occupancy. The term "ready for occupancy" is commonly defined as either the completion or substantial completion of the work to be performed by the landlord. The term "substantial completion" may be defined as the completion of the landlord's work such that only minor details of construction and mechanical adjustment remain to be done and all utility services are available to the tenant; the date of issuance of a certificate of occupancy by local public authorities, or of a certificate of readiness by the landlord's architect, tenant's architect, or a third-party architect; or as the date on which the tenant can commence its business operations without material interference by the landlord.

To protect the tenant, the lease should provide that the tenant may terminate the lease if the leased premises are not ready for occupancy by that specific date. Landlords who object to such provisions may compromise and include a termination provision as long as the specific date can be extended for any period of delay caused by strikes, shortages of materials and labor, changes requested by the tenant in the work to be performed by the landlord, and similar matters beyond the reasonable control of the landlord.

To further protect the tenant from counterclaims by the landlord that the tenant's request for additional work caused the landlord to be late in delivering the tenant's space, any tenant requests for additional work should include a request that the landlord state the days of delay (if any) attributable to the request for additional work.

The use of the term "change order" in and of itself connotes a change. For this reason, tenants are well advised to use the term "request for additional work," which more clearly describes the transaction.

Existing Premises

In many states, unless a lease provides to the contrary, the landlord has no duty to put a tenant in actual possession of the leased premises at the commencement of the lease term. In these states, because the tenant has only the right to possession of the leased premises at the commencement of the lease term, the tenant must, at its own expense, evict a prior tenant that has violated its lease and not vacated, in order to obtain actual possession of the premises. Depending on the terms of the lease, the tenant might also be required to pay rent to the landlord while the prior tenant remains in possession.

Most leases of existing space provide that the commencement of the term of the lease will be delayed, and that the landlord will not be liable in damages to the tenant, in the event that a prior tenant fails to vacate the premises. If the prior tenant is holding over beyond the termination date of its lease because of a legal dispute with the landlord, the tenant might remain in the premises, rightly or wrongly, for a considerable period of time. Therefore, tenants should insist on the right to terminate the lease if the holdover tenant is not removed by the landlord by the date that the lease would otherwise commence. In the event that a tenant elects not to terminate the lease, the landlord should be required to bear all costs of removing the prior tenant, and all rent should be abated until the new tenant has actual possession of the leased premises.

Tenants who are moving into older buildings that are in the process of being renovated for their occupancy will want the lease to include clauses that specify the elevator service, security and safety features, and other issues such as working hours for the tradespeople, use of jack hammers, and the like, during the renovation process. In addition, the lease should include a schedule and date of substantial completion of the base building renovations and, realizing that such request will be met with great resistance by landlords, a final penalty (such as rent abatement or increased tenant improvement allowance) due to the tenant if the schedule slips. A representation as to asbestos abatement and accessibility to the handicapped is also advised.

Damages

Typically, office leases contain exculpatory clauses whereby the landlord is not liable to the tenant for damages as a result of its failure to deliver possession of the leased premises by reason of a prior tenant or other causes beyond the landlord's control. Tenants should seek to require that landlords be liable for losses, costs, and damages suffered or incurred by the tenant on account of the landlord's failure to complete its work on a timely basis or to deliver actual possession of the premises to the tenant. In addition to the other types of damages discussed, damages that could be suffered by a tenant include the difference between the below-market rent under the lease and the fair market rental value of the premises; penalties or premium rents due to the tenant's current landlord; moving costs; expenditures for office equipment; double handling of new office equipment en route to the new office facility; costs associated with double billings for telephone, computer, and printing equipment and services during the delayed transition period; and reduced profits. The liability of a landlord to a tenant for money damages in such circumstances, however, is likely to be a matter of considerable negotiation.

If the tenant's use of space is delayed through no fault of the tenant—for instance, because of a roof leak, a lack of elevator service, or some other delay caused by the landlord or the landlord's contractors—it is likely that the tenant's architects and space planners and their consultants will be called upon to provide additional services over a longer period of time and, accordingly, the tenant may be obligated to pay for these additional professional services. Tenants are well advised to include these consequential costs and expenses as a potential reimbursable claim against the landlord, in the event that the occupancy is delayed through no fault of the tenant.

The Assumption of Excessive and Costly Maintenance and Repair Obligations

Under a net lease of an entire office building, the tenant is usually responsible at its sole cost and expense to perform all maintenance obligations and to make all structural repairs. In a multitenant office building, net leases are not common, and maintenance and repair obligations are allocated between the landlord and tenants. Although landlords of multitenant office buildings are responsible for performing certain maintenance and repair obligations, they may attempt to pass through to tenants the costs of performing many of these activities. The lease must clearly allocate and define these particular maintenance and repair obligations of the landlord and tenant, not only because of the possible liabilities of a tenant to the landlord, or to other tenants and persons (such as office building visitors) for failing to perform these obligations, but in order that the tenant can determine and evaluate the likely expense of performing such obligations.

In General

Unless a lease contains an express covenant by the landlord to make repairs or to maintain the leased premises, the landlord generally has no obligation whatsoever to perform any repair or maintenance activities. Office leases commonly require the tenant to maintain the leased premises in good condition, subject to certain exceptions such as reasonable wear and tear and damage by fire and other casualties not occurring through the negligence of the tenant or its agents.

At a minimum, tenants in multitenant office buildings should require the landlord to repair and maintain structural aspects of the leased premises such as the foundation, outer walls, and roof. Landlords should be responsible for such items because of the costliness of performing these obligations and the likelihood that structural repairs are also likely to affect other leased premises in the building. In the event that the tenant agrees to be responsible for certain structural repairs, the lease must provide that the tenant will not be responsible to perform any repairs or alterations, or perhaps those costing in excess of a specific dollar amount, ordered by public authorities. Similarly, the landlord should agree to be responsible for the maintenance and repair of common areas such as hall corridors and stairways, and for plumbing, heating, and electrical systems. In no event, however, should tenants be obligated to perform any repairs in connection with casualty or loss covered by the landlord's insurance coverage.

Definitions

If the lease allocates repair and maintenance obligations between landlord and tenant, each of the major terms involving maintenance and repair obligations must be clearly and specifically defined. For example, if the term "structural" is not defined, disputes are likely to develop as to whether the landlord or the tenant is responsible for repairs to flooring; plumbing; sprinkler systems; electrical, heating, and other common facilities that also run through other tenants' space; and the common areas of the office building. If applicable, the lease should specify whether the tenant's repair obligations extend to and include exterior walls and common walls that may abut several tenants' premises. Moreover, tenants in newly constructed buildings should not be responsible for repairs necessitated by faulty work, defective materials of others when the building was constructed, or deterioration due to normal wear and tear.

Frequently, a new building will leak or otherwise cause damage to the tenant's interior fit-out work in progress prior to or just after substantial completion. Just as frequently, one tenant's fit-out work in progress, performed by such tenant's contractors approved by the landlord or by the landlord's renovation contractors, will cause damage to a neighboring tenant's fit-out work in progress. There are also many cases where one tenant will need access into the ceiling of the tenant below, to install certain pipes or wires, or where the going and coming of the building tradespeople will cause damage or theft to the tenant's property. All of these instances should be addressed in the lease, to properly and specifically allocate risk of loss or damage between the landlord and tenant.

Damage Caused by Casualty

The lease must specifically address rights and responsibilities in the event of a fire or other casualty. If the office lease does not adequately address these issues, the tenant might remain liable for rent or be responsible for significant structural repairs, even in the event of a catastrophic loss.

In the typical multitenant building lease, the landlord is responsible for repairing casualty damage to the building, and may elect either to perform such repairs or to terminate the tenant's lease if the repairs cannot be completed within a certain period. Rent typically abates during the period when the landlord performs repairs and the tenant is denied possession. Under a net lease, a tenant will be responsible for rebuilding, and rent will not abate during the period when the tenant cannot use the leased premises.

Some leases provide that the tenant will be responsible to the landlord for the cost of repairs and restorations, and/or that the tenant's rental obligation will not be abated, if the casualty causing such damage has occurred due to the negligence of the tenant, its agents, contractors, employees, guests, or invitees. Because the risk of casualty loss is insured against by the landlord and/or tenant (naming the landlord as a named insured and/or loss payee), the landlord's express covenant to make repairs at its sole cost should not be affected by the negligent acts of the tenant, its agents, or such other parties. If the landlord's obligation to either repair casualty damage or terminate a tenant's lease is negated by the tenant's negligence, the tenant may be responsible to pay rent during the balance of the lease term while it cannot occupy the leased premises and/or be responsible to repair the office building.

Yield-Up/Surrender of Leased Premises

Under most net or "semi-net" office leases, the tenant is required to surrender the leased premises to the landlord, at the expiration or sooner termination of the lease, in the same condition as they were at the beginning of the lease, except for ordinary or reasonable wear and tear and deterioration. Tenants, especially those occupying older buildings, may desire to take photographs and otherwise document the condition of the leased premises at the beginning of the lease term. Assuming that other provisions of a lease do not expressly impose broader repair obligations on the tenant, a tenant is generally not liable under this clause to repair damage caused by accidental fire or other casualty not caused by the negligence of, or waste permitted by, the tenant. Covenants to repair contained in other portions of the lease may, however, require the tenant to perform repair obligations regardless of fault or accidental origin.

In some jurisdictions, the covenant to surrender will be read together with covenants concerning maintenance and repair obligations and casualty loss. Expressed and specific limitations on the repair and maintenance obligations of the tenant will also limit the tenant's obligations under the surrender clause. For example, if the landlord is responsible for all repairs caused by any casualty loss, but the surrender clause does not except damage caused by any casualty loss, the surrender clause would not be read to require the tenant to repair any casualty loss. In other jurisdictions, covenants to repair and maintain the leased premises and casualty loss provisions will be treated as separate from the covenants contained in the surrender clause, raising the possibility that the tenant may have liability to perform certain repair obligations, on termination or expiration of the lease, in excess of the obligations set forth in the repair and maintenance clauses of the lease.[4]

Regardless of the jurisdiction, however, the surrender clause should be consistent with lease provisions concerning casualty loss and repair and maintenance obligations and should, if consistent with such provisions, be modified also to except damage caused by fire and other casualty and by condemnation. For reasons previously discussed, tenants in multitenant buildings should not agree to any qualifications to the surrender clause which only except damage caused by casualties, provided that such casualties do not occur through the tenant's negligence.

The Failure to Require Landlord to Give Tenant Notice of, and Right to Cure, Alleged Defaults

If a tenant defaults in the performance of its obligations under a lease, the landlord is entitled to exercise various remedies. These remedies may include the termination of the lease, the seizure and sale of property on the leased premises, or the payment on the date of demand of all rent due to be paid over the remaining balance of the lease term.

Given the harshness of landlords' remedies in the event of tenant defaults, tenants must require the landlord to notify the tenant in writing of all alleged defaults under the lease and to give the tenant an opportunity to cure the alleged default before the landlord can exercise its remedies.

As to this notice requirement, the lease should specify the date upon which the cure period will commence. Landlords will prefer that the cure period commence on the date the notice is personally delivered to the tenant or the date that the notice is sent by mail to the tenant. Tenants should either insist that the cure period commence on the date that the notice is actually received, personally or by mail, by the tenant. Or, if the cure period commences on the date the notice is sent, tenants should require that the cure period be long enough to provide the tenant sufficient time to cure the default after receipt of the notice and that the notice be delivered to the tenant's address in a timely manner.

Leases should provide different cure periods for monetary, as opposed to nonmonetary, defaults. Tenants should have at least 10 to 15 days after notice is

received to cure a monetary default. A reasonable cure period for a nonmonetary default is 30 days. If, however, the default is of such a character that it cannot reasonably be cured within the 30-day period, the cure period should be extended for as long a period as is reasonably necessary to cure the default, provided that the tenant has undertaken within the 30-day period such action as can reasonably be taken toward curing the default and prosecutes such curative action to completion.

To prevent tenants from abusing notice and right to cure provisions, landlords often insist that the landlord not be required to provide notice of an alleged default to a tenant after a certain number of defaults within any lease year. If such provision becomes operative during the lease term, the tenant would not be entitled to cure the default and the landlord could immediately elect to exercise its remedies under the lease.

The Failure to Obtain a Broad Use Clause

All leases contain a clause that sets forth the uses that a tenant may make of the leased premises. The use of the premises for any purpose other than a permitted purpose under this clause would constitute a default under the lease.

Landlords and lenders may have several reasons to desire to limit the use of the premises in an office building. They may wish to maintain compatible uses among all tenants; to limit the volume of traffic associated with particular uses, in order to reduce maintenance and operating costs and to minimize disruption of the business activities of other tenants; and to permit only "high-quality" tenants to occupy the building.

Although tenants may share many of these interests, an office building tenant must carefully examine the use clause in terms of its immediate and future business plans. A requirement that the tenant use the premises solely for a narrowly defined, immediately contemplated use could limit the tenant's ability to operate its business on the premises as the business develops and grows over time.

Recent legislation on the subject of energy conservation, and current discussions on the subject of "sick buildings," are causing landlords to question a tenant's in-fact use and occupancy. Tenants who require heavy central files or libraries, specialized air conditioning, or special fire-protection systems, such as Halon®, for

---

[4]See 1 M. Friedman, *Friedman on Leases,* § 18.1 (1985 Supp.) (hereinafter referred to as "Friedman").

their computer installations; tenants who require photocopy, photostat, or blueprint installations; tenants who require art departments or paste-up workstations where glues and paints are to be used; and tenants with large conference or dining facilities that may be construed by the building code to be a "place of public assembly" are well advised to specify these intended uses in their lease. The landlord should represent in the lease that these intended uses are acceptable to the landlord, are permitted pursuant to the certificate of occupancy, and are within the structural and mechanical system capabilities of the building.

Failure to state these intended uses may materially reduce the tenant's quiet enjoyment, if, after the tenant commences business operations, the landlord determines that these uses are not permitted under the lease or are not consistent with the building's capabilities (or constitute a violation of rules and regulations applicable to the building).

In addition, if at any time during the lease term the tenant desires to assign the lease or sublease the premises, a narrow or restrictive use clause could limit the number of prospective assignees and sublessees. Regardless of the particular business activity of the tenant (e.g., securities dealer, accountant, or management consultant), the lease should permit use of the leased premises for "general office use," if not "any lawful use."

The Failure to Delete "Absolute Prohibition against Assignments and Subleases" Clauses

At almost any time during the lease term, a tenant might desire to assign its lease to a new tenant or to sublease all or a portion of the leased premises. Business may be so successful that the tenant may want to relocate its entire office to a new office containing more space or, for other business reasons, may want to conduct a sale of all of its stock or assets. A business may be so unsuccessful that a tenant may have to assign the lease or sublet space, to avoid suffering continued business losses and eventual default under the lease. A tenant may simply desire to move to a new location in response to demographic or market changes or to keep pace with competitors.

An assignment involves the transfer to another tenant of all the tenant's right, title, and interest in the lease for the full unexpired term. The new tenant, or assignee, virtually "steps into the shoes" of the old

tenant and the assignee is directly liable to the landlord under the lease. The old tenant, or assignor, no longer has any rights to occupy the leased premises, but remains liable for defaults under the lease unless the landlord expressly releases the assignor from such liabilities.

When an existing tenant, or sublessor, sublets the leased premises to a new tenant, or sublessee, the sublessor transfers less than all of its right, title, and interest in the lease. For example, a sublessee typically occupies the leased premises for a term less than the remaining term under the prime lease between the landlord and the sublessor. Other sublease terms, such as the minimum rent payable by the sublessee, may also be different from the rent payable by the sublessor to the landlord under the prime lease. The sublessee is not directly liable to the prime landlord under the prime lease and the sublessor remains directly liable to the prime landlord under all the terms of the prime lease.

In general, a tenant may assign its lease or sublet the premises absent an agreement to the contrary. Office leases, however, typically forbid any assignment or subletting without the landlord's consent. Landlords do not want to permit tenants to freely assign the lease or to sublease the premises for various business reasons. Landlords want to review the financial responsibility, reputation, and business of the proposed assignee or sublessee, to determine whether it will be able to perform the financial and other obligations under the lease or sublease, and whether the proposed use of the space and the character of the tenant conform with the character and image of the office building. Mortgage lenders also object to the free assignability of leases or subletting of space, especially where the lender has relied on the credit of a particular tenant. Both the landlord and lender fear that the economic security of the lease is threatened by the ability of the tenant to freely assign a lease or to sublet leased space. Where major tenants are concerned, a lender may prohibit the assignment of a lease without the lender's and landlord's prior consent.

Many assignment clauses state only that the tenant shall not assign the lease or sublet the premises, in whole or in part, without the prior consent of the landlord. Other clauses, however, attempt to clarify what transactions are included within the meaning of the term "assignment." Some leases may expressly prohibit an assignment resulting from a merger of two companies whereby a successor corporation succeeds to the rights of a corporate tenant in and to a lease, or from a corporate consolidation or other reorganization. The transfer of all or part of the partnership interests of a partnership tenant to a new person(s), or any other transfer of control of a tenant by a person controlling the tenant to a person(s) that did not control the tenant as of the date a lease was initially executed, might also be deemed an assignment. Accordingly, the lease should contain carefully drafted language as to what is considered an "assignment."

The most common, but perhaps the least satisfactory, way of accommodating the landlord and tenant is to provide that the landlord's consent to assignments and sublettings shall not be unreasonably withheld or denied. Unfortunately, disputes may arise as to what is and is not "reasonable."[5]

More preferable approaches are for the landlord to consent in advance to certain specific types of assignments, subletting, or other transfers of the lease, or to obtain a covenant that the landlord will consent to assignments, sublettings, or transfers that satisfy certain conditions. For example, the landlord might agree in advance to all assignments or sublettings to a corporation of a certain net worth. Alternatively, the landlord might covenant to consent to assignments of the lease in connection with certain transactions, such as the sale of all or substantially all the stock or assets of the tenant, or the merger or consolidation of the tenant, provided that the assignee is of good repute and financially capable of performing all obligations under the lease and/or employs certain specified executives of the assignor for a certain minimum term.

Tenants should be aware that landlords, especially in tight rental markets, may condition the tenant's right to assign the lease or sublease the leased premises, in whole or in part, on the prior right of the landlord to terminate the lease as to so much of the premises subject to the assignment or subletting. This type of provision is commonly referred to as a "take-back" clause. Such provisions enable landlords to recapture space that may be renting at far less than the then market rate. The landlord's right to terminate the lease could, however, eliminate a major asset otherwise included in the sale of a business.

Tenants should be careful of a clause giving the landlord a right to share in, or possibly receive all of, any "profit" or "excess" that may inure to the benefit of the tenant as a result of an assignment or subletting. The terms "profit" and "excess" are commonly defined as the difference between the rent and other charges payable under the prime lease and the rent and other charges payable by the assignee or sublessee, including any lump-sum payments or premiums paid by the assignee or sublessee. Profits and excess must be clearly defined, and tenants should be able to recover all out-of-pocket costs incurred in connection with securing an assignee or sublessee, such as brokerage commissions and fees, legal fees, and costs for renovations to the premises as required by the assignee or sublessee.

The Failure to Obtain a Nondisturbance Agreement

Multitenant office building leases commonly provide that the lease and the tenant's rights to occupy the premises are subordinate in lien and priority to any then existing and future mortgages encumbering the office building. In the absence of such a clause, if a lease is executed prior to the creation of the mortgage, the interests of the mortgage lender are subject and subordinate to the rights of the tenant under the lease. In the event of the landlord's default under the mortgage loan and a foreclosure proceeding under the mortgage, the lender or any purchaser of the office building in the foreclosure proceeding could not terminate the lease, and the lease would be binding on the lender or such other persons. If, however, a lease is executed subsequent to the creation of a mortgage, the lease is subject to the mortgage and will generally terminate following a successful foreclosure proceeding by the mortgage lender.

Subordination clauses make it easier for existing landlords to obtain additional mortgage loans and to refinance existing indebtedness, and for purchasers of office buildings to obtain financing, by assuring lenders that all leases will be subordinate to the mortgage. Some lenders, however, may insist that prime leases on favorable terms with major tenants be prior to the mortgage loan so that such leases are not automatically terminated in foreclosure proceedings. The risk of a subordination clause to the tenant is that, regardless of the fact that the lease was executed prior to the creation of any mortgage, the lease would be junior to all such mortgages in terms of priority and would be subject to extinguishment in a foreclosure proceeding. A tenant that installed substantial

---

[5]See Friedman at § 7.304(b), (c), for a discussion of various cases concerning the reasonableness standard.

improvements in the leased premises would, on extinguishment, lose not only the value of the lease over the remaining term of the lease but the value of the improvements as well.

To protect against the extinguishment of a lease in the event of a foreclosure, a tenant should not agree to subordinate its interest in the lease to any mortgage loans unless each such mortgage lender executes a nondisturbance agreement. A nondisturbance agreement typically provides that the lender and its successors and assigns shall not disturb the tenant's possession of the leased space, provided that the tenant is not in default under the lease. Tenants should require the landlord to obtain a nondisturbance agreement from the existing lender, even in cases where the lease is in fact subordinate to a mortgage, because the lease is executed subsequent to the creation of the mortgage.

The Failure to Limit and Clearly Define Additional Rental Payments

Annual base or minimum rental payments are usually determined according to a certain cost per square foot. For short- or medium-term leases, base rent is usually a fixed amount for the entire term or it increases periodically according to specific amounts. For long-term leases, the base rent may be adjusted annually throughout the lease term or commencing on an agreed-on date, according to changes in an index such as the consumer price index (CPI).

In addition to fixed, base, and minimum rental payments, tenants in a multitenant office building are typically required to make additional rental payments. These additional rental payments vary from lease year to lease year and represent each tenant's share of the increase in the costs of operating the office building. Additional rental payments include charges for increases in the cost of items such as real estate taxes, utilities, insurance, and maintenance charges. Under a net lease, the tenant(s) would be directly responsible for all of these costs, among others, and not just the amount of the annual increase in such costs.

Additional rental payments represent a significant and variable lease expense. Therefore, in reviewing an office lease, tenants must determine: (1) exactly what charges are to be included in each additional rental payment category, and (2) how the tenant's share of such costs will be determined.

Real Estate Taxes

Real estate taxes are commonly defined to include real estate taxes and real property assessments levied against the office building in which the leased premises are located and the land on which the building is situated. Tenants must be certain that the landlord's inheritance, estate, succession, transfer, gift, franchise, income, and capital stock taxes, and penalties and interest for the landlord's failure to pay real estate taxes on a timely basis, are not included in the definition of real estate taxes.

Under many office leases, tenants are required to pay their proportionate share of real estate tax increases over real estate taxes for a specified base year. In these cases, the lease should expressly specify the base year and the amount of real estate taxes paid by the landlord in that year. In some instances, a base year is not used and tenants will pay to the landlord, as part of the base or minimum rent, a specific dollar amount for taxes. If the real estate taxes exceed the aggregate dollar amount payable by all tenants, the tenants will be responsible for their proportionate share of the excess. In some instances, a specific portion of base rent is not directly applied to real estate taxes, but tenants are obligated to pay their proportionate share of the amount by which real estate taxes exceed a certain dollar amount. Tenants may attempt to limit their exposure to large, unanticipated tax increases by establishing a maximum annual real estate tax increase payable by the tenant.

Tenants in buildings undergoing construction or in recently completed buildings should pay close attention to whether base year real estate taxes are based on actual occupancy or projected full occupancy. If, for example, base year taxes reflect taxes for an unfinished building or a tax moratorium period, then the base year figure will be biased downward and the tenant will pay a higher annual tax payment throughout the lease term than if base year taxes were for a finished building. Tenants should attempt to define the base year and base year tax amount according to the actual real estate tax assessment for the year in which the building is first assessed as completed or in which a specified minimum occupancy is achieved. For the foregoing reasons, where a base year is not used, tenants should also carefully review the landlord's assumption as to the fixed amount (whether or not included in base or minimum rent) above which tenants must pay their proportionate share of real estate taxes. Similarly, tenants must pay attention to the land and buildings on which taxes are based and should exclude from the escalation base new buildings on the office building site and additions to existing buildings, if such additions do not directly benefit the tenant or create additional rentable space in the building where the leased premises are located.

The possibility exists that the real property on which the building is situated will be assessed for its share of public improvements. Therefore, the lease should provide that any taxes or assessments that are payable in installments should be paid by the tenant over the longest period of time permissible by law and that the tenant should be responsible only for those payments accruing during the term of the lease.

Major tenants, or a specific number of tenants acting collectively, may be able to obtain the right to contest, by appropriate proceedings, the amount or validity of any real property assessment or real estate tax increase applicable to the leased premises. Such tenants typically have the right to postpone or defer payment of the tax, provided such postponement or deferment does not subject the office building to a lien for nonpayment. The exercise of this right may be subject to obtaining the consent of specific mortgage lenders.

In addition, tenants must pay close attention to the formula pursuant to which each tenant's "proportion-ate share" of real estate tax increases is determined. If the proportionate share is determined by dividing the square footage of the leased premises by the square footage of all "leased" space in the office building, then the tenant bears the risk of unleased space and the tenant's share of real estate taxes will increase to the extent that the landlord is unable to rent space in the building. Therefore, proportionate share should be determined by dividing the tenant's square footage by the amount of "leasable" space in the office building.

Utility Costs

Until the energy crisis of the mid-1970s, landlords typically required tenants to pay the landlord (rather than contract directly with the appropriate utility providers) for the cost of providing water, gas, electricity, and other utilities to the leased premises. Recently, however, many newly constructed office buildings have been wired so that full-floor tenants and even partial-floor tenants can be separately metered by the local utilities or submetered by an independent metering company. Absent tenant utility meters, landlords may require the

tenant to pay, as part of the base or minimum rent, a specific amount per square foot of space in the leased premises on account of electricity charges (typically based on a consultant's estimate of a tenant's electricity consumption). Where there are no tenant utility meters, tenants' interests will best be served if the leased premises are submetered for electricity (sometimes at the election of the landlord and at the cost of the tenant during the lease term) so that the tenant's payment to the landlord for the cost of electricity can be verified against actual consumption in the leased premises. Alternatively, tenants may be required to pay their proportionate share of all utility costs incurred by the landlord or some calculation of usage above a specific dollar amount. In addition, tenants typically pay their proportionate share of the cost (excluding costs charged directly to tenants) of providing water and sewer service, electricity, and other services to the entire office building.

If the landlord bills the tenant for electricity charges on a rent inclusion basis without the benefit of submetering, however, tenants must be assured that they will not pay in excess of the cost charged the landlord by the applicable utilities. In larger office buildings, the landlord typically contracts for electric service at a discounted high-tension rate, which is lower than the rate the utility company may charge for the standard 120–240-volt current typically provided to a low-voltage commercial customer of the utility. Landlords should agree to bill tenants for all utilities at either their high-tension discounted rate or at the same low-tension rate the tenants would have been billed by the utility company providing such service. Absent a tenant submeter, tenants that pay for utilities on a rent inclusion basis will have no empirical means of verifying the landlord's estimate of the tenant's consumption rate. These tenants will be well-advised to include a lengthy lease clause providing for periodic energy audits by outside consultants, to verify consumption and set the rent inclusion dollar costs.

Without a tenant meter or a periodic energy audit, tenants might find that they are in fact responsible for a share of that portion of utility costs attributable to abnormally high consumption by other tenants. Other tenants that have an unusually large number of employees or use special equipment such as computers, for example, may consume electricity and other utilities in excess of that customarily demanded by tenants for normal purposes during business hours. Some tenants may consume excessive amounts of electricity and other utilities because of frequent operations on weekends or operations beyond regular business hours during the week.

A tenant meter or submeter costs less than $2,000 to install. Because the above-noted consultant verification service is very cumbersome and costly, most tenants are well-advised to insist on a submeter clause in their leases.

By using a submetering technology and appropriate lease terms, a tenant can negotiate a pay-as-you-go clause for overtime air conditioning and heating, rather than the dollars-per-overtime-hour clause that is typically found in a landlord's form lease. Both the air handling fans and the chillers or heaters serving these fans can be metered just prior to entry into the tenant's space, so that accurate accounting of overtime use and requirements can be made.

Operating/Maintenance Expenses

Office building tenants are commonly required to pay their proportionate share of the costs of operating and maintaining the office building complex. As with real estate taxes, some tenants may be responsible for their proportionate share of various increases over operating costs for a specific base year. Other tenants will be responsible for their proportionate share of the operating cost increases in excess of a specified base amount per square foot of the leased premises (which amount may or may not be paid to the landlord as part of the base rent).

Operating costs typically include, among other things, the cost of insurance carried by the landlord; utility costs not otherwise billed directly to tenants; the cost of repairs, maintenance, and replacement (except to the extent paid with insurance proceeds); the cost of janitorial services, nightly cleaning, and snow removal; management fees; security; wages and salaries of all persons engaged in the maintenance, repair, replacement, or operation of the building; and fees for necessary government permits. Operating costs may also incorporate real estate taxes and utility costs. Broad operating-cost clauses should be avoided, and all operating costs to be passed through to tenants as additional rental charges should be specifically mentioned.

Operating costs should not include the following items: payments of principal and interest pursuant to any loan affecting the building; salaries of executive officers of the landlord; brokerage commissions and advertising costs; uninsured casualty losses; deductions for depreciation and other noncash expenditures; expenditures for capital improvements (some landlords may attempt to include only those expenditures that reduce operating expenses or are required by a public authority, or may include capital expenditures on an amortized basis); alterations, improvements, and other nonroutine services provided to individual tenants; and costs and fines attributable to the landlord's violation of any governmental rules, regulations, statutes, and ordinances.

As with real estate taxes, if the tenant is to pay its proportionate share of operating expenses, the proportionate share should be determined by dividing the space of the leased premises by the leasable area of the building, thereby causing the landlord to bear the risk of vacancies. In addition, if the building has been recently completed and tenants are obligated to pay their proportionate share of operating expenses in excess of expenses in a specific base year, their share should be based on full occupancy. If tenants are obligated to pay their proportionate share of any excess above a fixed dollar amount (whether or not included in base or minimum rent) for operating expenses, the tenant must determine the reasonableness of the estimate of the fixed amount.

Tenants leasing space in older buildings under substantial renovation will want to exclude those renovation costs from the operating cost calculation, regardless of whether they are capital improvement costs.

Books and Records

Landlords typically require each tenant to pay, with each monthly payment of basic or minimum rent, one-twelfth of estimated additional rental payments for the then current lease year. Soon after the end of the lease year or some other designated date(s), the landlord determines whether the amount paid by tenants for additional rent during the preceding lease year or such other period exceeded or was less than the actual cost of such charges. The landlord will either require each tenant to pay a share of the amount by which the actual cost exceeded the amount paid by the tenant or will apply the amount of the excess toward future additional rent. To avoid grossly excessive estimates of operating costs, tenants and landlords should agree to a precise formula for estimating annual operating costs, such as an amount equal to a fixed percentage of operating costs for the immediately preceding year.

The landlord should be required to keep accurate books and records of utility costs, real estate taxes, and operating costs. In addition, the landlord should be required to deliver a reasonably detailed list of expenses to the tenant, along with the landlord's statement as to the difference, if any, between projected additional rental costs and actual costs. Tenants should request access to the landlord's books and records for the purpose of verifying the landlord's statement of costs. Tenants may be able to require the landlord to pay for the fees of a professional auditor if a significant discrepancy is revealed between the landlord's statement of costs and actual costs (commonly defined as a specific minimum percentage).

The Failure to Provide for Automatic Termination of the Lease on Expiration of the Lease Term; the Failure to Provide for a Tenant's Election to Terminate the Lease in the Event of Casualty or Condemnation

Automatic Termination

Notwithstanding the fact that a commercial lease has a definite term and expiration date, some leases provide that, in order for the lease to be terminated, either party must give the other party written notice thereof by a certain time prior to the end of the stated expiration date of the lease. If such notice is not given by either party, the lease continues, on the same terms and conditions as were in force immediately prior to the end of the term, for a further specified term and for additional renewal periods, unless and until terminated by either party prior to the then current renewal term of the lease.

The obvious risk to the tenant is that it might fail to give notice of termination by the specified date and, if the landlord fails to terminate the lease, be required to occupy the leased premises for an additional term. It is not uncommon for additional terms to be one year in length. To avoid this risk, extension of term clauses should be revised to provide that the lease shall automatically terminate on the last day of the lease term without the necessity of notice from either party to the other, unless a tenant exercises any options to renew the lease as specifically provided for in the lease.

Casualty/Condemnation

Commercial office leases typically provide that if the office building is damaged by fire or other casualty such that the leased premises are rendered unfit for occupancy, then the landlord may elect to terminate the lease within a certain period of time after the occurrence of such damage. If the landlord does not elect to terminate the lease, the landlord is obligated to repair the building and the tenant is no longer obligated to pay rent during the period when the tenant is deprived of the leased premises.

If the landlord elects to repair the building, tenants typically have no assurance of a date by which they can reasonably expect to regain possession of the leased premises and to be able to continue normal business operations. Therefore, casualty clauses should be revised to provide that a tenant can terminate the lease if the tenant reasonably determines, within a specified period of time after the occurrence of the damage, that more than a certain number of days would be required to complete the repair of the building. The lease should also provide that the tenant may terminate the lease if the landlord fails to complete the repairs within a designated period. The ability of the tenant to terminate the lease and the length of the repair period are likely to be items of considerable negotiation.

Office leases commonly provide that, in the event that all or a portion of the office building is taken or condemned, the lease terminates as to the part so taken on the date that the condemning authority takes title to such property, and all rental payments are thereafter abated proportionally. Unless the lease is terminated by the landlord, the landlord typically remains liable to make repairs and alterations that will restore to useful condition the portion of the leased premises not taken. In some leases, if the balance of the leased premises is rendered "untenantable" (or such that the tenant cannot make use of the premises in connection with the normal operation of its business), the landlord has the option to terminate the lease.

In other leases, the landlord may have the right to terminate tenant leases following any partial condemnation to the building, even without regard as to whether the leased premises are affected.

The lease should therefore provide that the tenant may also terminate the entire lease if, in connection with a partial taking, the portion of the leased premises not taken is rendered untenantable. To minimize disputes as to what is and what is not untenantable, the landlord and tenant could also condition the tenant's termination right on the taking of a specific percentage, such as 25 percent, of the entire office building or leased premises and/or parking lot. In addition, the tenant should have the right to terminate the lease if the landlord elects to repair the leased premises but fails to complete the repairs within a designated period of time.

The Failure to Describe Adequately Ownership of Tenant Improvements and Fixtures

Ownership of tenant improvements and fixtures is an important matter, upon the expiration or termination of a lease. Many commercial office leases provide that all fixtures, equipment, improvements, alterations, and additions attached to or built into the leased premises before or during the term of the lease by the tenant, or by the landlord at the expense of the tenant, shall become the property of the landlord and remain at the leased premises or, at the landlord's option, shall be removed at the sole cost of the tenant before the expiration or sooner termination of the lease. These provisions generally pertain to items affixed to the premises and do not govern personal property such as desks, chairs, files, and other similar office equipment. Tenants should, however, read such clauses carefully to determine what items are subject to these provisions.

Tenants must be aware of the possible loss of valuable improvements when the lease is terminated or expires. For example, under a typical clause, tenants might be forced to leave behind items such as movable office partitions, workstations, built-in cabinets, light fixtures, display cases, security systems, paneling, shelving, tenants' LAN computer and telephone systems, and air conditioning and cooling equipment. Because the tenant fit-out industry is relying more and more on factory-made modular components that are easily moved or removed, each tenant should specify particular items that can be removed at the tenant's cost and expense, upon lease termination or expiration.

If the landlord is paying for these items as part of the workletter or landlord fit-out allowance or budget, the landlord will be entitled to just compensation for the unamortized portion of the costs of the items the tenant may wish to remove. For this reason, the landlord should state the amortization schedule and the method for calculating the tenant's reimbursement to the landlord, in the event that (1) the tenant wishes to remove the fit-out items or (2) the lease is terminated or not renewed until these capital improvements provided paid for by the landlord are fully amortized.

As with other provisions of a typical office lease, tenants should attempt to resolve all ambiguities regarding the items that may eventually be owned by the landlord. For example, most leases provide that all "fixtures" shall become the property of the landlord. Courts generally apply a number of factors to determine whether an item is a "fixture": whether an item is physically attached or annexed to the premises such that removal of such item would damage the premises; whether the item is well adapted to the premises; and/or whether the party that installed the item intended that the item form a permanent part of the premises. As such, fixtures are deemed a part of the realty.

Fixtures that are necessary for the operation of a business, however, are considered "trade fixtures" and, absent a clear indication to the contrary, tenants are entitled to remove trade fixtures during or at the conclusion of a lease. Therefore, because of the ambiguity as to whether the term "fixtures" in a lease is intended to overcome the trade fixtures doctrine and include trade fixtures within the property to be retained by the landlord, and because the tenant fit-out industry is providing more easily removable components, tenants and landlords should clarify whether trade fixtures are subject to clauses governing ownership of such improvements.[6]

The Failure to Limit the Cost of Insurance and Liability to the Landlord's Insurer

Insurance clauses in a lease are very important. At a minimum, these clauses require the tenant to obtain and maintain specific types of casualty insurance and comprehensive liability insurance at the tenant's sole cost and expense. Casualty insurance protects the insured against property losses suffered on the leased premises from risks contained in what is commonly referred to as a "fire and extended coverage endorsement." Landlords may require additional endorsements to cover additional risks and perils. Comprehensive liability insurance protects the insured against claims by third parties attributable to the acts of the insured and its agents. Leases typically require that the landlord be added as a named insured to such policies, to the extent of the landlord's interest under the lease.

---

[6]For a general discussion of the law of "fixtures" and "trade fixtures," see R. Kratovil, *Modern Mortgage Law and Practice* 179–180 (1972); and M. Garfinkel, *How Objects Become Fixtures,* 1 Practical Real Estate Lawyer 19 (January 1985).

One of the major reasons that tenants have recently started to examine insurance clauses more critically than in previous years is the increasing cost of insurance. A tenant must determine whether all of the insurance requirements contained in the lease are necessary. Tenants should also determine whether the required minimum limits of coverage are acceptable and should reduce excessively high minimum insurance requirements. Similarly, tenants should delete insurance clause provisions that require the tenant to obtain other types of insurance with respect to the leased premises, in such amounts as the landlord may request (reasonably or otherwise). In addition, tenants should attempt to delete broad provisions permitting landlords to increase specific minimum coverage limits of insurance contained in the lease.

The tenant is responsible for maintaining liability insurance and casualty insurance covering loss to the leased premises and the tenant's leasehold improvements, but landlords typically maintain casualty insurance and public liability insurance covering the portion of the office building not insured by the tenants' insurance carriers. The lease should contain a covenant by the landlord to maintain certain insurance coverage. Under a net lease, the responsibility for all insurance costs associated with the entire building is on the tenant(s).

If the landlord is obligated under the lease to provide casualty insurance (the cost of which is typically passed through to tenants), the tenant should seek a "waiver of subrogation" clause. Under the doctrine of subrogation, when an insurer pays a claim to its insured, the insurer inherits all of the rights that its insured had against the third party that caused the damage.[7] In the absence of a waiver of subrogation

clause, if a tenant negligently caused a fire that damaged the entire office building, the landlord's insurer would be subrogated to the landlord's right to sue the tenant, after compensating the landlord under the landlord's insurance policy. If the landlord is a named insured under the tenant's insurance policy, the landlord need not require a waiver of subrogation from the tenant's insurer because an insurer generally has no right of subrogation against its own insured.

In addition to obtaining a waiver of subrogation from insurers, it is not uncommon for a landlord and tenant to enter into a mutual release pursuant to which each party releases the other from any and all liability for loss or damage inflicted on the property of the other without regard to negligence, provided that the release does not affect the right of an insured to recover under its insurance policy. If the landlord has released its claims against a tenant, the landlord has no rights which the insurer may be subrogated to, upon paying a claim.

Tenants should make certain that the waiver of subrogation is not limited to the amount of insurance proceeds actually recovered; some landlords may have substantial deductible clauses in their policies, may be underinsured, or may be "self-insurers." Tenants must not confuse a waiver of subrogation by the landlord's insurer with a release by the landlord, and must be certain to obtain the waiver of the insurance companies' rights to proceed against the tenant and a release by the landlord of its right of recovery against the tenant.[8]

---

[7] See E. Halper, *People and Property: Waiver of Subrogation Clauses,* 14 Real Estate Rev. 58 (Spring 1984).

[8] *Id.* at 61–62.

Selected Bibliography

Antill, James, and Ronald Woodhead. *Critical Path Methods in Construction Practice.* New York: John Wiley & Sons, 1982.

Binder, Stephen. *Corporate Facility Planning.* New York: McGraw-Hill, 1989.

Burstein, David, and Frank Stasiowski. *Project Management for the Design Professional.* New York: Whitney Library of Design, 1982.

Compensation Guidelines for Architectural and Engineering Services, 2d Ed. Washington, DC: American Institute of Architects, 1977.

Coxe, Weld. *Managing Architectural and Engineering Practice.* New York: John Wiley & Sons, 1980.

————. *Marketing Architectural and Engineering Services.* New York: Litton Educational Publishing Co., 1979.

Crosley, Mark L. *The Architect's Guide to Computer-Aided Design.* New York: John Wiley & Sons, 1988.

Cushman, Robert F., and Neal I. Rodin. *Property Management Handbook.* New York: John Wiley & Sons, 1985.

Harris, Cyril M. *Dictionary of Architecture and Construction.* New York: McGraw-Hill, 1975.

Klein, Judy Graf. *The Office Book.* London: Quarto Marketing Ltd., 1982.

Kliment, Stephen A. *Creative Communications for Successful Design Practice.* New York: Whitney Library of Design, 1977.

Moscove, Stephen, and Arnold Wright. *Cost Accounting with Managerial Applications.* Boston: Houghton Mifflin, 1989.

Ouchi, William. *Theory Z: How American Business Can Meet the Japanese Challenge.* Reading, MA: Addison-Wesley, 1981.

Panero, Julius, and Martin Zelnik. *Human Dimension and Interior Space.* New York: Whitney Library of Design, 1979.

Propst, Robert. *The Office.* Zeeland, MI: Herman Miller, 1968.

Saphier, Michael. *Planning the New Office.* New York: McGraw-Hill, 1978.

Siegel, Harry, with Alan Siegel. *A Guide to Business Principles and Practices for Interior Designers,* Rev.Ed. New York: Whitney Library of Design, 1982.

Staebler, Wendy W. *Architectural Detailing in Contract Interiors.* New York: Whitney Library of Design, 1988.

Stasiowski, Frank. *Negotiating Higher Design Fees.* New York: Whitney Library of Design, 1985.

Steele, Fred I. *Physical Settings and Organizational Development.* Reading, MA: Addison-Wesley, 1973.

Stein, J. Stewart. *Construction Glossary.* New York: John Wiley & Sons, 1980.

Stitt, Fred A. *Systems Drafting.* New York: McGraw-Hill, 1980.

————. *Systems Graphics.* New York: McGraw-Hill, 1984.

Sugerman, Alan D., Robert F. Cushman, and Andrew D. Lipman. *The Commercial Real Estate Tenant's Handbook.* New York: John Wiley & Sons, 1987.

Sugarman, Alan D., Andrew D. Lipman, and Robert F. Cushman. *High Tech Real Estate.* Homewood, IL: Dow Jones-Irwin, 1985.

About the Authors

Larry C. Baucom, Esq., the senior partner of Jones Lang Wootton, is responsible for the firm's leasing and marketing operations in the United States. Developing marketing strategies and acting as the leasing agent for properties purchased by off-shore investors are among his most significant duties. Mr. Baucom holds a bachelor's degree in engineering and an MBA, with specialties in finance and marketing.

C. Jaye Berger, Esq., is the founder of Law Offices of C. Jaye Berger, a New York-based firm that specializes in building construction and real estate matters. Ms. Berger's firm represents interior designers, architects, contractors, owners, and developers. She has lectured on legal issues across the United States for organizations such as ASID and AIA. She teaches a CEU credit-approved course for ASID members on legal and business issues in the design industry, and has represented clients in arbitration hearings. She is an approved arbitrator.

Her articles have appeared in *Progressive Architecture, The Designer,* and *Interiors.*

Robert F. Cushman, Esq., coeditor, is a partner in the national law firm of Pepper, Hamilton & Scheetz and a recognized specialist and lecturer on all phases of real estate and construction law. He serves as legal counsel to numerous trade associations and construction, development, and bonding companies. Mr. Cushman is the editor and coauthor of *The Construction Industry Formbook* (Shepard's, Inc., 1981), *The Dow Jones Businessman's Guide to Construction* (Dow Jones-Irwin, 1980), *Construction Litigation: Representing the Owner* (Wiley, 1984), and numerous other articles. A member of the Pennsylvania bar and admitted to practice before the Supreme Court of the United States and the U.S. Claims Court, Mr. Cushman has served as executive vice president and general counsel to the Construction Industry Foundation. He is a member of the International Association of Insurance Counsel and a charter member of the American College of Construction Attorneys.

Karen Daroff, IBD, coeditor, *Interiors* magazine's 1990 designer of the year, is president and principal-in-charge of design of Daroff Design Inc. (DDI), founded the firm in 1973. Her award-winning design firm is comprised of four interlocking groups of professionals: DDI Strategic Facility Consultants, DDI Interiors, DDI Architects, P.C., and DDI Graphics. DDI collaborates with developers, architects, engineers, and other professionals in the design of offices and other commercial facilities, including the areas of tenant planning, interior architectural renovation, and adaptive reuse. A graduate of Moore College of Art and Design, Philadelphia, Ms. Daroff holds a BFA in Interior Design. She serves on the board of the Greater Philadelphia Chamber of Commerce and is a trustee of the Moore College of Art and Design. She has also served on the executive committee of the Mayor's Small Business Advisory Council and the Philadelphia Art Commission.

Joel J. Goldberg, Esq., is an associate in the Washington, DC, office of Venable, Baetjer, Howard & Civiletti. He received a BA (1975) from Rutgers University and an MPP (1977) and JD (1982) from the University of Michigan.

Mr. Goldberg is a member of the American, Pennsylvania, and District of Columbia Bar Associations. He practices in the areas of real estate development, leasing, acquisition, disposition, construction, finance, and partnership law.

Gary Goldman, Esq., is associate corporate counsel for CDI Corp. in Philadelphia. He received a JD (1976) from Villanova University School of Law, where he was the associate editor of the Law Review. Mr. Goldman is a member of the American and Philadelphia Bar Associations as well as the American Corporate Counsel Association. His writings have appeared in *Labor Law Journal* and *The Practical Real Estate Lawyer,* and he has been listed in *Who's Who in American Law.* His 1989 book, *Drafting a Fair Office Lease,* was published by the American Law Institute–American Bar Association.

Jay R. Hendler, AIA, is a licensed architect in California, with experience in a variety of architectural commissions. He has collaborated on designs with such internationally acclaimed architects as Philip Johnson and Arthur Erickson. In the field of renovation architecture, Hendler's projects include the award-winning Neiman-Marcus Rotunda on San Francisco's Union Square and the publicly acclaimed Monadnock Building. Hendler was also the architect in charge of adapting the Metropolitan Life Building for reuse as a five-star luxury hotel. His credentials further encompass major banking, commercial office, shopping center, and single- and multifamily residential and resort projects. A principal/owner for many years at Whisler-Patri Architects, Hendler has coauthored a chapter for the book *High-Tech Real Estate,* and has addressed the Industrial Development Research Council and other professional groups on the subject of "intelligent" buildings and rehabilitation design.

A member of the American Institute of Architects, Hendler is also a member of the National Trust for Historic Preservation, the Foundation for San Francisco's Architectural Heritage, and the Building Owners and Managers Association. He serves on the Washington State University Architectural Advisory Council and has for many years taught courses in architectural rehabilitation at University of California Extension. Hendler is a graduate of Washington State University, where he earned a Bachelor of Architecture with honors and was elected to the honorary architectural fraternity, Alpha Rho Chi.

Barry M. Nealon, Esq., senior partner of Jones Lang Wootton, is responsible for the firm's portfolio and direct management in the United States. An extensive part of this responsibility relates to the management of U.S. real estate assets for off-shore clients. Educated in England, Mr. Nealon is a qualified Chartered Surveyor. He has served as an Executive Director of the firm's United Kingdom management operations.

Piero Patri, FAIA, president of Whisler-Patri, has served as principal-in-charge of Whisler-Patri's mid- and high-rise commercial and residential projects over the past 25 years. He has also been responsible for many of the firm's research and development and office park projects.

Mr. Patri has directed the design of more than 4 million square feet of "intelligently" planned office space, including new construction, rehabilitation of existing facilities, and interior design commissions.

James E. Rappoport, AIA, co-editor, is executive vice president of Daroff Design Inc. (DDI), the Philadelphia-based architectural and interior design firm. While serving as principal-in-charge of DDI Strategic Facility Consultants, he supervises the firm's planning-intensive projects, providing consultation to major corporations, development investors, and other architectural and interior design firms. His areas of expertise include facilities programming, planning and management, economic analysis of real estate projects, operational and procurement methods and procedures, and related tax issues. Rappoport earned a BA in architecture from Cornell University and an MA in architecture and urban design from Columbia University. He has also completed postgraduate courses in urban economic analysis and public administration.

Richard C. Reisman, is vice president of Interland, a major developer and owner of real estate in northern California. He is responsible for all development activity for the company's new and ongoing projects in the San Francisco area.

Reisman joined the company in early 1988 as Senior Development Officer. Prior to joining Interland, he practiced architecture for 12 years and was facilities vice president for a medical clinic development firm in San Francisco. Reisman has been a Planning Commissioner in Foster City and has published chapters and articles on specialized aspects of building development.

Daniel W. Winey, AIA, is Design Director of Gensler & Associates in San Francisco, California. In his role as the firm's director of interior architecture, Winey oversees all activities within the interior design studio and provides guidance to individual project teams at critical junctures of project development. He also oversees activities of the computer-aided design and drafting (CADD) group and the facilities management services group.

Index